THE BOOK IN THE RENAISSANCE

ANDREW PETTEGREE is Professor of Modern History at the University of St Andrews and founding director of the St Andrews Reformation Studies Institute. Formerly a literary director of the Royal Historical Society, and currently director of the Universal Short Title Catalogue project, his previous books include *The Reformation World* (2000), *Europe in the Sixteenth Century* (2002) and *Reformation and the Culture of Persuasion* (2005).

D1003470

The

BOOK IN THE
RENAISSANCE

ANDREW PETTEGREE

YALE UNIVERSITY PRESS
NEW HAVEN AND LONDON

Published with assistance from the foundation established in memory of Oliver Baty Cunningham of the Class of 1917, Yale College

For information about this and other Yale University Press publications, please contact:
U.S. Office: sales.press@yale.edu   www.yalebooks.com
Europe Office: sales @yaleup.co.uk   www.yaleup.co.uk

Set in Minion Pro by IDSUK (DataConnection) Ltd
Printed in the United States of America

Library of Congress Cataloging-in-Publication Data

Pettegree, Andrew.
   The Book in the Renaissance/Andrew Pettegree.
   p. cm.
   Includes bibliographical references and index.
   ISBN 978-0-300-11009-8 (alk. paper)
   1.   Book industries and trade—Europe—History—16th century. 2   Book industries and trade—Europe—History—To 1500. 3.   Printing—Europe—History—16th century. 4.   Printing—Europe—History—Origin and antecedents. 5.   Books—Europe—History—1450-1600 6.   Renaissance. 7.   Reformation—Europe. 8.   Europe—Intellectual life. I.   Title.
   Z291.3P48 2010
   070.5094—dc22
                                                                                                1175255166

A catalogue record for this book is available from the British Library.

ISBN 978-0-300-17821-0 (pbk)

Contents

Part IV
New Worlds

ILLUSTRATIONS

Maps

PRELUDE

In 1490 two friends went for a stroll through the streets of Venice. One, Sararisius, was a native of the city, his friend Juliarius a visitor. Sararisius had a meeting with other Venetian patricians at San Marco; as they made their way there the two men amused themselves by sampling the riches of Europe's greatest trading city. As they walked along the Merceria even so urbane a figure as Juliarius was amazed by the stalls of the booksellers: great mounds of printed texts heaped up and displayed for sale. He stopped to look and was soon engrossed; Sararisius was forced to leave him while he conducted necessary business. When he returned, several hours later, he found Juliarius still browsing the books, and surrounded by piles of his purchases. It was only with difficulty that he was persuaded to move on to their engagement.

This scene, imaginatively described by another urbane Italian, Marcantonio Sabellico, in the preface to his treatise on the Latin language, encapsulates all that humanist intellectuals sought in the new world of printed books.[1] Fifty years previously, before a cranky German businessman had concluded his experiments with techniques of making 'mechanical books', it would have taken a lifetime to assemble the collection that Juliarius could purchase in one good morning's hunting on the Merceria of Venice. Printing did not invent the book: medieval Europe was full of books. But before the fifteenth century all books had to be meticulously hand-copied, with quill and ink, from other precious texts. Now, suddenly, in the second half of the fifteenth century, books were available in a wild profusion. It was no wonder that men like Marcantonio Sabellico believed that the world of knowledge – their world – was transformed for ever.

Step forward eighty years and we enter a very different world. In 1570 Lucas Cop stood before the Geneva Consistory, the body of men charged with defending the morals and religious observance of Calvin's city. Lucas was the bad boy of the family of one of the city's pastors, Michel Cop. Respect and embarrassment for the boy's late father may have delayed the denouement, but the boy's reckless and defiant behaviour eventually made confrontation inevitable. For Lucas had been reading books. Not the books of which the city's fathers approved, and which the city's presses turned out in large numbers, such as bibles, church orders and improving moral tracts. Lucas was addicted to literature.

Between 7 and 10 December 1570 Lucas Cop was interrogated at the city's prison.[2] Without hesitation or embarrassment he confessed his preferences: the lascivious love poetry of Catullus, the romantic verse of Pierre de Ronsard and Jean-Antoine de Baïf, Castiglione's cynical handbook of court life, *The Courtier*. Most provocative of all was his love of Rabelais. This was not a book on sale in Geneva; Lucas had obtained a copy from a bookseller of Lausanne, and he read it in the company of other young friends. According to one of them Lucas even carried it with him to church, in place of his copy of the Psalms (this caused trouble for the bookseller who had bound it up for him, presumably in a style likely to facilitate this deception). Lucas had showed a degree of interest in the official literature favoured by the Geneva Church, such as copies of Calvin's sermons and commentaries: but only because he stole copies from a bookseller to exchange for profane literature.

Lucas Cop was ordered to be whipped in the presence of all his fellow scholars at the city school and forbidden to travel outside the city. His accomplices escaped with lighter punishments. The affair sheds a vivid light on a new book *demi-monde*, with texts furtively exchanged outside the city gates, read and hand-copied in private circles. Both Cop and Pierre Enoch, another member of his secret reading circle, offered the defence that some of the disapproved texts had come from the libraries of their distinguished fathers: works of Ovid, for example, and the Latin poet Martial. Such libraries also undoubtedly contained the modern French poets. But what the fathers collected their sons should not necessarily read. The relaxed, engaging humanism of the first age of print was confronting the sterner climate of the age of confessional orthodoxy. Those who would not bend, like Lucas Cop, must be broken.

These two vignettes, so different in tone and outcome, capture much of the paradoxical quality of the book world of Renaissance Europe. For forty years after Gutenberg displayed his new invention to an admiring public, the printed book was carried along on a tide of optimism. The new technology spread with amazing speed: from Mainz through the cities of the German Empire, across the Alps to Italy, the epicentre of the Renaissance; north and east to France, the Low Countries, England, Poland and Bohemia. By 1490 printing presses had spread the new art to over 200 cities in every part of the continent.

Yet even as this expansive geography of print was being plotted, book industry professionals received the first indications that blind faith in the new technology would be misplaced. There were simply not enough readers to absorb this new torrent of books. Not that this would have been readily apparent to a complaisant, triumphant humanist like Marcantonio Sabellico, who would, it must be said, also have had little sympathy for the plight of a rebellious boy like Lucas Cop. Men such as Sabellico welcomed a world full of books only because it provided a greater variety of texts for people like themselves. This was a more limited vision than they would have recognised. It was also an impossible dream, and potentially ruinous for the printers and booksellers who tried to make it a reality. The scholarly community was not yet large enough to absorb the many thousands of copies placed on the market by those eager to share the craze for the new technology. Publishers found themselves with unsold copies, and many of the first printers were quickly driven into bankruptcy.

Ultimately print would survive only by developing new types of book for new types of reader: texts of a type and variety unimaginable in Gutenberg's day. The enormous diversification of this book market is the second part of the story of the Renaissance book world: a world shaped less by the idealism of scholars than by pragmatic businessmen for whom the only books that mattered were those that turned a profit. In the process print pushed into areas of society previously untouched by the medieval manuscript. New markets sprang up, for news, controversy, popular science and medicine, as well as the literature and poetry that led Lucas Cop into such difficulties. These new markets, mostly of books in the vernacular languages, flourished side by side with the still buoyant market for texts in Latin, the international language of scholarship. Gradually they brought book ownership within the compass of a whole new public. They also raised urgent concern about how access to this new more inclusive world of print should be regulated, both to protect the investment of the printers, and to protect readers from themselves.

Much of this new literature was worlds away from the expensive scholarly texts so lovingly crafted for sale in the markets of Italy, France and Germany in the fifteenth century. Many of the new genres were cheap, short and disposable. They were intended for everyday use, not to take their place in a humanist library. Many were used to destruction, to the extent that the whole edition is now completely lost. It is very common for just one copy of a sixteenth-century almanac, pamphlet or school-book to survive. Sometimes we know it only from a reference in a bookseller's catalogue or publisher's accounts: the book itself has disappeared altogether.

These scrappy little books are to historians among the most interesting productions of the sixteenth-century printing press. But they were not immediately thought of as worthy of a place in a respectable collection; often we owe their survival to the interest of collectors who in their own day would have been thought of as distinctly eccentric.[3] Now these small books are very precious, but four centuries of hard living has dispersed them throughout thousands of libraries around the world. This fact – that much of the output of the first age of print was seen at the time as being of no consequence – has meant that it has until now been very difficult to write the whole history of the first age of print. The books we know best are those that were collected into libraries. On the whole these were the largest, most scholarly and most valuable, the sort cherished by scholars and rich collectors, then and now. Scholars who have written of the print revolution of the sixteenth century have likewise tended to concentrate on the most eye-catching achievements of the new art: the great multilingual bibles, notable achievements of scientific publishing, milestones of scholarship, the most richly and lavishly illustrated texts.[4]

The more mundane productions of the press inevitably attracted less attention and admiration. But such books – almanacs and calendars, prayer books and pamphlets – were the bedrock of the new industry. They also offer the most eloquent window into the thought world of the sixteenth century's new generations of readers.

How can one assess the full extent of this trade, when so many of these publications have been almost completely lost? Happily this is one respect in which the new technological revolution of the twenty-first century has come to our aid. Tracing the sole surviving copy of these little books had been an almost impossible task. Now though, the sudden proliferation of online resources, catalogues and search engines allows us to gather together a vast amount of data that will permit us to match and compare information on almost all the books known to have been published in the first age of print – wherever they may be. This book represents a first attempt to take advantage of these global searches.[5] The results are profound. We can for the first time chart a coherent narrative of print, from the first experiments of the 1450s to the dawn of a mass information society. For all the twists and turns, reverses, disappointments and misunderstandings, it is an arresting story.

By the year 1600, 150 years after Gutenberg's Bible was first exhibited at the Frankfurt Fair, Europe's presses had cranked out something in the region of 350,000 separate titles: a cumulative total of some one hundred million individual copies. The impact of this torrent of print was enormous, but it was possible only because of the development of a multifaceted and sophisticated international industry that totally reshaped both the medieval book world and the reading public. This book is the story of that transformation.

PART I

BEGINNINGS

CHAPTER 1

THE BOOK BEFORE PRINT

In 1458 a young Magyar nobleman named Matthias Corvinus became the unlikely new King of Hungary. Within two decades Corvinus had made Hungary the dominant power of central Europe. Now at the height of his powers, the king wished to mark his triumph by making his court, and his capital Budapest, the equal of Europe's more established dynasties: so he resolved to build a library. Agents were dispatched to Florence, the centre of the European book trade, to commission the finest manuscripts. Italy's most accomplished illuminators were retained to embellish the new texts. In just seven years the scribes of Florence created for Corvinus over 2,000 volumes. All were shipped to Budapest, and added to a collection that fast became one of the wonders of European culture.

The library of Corvinus is now gone: indeed, it scarcely outlasted the king's death in 1490. When the Turks conquered Hungary in 1526 the plundered remains of the library were removed to Constantinople, and were subsequently lost. In 1877 what had survived in the Sultan's library, a remnant of some thirty-five volumes, was returned to the new Hungarian National Museum, among scenes of wild national celebration.[1] There is nothing unusual about Corvinus's collecting mania: most of Europe's rulers in the fifteenth century collected books along with other works of art. But what is remarkable is that the largest part of this collection of costly hand-copied manuscript books was accumulated in the last fifteen years of his life, at the very end of the fifteenth century: that is, a full forty years after the invention of printing.

For all the fanfare that greeted the first printed texts, hand-copied manuscript books had been an integral part of European society for many centuries. By the late medieval period Europe was full of books: books for churchmen, for scholars, for schoolboys, as well as the large decorated texts favoured by nobles and princes. The arrival of the new technology of print did not put an end to this older tradition. Rather, print made its way into a world where demand for texts had already created an intricate, sophisticated market of production, exchange and sale. To succeed, print would have to match up to demanding standards. In the first decades after Gutenberg's invention, it was not entirely clear that it could.

The origins of the book

Go into any museum of medieval Europe and you will find books: finely crafted bibles and ecclesiastical texts often richly bound in gold or ivory, their pages decorated with gold leaf and coloured illuminations. These magnificent artefacts, among the most precious remains of the age, were the culmination of a long process of evolution reaching back over many centuries.

The invention of the book was the achievement of late antiquity or the early Christian era. It came just in time to save the record of the literary culture most admired by the humanist scholars of the Renaissance, that of Greece and Rome. The ancient Greeks disseminated their learning in an oral culture; texts were written down to give them fixed form, and to assist in committing them to memory. This learning was first plundered and then adopted by the Romans, whose society was distinguished at its upper levels by a culture of literacy; literacy was also, to judge by the ebullient graffiti discovered at Pompeii, quite widely spread through society.[2] Those with sufficient funds could create their own collection of texts: for example, the statesman author Marcus Tullius Cicero built a considerable personal library. But in this era the means of recording knowledge was seriously deficient. Texts of any length were recorded on scrolls, with the text inscribed on one side of a long roll, moving longitudinally in columns left to right. The reader would unroll it gradually, grasping the roll in the right hand and unrolling it with the left. The text could only be read in one way, in the order in which the words were recorded.

These texts were written on papyrus, a material made from the stems of an abundant marsh plant that grew along the River Nile. The stems were split open and formed into flat strips that could be joined together to make sheets of any desired length. Papyrus was cheap and easy to manufacture, and created a versatile and practical writing material. However, outside the dry climate of Egypt and Greece it proved to be very perishable, and especially susceptible to damp. In Rome, and elsewhere in the northern reaches of the Empire, texts had to be continuously recopied to preserve them. Fire would rapidly consume any collection of scrolls. Today, papyri survive mostly as isolated shards, little more than an evocative fragment of the first written literary culture.

That the wisdom of the ancients survived at all we owe to two major changes in the third and fourth centuries: the replacement of papyrus with parchment, and of the scroll with the codex. The codex takes its name from the physical form of the tablets of wax or slate developed in the Roman Empire as a portable writing surface. This was ideal for note taking: two tables, hinged, could be folded away, protecting the writing until it could be transcribed. In the third century the practice emerged of recording text on rectangular blocks of papyrus, which could be stitched together along their long side to create a longer text. This development was closely linked with the growth of Christianity: Christian texts were invariably distributed in this new form.

The substitution of the codex for the scroll was a gradual process but its intellectual impact was as profound as would be that of the invention of printing many centuries later. The codex was popular because it was convenient. It took up less space than a scroll, not least because both sides could be written on, it was less easily damaged, and a damaged part could be more easily substituted and replaced. A collection can be stored, stacked or shelved in such a way that different volumes can be readily distinguished. Codices are far more practical than scrolls for the accumulation and organisation of a library. The codex can be separated into parts to be copied; different texts can be assembled into a collection in a desired order, and that order can easily be changed. In other words, it is flexible and durable.

A codex is not only practical: it also permits a far more sophisticated intellectual engagement. A codex allows for different sorts of reading. Where a scroll is intended for consecutive reading, a codex can be browsed. As the reader can move from one part of the text to another in a manner of their own devising, forwards or backwards, this encourages reflective thought. A codex provides not merely a narrative but a research resource.

All these circumstances, practical and intellectual, help explain why the codex (or, as we think of it, the book) has remained so popular and resilient. In the centuries that followed its introduction, the book evolved and developed, but it retained these essential features of the first years. A book consisted of several sheets gathered together, the text arranged on successive pages, to be read front to back or browsed at choice. It is an invention that has stood the test of time.

The success of the codex depended also on the substitution of a more durable writing medium for the brittle, perishable papyrus. Papyrus was gradually replaced by parchment, made from the treated skins of soft-skinned animals such as sheep. The highest quality was made from the skin of very young calves, and is known as vellum. The process of manufacture was intricate and skilled. The animal had to be skinned, and then the skin was washed and stretched; superfluous matter such as hair was then carefully scraped away. The result was a smooth flat surface which took writing easily and well. Scribes learned to love the sensitive flexible surface, on to which they could transfer their writings with pens fashioned out of bone or bird feathers.

Parchment was also hardy and durable, allowing for the manufacture of longer and more highly decorated texts. The disadvantage was that its raw material was in limited supply, and expensive compared to the abundantly growing papyrus. For this reason a text thought to be redundant was often washed or scraped off and the parchment reused. With the passage of time the faint remains of the original writing sometimes reappear, on occasions allowing the under-text to be deciphered. A text of this nature is known as a palimpsest. These shadow texts provide a glimpse into some of the oldest surviving writings, reaching back through fifteen hundred years of written records.

The preservation of learning

The rise of the codex was a triumphant achievement of what was otherwise a bleak period for the European cultural heritage. Literacy declined sharply in the fifth and sixth centuries.[3] The collapse of the Roman Empire in the west opened the real possibility that the accumulated literary and scientific heritage of the classical era could be lost. Education and the preservation of a literary culture depended increasingly on the institutions of Christianity, and the Church of this period was not overly sympathetic to the pagan scholars of antiquity. Despite this, it would be in the abbeys and monasteries of the Christian West that a vestige of literacy was preserved.

As the social institutions of the late Roman Empire fell into disarray, monasticism became the refuge of literacy. In the monasteries and abbeys around Europe books were gathered, ordered and preserved, often without explicit concern for their contents. Much classical learning was preserved in this way.[4] In the scriptoria, or writing rooms, of monasteries, books were written and texts copied. Monastic scribes concentrated their efforts on replicating the text of Scripture. Books came to play an increasingly important role in spreading the faith. As the Christian missionaries took the news of eternal life to the far reaches of Europe, it was important that they should be able to exhibit tangible images of the new religion. It was also important that these should be impressive. The Christian missionaries to Britain took 'all such things as were generally necessary for the worship of the church', including ecclesiastical garments, ornaments, relics 'and very many books'.[5] Soon the monasteries of Britain and Ireland were themselves leading centres of production. These books were then transported back to continental Europe as part of the Anglo-Saxon mission (the only time, incidentally, when the British Isles would be a net exporter of books until the eighteenth century).

The manuscript culture of the early medieval period reached its apogee with the extraordinary and richly decorated volumes produced during the Carolingian revival of the ninth to the eleventh centuries. The Empire created by Charlemagne and his successors embraced both the remnants of Roman civilisation south of the Alps and the broad spaces of Gaul and Germany. The creation of an embryonic bureaucracy to manage this enormous space stimulated the development of a new uniform handwriting, the Carolingian minuscule. The Carolingian minuscule was small, neat and very simple, its letters easily formed and easy to copy, rounded with tall, vertical strokes above and below the line. It was quick to write and read, and it was phenomenally successful. Soon it had replaced both the insular script of the missionary age and the archaic Roman handwriting which had often been written without word division or punctuation (the so-called *scriptura continua*). The majority of the classical texts discovered in the Renaissance were in the new Carolingian script. Humanists, wrongly thinking this represented original Roman handwriting, imitated it and in due course it became the model for the Roman type that gradually superseded the Gothic script of the late Middle Ages. To this extent we all still use the script first developed in the Carolingian Empire.

Obviously not all the products of the monastic scriptoria had the grandeur of the majestic texts designed for the Imperial court. Monastic scribes turned out a large number of books for everyday use, especially service books and texts of Scripture. Monastic houses needed several bibles, to be stationed in the chapel, the dormitory, the refectory, and even in the cloister, where monks walked and meditated. Other copies in smaller formats were used for private study. Monastic life also required many different service books: these survive far less frequently, as they were in constant use. Monastic production of bibles reached its high point in the twelfth century, by which time the market was effectively saturated. Monastic scribes then turned their attention to the works and commentaries of the writers of the early Christian era known collectively as the Church Fathers. All of this activity required not only organisation but a phenomenal quantity of parchment. Even a text of relatively modest size would require the skins of twenty to forty animals. A massive lectern bible, or a volume like the Newberry Library's twelfth-century Augustine (762 individual leaves) could consume several hundred. The production of books in these monastic centres thus required the co-operation of large numbers of people from the surrounding countryside, especially the farmers who reared animals for slaughter, and those who treated the hides. The creation of books employed many besides those who occupied their days with ink and writing implements.

The rise of the universities

At the end of the twelfth century Europe's book trade moved to new centres of writing and scholarship in the cities, a change that was closely connected with the rise of the universities. Universities had their origins in cathedral schools, where famous masters gathered around them small groups of scholars, for the teaching of theology, grammar and other subjects. The reputation of these cathedral schools inevitably rose and fell with that of their principal teachers. Universities were created when *ad hoc* seminars were replaced by fixed, permanent institutions, with a structure, statutes, and a deed of foundation. This was the achievement of the thirteenth century. In an extraordinary wave of intense creativity the new universities were planted north and south of the Alps (principally at Paris and Bologna), in Spain, and in England at Oxford and Cambridge.[6] Soon the students gathered in these places were studying an established and regular curriculum. Their need for textbooks brought about a significant change in the methods of book production.

The unrivalled centre of the new academic culture was the University of Paris. Already by the mid-thirteenth century Paris was drawing students and teachers from all over Europe. Instruction was rapidly systematised into four main areas of instruction, or faculties: arts (which encompassed a range of subjects such as grammar, mathematics, music and logic), law, medicine and theology, all of which required a great number of books. The study of theology inspired a major shift in the manufacture of the scriptural text. The large, monumental lectern bible was superseded by a compact, often largely undecorated text in small format. The format and order of the biblical text became standardised. The new bible manuscripts met a discernible need, and soon conquered the market. They were turned out in such numbers between 1240 and 1280 that manuscript bibles from the fourteenth and fifteenth centuries are a comparative rarity. The market had been saturated.

The medieval university curriculum made use both of the inherited salvaged learning of the classical era and of newly written books. In Paris the enormously diverse corpus of the writings of Aristotle enjoyed a huge vogue from the late thirteenth century onwards. Of the modern authors, the greatest was undoubtedly Thomas Aquinas, who wrote many of his finest works while teaching in Paris. Teaching was based on a dialectic method, with the teacher citing a mass of authorities in support of a proposition before stating the opposite case and providing resolution. But first students had to be made aware of the authorities. In the early days, when copies of the crucial texts were in short supply, the master had to work through them at dictation speed. This naturally frustrated the more gifted students so a new system was devised whereby students might supply themselves in advance with copies of the necessary texts.

Under this system, known as *pecia*, privileged booksellers were permitted to rent out specially made exemplar copies of the set texts. The master copies were checked for accuracy by the university authorities before the exemplars were loaned out in parts, a section at a time. The student copied them, or had them copied, before returning them. The system allowed for the multiplication of copies while preserving accuracy.[7] Of course it broke down if the students made unauthorised copies of each others' texts: an obvious temptation, since this avoided payment of the fee for renting out the master copy.

These are mundane, working texts, and they were generally used to destruction. Few survive. But the mass production of texts for a student market was a significant development of the book market. In university towns like Paris we can talk of books being manufactured in a proto-industrial process.[8] By 1300 Paris had around thirty booksellers, congregated around the university. The production and sale of books was now the full-time occupation of a new breed of workmen.

Scholars and noblemen

In the two years between 1347 and 1349 Europe was devastated by a new scourge: bubonic plague. The outbreak spread swiftly across Italy, France, Spain, England and Germany; even the outlying and thinly populated lands of Scandinavia were not spared. The impact on Europe's cultural life was traumatic. At least 30 per cent of the mainland population of Europe died in this first great epidemic. Although there was never again an outbreak of quite this severity, the plague returned with erratic frequency many times over the next two hundred years. Mortality was particularly severe in the cities, the major centres of book production, and the epidemic deprived universities of their students and masters. For those who survived there was a glut of texts, even if no one survived to teach the courses. The devastation of the rural population caused a crisis in farming, forcing up wages and severely restricting the disposable incomes of the monastic and lay landowners who had been the main customers for rich illuminated manuscripts. This further depressed the book market.

The European economy, and the population of the devastated towns, gradually recovered. The book trade then embarked on a period of remarkable growth, a late medieval flowering that lasted up to and beyond the invention of print. Three aspects of this late medieval manuscript tradition deserve special attention: humanist scholarship, court culture and lay devotion.

Humanist scholarship emerged as a significant force in the book world towards the end of the fourteenth century. The inspiration was Francesco Petrarch (1304–74), scholar, collector and man of letters. Petrarch lived for much of his youth in Avignon, a cultural centre well placed for investigative sorties into the large monastic and cathedral collections of northern Europe. A manuscript from Chartres Cathedral provided him with the crucial texts for a reconstruction of the works of Livy; other libraries yielded works by Seneca and Cicero. Petrarch's most significant discovery, however, was made in Italy, in 1345, when he unearthed the text of Cicero's *Letters to Atticus* in the Chapter Library at Verona. During the course of a long life Petrarch accumulated an impressive library, which he persuaded the city fathers of Venice to accommodate, on the promise that it would be bequeathed to the Republic. Although this promise was not kept, Petrarch was readily forgiven by those inspired by his example as a scholar and as a collector. Among them were a trio of Florentines, Coluccio Salutati, Niccolò Niccoli and Poggio Bracciolini. Coluccio assembled a large collection of books, including Cicero's previously lost *Epistulae ad familiares* (Letters to Friends), discovered in the library at Vercelli.[9] Like all true collectors Coluccio and Niccoli assembled books with a magnificent disdain for cost and consequences. Niccoli consumed a considerable fortune in assembling his library, and died heavily in debt. His collection was rescued by the Florentine magnate Cosimo de' Medici, who paid off Niccoli's creditors and donated the library to the monastery of San Marco.

Like Petrarch before him, Poggio Bracciolini scoured the great collections of northern Europe for lost texts. His best opportunity came while he was employed on Papal service at the Council of Constance. Between sessions of the council he travelled widely, rummaging through the libraries of monastic houses and browbeating the hapless custodians into parting with their texts. Bracciolini treated his victims with a lofty Italian disdain. Describing the northern librarians as 'barbari et suspiciosi' was not likely to win friends, and he did not always succeed in liberating the choicest texts. The monks of Cluny were sufficiently impressed by his credentials to give up their Cicero, but those of St Gallen would not be parted from their Quintilian, the first time the

Fig. 1 Boccaccio's vision of Petrarch. Petrarch was the hero and inspiration of generations of humanists: writers, scholars and book collectors.

complete text had been rediscovered. In the end, Poggio was allowed to borrow it to have it copied.

The texts repatriated to Italy were eagerly discussed, studied and copied. The number of people involved in these humanist ventures was still small, but with the help of influential patrons in the fifteenth century they were increasingly able to shape the intellectual agenda. When men like the Florentine magnate Cosimo de' Medici decided to build a library, scholars seized the opportunity to proffer advice, and searched out copies of the desired texts. The demands of aristocratic patrons, who wished to build a comprehensive library very quickly, produced a new revolution in copying practice. The new humanist rounded script, based as they thought on the authentic Roman (but, as we have seen, in fact on Carolingian minuscule) was a beautiful lettering, but required care and precision. For the rapid copying of many texts, scribes began to develop a cursive script of linked letters, which did not require the quill to be lifted from the page as each letter was completed. This was the origin of italic, the second great calligraphical legacy of Florentine humanism to the culture of print.

The activity of the Florentine humanists injected an enormous energy and zest into the previously active but rather predictable book world of the Italian cities. So too did the competitive collecting of Italy's princes. This collecting instinct, so deftly encouraged by Florentine scholars, was common to all of Europe's major rulers. At the start of the fifteenth century they increasingly applied this to the collection of books. Of course books had been central to the articulation of wealth and power for many centuries, stretching back to the Carolingian Empire. A richly crafted, gilded bound volume was a proud possession and object of majesty from the time of Charlemagne to that of King John II of France, who rode into battle at Poitiers in 1356 clutching the royal bible (the French lost the battle, and the bible is now in the British Library in London).[10] The significant change in the late fourteenth century was the shift from the possession and exhibition of single prized volumes to the building of a collection of considerable size.

The most spectacular developments were in Italy and in northern Europe. Here the competing and closely related ruling houses of France, Brittany and the Burgundian Low Countries, together with their aristocratic followers, provided a tremendous marketplace for the best work of a rich and opulent craft tradition. The artistic workshops of Paris, Flanders and Brabant created exquisite artwork for the miniaturised medium of the manuscript book, blending text and illustration into a harmonious whole. Each one of these carefully planned and painstakingly executed volumes was a potential masterpiece. The workshops of Bruges and Ghent also benefited from the temporary rupture of the Paris book world following the English victory at Agincourt in 1415 and the occupation of Paris (1420). Many of the French capital's leading bookmen relocated to other towns in France, leaving the workshops of the Burgundian Low Countries unchallenged in the production of the highest-quality work.

Aristocratic patrons desired different books from those created for students, scholars and clerics. Such households valued texts that were uplifting, edifying

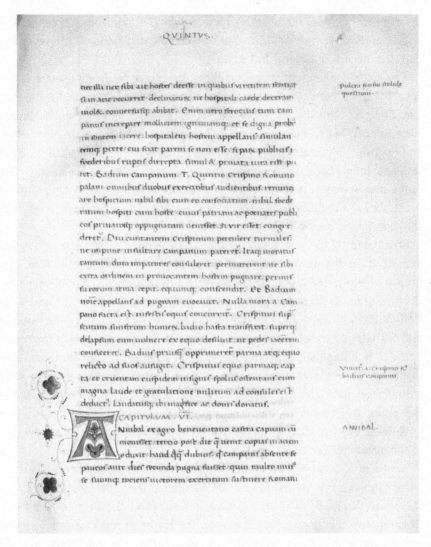

Fig. 2 Humanist script: neat and clear, and the ancestor of the 'Roman' type in which modern books are printed. From a manuscript of Livy, *c*.1450.

or amusing and that reflected the values of their societies. Alongside the classical authors everywhere in vogue, aristocratic buyers accumulated bibles, the lives of saints and other moralistic pieces. They also bought books intended purely for entertainment, such as chronicle histories and chivalric romances. As many of these books were intended to be read aloud and enjoyed collectively, the texts were in vernacular languages, rather than Latin. The most significant development of this vernacular tradition was in France, where the new recreational literature included original compositions, such as the hugely popular *Roman de la Rose*, as well as new variations on the venerable chivalric legends of Roland and Arthur.

The vogue for French vernacular literature spread far beyond the French-speaking lands. For example, the two most popular and influential imaginative travel narratives of the late medieval period were written in French, though their authors, Marco Polo and John de Mandeville, were respectively Venetian and English.[11] The major Italian collectors were eager to get their hands on the fashionable vernacular literature. Borso d'Este, Duke of Ferrara, wrote requesting 'as many French books as possible, especially the story of the Round Table, for I shall receive from them more pleasure and contentment than from the capture of a city'.[12]

Stimulated by the availability of these new genres, the princes of Europe embarked on the accumulation of libraries of very considerable size. The library of Philip the Good, Duke of Burgundy, had grown to 900 items by the time of his death in 1467. Mary of Burgundy, only daughter of Charles the Bold, had over 500 books.[13] By the second half of the fifteenth century nobles and officials in the ambit of the court were following the example of the ruling house by building their own collections. Their choices from the same canon of historical, literary and didactic texts were a further stimulus to large-scale manufacture in Bruges and Ghent, but also in Lille, Tournai, Valenciennes and the rising metropolis of the Low Countries, Antwerp. In the north the ecclesiastical city of Utrecht was surpassed by new centres of book production in the major cities of Delft, Haarlem and Leiden.[14]

Aristocratic collectors accumulated many devotional and liturgical works, some exquisitely decorated for private devotional use. The most common of these was the Book of Hours, known in English as the Primer. The Book of Hours was a collection based around the Hours of the Virgin, a series of prayers and psalms to be said at the canonical hours (the eight services of the monastic day).[15] Its equivalent in the ecclesiastical world was the breviary, the universal handbook of priests and monks in their private devotion. The Book of Hours was intended exclusively for the pious lay person. The compendium of prayers was accompanied by certain useful tables, such as a calendar of the church year. The collection would be rounded out by a selection of prayers, devotions and biblical readings of local resonance or particularly requested by the purchaser. As this suggests, these were highly personal collections. In many surviving examples the basic Hours were accompanied by small devotional works chosen from a developing corpus of popular texts, the life of St Catherine or the *Fifteen Wounds of Our Saviour*. This tradition would be

Fig. 3 Illustrated Books of Hours were turned out in huge numbers for the use of pious lay people in the age before print. The main centres of production in Paris and the Low Countries also supplied a healthy export market.

continued into the print era, when the purchaser of a Book of Hours could specify choices from a range of small texts the bookseller kept in stock to add to the volume before it was bound up.

In the workshops of northern Europe the production of Books of Hours became an immensely lucrative part of the book trade. All the major aristocratic patrons commissioned examples, of which the most famous by far is the *Très riches Heures du duc de Berry*, now in the Musée Condé in Chantilly. This was the highlight of an aristocratic collection of around 300 manuscripts. (The Duc also had fifty swans, 1,500 dogs, ten castles, a monkey, an ostrich and a camel.)[16] The *Très riches Heures* was far from being a typical example of the genre, and the duc de Berry far from a typical owner. The market flourished because many modest urban households also owned a Book of Hours: surviving documents show that this was very often the only book owned by its purchaser.

The size of the market encouraged the development of something close to industrial production. The centre for the fabrication of Books of Hours was Bruges, with large numbers destined for export to England. The market and mode of manufacture mirrored that of the production of books at the height of Parisian output in the fourteenth century. The aristocratic demand for popular works, and the steady demand from established clerical customers for missals, breviaries and other essential accoutrements of worship, meant that the manufacture of manuscript books by the fifteenth century was an industry of very considerable size. It is difficult to be more precise than this. Manuscripts are, by definition, unique items. But the scattered data available suggests that many texts were produced in hundreds, if not thousands. In the Low Countries, the northern heart of the manuscript trade, output rose steadily through the fifteenth century, reaching a peak between 1490 and 1500: well into the age of print.

The persistence of manuscripts into the age of print should not surprise us. Although we are now encouraged to think of manuscripts and printed books as two distinct and separate entities, this is a cast of thinking entirely foreign to the period. Scholars and noble collectors would mix and bind together texts they had acquired according to a highly personal order. These bound volumes might contain manuscripts that had been purchased along with items the owners had copied themselves and texts that had been copied for them. The habit of purchasing and ordering according to personal preference continued after the invention of printing: many volumes from the first century of print mixed manuscripts and printed items quite indifferently. Manuscripts were not simply copied from other manuscripts, but sometimes even from early printed editions.

It was said of Federico da Montefeltro, Duke of Urbino, that he would not allow a single printed book in his library. If this was true, he was certainly an exception. Owners seem not to have cared a great deal whether their book was a manuscript or printed, so long as they obtained the desired text. There was no clear hierarchy of merit between manuscripts and print, particularly as, in the early years, printed texts were so closely modelled on manuscripts in their visual appearance. The extent of this mixing of texts in fifteenth-century book ownership is unfortunately totally obscured by the efforts of over-zealous nineteenth-century librarians, who carefully disbound many of these volumes.[17] The search for order in library science demanded that manuscripts and books should form part of separate collections, and so this crucial piece of evidence of how fifteenth-century owners organised their collections was carefully, lovingly, destroyed.

Paper

By the mid-fifteenth century the European book market was already very large. Aristocratic collecting opened up new markets for scribes and booksellers, and the expansion of the European university network increased traditional demand among scholars, students and theologians. The expanding functions of government required more notaries, secretaries and literate public officials, stimulating a rapid growth in the number of schools. All of these people required books, competing for a supply of the precious raw material – parchment – on which books depended. Parchment was expensive and the supply relatively inelastic; there were only so many suitable animals to be skinned. The continued expansion of the book market would have been halted if it had not been possible to find a cheaper, more plentiful alternative.

Paper was an invention of the Eastern cultures, where it had been known and used for many centuries. It entered Europe via the Levant and Islamic Spain, where the process of manufacture was mastered in the twelfth century. The raw material, before the introduction of paper made from wood pulp in the nineteenth century, was linen rags. These were collected and then mashed together into a pulp which was mixed with water into a substance with the consistency of a thin gruel. A rectangular griddle with a base of wire mesh could then be lowered into the mix, and a film captured in the base. This would be delicately jiggled to create an even covering; as the water drained away it left a thin sheet which could be removed and dried to create paper.

This was a complex and intricate operation, demanding considerable skill to capture the right thickness of mulch. The process needed an abundance of running water to power the hammers that smashed the rags. Obviously it also required access to a steady supply of suitable waste clothing. These were conditions that existed in or close to many of Europe's largest centres of population, and soon the process was spreading far beyond Spain. In the thirteenth and fourteenth centuries paper mills were established in northern Italy, southern Germany and in France in Normandy and Champagne. These locations were strategically close to the major urban centres that made most use of parchment. Soon paper became an acceptable substitute, especially for the more mundane purposes of bookkeeping and correspondence. Initially there was some resistance to the use of paper in books. Parchment was more hard-wearing, and especially for a richly illuminated or decorated text the shiny surface of parchment continued to be preferred. But paper was also hardy and durable, as anyone who has handled a book made with the fine rag-based paper of the fifteenth century will testify. It was also more flexible, less brittle, and more easily folded. Sheets were even and regular, and stacked well for transportation. Soon large quantities were being traded, especially into the chillier northern lands where the ubiquity of woollen clothing restricted the supply of suitable rags.

The quantity of paper manufactured increased rapidly in the fourteenth and fifteenth centuries. More important, it could be multiplied many times over as the supply of rags from clothing was virtually unlimited. Envisaged as a practical response to the need for a larger supply of an expensive resource, it became a fortuitous but vital precondition of the technological revolution about to transform the fifteenth-century book industry.

The development of paper came at a critical moment for the expanding late medieval economy. Books were becoming a more important part of a developing network of international trade. The collecting mania of the upper echelons of European society resulted in large numbers of manuscripts being shipped around Europe. Scholars and aristocratic collectors could make use of the increasingly sophisticated business networks that linked Italy and the markets of the Levant with France, Germany and the Low Countries. The opening of the St Gotthard Pass through the Alps provided a direct connection between Venice and the major trading cities of south Germany: Nuremberg and Augsburg. From the late fifteenth century these south German Imperial cities were enjoying a period of rapid economic growth, with Augsburg now a centre not only of trade but of banking. The institution of letters of credit, accepted in lieu of cash and convertible to other currencies, was a further crucial step in the development of international trade.

During the fourteenth and fifteenth centuries the volume and value of international trade increased exponentially. The most visible manifestation of this commerce was the great trade fairs, usually biannual occasions, where the traders of Europe would gather to buy and sell, to haggle, gossip and lay plans for future enterprises. The preparation of the largest fairs, at Lyon and Frankfurt, was the work of many weeks. Caravans of loaded mules would make their way across the Alpine passes to warehouses in Augsburg, Nuremberg and Basel. From here merchants progressed almost as small armies, their wagons grouped together for protection and company. In 1374 the merchants of

Nuremberg travelled to Frankfurt in a party 500 strong, with 250 laden wagons and 300 horses.[18] From the second half of the fifteenth century their loads would also include cargo of the new printed books.

Vespasiano and his clients

The development of the major overland trade routes was the final necessary condition for the development of an international book market. The new European economic system linked together major population centres in Italy, Germany, France and the Netherlands. The increasing wealth of the leading figures in European society created the surplus income necessary for the accumulation of fine things. The rise in lay literacy created interest in books, and supplied the community of scribes and scholars who acted as copyists. All the conditions were in place for a rapid increase in the volume of books in circulation, fuelled by the new interest in books among many of Europe's political and cultural elites. What was possible with this happy conjunction of cultural and economic circumstances is brilliantly illustrated by the remarkable career of the Florentine bookseller Vespasiano da Bisticci.

Vespasiano was not a well-educated man. He knew no Latin, and, most unusually for someone moving in his circles, he was prepared to admit it. Vespasiano began his career as a *cartolaio*, a dealer in paper or parchment. A business of this sort quite naturally expanded to include manuscript texts. By the 1440s Vespasiano was proprietor of a shop where members of Florence's humanist community were happy to drop by to browse, read, and pass the time. Some became firm friends, and through these connections Vespasiano was introduced to the scholars and churchmen who accepted work copying manuscripts. Vespasiano became known as someone who could provide manuscripts of the highest quality. When Federico, Duke of Urbino turned his mind from war-making to building a library, it was Vespasiano he commissioned to furnish it. The work occupied fourteen years, not surprisingly since Federico had resolved, 'to do what no-one had done for a thousand years or more: that is to create the finest library since ancient times.'[19] Vespasiano would perform a similar service for Cosimo de' Medici, sending him a systematic catalogue that became the plan of the new library.

Supplying such eminent clients, at times simultaneously, required Vespasiano to create and manage a network of copyists and illuminators. The scale of the enterprise almost beggars belief. For Cosimo, anxious to build his library very quickly, Vespasiano engaged fifty-five scribes, who completed 200 rich volumes in under two years. Vespasiano was responsible for supplying over half the 1,000 manuscripts in the library of Federico of Urbino. In the same period the Vatican library expanded to around 4,000 volumes.[20]

Vespasiano's most famous clients had to compete with other visitors who came to Rome and Florence intending to build a library: men like William Gray, Bishop of Ely, who returned to England with a magnificent library assembled with Vespasiano's assistance (152 of his manuscripts are now in Balliol College, Oxford). Through these visitors Vespasiano's network spread far and wide throughout Europe, even before Vespasiano became intimately involved in the plan to create a library for Matthias Corvinus, King of Hungary.

Corvinus began to collect seriously around 1485. In 1487 his librarian, the Italian Taddeo Ugoleto, was dispatched to Florence to snap up what was available and commission new manuscripts. From these years date some of the finest works in the library. By the time of the king's death in 1490 some 2,000 manuscripts had been assembled in Budapest. Another hundred, unfinished and unpaid for, were left in various stages of production in Florence.

'Matthias is dead. There will be a glut of copyists.'[21] Such was the complaisant and uncharitable response of another prodigious bibliophile, Lorenzo de' Medici. But the monopoly of Italy's finest calligraphers and illuminators that Lorenzo anticipated was short-lived, since he himself would die in 1492. Vespasiano had chosen a good moment to retire and write the memoirs of an eventful life, including accounts of the great men he had served and admired. From this point on, the library played a diminished role in the conspicuous display of Europe's ruling houses. In the finest collections, that of Francis I of France for instance, hand-copied manuscripts would retain a special allure into the sixteenth century and beyond. But that did not prevent many of Europe's rulers from taking an equal interest in the new technological marvel of printing.

The increase in manuscript production during the course of the fifteenth century had demonstrated a great demand for books, fuelled by the humanist desire for accurate scholarly versions of rediscovered texts. But, as the diverse book market of the Italian cities had discovered, it also set demanding standards. In the courts and cities of Europe, a book was not merely a source of information and a repository of knowledge, but a prized and valued artefact. The relationship between owners and their books was one of some intimacy. Care was taken in the presentation, beautifying and conservation of a text. All of this established a high threshold of expectations when across Europe men began to interest themselves in mechanical techniques that might speed the production process and help them meet the ever-expanding demand for books.

CHAPTER 2

THE INVENTION OF PRINTING

T HE INVENTION of printing was not the work of scholars. Scholars in the fifteenth century had all the books they needed: their attention was directed to the borrowing, copying and bargaining necessary to obtain more texts. It required hard, practical men, often men of little education, to see the potential of a new method of copying that would bring many hundreds of texts simultaneously to the marketplace. It was also men of this stamp who perceived how the techniques of medieval craft society could be applied to achieve this.

Experiments with new techniques of mechanical copying seem to have begun around 1430. In 1444 and 1446 a certain Procopius Waldvogel of Prague was recorded in Avignon, where he was promising to teach a method of artificial writing (*ars artificialiter scribendi*). But it would be another decade before Aeneas Sylvius Piccolomini, later Pope Pius II, could report having seen at the Frankfurt Fair the pages of a bible produced without a human scribe.[1]

These pages were the work of a German merchant speculator, Johannes Gutenberg. And Piccolomini was right to think that what Gutenberg had achieved was remarkable. Gutenberg had brought together several processes well known in medieval craft society to create sheets of text 'written' with individually cast metal letters. It was a process that would provide the crucial technological apparatus for an infinitely expanded production of books.

But Gutenberg could not make it pay. He died bankrupt and disappointed, defeated by the complexities of a market not yet adjusted to absorb many hundred copies of identical books. Making the new invention a commercial proposition was the crucial and most critical challenge facing the new book entrepreneurs. It would defeat many who plunged into the new art before the end of the fifteenth century.

Gutenberg

Johannes Gutenberg was born some time between 1397 and 1403, in Mainz, a small German trading city on the Rhine.[2] His father, a cloth-maker, was a member of the Mainz patriciate, and he ensured that Johannes received a sound education. As a young adult Johannes worked mostly away from the city, largely in Strasbourg, where in 1437 he was reported to have been teaching the cutting and polishing of precious stones: probably he trained as a goldsmith.

In Strasbourg Gutenberg involved himself in several imaginative ventures that revealed the entrepreneurial flair he would later bring to his experiments with print. They also established an unfortunate pattern that business associations he optimistically entered into would collapse in acrimony and litigation. The legal documents that resulted from these cases have proved vital in reconstructing what we know of how the first experiments in printing were conceived.[3] Around 1438 Gutenberg established an ambitious scheme to manufacture pilgrims' badges for the forthcoming pilgrimage to Aachen, a great medieval shrine. These badges were simple decorative metal brooches, about four inches in length, into which a small mirror could be inserted. The partners undertook to make the impressive quantity of 32,000 of these brooches, which they intended to sell for half a gulden each. Alas for their scheme, they had miscalculated the date of the pilgrimage by a year: it would not in fact take place until 1440. Gutenberg thus had an early painful experience of the difficulties that would arise when capital had been expended, but with an awkward interval before any return could be expected from sales. This would be a recurrent problem for all those who undertook large, complex projects in the new age of print.

Gutenberg's experiments with printing may have begun in these Strasbourg years. Surviving documents include enigmatic references to terms that would later be resonant in the context of print, such as 'presses' and 'formes'. These may be connected with the pilgrims' mirrors; nothing further is known of Gutenberg's whereabouts between 1444 and 1448. But by 1448 he was back in Mainz, accepting a loan from his cousin Arnold Gelthus. This was the first of many financial transactions that underwrote his experiments with printing, which now seem to have begun in earnest.

None of the work of the first press bears Gutenberg's name. The custom of identifying the responsible printer, usually in a statement at the end of the text (known as the colophon) developed only a decade later. Nor are we helped by the fact that the books printed in Gutenberg's earliest type, the so called DK type, have survived only as fragments. These include at least twenty leaves taken from apparently different printings of the *Ars minor* of Aelius Donatus, the most popular school-book of the day, and several other small pamphlets and broadsheets. Gutenberg's partner, the financier Johann Fust, later reproached him for having diverted his presses from the business of the Bible for these more prosaic tasks, but in this, at least, Gutenberg's instincts were sound. For printing small, popular texts of this sort was a sensible way to ensure some income and keep an enterprise solvent while larger works passed through the press. Gutenberg may have produced several thousand copies of these school-books before he embarked on his Bible. If so these humble, now largely lost editions deserve to be honoured as Europe's first printed books; and it was in this initial project that Gutenberg resolved the complex technical challenges that lay behind the new art of printing.

The invention of printing

In conceptualising the printed book, Gutenberg had several models on which he could draw. There already existed a technique for reproducing short, simple texts cut into wood, from which copies could be reproduced by rubbing through on to a piece of paper or parchment. This technique, mixing text and woodcut illustrations, was used in particular for the production of devotional texts or images. These were usually sold as single sheets, but a number of woodcuts could also be gathered together to form a primitive book. One example was the series of woodcuts with inscribed text on biblical themes, known as the Bible of the Poor. A surviving example from the British Library consists of some 120 pictures from the Old and New Testaments with pertinent verses from Scripture.[4] The genius of print was to recognise that if the letters could be produced separately, then they could be arranged into an infinite number of new combinations, and constantly reused. Equally important was the recognition that an efficient mechanism would produce the image by pressing down the paper on to the inked type, rather than, as had been the case with the earliest block-books, by rubbing through (the technique practised in Asia for many centuries).[5] But first the type had to be created. The critical core of this process was the invention of the mould for hand-casting of individual pieces of type. This mould was a complex wooden frame into which a soft metal alloy could be poured and from which set type could then be released.

The process began with the tracing of the image of a letter on to the head of a rectangular piece of hardened steel. The background, non-printing areas would then be filed away to leave the character exposed: this was the letter

Fig. 4 Block book Bible. Here the text was cut into the wood block along with the illustration. The technique allowed the production of books of great beauty and utility; but it lacked the flexibility of print. This example was manufactured in the Netherlands, *c.*1430.

punch. It could then be driven with a single hammer blow into a bar of copper, yielding a sunken impression: the matrix. The matrix was then placed in the base of the hand mould; pouring in soft alloy, a compound of lead, tin and antimony, produced a column, ideally about an inch tall, with the letter standing proud and clear. Once the technique had been routinised, such characters could be produced at the rate of about four a minute. The emerging body of type would have to be filed to ensure that the types were of identical depth: this was essential for ensuring an even impression on the paper.

The second major technical component, the press, seems to have required the application of rather less in the way of ingenuity. Just as the creation of the type punch and matrix drew on the established arts of metal work and coin-making, so the press was based on familiar structures: the winepress, or a press for printing textiles from wooden patterns. The printing press consisted of two moving parts: the carriage on which the forme of type was placed and the screw, which caused a metal plate to press the paper down on the type as the pressman articulated a lever through ninety degrees. In presses that have come down to us this screw is made of metal: in the Gutenberg era it might conceivably have been made of wood. The pressure required was considerable: the whole frame of the press was therefore often secured to the superstructure of the print room by vertical struts.

With the press built and the type cast the task of creating a printed sheet could begin. First the individual pieces of type had to be set in a wooden frame or 'forme'. This was the job of the compositor, who sat with cases of type, setting up a line at a time from a manuscript copy text, placing the type first in a

Fig. 5 The type-caster's workshop, showing the moulds, chisels and vessels for the liquid metal that would be poured into the matrices to make the individual characters.

handheld compositor's stick before transferring it into the forme. The larger-format books would be from this point of view the simplest task, for here a forme consisted of just two pages of type for each side of paper. When one sheet was complete the forme was affixed to the carriage of the press. The mechanical task of printing off the desired number of copies normally required two pressmen. One would fix the paper into its frame to be lowered on to the type, which the second man meanwhile covered in an even coating of ink. The carriage would then be slid under the press and the screw rotated to press the paper down on the inked type: two impressions were required, one for each leaf of the folio sheet.

This was the ideal process, but it would be many years before it became the unvarying routine of the print shop, and there were many technical problems to be solved along the way. To take the ink the paper had first to be damped; after impression the printed sheets had to be allowed to dry, but in such a way that the reverse side could be printed without the ink smudging or showing through. The reverse also had to be printed before the paper had dried out completely. Although early illustrations seldom show this, presumably early print shops must have been cluttered with half-dry sheets, suspended like

Fig. 6 This outstanding surviving example of an early press shows the carriage open, exposing the type laid out on the forme below. Hanging from the side of the press is the soft sponge used to ink the type. Beams anchor the press to the ceiling of the workshop.

clothes on a clothesline until they were dry enough to be stacked between felt. Then there was the problem of the ink itself. The early typographers had to develop a very specific sort of ink: rich and sticky; sufficiently viscous to be easily spread, but giving an even impression and drying quickly before the paper had dried through. This was one of the great triumphs of the early Mainz typographers, who contrived (from soot, varnish and egg white) a superb black ink, rich and pure, and free of any tendency to stain. Subsequent attempts to cut cost led to a considerable reduction in the quality of printer's ink.

One can only imagine the sense of triumph as the first examples of the new printed sheets were stacked up and arranged into finished books. If the first book was indeed a now lost copy of the popular school grammar known as the Donatus the finished product would have emerged relatively quickly as this text was only 14 leaves or 28 pages long. The first books then vanished from sight, probably sold to local customers to whom they may have been virtually indistinguishable from the thousands of manuscript school-books already in circulation. The crudeness of the type, cut explicitly to resemble a manuscript hand, and the unadorned simplicity of the text on the page, must have assisted this process. Certainly if Gutenberg's first customers were aware of the momentousness of his achievement, they left no comment: until, that is, the publication of the Gutenberg Bible.

The Gutenberg Bible

One can well understand why Gutenberg, conscious of what had been accomplished, should now have hankered after a master-work to announce his great invention. That said, the choice of the Bible for this purpose is far less obvious than it may now seem. The first half of the fifteenth century had seen a large increase in book production in many parts of Europe. But the high point of manuscript production of bibles had been reached and passed in the thirteenth century. If gentry or noble households acquired any religious texts in the first half of the fifteenth century then these were far more likely to be Books of Hours. Institutional customers like monasteries had most need for liturgical texts, missals and lectionaries.[6]

The liturgical book most obviously in demand was the missal, used by all priests in celebrating the Mass. Church reformers such as Nicolas of Cusa had already spoken out for the creation of a correct and reliable text, to ensure that the Mass was performed in a proper manner throughout the Western Church. In 1451 Nicolas of Cusa was in Mainz, as the papal delegate to the fourteenth general chapter of the Benedictine Order, which had been summoned to pursue an agenda of monastic reform. The design of the DK type may indeed suggest that a missal or psalter was the original goal of Gutenberg's enterprise, and liturgical publishing of this sort would be the mainstay of the first generation of German printing. But Gutenberg resolved on a bible, and around 1452 he set about raising the additional funds necessary for such a giant undertaking.

A task of such complexity required a business of far more sophistication than the small workshop employed for the rudimentary school-books. In many respects the co-ordination of this venture is Gutenberg's greatest achievement. For the new project Gutenberg moved to a larger a workshop with four, and later six, presses. The Bible required new fonts of type to be cut, and to imitate the appearance of a manuscript bible Gutenberg proposed to use a far greater range of characters than would later be standard. Examination of the physical copy has established that four (and later six) compositors were simultaneously at work setting up type.

Printing could now begin – once a stock of paper, or vellum for the luxury copies, had first been acquired. This again meant a very substantial financial outlay, which Gutenberg could not have contemplated without taking a partner: this was Johann Fust, with whom he subsequently fell out. The surviving copies of the 42-line Bible reveal evidence that the ideal manufacturing process was only gradually discovered, through a process of trial and error. The first leaves have pages of 40 or 41 lines of type, and only from page eleven onwards does 42 lines become standard (an economy of around 5 per cent in paper and vellum). Gutenberg at first clearly had in mind that the required red page headings should also be inserted mechanically: this called for each sheet to be placed in the press again, this time with the appropriate parts of the forme inked in red. This proved too intricate and was soon abandoned: the headings were instead left for hand rubrication once the printed book was complete.

With the technique in its infancy, work progressed slowly. If each press were able to make between eight and sixteen impressions an hour, then the printing of the 1,282 pages of an edition of 180 copies would have taken roughly two years – a very considerable time for capital to be tied up before sales allowed the partners to recoup their investment. The work required constant injection of new funds. The logistical requirements were beyond anything previously experienced in a book world accustomed to manuscript books emerging from the copyist one at a time.

Gutenberg's nemesis

The Gutenberg Bible was an immediate sensation. When Piccolomini visited the Frankfurt Fair in 1454 he was able to view trial sheets but not a complete copy because the whole edition was already sold out. The astonishingly high rate of survival – of an estimated print run of 180 copies a full fifty can be identified today – suggests that from the very beginning this was a book that was cherished and treated with awe. Most of the initial buyers were monasteries and ecclesiastical customers in the immediate vicinity of Mainz, though Piccolomini dispatched samples to the Emperor for his inspection. Institutional customers would have had access to the calligraphical expertise which added the rich decorative illumination that adorns most of the surviving copies. They would also have been able to afford the very high cost. Customers paid around 20 gulden for a paper copy of the Gutenberg Bible and 50 for a copy on vellum. By way of comparison, a stone-built house in Mainz would have cost between 80 and 100 gulden; a master craftsman would have earned between 20 and 30 gulden a year.[7]

These costs would not have seemed outlandish for ecclesiastical institutions used to paying high prices for richly decorated manuscripts. But recouping the purchase price from a mass of individual customers or intermediary agents was inevitably a slow process; too slow to save Gutenberg's partnership with Fust. As soon as the Bible was published, Fust sued for return of his loans. Gutenberg could not pay. The case went to court, and Gutenberg lost. To meet his obligations he was forced to surrender his only substantial asset, his printing shop. For the next seven years, until his own death, Fust continued to run the press, now in partnership with Peter Schoeffer, his future son-in-law and eventual successor. Gutenberg faded from the scene. He would not be the last printer to learn that large complex projects carry the greatest risk, as well as the greatest renown. Although the Bible was a technical triumph, it effectively ended Gutenberg's active career as a printer. The future of print lay with Fust and Schoeffer.

Although Gutenberg is rightly honoured as the visionary force behind the new typographical invention, the partnership of Fust and Schoeffer also played a crucial role in ensuring the eventual triumph of print. For it was Fust and Schoeffer who would first place the business of print on a sound commercial footing. For this the partners were well matched. Fust provided the capital resources, and had a practical financial sense, as his ruthless dispatch of Gutenberg had demonstrated. Schoeffer, meanwhile, was the technical genius, who developed the design and manufacture of type beyond the clumsy and somewhat crude typefaces of the first experimental books.[8]

Originally a calligrapher in Paris, Peter Schoeffer had been recruited to work with Gutenberg and Fust as foreman in the print shop, and almost certainly to assist Gutenberg in solving the technical problems of designing and casting type. But whatever his loyalties to Gutenberg, when the partners fell out he stood as witness for Fust; his evidence may indeed have played a decisive role in deciding the case.

The new partners announced their enterprise with a publication as eye-catching and impressive as the Gutenberg Bible: the famous Mainz Psalter of 1457. Printed in a range of new typefaces designed and cut by Schoeffer, the Psalter was a technical masterpiece, printed in no fewer than three colours: black, red and blue. It was an unabashedly luxury item: all of the surviving copies are printed on parchment. At this stage the partners seem determined to test the technical limits of the new invention. Three-colour printing, which required the paper or parchment to be placed on the press for three separate inkings, all carefully aligned, was never a truly commercial proposition. But over the next years the new firm published a range of titles that revealed a shrewd sense of the potential of the new market for printed books. At first, their books were directed to an exclusively clerical audience. The Mainz Psalter was followed in short order by a further Psalter for the Benedictines of Bursfeld, and a series of liturgical texts. From 1460 there followed editions of Canon Law and staple texts of Roman law, such as the *Institutions* of Justinian. Other early editions included theological works by Thomas Aquinas and early Christian authors: two works by Augustine were published in 1460.

In 1462 another lavish Bible was printed, the two-volume 48-line Bible. Although not a slavish copy in typographical terms, this edition was clearly set up from a copy of the printed Gutenberg Bible. In this very important respect, therefore, the influence of Gutenberg's prototype proved to be remarkably enduring. Gutenberg seems to have given little thought to his choice of a copy text: he used one of many manuscripts of the Latin Vulgate (the fifth-century translation attributed to Jerome).[9] Yet this unconsidered aspect of the printed book proved extremely influential. Virtually all of the Latin Bibles subsequently published in the fifteenth century (a total of some 94 editions, 81 in plain text and 13 with an accompanying commentary) took a printed bible as their model. The earliest editions used a copy of Gutenberg's Bible as their copy text: later fifteenth-century editions used either Gutenberg or one of these early imitators. Unwittingly, therefore, Gutenberg played a major role in fixing the text of the Vulgate as the standard authorised text of Scripture. This would cast a long shadow over sixteenth-century efforts at revision.

These books were expensive, luxury items. Almost all were still in a large-folio format. The three Mainz Bibles were printed in an especially lavish manner, on a large sheet of 40 centimetres which became known as Royal folio, later largely superseded by the more economical Chancery folio

(30 centimetres) for all but the most expensive projects. Often a significant proportion of their print run was on parchment. All of this required heavy investment, and Schoeffer was sensible enough to take on simpler jobbing work to assist with cash flow. In addition to the theological and liturgical works that were their mainstay, the press published large quantities of single-sheet broadsheets and certificates. These included a large number of letters of indulgence, certificates granting the purchaser a remission of punishment in the afterlife in return for pious donations. Indulgences were proclaimed by the Pope to assist with specific fundraising projects: the building of a church, financing wars against the Infidel. Later they would achieve fame when Martin Luther spoke against them, but in the fifteenth century Christians had no such misgivings. Demand seemed to be inexhaustible and many early printers earned valuable fees by printing them.[10]

Fust and Schoeffer also published a number of other official notices, including broadsheet manifestos for both Adolf von Nassau and Dieter von Isenburg, rivals in the increasingly bitter contest to be named Archbishop of Mainz. The harrowing denouement of this conflict, when troops of the victorious Adolf sacked and burned large parts of Mainz, brought a temporary cessation of the press; but by 1465 the partners were back in business, turning out new editions of their expanding range of titles.

In 1466 Fust departed for Paris, taking with him a large stock of books, which he hoped would find a new market there. Once again the partners had been shrewd. News of the invention was spreading rapidly through Europe, and scholars in the largest centres of learning were indeed eager to own copies of books produced by the new technique. When Fust died of the plague in Paris, Schoeffer hurried after him to ensure the future of the business in the French capital. His new representative in Paris was another German, Hermann von Stadlohn, and although Stadlohn succeeded in reviving the trade, his death shortly after this caused Schoeffer great difficulties. The property of a foreigner dying in France was by custom forfeit to the crown, and this fate now befell Schoeffer's Paris stock. It was only after representations from the Archbishop of Mainz and the Emperor that the French king, Louis XI, agreed to compensate Schoeffer for the loss. The legal documents drawn up in connection with this case offer an awesome demonstration of the huge sums now bound up in the business of books. The French king promised restitution of a sum of 2,245 gold talers, or 11,000 livres. This was the equivalent of the annual income of one of the leading noblemen of France.

In the two decades that followed this case Schoeffer continued to turn out a steady stream of new publications, mostly in the genres that had proved so successful for his partnership with Fust: missals, Canon Law and theology. In all, he published over 250 editions, as well as at least a hundred single-leaf broadsheets: and these surviving ephemeral items were probably only a small fraction of a much larger business. But if Schoeffer had demonstrated that the business of print could be a richly rewarding one, the potential of the new market was not lost on others eager to win a share in the profits. Even before Fust's death in 1466 Schoeffer faced competition from other German workmen keen to try their hand at printing.

The spread of print

The first press established outside Mainz was probably that operated by Albrecht Pfister at Bamberg around 1460. Pfister had obtained Gutenberg's original DK types, presumably because they were regarded as outmoded and redundant by the new owners of Gutenberg's shop. Pfister published his own edition of the Latin Bible, as well as a number of small, more popular works in the German language. These included Johann von Tepl's *Der Ackermann aus Böhmen* (The Ploughman from Bohemia), a long narrative poem now regarded as the most significant printed text of early German humanism. These promising beginnings would not be maintained in Bamberg, which by the later decades of the fifteenth century was almost exclusively concerned with the publication of liturgical works. Of greater significance in the long term was the establishment of presses in the two great regional trading centres of the Rhineland, Strasbourg and Cologne.

The sack of Mainz in 1462, which induced workmen from the temporarily suspended Fust/Schoeffer enterprise to seek employment elsewhere, is sometimes seen as a major turning-point. But in truth it could hardly be expected that the techniques of the new art could be confined to Mainz, once purchasers of books began to recognise the potential of the new invention. Print had reached Strasbourg some years before the Mainz calamity. A printed Bible published by Johann Mentelin in Strasbourg is known to have appeared by 1460, the date given by an illuminator for his work rubricating the text. Mentelin published mostly editions of the Church Fathers, but he was also responsible for a milestone work, the first printed edition of the Bible in German (1466).

Printing certainly reached Cologne thanks to a man who had learned his trade from Fust and Schoeffer, Ulrich Zell. Having established his own press in 1464, Zell swiftly achieved a substantial output, mostly of theological texts, and also some editions of the classics. As befitted Cologne's status as home to a distinguished university, almost all of his works were in Latin. Cologne developed a special reputation for its theological literature, but the key to its emergence as a major centre of production lay in its role as a leading place of trade on the Lower Rhine.

It was swiftly becoming clear that it was the centres of trade, rather than of learning, that would provide the best locations for production of printed books in the fifteenth century. Rather against expectations print did not flourish in many places that boasted a distinguished medieval university. There was virtually no printing in Tübingen or Heidelberg; in England it would be London, rather than Oxford or Cambridge, that monopolised print. Large commercial cities proved more fertile territory. Print shops were established in Basel and Augsburg in 1468 and in Nuremberg in 1470. In the next thirty years these three southern hubs of German commerce, along with Strasbourg, Cologne and Leipzig, would come to dominate the production of German books.

Established trading cities enjoyed important advantages in the new commerce of books. They were natural distribution points for a business that would rely on moving books into markets a long way from the point of production. Importantly too, many of those who entered the new trade in these places were able to bring to the business of books considerable commercial expertise and substantial capital resources.

The physical appearance of books evolved rapidly in these years. In the first experimental years, the Mainz typographers had modelled their books very closely on their manuscript exemplars. This had led to a relatively easy acceptance of print in the existing established markets, where the appearance of the first printed books was simultaneously both thrillingly new and reassuringly familiar. But it also led to significant missteps in terms of the technology. The attempt to replicate all aspects of the finished manuscript through mechanical process had encouraged experiments in two-colour or even, as we have seen, three-colour printing. This was painfully slow: it required each printed sheet to be returned to the press for the decorative features to be imposed in a different ink. It was intricate and expensive work, and it was hard to ensure that the second impression was exactly aligned. It soon became clear that it was far better to leave these tasks to the established experts, the calligraphers, who would then hand back the unbound sheets to be made up as a finished book.

Such a compromise characterises most of the production of the first twenty years of print, until printers found other ways to adorn the appearance of their books. The illuminated headings and decoration familiar from the manuscript age played an important role in leading the reader through the text and in breaking up the text. To achieve a similar effect printers began to experiment with new arrangements of type, using large fonts for headings and substituting decorative woodcuts in the blank spaces previously left for hand-executed decorative initial letters. Books of the Fust/Schoeffer press frequently used several of the fonts at their disposal. This was only part of the necessary adjustment from manuscript to print. Ultimately printers had to train readers to accept a book printed in just one colour.

Illustration

In the first generation of print many printers cut their own types: Schoeffer, a precocious master in this field, cut a number of new fonts that enabled the Mainz books to experiment with a pleasing variety of arrangements of text. Fust and Schoeffer were also the first to experiment with the use of initial letters printed from wood blocks. It helped that the introduction of print coincided with a golden age of German woodcut art. The development of the woodcut precedes the invention of print by several decades: perhaps by as much as a century.[11] In this earliest period woodcuts were used largely for the manufacture of playing cards, and for the making of pictures of saints and other religious subjects. Ulm, near Augsburg, was renowned in the early fifteenth century as the chief centre for the making and distribution of playing cards throughout Europe.[12]

The first sustained experiment with woodcut illustrations was pursued by Pfister at Bamberg, who embarked on a type of book production radically different from that of the Mainz presses, directed to a largely popular market and mostly in the German language. To attract these buyers eye-catching illustrations were an obvious advantage, and Pfister invested heavily to produce this new effect. *Der Ackermann aus Böhmen* (The Ploughman from Bohemia) had five full-page woodcuts, and *Der Edelstein* (The Precious Stone), a series of fables in German, no fewer than 103. Three editions followed of the Bible of the Poor, two in German and one in Latin. This text was the traditional favourite of woodcut artists, but now the texts previously painstakingly cut into the wood blocks were replaced with movable type. A further biblical subject, the *Four Histories* (of Joseph, Daniel, Esther and Judith) was decorated with fifty-two oblong woodcuts. The cuts designed for Pfister's books were purely in outline, with little background shading. The style suggests they were intended for hand colouring, and may indeed have been coloured in the shop before sale.

After Pfister ceased production in Bamberg the main focus of book illustration moved south, to Augsburg and Ulm, the established centres of woodcut production. In 1471 Günther Zainer, one of the earliest to establish a print shop in Augsburg, began a remarkable series of illustrated books, including two magnificent editions of Jacobus de Voragine's compendium of saints' lives, the *Golden Legend*. In 1475 he published a magnificently illustrated German Bible, initiating a tradition that would continue until the Reformation. Almost every vernacular Bible published in Germany from this date until Luther's Reformation translation was copiously illustrated.

Zainer's illustrated books stirred up a great deal of discontent among the local artistic community. Those involved in the local production of block-books sensed the danger posed to their craft by books that integrated text and pictures, and they were initially successful in preventing his attempts to print. Zainer was ultimately given permission to print only on the understanding that he employed as illustrators the woodcutters of the guild.

In Ulm, meanwhile, his kinsman Johann Zainer was able to exploit the tradition of playing-card manufacture to create some exquisite illustrations for early Latin editions of Boccaccio and Petrarch. His example was followed by Heinrich Knoblochtzer of Strasbourg, who published lavishly illustrated copies of a number of popular literary works, including the *Belial* of Jacob de Theramo, the *Mélusine* of Jean d'Arras, and the *Fables* of Aesop.

So far illustration was largely confined to books of this type, a relatively small proportion of overall production at this stage. But more generic decorative features such as woodcuts, initials and border panels could find their way into the mainstream scholarly and religious texts, and did so more often in the last three decades of the fifteenth century. Through these features and the increasingly deft handling of different arrangements of type, capitals and headings, buyers of books were gradually weaned away from the expectation that a finished book required hand decoration.

Publishers of printed books began to deviate even more boldly from the manuscript prototype. Symbolic of this change was the introduction of a design feature, specific and original to the printed book: the title-page.[13] In the manuscript era books had characteristically announced their subject in the first lines of the text, often with the formula, *incipit* (literally, 'here begins'). The first printed books followed this practice. But as books were manufactured in ever-larger numbers this came to seem unsatisfactory. The precious printed sheets were now being transported, unbound, over large distances, with consequent danger of damage to the top or outer sheet. A far larger selection of texts was also available for purchase. For both of these reasons it was sensible to provide printed books with a top sheet that provided protection for the text, and a swift means of identifying the work inside. This was the title-page. In the very first printed books it was usually a blank wrapper, before printers began to use the space to provide a short description of contents. It was only towards the end of the fifteenth century that the title-page started to take on its mature form, offering a full view of what the reader might expect of a book and advertising its particular virtues. This longer description often stressed that the text was complete and accurate, or that a new edition had been freshly and wholly revised. The eloquence of the title-page announcement did not necessarily correspond to the accuracy of these claims.

The merchant publisher

In the last quarter of the fifteenth century, print spread far and wide through the German Empire, and beyond. Print reached Lübeck in 1475, and Vienna in 1481. A press was established in Hamburg in 1491 and Danzig in 1499; eastwards print reached Buda in 1473, Cracow in 1474 and Breslau (Wrocław) in 1475. In all, presses were established in some sixty-four places in Germany and central Europe before the end of the fifteenth century. But the crucial development of these years was less the mosaic of print towns, impressive though this was, than the establishment of major centres of production in the three great trading cities of the German south: Augsburg, Nuremberg and Basel.

Although those involved in the book trade in the three cities often co-operated closely, their publishing profile was quite distinctive. Basel, home to a distinguished university and a renowned group of humanist scholars, published mostly for these academic and ecclesiastical markets. Nuremberg publishers, too, could afford to publish rich, expensive editions. In the last decade of the fifteenth century Nuremberg was a town of around 50,000 inhabitants, and after Cologne the largest in the Empire. It was renowned for its role in the international book trade. Augsburg, in contrast, catered for a more local, regional trade, and for a more commercial burgher readership.[14] Very unusually, more than 60 per cent of the 1,252 editions published in Augsburg in the fifteenth century were in German. This is in contrast to the overwhelming domination of Latin in the production of early printed books overall.

These merchant communities, with their extensive resources and experience of major capital investment, would play a decisive role in the development of the German book industry. Their business experience allowed the emergence of a new phenomenon in the book world: the merchant publisher. Merchant publishers were men who commanded the capital necessary to underwrite large, ambitious projects that required careful preparation and a sophisticated network to ensure sales. In Basel, the dominant figure in the industry was Johann Amerbach, the son of a wealthy Franconian merchant. He quickly joined the merchant elite, founding a printing house that played a large role in

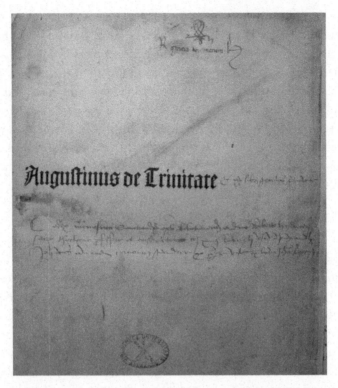

Fig. 7 Augustine, *De trinitate*, Basel, 1489. The median state of the title-page. The blank wrapper has been replaced by a terse identification of the text with no attempt at decoration.

establishing Basel in the first rank of learned publishing. His enterprise prospered greatly from his close association with Anton Koberger, the quintessential merchant publisher and leading figure in the Nuremberg book industry.[15] Koberger published over 200 works between 1480 and 1500, but he also underwrote ambitious schemes for the publication of large learned works commissioned from printers in other cities. By 1480 the productivity of his shop had dwarfed that of Schoeffer in Mainz; his operations were so extensive that in 1493 he received permission to lay in his own water supply for the row of houses he had purchased in one of Nuremberg's most prestigious quarters.[16] The pipes traversed the town at shoulder height, and were only taken out of service at the end of the nineteenth century.

The claim that Koberger's shop operated two dozen presses probably reflects the characteristic imprecision of the age with regard to numbers, but this was certainly a venture on an industrial scale. His investment was enormous: books published by Koberger used more than thirty different typefaces during the lifetime of the firm. Augsburg had no similarly dominant figure in the printing industry, but it was still of sufficient size to turn out large numbers of books in sizeable editions, such as the 12,000 broadsheets supplied by Johannes Bämler to a single customer in 1480.[17] Augsburg led the way in the output of small, relatively ephemeral books, such as almanacs and news pamphlets, and quickly established the leading role in the book trade of the region. Despite promising beginnings, printing in Ulm soon withered in the face of competition from its larger neighbour, and the same is true of fitful printing houses in other cities round about: Nördlingen, Reutlingen, Tübingen and Memmlingen. None could sustain a profitable business fit to compete with the regional giants.

Peter Drach

The growth of the German book market encouraged an increasing degree of specialisation, as printers avoided books that they knew were adequately catered for by other publishers. The robust trade in books also encouraged the rise of a new class of trader: the specialist book merchant.

We can learn much about the functioning of the book trade from many fragmentary sources. Scholars, publishers and book collectors maintained a lively correspondence about books, sharing information on recent publications, arranging consignments of books, and asking after titles they wished to obtain. However, the world of the book dealer would have remained largely in the shadows but for the relatively recent discovery of a remarkable source: the account book of the Speyer book dealer Peter Drach.[18]

This account book was discovered in the binding of three sixteenth-century books, where the manuscript sheets had been used as 'printer's waste' to bulk out and stiffen the boards behind the leather or pigskin that made up the book's binding. In itself, this was not unusual. Paper was too precious a commodity simply to be thrown away, so printers routinely sold bookbinders spoiled sheets or unwanted surplus from a print run for use in this way. The examination of original fifteenth- and sixteenth-century bindings during restoration and repair has revealed parts of many otherwise lost printed items, often fragments of school-books, or broadsheet edicts and announcements regarded at the time as too ephemeral to be worth collecting. So it was with Drach's account book, which disappeared into the binding of books imported from Lyon to Speyer some time after 1562. The sheets that have been rescued, though extensive, were not the whole book. What survives is probably only a third of the original. But this is enough to give a vivid picture of a fascinating business.

Peter Drach was a member of an established merchant family in the prosperous Rhineland town of Speyer, where his father, Peter Drach the Elder, had established one of the first printing presses. His son inherited the business in 1480, and ran it until his death in 1503. But increasingly Drach's business was focused on selling books. Speyer was well placed geographically, between the major print centres of southern Germany and the Rhine, but Drach built a business that ranged far beyond this regional trade.

Drach's bookselling business was extremely profitable. The surviving portions of his account book record the delivery of 17,155 books, an average of 1,200 a year. Drach had good regular business with the university towns of Heidelberg and Tübingen, though he sold more in Tübingen, where there was no local competition, than in Heidelberg, which had its own printers. He dispatched books to booksellers in Lübeck and Cologne, to Breslau and Halberstadt in the east, and south to Landshut and Ulm. Drach conducted much of his business, and met potential customers, through the two major trade fairs at Frankfurt and Leipzig. Almost two-thirds of all his books were delivered to Leipzig, which functioned as an entrepôt for Drach's important markets in Bohemia and Moravia.

Drach operated at the top end of the market. Most of the books he sold were intended for the use of the clergy, and he sold many theological works and books of Canon Law and liturgies for use in church to institutional customers. Individual purchasers bought collections of sermons and dictionaries. Among the sermons that sold well were the works of Bernard of Clairvaux, and the near contemporary German Dominican author, Johann Herold. Interestingly, despite the importance of the clergy in Drach's extended customer base, the texts of the Bible do not feature particularly strongly in his accounts.

Drach's accounts offer a revealing snapshot of the German book market as it had developed in the last twenty years of the fifteenth century. Of course Drach was only one dealer, and his stock is not representative of the whole corpus of available titles. Works by classical authors and recent humanist literature are scarcely represented; other booksellers developed the market in vernacular books that Drach largely ignored. But Drach's inventory does give us an illuminating insight into several aspects of overall production of books in Germany in this era. Three features, in particular, stand out. The first books published in Germany overwhelmingly concentrated on religious themes; they were mainly the works of authors of the preceding centuries rather than their own day; and most of these earlier works were also by non-German authors.

German presses turned out multiple editions of the Church Fathers, Augustine, Jerome, Chrysostom and Gregory. There were many editions too of the theological authors of the medieval period, pre-eminent among them Thomas Aquinas, Jacobus de Voragine, Bonaventure, Gratian and Peter Lombard. Most of these were Italian. Only when we consider authors writing in the century immediately before the invention of print do German authors make more of an impact. Many were Dominican or Franciscan authors active in the composition of sermons and confessional literature, such as Johannes Nider or Johann Herold.

German printers of the fifteenth century also published extensively in other genres such as history, law and philosophy. But even here, the prestige of older authors severely handicapped attempts by newer writers to obtain a hearing. The encyclopaedias, medical books and histories of the thirteenth and fourteenth centuries continued in vogue, and were frequently reprinted, at least until the last decade of the century. For contemporaries seeking to make their name through the new genre of print, the fifteenth-century German presses offered relatively slim pickings. This would be an enduring problem that blighted the careers of many contemporary poets and scholars hoping to make a living in the rising tide of book production. The innovative spirit demonstrated by German publishers in developing the form of the printed book and in constructing an advanced business network contrasts with pronounced conservatism in their choice of titles. This was indeed the secret of their success. But it is a warning against too automatic an association of print with the triumph of the new.

The Nuremberg Chronicle

By the end of the fifteenth century the book had come a long way since Gutenberg's first experiments with print. Printers had mastered a complex arrangement of type and decorative material to render hand illumination and decoration redundant in all but the most valued copies. They had developed a range of typographical material and publication formats for a market developing cautiously beyond the traditional purchasers of books. They had exploited the potential of the new genre for new design features, such as the title-page, which differentiated the printed book decisively from its manuscript forebear. Most of all they had developed complex mechanisms of finance and marketing that allowed both the raising of capital for large, complex projects, and for these projects to be delivered to a marketplace spread across Germany and eastern Europe.

All of these features of the development of the book are evident in a project that epitomises the energy, ambition and pride of achievement of the German book world at the end of the fifteenth century: Hartmann Schedel's *World*

Chronicle, the Nuremberg Chronicle.[19] This was not an especially original work; in large part it is an essentially unaltered reworking of earlier histories. But the ambition to place Nuremberg at the centre of an encyclopaedic rendering of world history from the Creation made it an especially important project for the city's merchant elite. Intellectual ambition was matched by the opulence and complexity of the planned volumes. The whole venture was financed by two wealthy Nuremberg merchants: the text was the work of the learned physician, Hartmann Schedel, while Anton Koberger was to be the printer, responsible for both the publication and distribution.

Most unusually, the contracts laying out these detailed arrangements have survived and we are able to reconstruct every aspect of the production of this prodigious book. A crucial role was played by the woodcut artists, Michael Wolgemut and Wilhelm Pleydenwurff. In addition to providing the woodcut blocks, which included intricately executed (if freely imagined) typographical views of Europe's major cities, the artists had to provide sketches showing how the text, woodcuts and decorative features would all appear on the printed page. To ensure that the printers followed them accurately, one or other of the artists was required to be in Koberger's workshop throughout the production process. This took two years, for although Koberger allocated most of his available presses (up to fifteen) to the project, this was a massive work: a large folio with 645 different woodcut blocks (since they were frequently reused, this amounted to over 1,800 separate woodcuts through the text).

Koberger printed at least 2,500 copies – 1,500 of the Latin and 1,000 of the German edition. This represented a staggering investment in paper alone. In addition the artists were guaranteed 1,000 gulden, as well as a share in any possible profit. It is no wonder that when Koberger finally finished this monumental task in 1493, he should have indulged himself by publishing a separate broadsheet advertisement. This also survives, bound in with the author's own copy of the Latin edition. Koberger did not underplay his hand:

> Nothing like this has hitherto appeared to increase and heighten the delight of men of learning and of everyone who has any education at all: the new book of chronicles with its pictures of famous men and cities which has just been printed at the expense of rich citizens of Nuremberg.

The broadsheet concluded with an exultant verse encomium:

> Speed now, Book, and make yourself known wherever the winds blow free. Never before has your like been printed.

A thousand hands will grasp you with warm desire
And read you with great attention.[20]

The hubris is perhaps excusable, for the Chronicle was a formidable statement of German self-belief. It epitomised the commercial sophistication, economic power and technical virtuosity that had brought the art of print to this extraordinary climax. In these terms the book was an undoubted success, and spread far and wide through the book-owning world. Even today it is one of the most widely owned books of the fifteenth century, with over 1,200 surviving copies registered, 800 of the Latin and 400 of the German edition. But the story of the Nuremberg Chronicle has an extra twist, a sobering and revealing codicil. The early success of the Chronicle inspired a rapid reprint. In 1496 the Augsburg printer Johann Schönsperger produced his own edition, now with 2,165 illustrations copied from the Nuremberg blocks, but completely re-cut. He followed this with a Latin edition in 1497 and a second German edition in 1500. These pirate editions completely spoiled the market for the Nuremberg original. When the contract between the printers was wound up in 1509, a considerable portion remained unsold.

The eventual failure of the consortium behind this publication was a reminder that a market dependent on frequent reprints of a limited number of tried bestsellers easily descended into ruthless and mutually ruinous competition. For those easily entranced by the technical virtuosity of the new invention, the world of books could be cruel. Even in the first generation many more fortunes would be lost than won.

CHAPTER 3

RENAISSANCE ENCOUNTERS: THE CRISIS OF PRINT

THE FIRST age of the printed book was undoubtedly a period of excitement and bold experimentation. But not everyone was convinced that the new invention represented a great leap forward for the book culture of the Renaissance. True, desired texts were now easier to obtain. But was such profusion necessarily to be welcomed? Was it possible that the flood of new writing had actually damaged the cause of pure letters? The case against books was made most eloquently by a dyspeptic Benedictine, Filippo de Strata, a member of the community of S. Cipriano in Murano. De Strata, like many early critics of the press, earned his livelihood as a scribe, copying mostly devotional works and occasional verse. But he was also a well-travelled man, a well-respected preacher, and he could rely on a hearing in high places. His diatribe against printing was addressed to the Doge of Venice. De Strata chose his moment well. His proposal, that printers be banned from the Republic, was made just as the industry seemed in danger of collapse in 1473.

De Strata's complaints were partly conventional. The flood of cheap books, he argued, was corrupting morals. The printers themselves were uncultured men. The refined scribe recoiled from the thought of his beloved books now being produced by ink-stained artisans, rootless servants and drunken foreigners. The only good thing that could be said for print was that these guzzling workmen had at least increased the income from wine tax. But de Strata also articulated fears that struck a chord with many of the elites that had thus far sustained the new technology: that a flood of cheap books encouraged the wrong sorts of reader.

This is what the printing presses do: they corrupt susceptible hearts. The silly asses do not see this, and brutes rejoice in the fraudulent title of teachers, exalting themselves with a song like this (be so good as to listen): 'O good citizen, rejoice: your city is well stuffed with books. For a small sum, men turn themselves into doctors in three years. Let thanks be rendered to the printers!' Any uncultured person without Latin bawls these things.[1]

De Strata's appeal, relying on the cultural elitism of those who had been able to afford costly manuscript books, could not in the end stem the tide. But many of those deeply committed to the new enterprise of print were soon disenchanted too. Within years of the establishment of the first presses in Rome and Venice, producers found they could not sell their books. Most of the first printers quickly went out of business. This turbulence established the dynamic of an extremely volatile and unstable book world. Printing spread with extraordinary rapidity, but the market could just as soon reach saturation. Inefficient producers were swiftly driven out of the market.

This was an age of experimentation and rapid technical advance. But the production of the new printed books required heavy investment, and many who had plunged with enthusiasm into this new world soon found themselves badly exposed. The essential problem was this: publishers and booksellers had embraced the printed book, but without fully comprehending how much had changed in the intimate and personal world of the manuscript book. Book producers in the age of print faced a totally different set of problems from those of the manuscript era. How many books should be printed? How should they be brought to the market? Would another printer attempt to spoil the market with a competing edition? The world of the scribe, where demand and supply were exactly aligned, offered no help with these questions. The implications of this quantum shift were slow to be understood. In the process, many who put their hopes in print found only ruin.

New markets

In the years immediately after the production of the first printed books the advantage lay clearly with those close to the first print shops at Mainz. For more than a decade the mysteries of the new art remained known only to a relatively small circle of pressmen and entrepreneurs. But in the peripatetic trade world of medieval Europe such a situation could not continue indefinitely. As quickly as the new invention spread through Germany, scholars and rulers in other parts of Europe also yearned to learn the secrets of the new process.

This was particularly the case in Paris, centre of the medieval book world and capital of one of Europe's proudest monarchies. By 1458 the King of

France had got wind of the new invention, and he dispatched to Mainz an experienced punch-cutter from the royal mint, Nicolas Jenson, to divine its secrets. Jenson was intended to bring back the new techniques to establish printing in France, but either the workers at Mainz proved too wily, or by the time of his return the king was dead. In either case Jenson disappears for some years before emerging as a printer, not in France but in Venice.

It would be another ten years before a printing press was established in the French capital: until that time the bookshop established by Mainz printers Fust and Schoeffer in Paris dominated the local market. The first press was finally established in 1470, thanks to two scholars at the university, who succeeded in persuading three Germans experienced in the new art to come to Paris and set up a press within the precincts of the Sorbonne, the theology faculty of the University of Paris.[2] These were the modest beginnings of what would become, with Germany and Italy, the third pillar of the world of early printed books. The book trade had flourished in France in the two centuries before print, sustained by steady demand from the royal court, the lawcourts and the university, all located in the French capital. It was natural that Paris should now emerge as a major centre of production of the new printed books.

In 1472 the firm of the immigrant Germans transferred from the Sorbonne to the Rue Saint-Jacques, which now became the centre of the new industry. For the next five years they turned out a succession of law books, works of theology and scholastic texts: standard titles for established users of such books. Their success tempted other businesses into the market. These included a number of men who would become important figures in the Paris book world: Pasquier and Jean Bonhomme both set up shop in 1475, and Jean Dupré in 1481.

Paris was home to a large and diverse book-buying community, sufficient to sustain several printing firms. It was also the capital of the most populous nation state in Europe. The printed book was established in France at almost precisely the moment when the French monarchy had finally thrown off the long shadow of the Hundred Years' War, the destructive conflict with England that had ravaged the French landscape and deeply undermined its economy. In the second half of the fifteenth century both the population and economic activity of France's numerous provincial towns were reviving strongly. These towns soon provided an important secondary market for the new printed books.

It was not long before print made its way to a number of these places: Lyon, Toulouse and Poitiers all had printing by the end of the 1470s; Caen, Troyes and Rouen in the following decade. In the first years these provincial

Fig. 8 After a slow start, Paris emerged as one of the leading centres of European typography. Especially in northern Europe Paris printers were extremely influential in the emergence of the design features we associate with the first age of print. Here the printer's mark points the way towards the full integration of text and decoration on the mature title-page.

presses relied heavily on the patronage of the Church. Many French dioceses had their own independent rites and therefore required liturgies customised for local use. Paris bookmen had provided fine breviaries and missals for their use in the manuscript era; this trade continued quite naturally in print. A key figure in the trade was Jean Dupré, one of the first Paris publishers to build a business on the scale of Schoeffer or Koberger. He specialised in

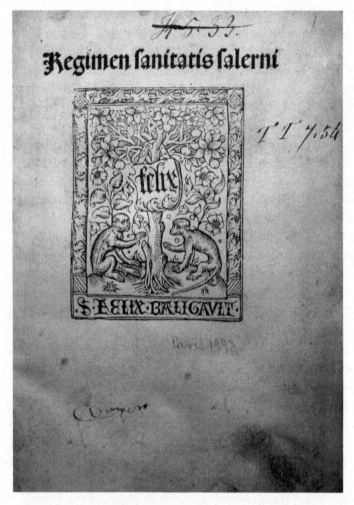

Fig. 9 An early Paris edition of a medical best-seller. Here the printer has achieved a better balance between text and illustration than in the previous example.

providing editions of liturgical works for diverse places throughout France. At first these were published at his shop in Paris but as the business grew it became sensible to establish a branch office, with a local printer, in such places where he already sold books, such as Abbeville, Rouen and Chartres. Later his enterprise would range further afield, to Angoulême, Nantes and Châlons-sur-Marne.

Paris printers played a dominant role in the development of this provincial print, but France sustained a second major centre of print culture at Lyon. Print came to Lyon in 1473 and by the end of the century the city had become a print centre of European importance. Lyon profited from its position at an established crossroads of European trade, with routes east into Germany and south across the Alps into Italy. In 1494 Lyon secured the restoration of its famous quarterly fairs; the injection of capital that followed passed naturally into the burgeoning book industry.[3] Lyon printers published a larger number of books in French than did the printers of Paris. These catered for Lyon's educated but not necessarily scholarly clientele (Lyon, in contrast to Paris, had no university). Lyon's publishers also developed a reputation for the publication of high-quality books on medicine and law, books that required both significant financial investment and access to a broad European market. Like their Paris colleagues, Lyon's book trade entrepreneurs assisted in the establishment of a range of subsidiary centres of print in towns round about, such as Narbonne (1491) and Uzès (1493).

Printing spread to more than forty towns and cities in the Francophone world before the end of the fifteenth century. Many of these lay outside the borders of the French kingdom: in Brittany (not incorporated into France until 1532), Lorraine, and the territories owned by the Dukes of Burgundy, the Netherlands and the Franche-Comté.

The Low Countries was one of the wealthiest parts of medieval Europe, and it rapidly emerged as another important early centre of print culture.[4] In 1473 Thierry Martens opened a small experimental press at Alost near Louvain; almost simultaneously Nicolaus Ketelaer and Gerardus de Leempt established a press in the northern Netherlands, at Utrecht. Neither of these first ventures was particularly long-lived. The Martens press soon migrated to Louvain, home to the only university in the fifteenth-century Low Countries. The Utrecht press was quickly superseded by a far more ambitious enterprise that flourished under the sponsorship of the Brethren of the Common Life in Deventer. Here Richard Pafraet established a busy and lucrative business, turning out numerous editions of the school-books of Aelius Donatus and Alexander de Villa Dei, two of the most popular and widely reprinted texts of the first era of print.

The commercial centres of Flanders and Brabant, meanwhile, catered for a rather different clientele. Presses were established in Antwerp, Ghent and Bruges to exploit the lucrative trade in literary texts for a largely bourgeois lay readership. Bruges, like Paris, had been a major centre of the manuscript trade, sustained by the expensive tastes of the Burgundian court and the local aristocracy. In the age of print its book production was eventually eclipsed by that of the commercial metropolis, Antwerp, but it did provide the location for the first typographical experiments of William Caxton. Caxton briefly operated a press in Bruges with a local man, Colard Mansion, and it was here that the first book in the English language was published, in 1473. In 1476 Caxton transferred his enterprise to Westminster, where, with support from a variety of noble patrons, he turned out a series of fine literary editions, almost exclusively in English.[5] The Caxton press was continued after his death by his one-time assistant, Wynkyn de Worde, but by now the press faced the competition of several other foreign-born printers who had decided to try the potential of the English market, most notably Richard Pynson, from Normandy. By the end of the century Pynson was established as de Worde's most substantial competitor, and the two firms would continue to dominate the small English market through the first two decades of the sixteenth century.[6]

Italy

The first experiments with printing on the Italian peninsula took place at a Benedictine monastery at Subiaco, around 50 miles from Rome.[7] Here, as in Paris, the influence of *émigré* Germans was an important catalyst. Most of the monks at Subiaco were German; the house's patron, and probably the guiding influence behind the venture, was Nicolas of Cusa. The Subiaco press published four books between 1465 and 1467, including editions of Augustine, Lactantius and Cicero's *De oratore*. The two printers, Sweynheym and Pannartz, were both men of the north: Sweynheym came from the Rhineland and Pannartz from Prague. In 1467 the partners moved their press to Rome. Germans were also responsible for the establishment of presses at Venice in 1469, and Foligno and Trevi in 1470. From this point the spread of the new art was quite spectacular. Within two years a press had been established in most of the largest cities in Italy: Ferrara, Florence, Milan, Bologna and Naples in 1471; Padua, Parma and Verona the following year. By the time print had arrived in Lyon and the Low Countries in 1473, twenty-four Italian cities had a functioning press. And when William Caxton opened his print shop in Westminster in 1476 that number had increased to forty. In all, some eighty towns in the Italian peninsula would play host to a printing shop before the end of the fifteenth century, and these included three of the ten largest centres of production in Europe: Venice, Rome and Milan. All told, Italy was responsible for almost a third of all books published throughout Europe in the fifteenth century.

The impact of the printed book was especially profound in the Republic of Venice.[8] In the second half of the fifteenth century Venice was at the apogee of its commercial power. The city had a population of 100,000 and ruled over a territory that included the university town of Padua. Despite the loss of large parts of its Mediterranean empire to the advancing Turks, it was still the southern entrepôt for Eastern trade, and this was the cornerstone of its vast wealth. Among its prosperous manufacturing trades Venice had established in the fourteenth century a leading role in the production of paper. All of this helps explain why, when printing arrived in Venice in 1469, it developed with rapidity unequalled in any part of Europe. The first printer of Venice, Johannes de Spira, began in 1469 with a modest four editions, a conventional selection of Latin classics: two editions of Cicero, a Terence and a Pliny. In 1470 there were at least four printers at work in Venice, responsible for a further twenty-three editions. By 1471 the number of new editions published had risen to eighty-five. This was a breathtaking rate of growth in a still relatively untested market. But the true boldness of the Venetian enterprise is only apparent when one considers that these eighty-five editions represented a third of the total output of printed books published throughout the whole of Europe in this year. All told, printers in the Italian peninsula printed almost 400 new editions in the years 1472 and 1473. This was almost double the output of printed books published in Germany in the same two years.

First doubts

In the fifteenth century Italy was both the acknowledged centre of cultural and intellectual innovation, and a major motor of the European economy. The spectacular growth of printing in the Italian peninsula reflects this. Print spread like wildfire, fuelled by the enthusiasm of a sophisticated urban market. But this enthusiasm was based more on fascination with the new technology than on rational calculation. It was still far from clear whether Italy's community of readers could deal with so large a volume of printed books.

A first sign that the printers may have misjudged the market came in 1472, when the two Rome printers, Sweynheym and Pannartz, petitioned the Pope for relief. They claimed that they had thus far manufactured some 20,000 copies of their printed texts; but they could not sell them. Their workshop, they complained piteously, was 'full of printed sheets, empty of necessities'.[9] Sixtus IV, a keen supporter of humanist scholarship, did what he could, but the funds he provided, in the form of a grant of benefices, sustained the press only for a further year. In 1473 Sweynheym and Pannartz closed their shop for good.

The difficulties confronting the Rome printers were not unique. The rapid expansion of printing throughout the peninsula in the 1470s was followed almost immediately by a period of painful adjustment. The first crisis of production hit Venice in 1473, immediately following the extremely rapid take-off period. Production fell to half the peak of 1471–72, and eight of the dozen printers working in the city were driven from the market. This particular crisis may have had local, political causes, but the printers seemed also to have misjudged the market. In particular the market was glutted with editions of classical texts, including multiple editions of works for which there were simply, as yet, insufficient readers. By the beginning of 1473 there were available three editions of Quintilian, Livy and Pliny, five editions of Juvenal and nine of Terence and Virgil. The thirty-eight editions of works by Cicero included nine printings of *Letters to Friends* and four of his treatise *De officiis* (On duties).[10]

As the printers struggled to dispose of their stock, criticisms of the quality of their work began to emerge. The scholars who shared the excitement aroused by Gutenberg's new invention did so for very specific reasons. They believed that print would make true texts, especially of the works of classical authors, more widely available. By this they meant that print would be employed to enable scholars and intellectuals to possess more books; humanists were less concerned that books should be made available to a broader range of the population. This is a crucial distinction; and it is in this context that the humanist criticism of print now developed. For it was swiftly realised that printed books had not necessarily produced more accurate editions.[11] The first printed books could not live up to the standard set by manuscript production in Italy. They were often dirty, smudged and inaccurate. They included too many mistakes. The inefficiency and carelessness of printers would be a repeated lament of authors throughout the era of hand-press printing, but in this first generation it had a philosophical edge: the charge that print had debased the book.

Florence

This ambiguous attitude to print may go some way towards explaining the relative failure of the printing press to gain a secure foothold in Florence. Florence was both the intellectual capital of the Italian Renaissance and a leading centre of production of manuscript books. Before print, the calligraphers and copyists of Florence had produced books of great beauty, and in great profusion. But the city's elites proved stubbornly reluctant to embrace the new art. Although an attempt was made to introduce printing into Florence by 1471, the first enterprises had all either failed or moved away by 1473. Florence was without a printing press altogether until a new press was established in the Convent of San Jacopo di Ripoli in 1476. This press at least enjoyed a measure of continuity, perhaps profiting from free labour among the monastic workforce. It turned out a range of cheap, commercial publications over the next eight years.[12] But Florentine intellectuals generally kept their distance. The contribution of Florence to original publications in the field of literary scholarship is strikingly modest: the city of Petrarch, Dante and Boccaccio seemed oblivious to the potential of print.

The difficulty facing printers in Florence was that no book likely to prove commercially viable could live up to the city's elevated self-image. The printer of the first book published in the city, the goldsmith Bernardus Cenninus, felt it necessary to claim that he had perfected the art of printing without any help. His book, published in three parts between 1471 and 1472, was thus a monument to Florentine spirit and ingenuity. It was indeed a beautiful book, made with special types that Cenninus had designed himself; but it was not a commercial success. A surprisingly small number of copies survive for such a luxury enterprise, and it was the only book that Cenninus published. Here lay the rub. Although Florentine publishers did produce a number of notable and eye-catching books, including a significant group of the earliest books printed in Greek, the city did not appropriate a sufficient portion of the more mundane commerce of print. Such quotidian productions proved below the notice of the traditional buyers of Florentine manuscripts. The Medici, in contrast to other princely patrons elsewhere in Europe, gave the press little support. When Marsilio Ficino, the first of the Florentine humanists to engage with the press, brought to completion his monumental edition of Plato, his only reward was that when Lorenzo the Magnificent commissioned a new edition six years later, he had it printed in Venice.[13]

This cultural disdain had the inevitable consequence that publishers could survive only by pursuing a ruthlessly pragmatic strategy. The one Florentine firm to enjoy sustained success, the Giunti, angled their output firmly towards a less literary market. Books like their Italian translation of the *Imitation of Christ*, were aimed at a large market of proven profitability.[14]

Up until the end of the fifteenth century fewer than a thousand books were printed in Florence, against almost 4,000 editions in Venice. If one counts only books in the scholarly languages, Latin and Greek, then Venice out-published Florence by a factor of fifteen to one. Amazingly, Florence, the cradle of the Renaissance, had turned its back on scholarly print. Fewer than 200 books were published in Latin in Florence before the end of the fifteenth century. In fact it was one of only two major print cities in Europe that printed more books in the vernacular than in Latin during this period (the other was Augsburg). The preponderence of printing in Italian was in part the consequence of the great upsurge that accompanied the brief ascendancy of the apocalyptic preacher Girolamo Savonarola in the last years of the century (1494–98). Savonarola's preaching of an impending apocalyptic judgment on a city corrupted by luxury convulsed Florentine politics. Those who crowded to hear his sermons would soon have the opportunity to read them as the Florentine presses cranked out numerous editions of his works.[15] This print surge prefigured the later experience of Germany during the fury over Martin Luther and sent a powerful signal to a city elite that had turned its back on book production. The ruling classes had paid a heavy price for their disdain of print. The lessons of the Savonarolan ascendancy in Florence would be well learned by Europe's other ruling powers.

The crisis of print

Florence was a special case, but it was not the only place where the new technology would be tested. As print became a familiar, and then an increasingly dominant presence in the previously relatively intimate world of book ownership, it became more obvious that all aspects of the business had radically altered. The book itself was changing. The earliest books were 'half finished goods' that required hand adornment: the provision of initial letters, headings and decorative paragraph markers. As the century wore on printers had gradually learned to print all these as an integral part of the text, but the result was a physical artefact ever more radically different from the familiar manuscript. Buyers had to be retrained to accept the monochrome finished article as an adequate substitute for the more dazzling manuscript.

In due course this would be achieved, but it took far longer for the producers of books to understand the new disciplines under which they laboured. In the first years printers were understandably preoccupied with the technical demands of the new art. But in some senses even when the book was printed, and the finished text stacked ready for the binder, the most challenging task still lay ahead: how to bring the book, now printed in 300, 400 or even 1,000 copies, to a host of individual purchasers: purchasers at this point unknown to the printer. This would seldom have happened in the manuscript age, when the man who commissioned a manuscript often knew the scribe personally: it was an individual and often very personal transaction. The buying of a printed book from a large stock was a very different thing. Purchasers had to be trained to understand that they desired a book that they had not personally commissioned. Sabellico's alluring vision of Juliarius browsing the book stalls of Venice in 1493 might have described what was by now a familiar part of the book trade – but it would not have conformed to the expectations of the book-buying public thirty years before.

It was the difficulties posed by this new marketplace that accounted for the failure of so many publishing ventures in the last third of the fifteenth century. The investment that a printer made in type, paper and wages was all directed towards a clear goal: the production of a finished artefact. But unless the edition was supported by a wealthy sponsor or patron, the costs could only be recouped once the books had been sold. For many printers this demanded skills for which experience in a workshop producing manuscript books offered little help, and a network of commercial contacts they did not possess. The pool of potential purchasers was large, but often widely dispersed. The desire of many printers to publish eye-catching, luxurious or innovative publications accentuated this problem, since books like this were the most difficult to sell to a clientele dispersed around Europe. Printers would often have to hold stock for a long time before the edition was sold out: this again, was a problem not anticipated by those familiar with the retail manuscript trade.

The bitter reality of the fifteenth-century expansion of print was that the rush of the new had brought print to many towns where the production of books was not commercially viable. The market was too large and too dispersed for the small producer. In the last two decades of the fifteenth century, as printing moved towards a more fully commercial basis, this brutal truth became more apparent.

During these years the geography of European print was radically transformed. Gradually, printing became concentrated in a small number of major centres of production; and within these centres, printing increasingly became the business of a small number of larger firms. The extent of this transformation has been masked by a focus on the rapid spread of print. Closer examination tells a different story.[16] In Italy, printing was known, at some point in the fifteenth century, in around eighty different places. But of these only eleven could sustain a printing press continuously through the period, and the four largest centres of print between them accounted for 80 per cent of the total output. The experience of smaller cities was quite different. Printing arrived in Treviso in 1471, and some eleven different printers worked in the town over the next twenty years. But when the last of these shops closed in 1494, it would be another ninety-five years before a printer worked in the town again.[17]

What was true of Italy was also true of other parts of Europe. Most of the presses established in provincial France lasted only a few years, and produced only a handful of books. In the first forty years of the sixteenth century just three towns in France – Paris, Lyon and Rouen – would sustain printing continuously.[18] Even in Germany by the last decades of the fifteenth century a small number of major centres of production had come to dominate the trade.[19] The publication of books outside these major metropolitan centres was becoming difficult. In Ulm, where printing had been established early, and initially flourished, four of the five printers active during the fifteenth century experienced financial difficulties, or bankruptcy. The man who survived was a printer who eschewed expensive projects in favour of a mundane production of single-sheet items for the city council.[20] To many printers this would have seemed an unworthy choice. But those who dreamed that printing would win them the respect and trust of their social betters faced more crushing disappointment, and often financial ruin.

In the last years of the fifteenth century the print world included many such dreamers. A number trailed hopefully from town to town establishing print shops that failed in every one. Jacobinus Suigus worked successively in San Germano, Vercelli, Chivasso, Venice, Turin and Lyon without conspicuous success.[21] Henricus de Colonia at different times ran presses in Bologna, Brescia, Lucca, Modena, Milan, Siena and Urbino.[22] The peregrinations of Johann Neumeister, the proto-typographer of Albi, took him to three different countries, but he never managed more than a handful of books in any of them. He first appears at Foligno in Italy around 1470. After a decade of inactivity he surfaces in Mainz, where he printed a single book before moving to Albi. The predictable failure of this venture drove him finally to Lyon, where he eked out a living to the end of the century.[23]

Nicolas Jenson

By the time print entered its third decade, the age of innocence was past. To survive, the new technology would have to establish a secure commercial base. In this, as in so much else, the largest centres of production led the way. In Germany we have witnessed the success of the first merchant publishers, Schoeffer, Koberger and Amerbach. In Venice we can follow this transition through the careers of two exceptionally influential typographers, Nicolas Jenson and Aldus Manutius. Jenson's eventful engagement with print had begun, as we have seen, with attempts of the King of France to divine the mysteries of print in the early 1460s. But it was in Venice that Jenson would eventually settle, and embark on his career as a printer.

Jenson's first ventures in printing followed the then customary concentration on the works of classical or humanist authors.[24] Nor did he show any great originality: of the seventeen literary works that Jenson brought to the market in the years before 1473, twelve had already been printed by somebody else. By 1473 the market was saturated. Jenson's business might have suffered the fate of other Venice contemporaries but for a rapid change of course. In 1473 he made two critical decisions that saved his business and effectively laid out the path that would carry Italian printing through the shoals of an increasingly uncertain business environment. Firstly Jenson entered into a formal partnership with two Frankfurt merchants, Johann Rauchfas and Peter Ugleheimer. The capital

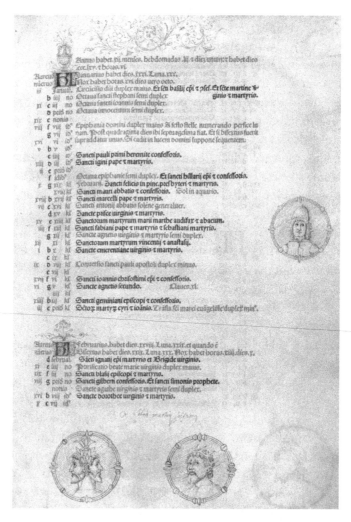

Fig. 10 Even those printers keen to embellish a reputation for high-quality books for cultured and learned customers did not despise more humble tasks. This calendar was intended for one of the liturgical publications of the distinguished Venice printer, Nicolas Jenson, in 1478.

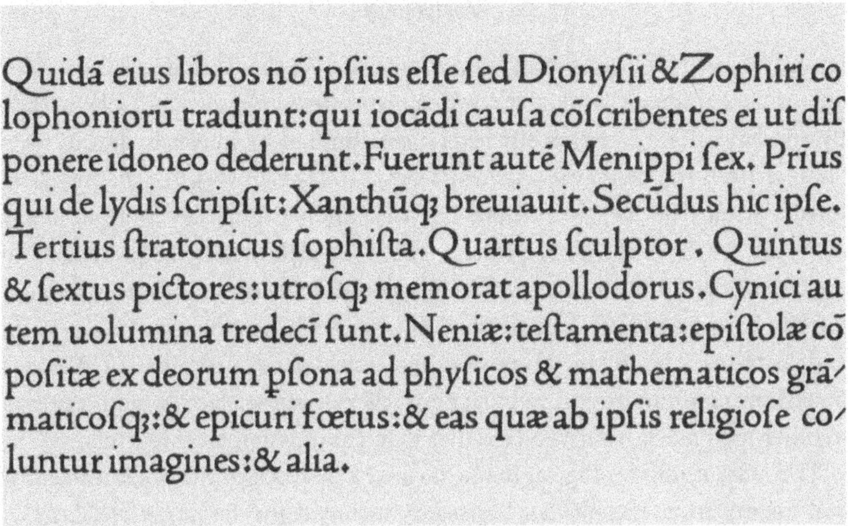

Quidā eius libros nō ipſius eſſe ſed Dionyſii &Zophiri co
lophoniorū tradunt:qui iocādi cauſa cōſcribentes ei ut diſ
ponere idoneo dederunt.Fuerunt autē Menippi ſex. Prius
qui de lydis ſcripſit:Xanthūq; breuiauit.Secūdus hic ipſe.
Tertius ſtratonicus ſophiſta.Quartus ſculptor. Quintus
& ſextus pictores:utroſq; memorat apollodorus.Cynici au
tem uolumina tredecī ſunt.Neniæ:teſtamenta:epiſtolæ cō
poſitæ ex deorum pſona ad phyſicos & mathematicos grā
maticoſq;:& epicuri fœtus:& eas quæ ab ipſis religioſe co
luntur imagines:& alia.

Fig. 11 An example of the famous Jenson Roman types.

injected into the business by this arrangement was used to reorientate
production towards a wholly different type of book serving specialist markets in
law, medicine and theology. Jenson rebuilt his business in the 1470s by
concentrating on publishing substantial texts required by particular groups of
professional readers. These included the four main texts of Canon Law, which
together constituted an indispensable codification of the decrees of the Church:
Gratian's *Decretum*, the *Decretales* of Gregory IX and the two supplements of
Boniface VIII and Clement V. These texts would be published in over 200
separate editions before the end of the fifteenth century. Venice printers also
published repeat editions of the foundational texts of Roman law, such as
Justinian's *Institutions*.

Jenson is best known to posterity for the Roman types in which his
early works were published. This was an apparently decisive break with the
tradition of black-letter or Gothic types modelled closely on the scribal
scripts, and Jenson's innovative designs have been widely admired, not least
by the Victorian artist William Morris, who adopted Jenson's new Roman
type as a model of typographical perfection; but in fact Jenson, in his
reconstructed business, swiftly abandoned these types and moved back to a
more conventional Gothic typeface for his great series of law books. Jenson
had the commercial sense to see that typographical innovation had moved
ahead of the market.

Bestsellers

Jenson's market strategy swiftly found imitators. As the fifteenth century wore on, printers gradually worked out which texts offered the most reliable market. By and large these were not the texts most admired by intellectuals, but texts familiar from the medieval scholarly world. Today the works of the medieval jurist Bartolus de Saxoferrato are not well known; but they were a steady bestseller for the first Venice printers, going through over 200 editions before the end of the fifteenth century.[25] Venice could dominate this market because the city lay close to four distinguished university towns: Bologna, Padua, Pavia and Ferrara. The financial power and established expertise of Venice's publishing community ensured that booksellers in these places would continue to order their stock from Venice rather than commission local reprints.

The market for theological books formed a bedrock of the book trade as it had before print. Established bestsellers included the *Imitation of Christ* of Thomas à Kempis, published in 172 printed editions before 1501, the works of the early church fathers, Augustine and Jerome, and the medieval scholastic Thomas Aquinas. The *Golden Legend* of Jacobus de Voragine was published in over 150 editions in the fifteenth century, though it proved more popular in northern Europe than Italy.[26] This was one of the most translated texts in fifteenth-century Europe, with editions in no fewer than nine vernacular languages. Books of Hours also played a larger part in the book trade in northern Europe.[27] In the Netherlands, by far the most frequently produced texts were school-books, especially the *Ars minor* of Aelius Donatus, and the much-criticised *Doctrinale* of Alexander de Villa Dei. We will never know quite how large this market was, because most books of this sort were used to destruction and many editions have vanished altogether. Most surviving works are known only from fragments discovered in the bindings of books.[28]

What of contemporary authors? The concentration on familiar bestsellers in the last years of the fifteenth century may have been the pragmatic choice for printers, but it did little for those who hoped to make a literary reputation in the new world of print. An author wishing to make a modest living through the business of books was far more likely to do so as the editor of a new edition of one of these established texts than by publishing his own compositions. In the field of literature, editions of the three great names of Tuscan letters, Petrarch, Dante and Boccaccio, dwarfed those of any living author.[29]

Even in printing the classics, printers had an ingrained tendency to play safe. The great Roman authors, Cicero, Virgil, Ovid, Seneca and Terence, were

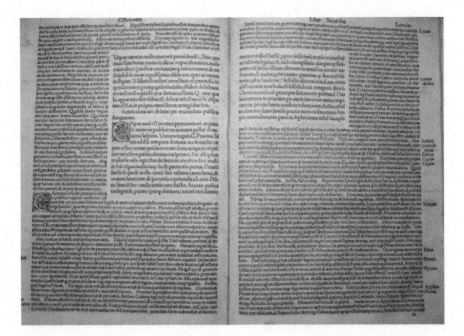

Fig. 12 Cicero, *De officiis*. A scholarly edition, with commentary. The early experiments with arrangement of text and commentary were not always easy on the eye. Here the text is almost submerged by the scholarly apparatus.

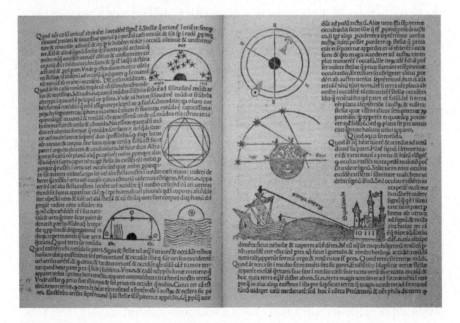

Fig. 13 The management of text and illustrations was in many respects easier in manuscripts than in print. This early Venice edition of Sacrobosco's *De Sphaera* presents an uneasy combination of densely massed text with woodcuts of mixed quality and relevance.

printed around a thousand times before the end of the century, altogether accounting for roughly two-thirds of the total output of classical texts.[30] All told, editions of the classical authors make up around 5 per cent of all printed books published in the fifteenth century: perhaps less than one would expect given their place in the humanist mythology of print.

Aldus Manutius

Conservative in their choice of texts, publishers pursued innovation through typographical subtleties and in the development of new configurations of text and typefaces. In this respect, special renown has always attached to the name of Aldus Manutius, Venice's most famous printer in the last decade of the fifteenth century.

Aldus Manutius came to Venice in 1490, a man in mid-career with an established reputation as a scholar and pedagogue.[31] Although his first books were not published until 1495, it seems he arrived in Venice with the express purpose of founding a publishing firm. Certainly the complexities of the task he had set himself would have necessitated a lengthy period of preparation. For Manutius was preparing the publishing programme with which his name is forever associated: bringing to the market a range of the seminal works of the Greek authors in the original language. This would include a range of basic pedagogic tools, such as works of Aristotle familiar from the university curriculum in Latin translation, along with various literary and medical works: books by Theocritus, Hesiod, Dioscorides and Nicander.

The intellectual agenda that lay behind this was set out in a short pamphlet penned by Manutius some time before, possibly before his arrival in Venice. Greek, he argued, was an indispensable aid to true Latin scholarship.

> How can one who does not know Greek imitate the Greek authors, who are the most advanced in every field of learning and from whom, as is known, everything that is worthy of praise has passed into the Latin tongue?[32]

The Roman authors Cicero, Horace and Quintilian are all cited in support of this proposition which urges the absolute necessity of mastering Greek literature.

In three great bursts of creative energy between 1494 and 1515 Aldus produced editions of ninety-four classical and post-classical authors. This total included the first Greek edition of thirty-one works, including writings of Aristophanes, Thucydides, Sophocles, Euripides, Demosthenes, Plutarch,

Pindar and Plato. Manutius thus diverged boldly from the pattern of cautious imitation that had formed the cornerstone of most successful publishing programmes. That he pursued this purpose in Venice was itself worthy of note, because to this point Florence had been the acknowledged centre of Greek scholarship. Manutius was clearly prepared to trade proximity to the famous scholars who lived in Florence for the capital resources and typographical expertise that only Venice could offer. This was shrewd. The technical problems associated with the development of a printed Greek alphabet were considerable, and the investment commensurately high. Manutius estimated the running costs of his printing house at some 200 ducats a month. It was therefore important that he was able to recruit not only a type designer of some genius, but a reliable financial partner, the stalwart Andrea Torresani. This partnership allowed Manutius to undertake some of the most ambitious books of the age, such as the impressive five-volume Aristotle. The Greek works formed the heart of Manutius's publishing programme, but he is now almost as famous for two further innovations: the publication of a series of Latin classics in a new italic script, and in a small octavo format.

The elegant italic, like the Greek type, was the achievement of the designer Francesco Griffo of Bologna, a man so important to the printer's enterprise that Manutius made a rather clumsy attempt to prevent him working independently. Manutius applied to the Venetian authorities for a privilege (in effect a copyright) on his Greek and italic types. Not surprisingly, Griffo objected to this restriction on his freedom to ply his art, and the two men quarrelled. Manutius was right to fear imitation, for it was the design brilliance, so much as the publishing programme itself, that secured the reputation of the firm. The Aldine classics were quickly recognised as a milestone in typography and scholarship, and scholars all over Europe sought to purchase Aldine editions. According to one excitable contemporary, Gerolamo Bologni, Aldus was 'the most glorious of all makers of books in any age' and 'the rescuer of Greek and Latin literature.'[33]

Whatever the undoubted distinction of his work, such outlandish claims invite a degree of sober reflection. The small-format Latin works published by Aldus were justly recognised as significant, but Aldus did not invent the octavo: books had been published in this format, north and south of the Alps, before the 1490s. Nor were his books particularly cheap. The pocket octavos do not seem to have retailed for significantly lower prices than other competing editions, and the definitive edition of Aristotle would have been one of the most expensive books on the market. It is certainly possible that Aldus was significantly less successful in turning a profit from this work than in earning the admiration of posterity. The production of the Aldine press was frequently interrupted, and the returns on his enormous investment seem uncertain.

New storms

The years 1499–1504 brought a general crisis in the Venetian printing industry, as the political difficulties experienced by the Republic led to a flight of capital and the collapse of the credit facilities that were essential to the running of the publishing trade.[34] Initially Aldus rode out the storm. It helped that his bank was one of the few that remained sound; in the short term Aldus would have benefited from the fact that many of his less robustly financed competitors in Venice were driven out of the market. But from 1504 the production of his firm fell off precipitously. In some respects Aldus was a victim of his own success. His italic type had attracted a great deal of attention: and imitators. By 1503 a number of pirate copies, many published in Brescia or Lyon, were cutting into his market. Aldus fired off a thunderous denunciation of the Lyon imitations, but in vain. The Lyon typographers had achieved what posterity has ascribed, with less justification, to Aldus: cheap, accessible editions of the classics.

The tribulation of the Venice industry at the turn of the century, and the trials of the Aldine press in the first decades of the new, are a reminder that the book trade, for all its energy and glamour, was still resting on uncertain foundations. If even so solid a pillar of the trade as Venice could experience so radical a reversal of fortune, then elsewhere the economics of the trade were even more bleak and forbidding. In the last decade of the fifteenth century the attempt to establish a printing press away from the established centres of production was almost doomed to fail, and this would remain the case for the first fifteen years of the new. Fifty years after Gutenberg's triumph print was an inescapable part of the book world. But it was still a world catering mostly for a moneyed and restricted readership, based on a familiar and rather conservative range of texts.

PART II

CONSOLIDATION

CHAPTER 4

THE CREATION OF A EUROPEAN BOOK MARKET

T HE EARLY years of the sixteenth century brought major changes in the European book world. The prolonged crisis that engulfed Venice, Europe's principal emporium of print in the fifteenth century, helped bring about a significant shift in the centre of gravity of European book production. Italy, which had outstripped Germany as the leader in the new world of print, fell back. New centres in the north, at Paris, Lyon, Basel and Antwerp, emerged to fill the gap.

These were also important years in the development of the book trade. Northern centres of typography may have seized the initiative, but they still depended on a pan-European readership to dispose of their texts. Merchants, booksellers and publishers gradually developed the necessary infrastructure. The industry began to develop mechanisms of order and control, of regulating competition and enforcing standards. A new trade like printing, which had no roots in the medieval guilds, had to evolve such structures as the craft developed.

At the same time a new generation of ambitious and creative book world professionals brought grace and style to perfecting the physical appearance of the book. In the first half of the sixteenth century the evolution of the book as an independent artefact reached its conclusion with the development of the title-page and other crucial features designed to assist the reader, such as dedications, an index and side-notes. New typefaces and greater typographical sophistication in the management of the printed page proclaimed the industry's growing confidence. The printed book had finally broken free of its roots in the manuscript world.

This was also the period when the book began to move beyond the conservatism of the late fifteenth century in terms of its subject material.

Cautious reliance on familiar texts had been a natural response to the turbulence that had imperilled the industry in that era: the new confidence of the early sixteenth century permitted more daring choices. Publishers and entrepreneurs could give more attention to bringing to the market new works by living authors, and new genres of book. The industry could respond to, and shape, the taste of a growing range of readers.

The eclipse of Venice

The turbulence in the Venetian print industry was symptomatic of a wider crisis that engulfed Italy in the first three decades of the sixteenth century. Successive French invasions and the defeat of Venice by the League of Cambrai (1508–10) brought turmoil to the Venetian economy and emptied the northern Italian universities. Both spelt ruin for the Venetian press. Scarcely had the Italian economy absorbed this calamity, when the Sack of Rome (1527) brought new disaster. It did not help that political circumstances conspired to bring new vigour to a number of northern markets at precisely this time. In Germany the Reformation vastly increased the number of books in circulation, and offered easy profits to grateful publishers. It also deflected towards the purchase of pamphlets part of the disposable income that might previously have been laid out for the products of the Italian press.

The potential importance of these developments, and the consequent problems that afflicted the Venetian industry, cannot be exaggerated. In the last three decades of the fifteenth century Venice had built an awesome primacy in the European book market. Venice was the centre of the book world by any measure: the number of editions, the total volume of output, the number of printers and publishers active in the book trade. To measure the full extent of this trade one has to bear in mind that a disprotionate number of the books published in Venice were very large. They would have consumed more paper, and more time on the press; they provided far more employment than smaller books that could be printed in a few days. This helps explain how Venice was able to sustain such a phenomenal volume of activity: between 1469 and 1500 some 233 different printing houses were at various times working in Venice.[1]

Books published in Venice reached into every corner of the European market, wherever printed texts were desired. Judging from the books now surviving in these countries, Venice commanded the market in Spain, Portugal, Hungary and Poland.[2] These were all outside the heartland of the European book world. Of course one cannot be certain that books now in

Polish or Portuguese libraries had arrived there in the fifteenth century, but there are other powerful indicators of the expansive reach of Venetian publishing. In the fifteenth century liturgical publishing was a mainstay of the industry. Many places around Europe had their own local rite, and when they wanted a printed edition it was often a Venice publisher who provided it. Venice printed more liturgies, primarily missals and breviaries, than any other place in Europe. This included the rites of thirty dioceses outside the Italian peninsula, from Esztergom to York, from Zagreb to Zaragoza.[3]

The difficulties in the Venetian market, and disruption to Venetian international trade, offered a tremendous opportunity to ambitious printers in France, Germany and the Low Countries. To develop their share of the international market they first required business practices robust enough to sustain a high volume of good quality printing. This was the achievement of the first decades of the sixteenth century. These were years in which the printers of northern Europe absorbed and appropriated the stylistic and technical advances made in Venice at the turn of the century. Northern printers also made their own, distinctive contribution, not least in developing structures of organisation and arrangements for the apportionment of work that allowed printers to coexist in the same marketplace. These mechanisms brought an element of stability to the industry and helped diminish the catastrophic rate of failure that had characterised publishing enterprises in the first era of print.

Amerbach

The international book market presented publishers with enormous opportunities. The efficient functioning of this market gave them access to a far larger pool of readers than was available locally, enabling them to take on larger, more varied and more expensive books. But success depended on the successful resolution of a range of practical questions. Firstly, what should they print: that is, which texts, in how many copies, and for which readers? How then should they bring them to their readers? Finally, how would they obtain payment? All of these issues posed real challenges, even for the most flourishing business. Success involved the careful establishment of an intricate network of relationships, often nurtured over many years through personal association, correspondence and the recommendation of friends.

A mass of surviving documentation allows us to investigate these business practices. Yet in all this material one resource stands out: the correspondence of the publisher Johann Amerbach.[4] Amerbach was the leading typographer of the emerging print centre of Basel, a city that built in the sixteenth century an

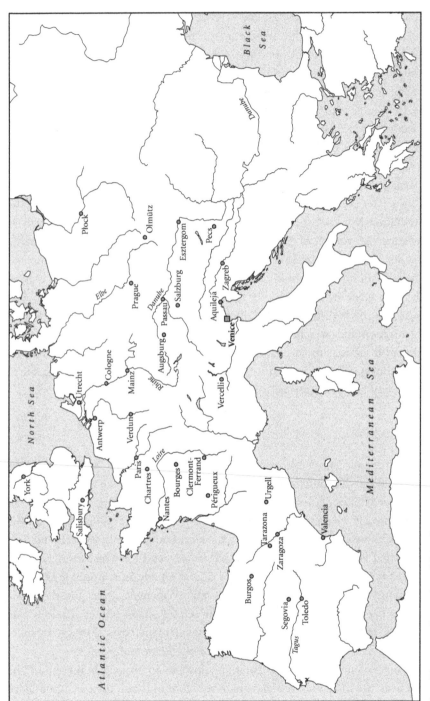

1 Publication of Missals in fifteenth-century Venice.

enviable reputation for scholarly publishing. His press published some 250 editions between 1478 and 1513. Amerbach's work included some of the most opulent scholarly editions of the day, including a three-volume edition of the complete works of Ambrose, and an eleven-volume Augustine.

At the heart of Amerbach's business was an enduring association with the Nuremberg publisher Anton Koberger. Koberger's printing house was one of the largest in Nuremberg, and as the years wore on he also concentrated increasing resources on large projects pursued in partnership with other printers. Amerbach was one of the most important of these connections, since he was able to take on the large high status projects with which Koberger wished to be associated. Koberger in turn had the distribution network to place these books in the marketplace. The partnership proved surprisingly harmonious, characterised by greater mutual respect and trust than one might expect in the higher reaches of so competitive a business.

Amerbach and Koberger were functioning at the very top end of the market where the level of investment required was often breathtakingly large. But the problems they faced, of managing their stock and bringing books to their customers, were common to the whole trade. From their correspondence we can learn a great deal about the mundane and arduous work that underpinned the development of the international book market.

Choosing titles

For any printer or publisher the first crucial decision was which books to bring to the market. In such a competitive business a single false step could easily spell disaster, and there was always a temptation to make conservative choices, printing proven bestsellers, or books for which there was a steady recurrent demand. But such a strategy had its dangers. Too many editions of the same works could quickly flood the market, as had been shown with the glut of classics in the 1470s. Even in the early sixteenth century publishers had to beware recurring crises of over-production. In 1503 Koberger warned Amerbach that the market in books for the clergy was dangerously overheated: so many books had been published that they were simply not buying any more.[5]

The best policy was often to ask friends what books they wished to have, and see if an edition was practical. Printers like Amerbach with a wide network of scholarly connections were never short of advice, though much of it was patently self-interested. The humanist scholar Jakob Wimpheling frequently offered suggestions, including invitations to publish his own trenchant and disputatious writings.[6]

Such connections required tactful handling. Amerbach was reluctant to become embroiled in Wimpheling's feuds, but the scholars with whom he corresponded rendered invaluable service, searching out manuscripts the printer needed for copy texts and then interceding with owners to loan them out. The owners were often monastic houses reluctant to lend precious possessions that they feared, quite justifiably, might face rough handling in the print shop. In return for their help, scholars hoped the printers might favour their own projects. Rather than cause offence, Amerbach often chose simply to ignore such importuning; the vagaries of the postal service gave him some room for manoeuvre here. For example, the aspiring scholar Rutgerus Sycamber had by 1498 written thirty small works, and he hoped Amerbach would print a selection. He wrote directly, and solicited the help of friends. By 1508 the number of these unpublished effusions had risen to 140, but the author remained hopeful.[7] It says much for Amerbach's patience and tact that although none of Sycamber's writings ever appeared with Amerbach's imprint the scholar remained a friend.

Most printers were to a large extent generalists: of the many projects put to them, they printed those they thought offered the prospect of profit. But for the most fortunate it could also be very lucrative to develop a known specialism. If a single printer or group of printers was known to command a particular market, interlopers could be deterred from entering it, however tempted. The best chance for market domination lay in publications with high initiation costs. The market in Books of Hours in Paris, the acknowledged European leader in production of such works, was dominated by a relatively small circle of producers.[8] Imitating the earlier success of Venice, they turned out not only generic Books of Hours, but also liturgical works in many individual diocesan rites.

Numerous books were printed as the result of direct commissions from an individual or institution. The latter were easy for a printer to accept, as the institutional sponsor would frequently underwrite the cost of the whole edition. The two most common undertakings of this type were the printing of broadsheet ordinances for the local authorities, and the printing of small devotional works for particular religious institutions.

Such jobbing work helped Amerbach with liquidity and cash flow while he pursued more ambitious ventures. Many early printers were also scholars, or wished to be regarded as such. The desire to be associated with a signature work, a notable first edition or a sustained series of standard texts was very strong. Amerbach was no exception, and he devoted much of his energy to a projected series of the complete works of the Church Fathers. This monumental undertaking was announced in the preface to the three-volume Ambrose that initiated the series. Years of arduous preparation, including a wide-ranging search for texts involving many of the scholars in Amerbach's circle, brought forth the masterly eleven-volume Augustine in 1506.[9] This astonishing monument of scholarship was published in an edition of 2,100 copies. Amerbach now turned to Jerome, a labour still unfinished at his death in 1514. The nine-volume set was completed by his successor Johannes Froben with the help of Erasmus.[10]

Reading the market

All printing projects involved critical judgements regarding how many copies should be printed. This was a crucial part of the publisher's art. Once an individual sheet had been printed off, the body of type used for those pages would be broken up and the type washed for reuse. It was therefore not possible, late in the day, to decide to print extra copies if the market seemed more promising. The temptation was always to print more, particularly with large texts where the time and effort of setting up the type again was disproportionately great. But this then risked the truly disastrous result of a large portion of the edition remaining unsold, with no return on the huge investment in plant, paper and wages.

The range of possibilities was rather narrower than might be thought. Printers reckoned in units defined by how many copies could be turned off the press in a full or half-day's work. Once the press was occupied with a particular book, it might as well use the full working day, since no other work could be started until the current work was off the press. By the sixteenth century an efficiently functioning press could print up to 1,500 sheets, front and back, in a full day.[11] This tended to be the normal range for the edition size of a large folio work, though printers were happy to print smaller editions of pamphlets of eight or sixteen pages because the effort of recomposing the type for a rapid reprint of these small books was much less significant. Sometimes these smaller books were printed on commission. A publisher or institutional customer would order 300, 400 or 1,000 copies of a text and pay for the whole edition. Not surprisingly, printers were very keen to have this sort of work.

The real problem lay in judging the market for big books. For large folio editions publishers had to be mindful that it might take several years for the edition to sell out, and indeed both publishers and booksellers seem to have been prepared to hold stock for long periods. Thus, while the efficient organisation of marketing and distribution was critical to profitability, this was inevitably a business that favoured the larger firms with deep pockets and steady access to credit.

Two other factors impacted on printers' plans: they had to have a reliable supply of paper, and they had to keep in mind other tasks in hand. Printers like Amerbach generally purchased paper in the immediate vicinity for everyday jobs, but would then look to the international market for the highest quality paper for special commissions. Like the book trade, trade in paper was conducted on credit, or by exchange. A bale of finished books might be exchanged for two bales of paper, an equation in harmony with most estimates that the cost of paper generally represented about half the cost of the finished book.[12] The wholesale cost of books followed fairly mechanically from the raw material costs; that is, principally the amount of paper consumed in making the edition. Later in the sixteenth century this would be subject to some adjustment to take account of the additional composition costs of books in very small formats.

For any print shop it was always difficult to ensure an even flow of work. Printers were loath to turn down commissions, but then if their shop were busy they would face a barrage of complaints from authors, booksellers or publishers keen to see their own books on the market. For a printer facing a backlog, there were two choices: to set up an additional press, though this was a long-term decision and possible only if there was enough floor space in the workshop (and indeed if the local guild regulations allowed it); or, particularly to deal with a sudden rush of work, they could subcontract the task to another printer. This became very common, especially in the larger publishing centres with many print shops.

Over the course of years, a successful printer or publisher might establish a whole network of relationships with others in the trade, taking in or putting out work as occasion demanded. Willem Vorsterman ran a highly successful printing business in Antwerp in the first half of the sixteenth century: in a long career spanning three decades he printed over 400 books of diverse sorts. During his career Vorsterman established connections that stretched throughout the Netherlands. At different times he printed for printers, publishers and booksellers in Ghent, 's-Hertogenbosch, Ieper, Zierikzee, Amsterdam and Leiden. He put out work to numerous Antwerp colleagues, and on occasions also printed for them.[13]

On other occasions a group of booksellers seeing a market opportunity would create a consortium to share cost and risk. This became almost the standard practice for the publication of expensive editions in Paris.[14] Such practices evolved most easily in the largest centres of typography, and in turn further enhanced the market advantage of the biggest cities. It is no accident that these decades witnessed the rise of Paris and Antwerp to a commanding place in the northern world of print.

Market protection

Despite market practices of increasing sophistication, the business of books was still very risky. Printers were keen to minimise the risk of competion and a lot could be accomplished by informal agreement. In 1485 the Strasbourg printer Adolf Rusch wrote to Amerbach in some anxiety. Four years before he had published a lavish Latin Bible, with annotations by Nicolas of Cusa. Rusch had now heard a rumour that Amerbach planned his own edition, and he begged Amerbach not to proceed while he still had stock in hand.[15] On this occasion Amerbach was happy not to jeopardise a valued business association; and perhaps prudence also spoke against a new edition while Rusch still had unsold stock.

Often, though, it was not possible to come to this sort of gentleman's agreement. From an early date therefore printers and publishers pursued a range of strategies designed to protect their markets, and the considerable investments they had made in bringing a book to the press.

The history of book regulation is normally studied as an aspect of the history of censorship, and this casts a long shadow.[16] So it is all the more important to emphasise that pressures for the regulation of print came overwhelmingly from within the industry itself. They reflected a concern to protect the position of established producers which was common to all medieval craft trades. Medieval guild regulations had three main purposes: to protect the quality of produce and the integrity of local systems of training such as apprenticeship; to protect tradesmen who had been trained locally against immigrant interlopers; and to encourage and reward innovation. In a new industry like printing there was no structure of training or apprenticeship to provide the quality controls and rewards for long service present in other crafts. Printers, seeking protection, asked local rulers to guarantee that no other printer would be allowed to publish a book that they wanted to print themselves.

The search for appropriate ways to regulate the industry began very early. In 1469 the Venice authorities offered Johannes of Speyer, the first printer to appear in the city, an exclusive monopoly on printing within the city for five years. Such a sweeping privilege was undoubtedly unsustainable, and would have stifled the development of the industry; luckily the printer's unexpected death the following year made the issue moot, and the experiment was not repeated. More common was the attempt to secure exclusive rights for a period of years to the publication of a particular book, or group of books, or to a particular technical innovation. As we have seen, Aldus Manutius in 1496 sought a twenty-five-year patent on the designs of his Greek type, which he obtained.

The precise mechanism that was used to apportion such privileges differed from place to place, but normally the producer (the printer or publisher) would approach the local authority, proposing that their rights to a work be protected for a stated period of years. In France such privileges could be granted by a range of authorities: the crown, the university or the local municipal authorities.[17] The petitioners would present a formal justification, stressing the expense incurred in procuring the text or the translation work, the further expense likely to follow, and the great benefit that would result from publication. If the request was granted (often for a shorter period than that requested), a version of this petition would be published in the book itself, often on the back of the title-page where it could not easily be overlooked. This printed summary would also state the penalties specified for any breach: always a fine, and sometimes additionally the confiscation of the offending press, types or woodcut blocks.

In time both the petitions and the privileges would become highly formulaic, and the Paris forms were widely imitated elsewhere in Europe. The problem for the printers, and for the authorities, was that a privilege was good only within the jurisdiction of the power which granted it. A Paris privilege could not prevent a competing Antwerp, Venice or Basel edition. We have seen the frustration of Aldus Manutius at the cheap imitations of his small-format classics that swiftly appeared in Lyon. Manutius could fulminate against their shoddy workmanship, but they were a real threat to his market in northern Europe. The problem was acute in the German Empire and to a lesser extent Italy, where printing towns a few miles apart would be in quite separate states or jurisdictions. The voluntary agreements between printers not to spoil each others' markets were only a partial answer. Ultimately publishers had to rely on the enlightened self-interest which dictated that in an efficiently functioning international market reprints were as risky to the pirate as to the original publisher. But within a single jurisdiction the system of regulation could work well, as it did in Paris, to encourage a logical apportionment of work in a large printing community. It relied on the authorities resisting the most extravagant demands, where printers sought the exclusive right to publish a large class of popular books. It relied also on the printers themselves being prepared to enforce the law by denouncing those who violated privileges and helping identify any printers who sought to disguise their responsibility by printing anonymously. This they proved all too willing to do. It was a harbinger of the role printers would play in enforcing controls when religious and political controversies added a new edge to the regulation of the marketplace.

Selling

We turn now to the last crucial part of the process. The choice of texts is made, the copies are printed. Now all that remains is to sell the books. Publishers often hoped to dispose of a considerable proportion of their print run locally and in doing this would enlist the help of authors, patrons or others who had taken an intellectual or financial stake in the project.

An author would often take a portion of the edition to distribute among friends. Sometimes it was possible to get a book published only if the author promised to underwrite the whole cost. As a young man in Paris, John Calvin was forced to liquidate part of his inheritance to pay for publication of his commentary on Seneca. His earliest correspondence includes letters to friends urging them to recommend the text.[18] The edition was not a success, and the ambitious author was left humiliated and impoverished. Calvin could take consolation from the fact that his experience was far from unique. In 1506 Johannes Reuchlin had brought to the press his milestone text on the Hebrew language, *De rudimentis Hebraicis*. Perhaps the more experienced printers had seen the difficulties ahead, because Reuchlin was forced to consign the work to Thomas Anshelm at Pforzheim.[19] He had to provide a substantial financial contribution – but even then the project was a disaster, and the book unsaleable. The desperate Reuchlin appealed to Amerbach, who agreed to do what he could. But after conversations with booksellers at the Frankfurt Fair, he confirmed the worst: no one would accept stock of such an untried book in a language that was totally unfamiliar. Amerbach could only advise Reuchlin to lay up his stock until Amerbach's own edition of Jerome appeared. Because Jerome's works were 'sprinkled throughout with Hebrew letters, sentences and even passages', its appearance would, he offered hopefully, 'make many learned men eager to learn Hebrew'.[20] To an author with 1,500 copies of an unsaleable book this must have been difficult advice. It would have been more so if Reuchlin had known that the promised edition of Jerome would not appear for another seven years.

For particularly notable texts a printer or publisher would sometimes prepare the ground with a printed advertisement. These mostly directed the potential purchaser to the bookshop or stall where a specific book could be obtained. The only surviving publisher's puff for a book published by William Caxton takes this form.[21] It is indicative of the importance attached to such advertising that by the early sixteenth century a title-page of a book published in Paris was far more likely to advertise the shop where a book was to be sold than the name of the printer. The printer's name was relegated to the colophon at the back.

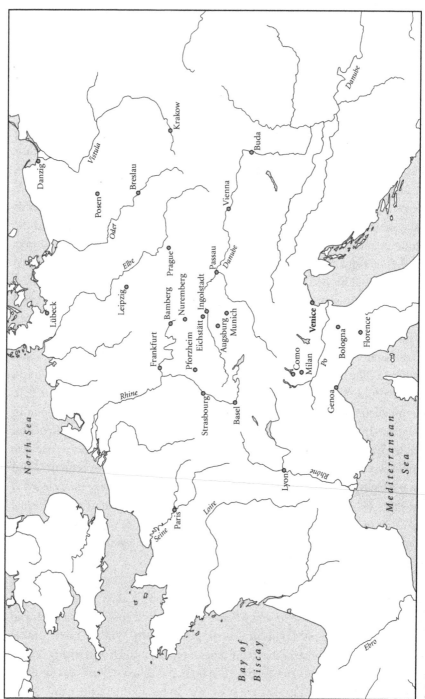

2 Sales network of the Nuremberg Chronicle.

Booksellers with permanent premises hung out shop signs like other tradesmen. An advertisement might therefore state that a book was available, 'from Jean le Tellier, at the sign of the Golden Unicorn, in the rue St Jacques'.

For publishers operating in the international Latin market the network of sales dovetailed naturally with other contacts with scholars, editors and authors. Scholars wrote to procure books at the same time as they offered news, advice and gossip about other books that they had seen on the market. Collectors asked publishers to send them parcels of books, which might include works that they knew had been published by other printers locally. They also wrote to ask for help in locating texts they very much wanted to add to their libraries.[22] At one level this was no more than a continuation of habits inherited from the manuscript age, when scholars cultivated anyone who could help them procure a desired text. Publishers, who travelled widely and saw many thousands of books, were ideally placed to help track down such elusive items. These small courtesies helped maintain good relations with the scholarly community. But to shift their texts publishers also cultivated connections with a network of booksellers located in every part of Europe.

If we wish to see how the book trade could ensure the efficient supply of books at a reasonable price to a widely dispersed readership, the occasional surviving correspondence with booksellers is vastly illuminating. In 1495 and 1496 Andreas Ruwe, a German bookseller settled in London, wrote twice to Amerbach to establish a regular connection.[23] He required multiple copies of the classic works of Roman law, works of theology, and anything Amerbach had recently published in the arts. Some works he asked for in surprising quantities: fifty copies each, for instance, of Augustine's *De civitate* and *De trinitate*. If he could not sell them Ruwe expected to be able to send them back. Such a spider's web of individual relationships required intricate management to keep track of consignments of books and ensure payment. For markets in which they expected to be able to dispose of large quantities of books the largest publishers would install their own local agent. Amerbach employed Peter Mettlinger as an agent in Paris at the time when the local Paris market was in its infancy in the 1480s. Koberger had fixed agents in a number of places, including Paris and Lyon.

A revealing indication of the extent of Koberger's business is provided by a document of 1509, drawn up as a final settlement of the contract between partners involved in the production and sale of the Nuremberg Chronicle.[24] This accounting reveals a network of outlets spread far and wide throughout Europe. We know that the Nuremberg Chronicle sold well, because there are at least 1,200 surviving copies logged in libraries today. But in 1509 there were still 600 copies unsold. For copies previously supplied debts were logged against the accounts of booksellers spread through the Germanic world: at Lübeck and Danzig, Passau and Vienna, Ingolstadt, Augsburg and Munich. Linhard Tascher still had to settle for just over a hundred copies sent to him at Posen and Breslau (presumably for sale in Silesia): eighty-three Latin and twenty-eight German. A separate consignment of mostly Latin copies had been dispatched to Cracow. The Koberger agency in Lyon had to account for forty-one copies, and several hundred had been dispatched to agents in Italy, at Bologna, Florence and Genoa. Peter Vischer, the agent at Milan, had received the largest consignment for distribution in the peninsula, of which almost 200 remained unsold. The Venice agent, Anthoni Kolb, had just thirty-four left. Bearing in mind that these represent the unsold residue of what had been a very large edition, the geographical reach of Koberger's enterprise was every bit as impressive as the Venetian network of the previous decades. The bold confidence with which Koberger had taken on the Italian market was especially striking, even if transalpine demand for this masterpiece of German typography had ultimately not matched expectations.

Koberger was exceptional in the extent of his business connections and their geographical reach. But the existence of these large parcels of books in distant agencies gives some hint of the vast quantities of books that by this point were being routinely shipped and transported around Europe. Books were a valuable and precious commodity, but they were also bulky and fragile, susceptible to damage, especially by water. Much of the bulk trade was conducted along the great rivers that linked Europe's major printing cities; otherwise books were dispatched by wagon, either packed into wooden barrels or wrapped in leather bales. The major trading towns were linked by established wagoning firms who would compete for business, but the publishers were themselves responsible for supplying the barrels, which they would have specially made for books. Amerbach's propensity to economise with cheap, flimsy wood was an issue that brought several protests from Koberger, who found several consignments had been damaged on the road from Augsburg to Nuremberg.[25] A large order of this sort would generally be transported in individual sheets, to be made up into finished books on arrival. This meant that if they did suffer water damage *en route* an attempt could be made to dry them out before the books were collated and bound.

The Frankfurt Fair

Such bilateral contracts were available only to the most established figures in the industry, and the biggest dealers. For the trade as a whole the movement of books around Europe's markets, indeed the whole business of books, revolved around the book fair.

Europe's trade calendar was crowded with fairs, and booksellers were well represented at most of them. For the most active publishers there was an established sequence of fairs through the warmer months of the year. The first of the year, also first in order of importance, was the Lenten Fair at Frankfurt. At Easter there were fairs at Leipzig and Lyon; August brought a second Lyon fair before the Autumn Fair at Frankfurt, which took place in the last week of September and the first week of October. Lyon held a further fair at All Souls, and Basel one in October. In Spain the market revolved around two fairs at Medina del Campo in May and October. There were also smaller regional fairs at places like Nördlingen, important for the book dealers of Augsburg and southern Germany, and small provincial fairs in France at which the Paris dealers would always be represented. The circulation of books around Italy was facilitated by fairs at Recanati, Foligno and Naples, the twice-yearly fair at Lanciano and Venice's Ascension Fair.[26]

This regular round oiled the wheels of business through the most productive months, when print shops had the daylight to work long hours. But one fair soon established primacy and a status in the book world that dwarfed all others. When printers spoke of 'the fair' they inevitably meant Frankfurt. The biannual fortnights, in spring and autumn, became fixed points in the calendar of all major figures in the industry.

Frankfurt was established as the home of a major book fair as early as 1475, and it would retain unchallenged pre-eminence as the centre of the international book trade for more than two centuries.[27] Frankfurt's domination rested on firm foundations. Firstly, as the seat of a major medieval fair, Frankfurt was used to the demands and rhythms of seasonal commerce. The city was blessed by an excellent situation, astride the Main, the main tributary of the Rhine. Hence the city was well situated for the main arteries of trade linking the commercial markets of Italy and the Netherlands, to north and south, and France and the Empire, to east and west. These lands were the major engines of the medieval European economy, and the major centres of the Latin book trade, along with the Swiss Confederation – also conveniently situated for trade with Frankfurt. The Frankfurt Fair, confirmed by an Imperial charter of 1240, already attracted large numbers of merchants to its twice-yearly gatherings in Lent and at Michaelmas. Many towns promoted such fairs, not least as a logical response to the notorious danger of travel in the era. Merchants could journey together, and between them pay for the necessary protection for their valuable merchandise. But few trade centres could rival Frankfurt for the opulence and international esteem of its fairs. Visitors from other lands, especially France, Italy and the Low Countries, were a familiar sight.

Even in the manuscript age merchants would certainly have brought books, along with other merchandise, to Frankfurt's fairs. Frankfurt merchants were closely involved in the earliest ventures in book production; here the city's proximity to Mainz, the scene of Gutenberg's triumphant experiments, was helpful.[28] Yet curiously, Frankfurt did not develop as an especially important centre of book production in the first years of print; perhaps the close observation of Gutenberg's financial difficulties was a cautionary experience.[29] Rather it was Frankfurt's experience of the mechanics of international trade – especially the credit and barter transactions that became its mainstay – that allowed it quickly to attract a large part of the trade in Latin books to its established fairs.

Frankfurt was also exceptionally well placed to act as a point of exchange for the trade in vernacular books within the German-speaking territories of the Holy Roman Empire. In this respect at least Frankfurt did face serious competition, from Strasbourg, on the Rhine, and Leipzig in Saxony. But Frankfurt would always have the advantage, not least because of the large number of foreign merchants gathered to view the Latin books on offer. The trade in German books developed as a subsidiary, though very important, aspect of this larger international trade. By the last four decades of the sixteenth century Latin titles made up on average 65 per cent of the books traded in Frankfurt, and German books around 30 per cent. Most of the Latin books were published outside Germany; the largest proportion of the German books came from Frankfurt itself, or other south German cities.[30] Frankfurt thus served two largely distinct, though interlocking markets: an international Latin trade, and a trans-German market in vernacular books.

Most major printers were represented at every fair, and often attended in person. Regulars had established stands where they could receive post, as Amerbach did 'at St Leonard's Church at the Sign of the Swan'.[31] The intercourse of the fair was important to publishers for a number of reasons. Conversation and chance meetings allowed them to establish new bilateral connections and inspection of the books enabled them to spot developing trends, identify shifting tastes or assess new opportunities. Publishers would also get a sense of what made books stand out among the masses on display. The fair thus played its part in encouraging the continuous small technical improvements and design innovation that characterise these years.

Publishers took with them large quantities of books to sell. The business model of scholarly books depended on the publishers being able to dispose of a large proportion at the first fair following publication. In 1534 the Zurich printer Christopher Froschauer took with him to the fair 2,000 copies of a work that he had printed in an octavo and a folio edition, and sold half of them. Printers organised their schedule to have important works ready for the fair, and their presses sometimes worked long hours at a frantic pace to ensure that deadlines were met. Authors grew accustomed to building their writing schedules around the rhythms of the fair. Calvin's correspondence is full of references to such pressures. He could, if need be, write extremely quickly, but on one occasion a polemical piece was dispatched without a planned final section, because otherwise it would have missed the fair. The end of the book contained the announcement, 'I will leave this topic [predestination] to the next fair'.[32]

Publishers used the fair to settle accounts with other producers or with the agents who acted for them abroad. This was far simpler than settling up for occasional parcels of books, or individual titles, dispatched at the request of a distant bookseller or individual purchaser. For these transactions booksellers and publishers drew on the mechanisms of international finance developed during the medieval period. Be advised, wrote Peter Mettlinger to Amerbach from Paris in 1482:

> that I have sent you 103 crowns in gold and thirty-three ducats via a bill of exchange with the Deacon of Basel; he should give them to you in crowns and ducats as I have lent him. Further, I have taken in sixty crowns and would gladly send them to you with Johann [unknown], but I am afraid it would be stolen from him on the road. I believe I will take in more at the Lyon fair, so that I will have 100 guilders altogether. If it suits you, I will send it to you at the next fair through a Basel merchant whom you would write to me about, or if you know other merchants who would get the money from me in Paris and bring it to you, that would be satisfactory to me.[33]

All of this depended to a large extent on trust: the business of books was a credit and debt economy. Even the most established figures in the industry could be embarrassed if bills fell due and they could not obtain payment. For this reason a large part of the business functioned by exchange: books for books, books for paper, books for manuscripts supplied by authors or in payment for editorial work. All of this explains how it was that printers, publishers and booksellers could build up such astonishing stocks of books, their own and those produced by others. When he died in 1522, the Paris printer Jean Janot possessed a stock of some 53,000 volumes.[34] This would not have been particularly unusual.

The creation of a functioning international book market was only one of a number of achievements of this seminal period, between 1485 and 1530, when the book industry finally achieved its mature form. The printed book was in the final stages of its development as a physical artefact, now recognisably distinct from its manuscript predecessor. Publishing as a craft had achieved a degree of professional respectability, but without full integration into the medieval guild structure. In many respects this was the ideal business environment for publishers, who were bringing out a large number of books, in a widening range of genres, for a gently expanding readership. With these new genres came a degree of specialisation, although more printers continued to undertake as large a range of work as was available to them.

This was an era when the book trade found its feet. Chastened by the experience of the early years of print, when commercial sense was too easily overwhelmed by the excitement of the new invention, print had now found a sound and workable model. At its heart were the printers and publishers concentrated in a relatively small number of major centres of production, from where books were transported and supplied to purchasers dispersed through Europe. For this the printers depended on a whole range of other figures essential to this market: wagoners, and those who specialised in international money transfers; booksellers and their travelling salesmen; authors, and those who supplied the editorial expertise that justified many new editions of familiar texts; last but not least, buyers and collectors. We can illustrate the workings of this extended community of buyers and suppliers by looking in more detail at three individuals whose engagement with books brought them into the public eye. One is an author, one a collector, and one a bookseller. None are truly representative, since ordinary figures seldom leave much trace in the documentary records. Yet each of their careers is highly revealing of the opportunities and pitfalls that attended the growth of the European book industry.

Erasmus

Our author is Desiderius Erasmus, revered in his day and ever since as the shining epitome of the new scholarship. Erasmus was almost certainly the first living author to make a substantial living from writing. Before Erasmus it was almost unknown for authors to profit directly from the publication of their books. Even after his death, few sixteenth-century authors would realise their hopes of living by the pen. Erasmus's genius, his lightning wit and genuine learning, caught the imagination in a way that few could hope to emulate. His numerous works were published in over 2,500 editions during the sixteenth century.[35] But Erasmus was also a deeply practical spirit. From our point of view the most interesting aspect of this extraordinary career is the clarity with which Erasmus discerned the needs of the marketplace, and his willingness to bend his authorial activity to its disciplines.

The major milestones of Erasmus's writing career are well known: *The Handbook of the Christian Soldier* in 1503; *In Praise of Folly* in 1511, the New Testament translation of 1516, successive editions of his collection of humorous and philosophical aphorisms, the *Adages*, from 1500. These works brought Erasmus enormous renown, and a diverse readership. In 1518 a delighted Erasmus regaled a friend with the tale of how, travelling down the Rhine, he had been recognised by the toll keeper, who had insisted on calling his wife and children to be introduced to the great author. Heaped up on his table, among his papers, were a number of Erasmus's books.[36] Although Erasmus wrote only in Latin, he was always happy to have his works translated into vernacular languages, and followed these translated editions with interest. Erasmus revelled in the fact that his work found a wide audience.

Erasmus was acutely aware of the role that the printer played in the success of a volume. Throughout his career he gave close attention to the production process, seeking out the best printers and working closely with them to ensure that the text was both elegant and accurate. In early years his two principal collaborators were the Louvain printer Thierry Martens and Josse Badius in Paris. Martens was an immensely experienced printer, and the principal supplier of books for Louvain University. In addition to many high quality Latin editions, he was the first printer in the Low Countries to print with Greek characters. He published, in 1503, the first edition of *The Handbook of the Christian Soldier*. During Erasmus's second sojourn in Louvain between 1516 and 1521 Martens handled a large part of the published output of this immensely fertile period. In Paris, Erasmus worked successively with the German immigrant Jean Philippe (who published the first edition of the *Adages*) and the scholar printer Josse Badius.

Although Erasmus was settled in England for many of the years between 1505 and 1507, and again between 1509 and 1514, he would always return to France if he had something to print. However generously Erasmus praised the intellectual companionship of his English friends, he was too shrewd to consign any of his writings to an English press. This was true even of *Moriae Encomium* (*In Praise of Folly*), written at the house of his friend, Thomas More, in 1509. The punning title paid tribute to this friendship and the English humanist circle that had made him so welcome, but Erasmus still had the book published in Paris (in fact he made the perilous cross-Channel crossing in person to see the book through the press). An instant bestseller, it was reprinted eighteen times in five years, and in five different European cities – but never in England.[37]

Erasmus's first trip to Italy in 1506 had brought him into contact with Aldus Manutius, then at the height of his reputation. The Venetian press established a standard against which Erasmus would subsequently measure all of his printers. As his New Testament approached completion in 1515 Erasmus turned his steps to Italy once more and it was only when he heard of Manutius's death that he allowed the Basel printer Johannes Froben to undertake publication. Froben's success established a relationship of confidence that would last through most of the following decade. Between 1521 and 1529 the Froben press published fifty-eight of Erasmus's writings. This gave Basel a primacy in the publication of Erasmus's works that was of enduring significance for the Rhineland city.[38] Erasmus was often present in Froben's shop, and his publications undoubtedly benefited very greatly from his involvement in, and close appreciation of, the technical aspects of printings. When Erasmus prepared his commentary for the edition of Jerome, he set out his manuscript in exactly the same arrangement as it would appear on the printed page, with a large space left for a woodcut initial letter. This made life far easier for the compositor.

In the early years Erasmus, like all authors, struggled to achieve recognition. He may well have had to provide some financial contribution for the first edition of the *Adages* in 1500, and certainly he did his best to encourage sales. But as his reputation grew, Erasmus ensured he was well remunerated for his work: only Aldus Manutius received a manuscript for free. In 1512, Badius set out careful and generous financial terms for the publication of their projects: 15 florins for a further edition of the *Adages* and 10 for the revision of the letters of Jerome.[39] In 1516 Froben persuaded Erasmus to let him publish his Greek New Testament by promising to match any offer he received from other printers. Later, as their relationship matured, Froben would buy a garden in Basel to provide Erasmus with a suitably relaxing environment for contemplation.

Printers lavished such care on the great humanist because they realised that his works were immensely profitable. In later years Erasmus was able to specify that none of his works should henceforth be published in an edition of fewer than 1,500 copies, but publishers were often ready to risk far higher print runs. In 1524 Froben published the *Paraphrases* in an edition of 3,000 copies. Even so, demand was so high that he was obliged to reprint twice the same year. All told, it has been plausibly estimated that more than one million copies of

Erasmus's writings were in circulation during his lifetime.[40] This level of productivity was not achieved without the closest co-operation between all those involved. Like most authors Erasmus was prepared to orientate his writing activity to the rhythms of the fair. In the frantic weeks leading up to it he shared the exhaustion and privations of Froben's workshop.

When Erasmus's works became mired in controversy in the 1520s, his greatest fear was that a work attacking him would appear without his having time to refute it before the fair. His opponent would then have six months to shape the critical response before he had time to respond. Both sides did their best to wrong-foot their opponents in this regard. Erasmus had finished his response to Hutten's *Expostulatio* in July 1523, but with Froben's connivance it was not put to the press until shortly before the September Fair, in case Hutten got wind of it. And nothing gave Erasmus greater pleasure than his success in outfoxing Luther, when the reformer published his attack on Erasmus in 1526. Erasmus received a copy of Luther's *Bondage of the Will* less than a fortnight before the spring fair. Luther must have anticipated a free run for his work. But Erasmus set to work, Froben cleared his presses, and working on six presses simultaneously had Erasmus's reply ready in time. It was an astonishing demonstration of literary virtuosity; but it was only possible because of Erasmus's extraordinary influence with his printers.

Luther was a worthy adversary, but other aspects of the controversial literature of these years shows Erasmus in a less flattering light. In 1518 Edward Lee, later Archbishop of York but at this point an obscure figure, arrived in Louvain as a student.[41] Erasmus's early friendship with Lee soured when the Englishman criticised his New Testament translation. Lee's criticism of a favourite project clearly struck a nerve, but even so it is hard to comprehend the virulence with which Erasmus pursued him. Having goaded Lee repeatedly in print with unflattering satirical references in 1519 and 1520, Erasmus then used his influence with publishers to prevent Lee responding. No Antwerp printer would risk publication of Lee's side of the controversy. Lee eventually found a publisher in Paris, but even admirers of the great humanist felt the incident reflected little credit on him.[42]

It is easy to assume that because Erasmus was later the victim of censorship he would himself have supported press freedom. On the contrary, throughout his career he was ready to exploit his influence and reputation to suppress works written against him. Often simple commercial pressures were sufficient to warn off publishers who hoped for Erasmus's favour. When Erasmus quarrelled with the great humanist Juan Luis Vives, Basel publishers withdrew from publication of the Spaniard's works, taking him up again only after Erasmus's death. On

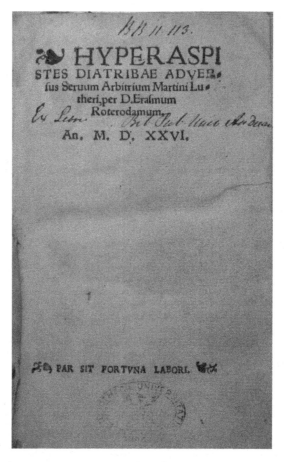

Fig. 14 Erasmus's response to Luther's *Bondage of the Will* was prepared in furious haste for the Frankfurt fair. As this brutally functional title-page shows, it needed little further advertisement than the names of the protagonists.

other occasions Erasmus intervened directly, as when he wrote to the magistrates of Strasbourg in 1531 asking that they take action to prevent the publication of a work by the spiritualist scholar Sebastian Franck. The entire print run, already prepared, was confiscated, with ruinous consequences for the publisher, Balthasar Beck. In his work Franck had written of Erasmus as a man unfairly branded as a heretic; Erasmus had failed to recognise the compliment.[43]

One might have imagined that Erasmus, a writer of true genius, would not have needed to resort to such tactics when his writings dominated the marketplace. Erasmus's close understanding of the production process was, as we have seen, a major part of his success. He was at one and the same time one of the most original minds of the century, and a truly commercial intellectual.

Fernando Colón

Fernando Colón was the son of the great explorer and discoverer Christopher Columbus, whose voyages and subsequent career as governor of the newly discovered territories brought the explorer renown and great wealth. The fickle vagaries of court politics would later bring him difficult times (he returned from one voyage disgraced, in leg irons) but these tribulations did not shipwreck the family fortunes. Fernando would in due course come into possession of a substantial fortune.

Fernando had no appetite to follow his father overseas. He eschewed the swamps and jungles of the newly discovered lands and gave himself to conquering another new world: the book world of sixteenth-century Europe. Fernando could not entirely avoid a public career. He was a page to Queen Isabella and later an adviser to Charles V, and it was on a progress around Europe with the court in 1509 that he first began to amass books and prints in large numbers. For the next decades most of his books were acquired in Italy; after 1520 he took advantage of his duties with the Emperor to travel to the Low Countries, Germany and London. Fernando's plans for his library were ambitious: he wanted to possess examples of all the books published throughout the continent. Even at this early stage in the history of print such an ambition lay outside the bounds of the possible, but Fernando still amassed an amazing collection. Thousands of books were gathered up from the marketplaces of Europe and shipped back to his estates in Spain. A large number still survive, in the magnificent Biblioteca Colombina in Seville, along with his systematic detailed catalogues.[44]

Colón's library contains many of the most prized editions of the day, and many exquisite manuscripts. But Fernando also possessed a rare fascination with the less esteemed output of the printing press: ephemeral pamphlets, and especially small books of religious devotion. These were books otherwise read and discarded, or literally used to destruction; very often the copy in the Biblioteca Colombina is the only one that survives.[45] Colón assiduously noted both where he obtained a book, and the price he paid for it. These careful manuscript annotations provide us with an almost unique opportunity to reconstruct the workings of the European book market; or at least that portion destined for the supply of books to the Iberian peninsula.

Colón bought over 2,000 books printed in France, even though he never visited Paris. More than half these French books he bought outside France.[46] Most were printed in Paris, and Colón's records demonstrate the extent to which Parisian books circulated freely through the major markets of Europe.

But even books published in the smaller provincial French towns, such as Rouen, seemed to have a wide distribution network. At different times Colón was able to purchase books printed at Rouen in London, Bruges, Ghent, Antwerp, Louvain and Cologne.[47] One of the biggest European book exchanges was in Lyon. Here Colón bought, in one enormous purchase, books published in over forty towns spread through Europe, including, somewhat perversely given their eventual destination, six places in Spain. Colón purchased other Paris and Lyon imprints in Spanish towns such as Valladolid, Medina del Campo, Burgos and Alcalá de Henares.

Colón's records allow us to document several other striking features of the European book market in these years. One was the extent to which a lively market in books had developed in many places which did not themselves have a large printing industry. There was no printing at all in Montpellier, for instance, before the last decades of the sixteenth century. Nevertheless, Colón was able to buy in the town a consignment of 750 books.[48] These included books published in twenty different locations in Italy. His Montpellier purchases demonstrate the continuing importance of Venice for the production of scientific and medical texts, for which the illustrious Montpellier medical faculty provided a steady demand.

Many of Fernando's books were purchased many years, indeed often decades, after their publication. In London in 1522 he bought books published in Louvain and Antwerp more than thirty years previously, and a Parisian edition of 1495. In Nuremberg in 1521 he found incunabula published in Strasbourg, Haguenau and Rome and further early Paris editions.[49] In this respect the books market had not entirely shaken off the habits and mind-set of the manuscript age, when the greater rarity of texts fed a lively second-hand market and encouraged sellers to value older texts. In the early sixteenth century booksellers could not afford to dispose of older texts simply because advances in design made them appear old fashioned.

Hieronymus Cloet

It is not at all easy to investigate the business of an ordinary sixteenth-century bookshop. Inventories of stock are rare enough, and usually composed in circumstances which complicate interpretation of their contents. Sometimes a business would be inventoried because it had gone bankrupt, in which case the inventory tells us more about unwise investments than popular stock.[50] Similarly, an inventory made after the death of even a very successful bookseller tells us precisely what books they had *not* been able to dispose of.

But occasionally a source comes to light which gives us a snapshot of a flourishing business in more normal operation; though admittedly in rather unusual circumstances. In 1543 the Louvain bookseller Hieronymus Cloet was arrested and interrogated on suspicion of heresy. The previous year a new inquisitor had been appointed in the university town of Louvain. His enquiries revealed the existence of a cell of suspected Lutherans. Many were arrested, interrogated, and the five ringleaders were later executed. The bookseller Cloet was caught up in the flurry of denunciations. To establish whether he was responsible for supplying heretical books a careful inspection was made of his stock. Fortunately no suspect texts were discovered; but thanks to this investigation we now have a detailed account of the stock of a well-established bookseller in a northern university town.[51]

Cloet's stock comprised precisely 2,546 books. Even though in many cases he had multiple copies in stock, he was still able to offer his customers an impressive 859 titles. Cloet catered mostly for the needs of those attending the lectures in the university, and especially of the recently founded Trilingual College. He supplied the required primary texts, but also grammars and vocabularies of the classical languages, and a wide variety of learned writers, historical and contemporary. Of the Roman authors Cicero, as usual, led the way, followed at some distance by Terence and Juvenal. Ovid and Virgil were less generously represented. Among modern authors Cloet's stock reflects the preponderance of humanist learning. Those in stock included incumbent professors and former students of the college, and also the man who had been its inspiration, Erasmus. Cloet stocked over 300 copies of Erasmus's works, confirming that the great man's death seven years previously had in no way diminished his popularity.

The clientele of this shop was overwhelmingly scholarly. Fewer than a hundred items, 4 per cent of the stock, were in either of the local vernacular languages, French or Dutch. The large proportion of titles were also very recently published; Cloet was not carrying a large amount of old stock. Almost all these recent scholarly editions were printed in the Low Countries, in France or Germany. This makes a very important point: by 1540 northern scholars could be supplied with all their requirements, whether editions of the classics, school-books or modern humanist writings, without recourse to Italy.

Cloet would have known what he had in stock. Yet he would still have heaved a sign of relief when the inquisitors drew a blank.[52] Cloet did not escape entirely. Two co-defendants attested that Cloet had debated some points of doctrine with them, including controversial issues such as the Real Presence. Protesting his orthodoxy, he was given the benefit of the doubt, and required only to pay the costs of his trial and incarceration. Cloet's troubles, even in orthodox Louvain, were an indication of the difficulties that faced the book trade in the new world created by the divisions of the Reformation. These were events that also had a momentous impact on sixteenth-century publishing.

CHAPTER 5

BOOK TOWN WITTENBERG

By THE third decade of the sixteenth century the general contours of the European book trade were fixed. In the fifteenth century twelve towns had been responsible for two-thirds of the total output of printed books: four in Italy; six in Germany; and two in France, Lyon and Paris.[1] This hierarchy proved remarkably enduring. Nine of these twelve cities were still major centres of production through the sixteenth century. The three newcomers to the top tier were all in northern Europe: Antwerp, the rising trade metropolis of the Netherlands, London, by dint of its domination of English printing, and Wittenberg.

Wittenberg had none of the attributes of the other major print towns. It was not a significant centre of population: at the beginning of the sixteenth century it probably only had around 2,000 inhabitants. It was far from the main centre of gravity of economic activity in northern Europe, along the Rhine and Danube basin. Even locally it lived very much under the shadow of Leipzig, with its established fairs and book industry. Leipzig also acted as the major gathering point of trade towards the east and, with Lübeck, to the Baltic.

Yet from these utterly unpropitious beginnings, Wittenberg succeeded in completely subverting the normal ordered hierarchies of the book trade. It introduced a new form of book, the *Flugschrift* or religious pamphlet, and an utterly original business model. Further, this transformation would have a lasting effect. Even though Luther died in 1546, in the second half of the sixteenth century Wittenberg retained its position as the largest centre of production of books within the German Empire. In the sixteenth century as a whole Wittenberg published more books than any of the established print centres in Germany.[2] Even in the seventeenth century, the three largest book production centres in Germany were Wittenberg, Leipzig and Jena, all tightly bunched in the previously unfashionable north-eastern provinces. All of this was the consequence of the turbulent movement of religious reform unleashed from Wittenberg in the third decade of the sixteenth century: the Reformation.

Wittenberg

The first printing press was established in Wittenberg in 1502, shortly after the inauguration of the new university.[3] The two events were closely connected, both parts of the programme pursued by the local ruler, the Elector, Frederick the Wise, to give his small capital city dignity commensurate with his lofty status in the Empire. The division of Saxony into two parts had left the only university in Leipzig, the largest city, outside Frederick's dominions. So Frederick determined to establish his own. However, attempts to build a commercially independent printing business solely around the needs of a university community seldom succeeded, and Wittenberg was to prove no exception: the students and professors always required a larger range of books than could be provided by a small provincial press. The first printers in Wittenberg laboured under the further disadvantage that they worked in the shadow of Leipzig, only 60 kilometres away, and Leipzig was an established centre of scholarly publishing. Almost anything Wittenberg scholars needed could already be obtained from Leipzig and its famous book fair.

Between 1502 and 1516 five printers worked briefly in Wittenberg, a sure indication that this work was unprofitable.[4] By 1507 the first printers had relocated elsewhere and it was recognised that if the university were not to be without a press then more tangible inducements were required. In 1508 the experienced printer Johann Rhau-Grunenberg was enticed to move from Erfurt by the promise of a house in which to set up his press: for a time it was in the Augustinian convent where Luther also lived. Rhau-Grunenberg at last succeeded in generating a modestly successful business, publishing almost exclusively the works of scholars associated with the university. An early work by Andreas Bodenstein von Karlstadt made use of Hebrew type; in 1513 an edition of the *Batrachomyomachia* of Homer was the first text of a Greek author to be printed in the city. As befitted a university printer, Rhau-Grunenberg published very little in German. But in 1516 he was persuaded to publish for the local town preacher, Martin Luther, an edition of the sermons of the German mystic Johann Tauler.[5] Luther had found a copy of Tauler's sermons during his years in Erfurt, and they were now published on Rhau-Grunenberg's press with Luther's own brief introduction. It was a deceptively unexceptional beginning to his publishing career.

Luther

In 1516, when he published the Tauler sermons, Luther was already a man of mature years. He could look back on a career of solid achievement, as a man respected in his order, his university, and in the town of Wittenberg, where he served simultaneously as professor and minister of the town church. A tendency to bleak introspection, increasingly reflected in a search for meaning in fundamental questions of theology, had not thus far impacted on his public career. Luther was a man esteemed in the small city of Wittenberg, cherished by his colleagues and by influential friends in the household of the Elector.

It is difficult to know quite what provoked him to so public an act as the writing and public display of 95 theses against indulgences in October 1517. Two years previously Pope Leo X had proclaimed an indulgence for the rebuilding of St Peter's Basilica in Rome, a conventional and pious cause. True, the preaching of the St Peter's indulgence around Wittenberg had been clumsy and venal, but the indulgence had the support of the most powerful local cleric, Albrecht of Brandenburg, Archbishop of Mainz and Magdeburg. Furthermore, Luther's own patron, Frederick the Wise, was known to be conservative in religion. His collection of relics, one of the largest in Germany, had been immortalised in the most ambitious publication of the Wittenberg press to date, a catalogue of the collection with illustrations by Lucas Cranach.

Even if we did not know the momentous consequences of Luther's action, the posting of the 95 theses would still have seemed impolitic to the point of recklessness. For with this attack on the indulgence trade, Luther was not only crossing one of the most influential churchmen in northern Germany. He was also attacking a genuinely popular church institution. Although the income from the St Peter's indulgence would ultimately assist the rebuilding of a church in Rome, many indulgences were obtained for the building of German churches. This was a significant and widely accepted means of raising funds for important local causes.[6] Other indulgences were proclaimed for the equally vital purpose of raising money for the war against the Turks. This was also a church tradition that had a particular resonance in Germany. We know this from the enormous numbers of indulgences printed in Germany in the seventy years before Luther's protest.

Printers had profited greatly from their support of this traditional devotional practice. Printed indulgences always consisted of a single sheet. Sometimes they were imposing broadsheets, intended for public display, to proclaim a papal grant to a local church or shrine. More often they were small rudimentary printed receipts, acknowledging an individual gift, with a space for the name of the pious donor to be inscribed. This was a straightforward piece of work for any printer, and offered a rapid return on minimal investment, since the entire print run would be delivered to a single client. This is the most ephemeral sort of printing, and surviving examples are rare, but clearly it was a massive market. Between 1498 and 1500 the great Benedictine monastery of Monserrat in Catalonia commissioned from local printers and from Johann Luschner in Barcelona more than 200,000 indulgence certificates. Only six examples still survive. In 1500 the Bishop of Cefalu in Sicily paid a Messina printer for an order of 130,000 indulgence certificates. All of these have disappeared.[7] Neither of these places was close to the heartland of European print: yet this was the sort of jobbing work that any competent printer could undertake. Of the 2,000 printed single-sheet items surviving from the fifteenth century over one third were letters of indulgence.[8] Ninety per cent of this material was published in Germany. This trade continued unabated into the sixteenth century. So when Luther proposed his theses he was tilting at a part of life that touched the lives of a vast number of Christians. He was also taking on an institution that brought solid profits to the printing industry.

Luther could, however, count on a sympathetic hearing from a number of educated scholars who felt that the overt commercialisation of the indulgence trade was bringing the Church into discredit. It is this that accounts for the rapid publication of the theses in Nuremberg and Basel, both important centres of humanist learning.[9] The theses were published both in broadsheet form, replicating the manuscript sheet as Luther would have posted it, and as a small pamphlet. The flurry of public interest led to some hasty work. The broadsheet edition published by Hieronymus Höltzel at Nuremberg in 1517 mis-numbered the theses by repeating the numbers 16 to 23. Readers of this edition would have thought Luther had posted 87 theses.

These were heady days for Luther and the press. The most surprising aspect of the developing publishing fury was the manner in which Luther discovered a quite unpredictable facility as a writer. Thrust into the public eye by the rush of publicity generated by the response to the 95 theses, Luther embarked on an astonishing burst of productivity. Nothing in his career, except perhaps his eloquence as a preacher, had prepared him for this, for Luther now engaged not only in the church controversies raised by his propositions, but also with a wider public audience. In 1517, the year of the 95 theses, Luther published a further three works. None had the success of the theses, and only his meditation on the penitential psalms would merit an immediate reprint. In 1518, however, he published no fewer than eighteen original works, all of which provoked wide public interest. A number were works of theology or sermons in Latin, addressing Luther's increasingly numerous audience among his fellow clergy and the lay scholarly public. But the greatest resonance was for Luther's sermon explaining his attack on indulgences, published in German.

The decision to pen his *Sermons on Grace and Indulgences* for a vernacular audience was in many respects the decisive moment of the Reformation, far more so than the posting of the theses. The formulation of the 95 theses could be defined as a normal, if bold, part of the usual process of academic exchange. Theses were propositions, to be defended and sustained, or withdrawn if overturned. But by appealing to a wider lay audience Luther passed a point beyond which the dispute could be contained within normal academic discourse. He also struck a surprising chord. The sermon went through an astonishing fourteen editions in the year of its first publication, and a further eight in 1519 and 1520.[10] After first publication by Rhau-Grunenberg in 1518, who printed three editions, it was reprinted in Leipzig, Nuremberg, Augsburg and Basel; in fact, all the major centres of German publishing with the exception of the determinedly orthodox Cologne. A separate work on the same topic warranted a further nine editions.[11]

By this point Luther was a major public figure, and the enthusiasm for his writings forced the Church into action. In 1518 he was summoned for interview by the Papal Legate, Cajetan, at Augsburg. In 1519 his debate with a leading champion of orthodoxy, Johannes Eck, led him into potentially damaging and increasingly fundamental criticisms of the Papacy. His excommunication in 1520 was by this time inevitable, but from the point of view of the authorities, too long delayed. Luther reacted with magnificent defiance, burning the Bull of Excommunication and excoriating the Pope and his agents.

Through all of these fast-moving developments Luther kept up an astonishing outpouring of writings: responses to opponents, articulation of his developing theological response to orthodox condemnation, and a large quantity of more measured pastoral theology. In all, thirteen works of this last type were published for the first time in 1519, along with numerous reprints of the writings of 1518. All were extremely short; four, six or eight leaves, and published in a convenient quarto. The longest, of eight leaves, would have occupied the press for no more than two days. An edition could be out on the streets and with its readers within a few days of Luther delivering the text. Of course Luther also continued to write in Latin, answering his critics and articulating his theological precepts. The dispute with Eck called forth at least three new writings. But although it was these controversial writings that most inflamed the church authorities, it was the short pastoral works in German that anchored Luther in the affections of his growing German public, and secured his reputation as a man of God. In the works of consolation and

Fig. 15 By publishing his sermon on indulgences in German Martin Luther consciously invited the general public to engage in this theological debate. This edition of Valentin Schumann comes from before the date Leipzig printers were forbidden to publish evangelical works – to their enormous regret.

admonition which poured from his fertile pen and the Wittenberg presses during these years Luther spoke as pastor to the German nation.

Book town Wittenberg

The massive public interest in Luther's writings presented an unprecedented opportunity for Wittenberg's printers. It was greatly to their advantage that many of Luther's early works were of precisely the type that offered the best opportunities of profit to a relatively under-capitalised and immature industry. Short works, swiftly realised, that sold out immediately: even the plodding Rhau-Grunenberg could scarcely fail to turn a profit. Luther clearly had mixed feelings about his first printer. Like many who worked with Luther in Wittenberg, Rhau-Grunenberg was an admirer and supporter; Luther acknowledged his piety, even when he grumbled about his printing. But Luther was never satisfied with how

Rhau-Grunenberg published his works. Like many authors Luther railed intermittently against his publishers, complaining of real or imagined imprecision or clumsiness. Usually Rhau-Grunenberg was the butt of these jibes.

> You would not believe how I regret and how I am disgusted by his work. If only I had never sent him anything in the vernacular! He has printed these things so shoddily, so carelessly, so confusedly that I keep these scruffy types and paper hidden away. Johann the printer never gets any better.[12]

Rhau-Grunenberg worked to his own pace and was not to be hurried. In truth, a more enterprising and dynamic man would have been overwhelmed by the sheer extent of public interest in Luther during these years. The Wittenberg industry needed to grow, and in 1519 Luther took a sensible initiative, inviting the experienced Leipzig printer Melchior Lotter to set up a branch of his business in Wittenberg.

Luther and Lotter had already by this time established a co-operative working relationship. Leipzig had shared generously in the publishing boom created by Luther's spreading reputation: works published in Wittenberg were almost immediately reprinted in Leipzig, and until 1519 Luther also dispatched a number of manuscripts to be published in the larger print centre, including more complex commissions such as the commentary on Galatians, a learned scholarly tome that might have overtaxed Rhau-Grunenberg. Lotter already shared in the profits of publishing Luther; in so rapidly developing a market he could also see the value of diversification. In 1519 he sent his son, Melchior Lotter the younger, to establish a print shop in Wittenberg. It was Lotter junior who published two of the great works of 1520: *To the Christian Nobility of the German Nation* and *The Babylonian Captivity of the Church*. The third, *Of the Freedom of a Christian Man*, was entrusted to Rhau-Grunenberg. It is typical of Luther that despite his grumbling he continued to use Rhau-Grunenberg, and sent him a portion of his original works until the printer's death in 1527. All three of these great writings sold phenomenally well. Lotter published *To the Christian Nobility* in an unprecedented edition of 4,000 copies. Even so, it sold out in five days. Fifteen further editions followed. *Of the Freedom of a Christian Man* went through eighteen editions in a single year.

The opportunities seemed boundless, and soon a number of new men were tempted to Wittenberg to set up their shops. Between 1523 and 1525 three arrived who would have a considerable importance in the development of the Wittenberg industry: Joseph Klug, Hans Lufft and Georg Rhau. Both Klug and Lufft printed a large number of Luther's writings, and other publications of the developing Reformation. Rhau, meanwhile, developed a significant niche market in hymnals and musical books. Lufft in particular formed a close and confidential relationship with Luther, especially after a precipitate fall from grace forced the younger Lotter to abandon Wittenberg in 1525. Lotter had been accused of battering one of his apprentices. Fined by the council, he suffered a far more severe penalty when Luther declined to offer him any more of his new works for publication. Starved of his lifeblood, Lotter had little choice but to leave.[13]

Among those tempted into the publishing industry during these years was one of Wittenberg's shrewdest businessmen, the painter Lucas Cranach. Cranach had been in Wittenberg since 1505, and in the intervening years he had built a large and versatile workshop. A close friend of Luther and a steadfast supporter, in the 1520s he would be responsible for the sequence of iconic portraits of Luther that marked the development of the Reformation: the visionary young monk, the disguised fugitive of the year in the Wartburg (the famous bearded portrait of Luther as Junker Jörg), later the Protestant patriarch and father. All of these images were mass-produced in the busy Cranach workshop, either as woodcuts or paintings. Cranach was thus responsible for some of the critical images of the developing Reformation movement. He was also heavily involved in one of the key publications, Luther's translation of the Bible. Luther had completed his translation of the New Testament during his year of protective custody in the Wartburg. On his return to Wittenberg the manuscript was entrusted to Cranach and Christian Dörning, who commissioned Lotter to print a large edition of several thousand copies. Even so, they had underestimated potential demand. A new edition was immediately put in hand, to be published in December. These two issues initiated a sequence of more than 400 editions of the Scripture text published in Germany during Luther's lifetime.[14] After the publication of the New Testament, Luther continued his work of translation, with the Pentateuch, the historical books of the Old Testament, and the Prophets. Although the Pentateuch was ready in 1523, thereafter progress slowed as other duties intervened, and the full text was not finally completed until 1534. But in many respects this worked to the advantage of the Wittenberg industry, since the publishers were able to keep up a steady flow of new works and imprints. The text was also swiftly reissued elsewhere in Germany. Nine editions of the New Testament were published in Augsburg and Basel in 1523 alone, and this same year the Luther text was translated for the first time into Low German, the dialect of northern Germany.

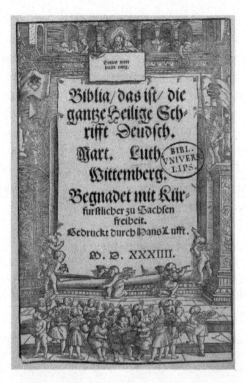

Fig. 16 One of several hundred editions of Luther's Bible published in Wittenberg. This is an edition of Hans Lufft published in 1534.

The bible editions are justly admired for their woodcut illustrations, designed by Cranach and executed in his workshop. Less celebrated, but no less important for the growing reputation of Wittenberg typography, were the beautiful woodcut borders with which the Cranach workshop had begun to adorn Luther's writings, and those of his Wittenberg lieutenants.[15] This design offered a radically new solution to the spatial problems of title-page ornamentation. The development of the title-page had progressed beyond the bare arrangement of text that had characterised its evolution in the first generation of print, and it was now quite common to have a woodcut either above or, more usually, below the text description. Printers had also employed further decorative features, such as sidebars or, on the largest books, a more elaborate frame.

In Cranach's workshop the border became a four-sided tableau, drawing the eye towards the simple bold black-letter text of the title. In the first years Cranach experimented with a number of these designs before settling on a repertoire that employed human or mythological figures in the side panels with Renaissance columns and decorative winding leaves. In later years more explicitly biblical themes would be developed, including a reworking of the iconic Lutheran image of the Law and the Gospel. It was Cranach's achievement to have reconstructed this narrative dichotomy to fit the vertical space of the title-page.[16] All of Cranach's designs, from the Renaissance borders to the biblical motifs, were widely imitated, and as much as the neat quarto format of the *Flugschriften* it was they that gave the works of the mature Wittenberg publishing of the 1520s its distinctive appearance. For those rummaging the bookstalls for the literature of the Reformation, the characteristic appearance of these elegant and boldly executed title-pages would have made them instantly recognisable. They were a visual representation of the confidence and ambition of the new evangelical movement.

Understanding Luther

In a few short years Luther's bold defiance and his facility as a writer had transformed Wittenberg. At the turn of the century, this was a small provincial

Fig. 17 Title-page by Lucas Cranach. Best known as a painter, Cranach's workshop also played a critical role in developing the title-page. This harmonious combination of text and frame became the distinctive livery of *Flugschriften*.

Fig. 18 One of the many works by Luther published in Wittenberg with an elegant title-page designed by Cranach. A near monopoly of supply of woodcut images in Wittenberg also helped make Cranach a rich man.

town. Thirty years later houses on the main streets of this thriving crowded city were being rebuilt in the new Renaissance style, as merchants and publishers reinvested the fruits of their industry.[17] But the benefits of this publishing boom generated by the Reformation were by no means confined to Wittenberg. Between 1520 and 1525 Wittenberg's bookmen published 600 editions, an incredible achievement for such a young industry. The growth of the German printing industry as a whole was even more spectacular. In these six years German presses turned out 7,764 editions, an increase of 340 per cent on the ten years previously, and more than four times as many books as were published in Italy during these same years.[18] It was an immensely profitable trade. Although many of the Reformation's controversial writings were relatively short, they sold out very quickly, and longer texts, such as the Luther Bible, also found a buoyant market. At least 100,000 copies of the New

Testament were published in Wittenberg during Luther's lifetime, and this represents a small proportion of the total output of scriptural texts.[19]

The Reformation controversies had a transforming impact on the German print industry as a whole. The best estimates suggest that between six and seven million evangelical pamphlets were placed on the market during the first decade of the Reformation.[20] What did contemporaries make of this outpouring of books? What indeed did they learn from them of Luther and his teachings? This is not so easy to say. Those who have studied samples of sermons published by supporters of Luther have been impressed by their doctrinal consistency, and by the emphasis placed on the exposition of Luther's teaching, particularly the core doctrine of justification by faith. But these are mostly Latin writings by educated men. The vernacular works that poured off Germany's presses in the years after 1520 reveal a more discordant cacophony of divergent voices.[21] Readers of these tracts could imbibe a bewildering variety of contradictory teachings, a disquieting harbinger of the later divisions and catastrophe that would afflict the Reformation movement.

How are we to reconcile these apparently opposing perspectives? Firstly it is unlikely that many ordinary people would have received their first impressions of Luther, or the controversies raised by his defiance, from printed books. News of the events in Wittenberg and elsewhere passed by word of mouth. Most citizens of the German cities were more likely to have heard the established order criticised or challenged from the pulpit, by ministers sympathetic to Luther's teachings. These preachers were the vital first readers, who ensured that his core theological ideas were articulated simultaneously and accurately in many German cities.

What then of the pamphlets in German and those who bought them? It seems that the broad mass of people who engaged with this literature took from it a range of less precise, but nevertheless powerful impressions. They believed that Luther was a holy man, and a humble one. They thought that he had been too hastily condemned, without a fair hearing; and they admired him for standing up to the powerful forces ranged against him. In this context the iconography of Cranach's first portrait of the tonsured monk, as a humble churchman with bible in hand, was particularly powerful. The evangelical call for simple Gospel preaching, 'rein Evangelium', the pure Gospel, struck a chord. The subsequent enthusiasm for the vernacular New Testament profited from, and further reinforced, this most powerful of Reformation slogans. The patriotic element of Luther's stand against the Papacy seems also to have resonated very powerfully, particularly in the critical months before the Diet of Worms in 1521.[22]

Most of all, contemporaries were impressed by the sheer scale of the public debate raised by Luther and his supporters. In this context the profusion of pamphlets became not only indicative of public interest, but a factor in shaping opinion. The sixteenth century was an era in which much decision making was collective. For the major events of the civic and church year, the citizenry would gather together, often outdoors. A sense of the will of the community would emerge. Justice was proclaimed and executed publicly, so that those present could affirm by solemn witness their support of the verdict. In an age before the establishment of police forces, no local authorities had the power to enforce their will on any truly recalcitrant population. Magistrates had to listen, and take note of any articulation of the public mood – in the marketplace, the town square, or in the churches.

Now they also had to contend with an unprecedented number of published pamphlets, and these too could move opinion, not so much by what they said, but because their sheer profusion seemed to indicate an irresistible desire for change. Contemporaries were deeply impressed by a sense that so many respected people in their own communities supported Luther; that he was not, as the church authorities would have wished them to believe, a maverick figure: as the Papal Bull of 1520 expressed it, a wild boar escaped into the Church's vineyard.[23] The evidence to the contrary, that Luther enjoyed the support of many respected people in their own local communities, was visible in the large numbers who took up their pens in Luther's defence. Between 1519 and 1529 the presses of Strasbourg published works in support of Protestantism by eighty-one authors. These included a large number by Luther and his Wittenberg lieutenants, but also the works of local ministers and lay people. In this first era of the Reformation, particularly before 1525, a strikingly large number of printed works were by lay men and women, many of them persons of respect in the local community.[24] These works were published as pamphlets in the familiar quarto livery of the *Flugschriften*. For those persuaded, by their minister in the pulpit or by friends and neighbours, that Luther was a force for good, the purchase of a Reformation pamphlet might be the first tangible gesture of commitment. It was a badge of identity available to many who might never previously have bought a book.

The German book industry

The first to benefit from this great increase in the book-buying public were, inevitably, printers in the established major centres of German typography:

Augsburg, Nuremberg, Basel and Strasbourg. Between 1522 and 1525 there were five reprints of Luther's works for every Wittenberg original. Although the Wittenberg publishing industry had expanded rapidly, the town remained towards the geographical periphery of the core market and production centres in the German south and west. For these markets local printers turned off new editions as soon as they could lay their hands on a copy of the text.

Some printers refused to take part in the new trade. In Strasbourg Johann Grüninger and in Nuremberg Anton Koberger stayed true to the old ways, and Cologne, a bastion of orthodoxy, largely avoided Reformation publishing. For the rest there were rich pickings. In Strasbourg, Protestant works made up over half the output of three significant printing houses, those of Wolfgang Köpfel, Matthias Biener (Apiarius) and Johann Herwagen.[25] In Basel Johann Froben turned briefly away from the scholarly editions that had made his reputation to publish a Latin compilation of Luther's early works.[26] Copies were dispatched for sale all over Europe. Froben reckoned that this was the most successful book he ever published; though the disapproval of Erasmus that he should have involved himself in publishing Luther might in the longer term have cost him dear. Froben managed to pacify Erasmus and avoided a rupture with the great humanist, the principal source of his prosperity.[27]

The enormous growth of the book market during these years stimulated a significant diversification in the German print industry. The vast demand for Reformation *Flugschriften*, and the ease with which they could be published, allowed print to be established, or re-established, in places which until this time had little or no experience of publishing books. Some were as tiny as the Saxon village of Grimma, where between 1522 and 1523 Nikolaus Widemar operated a small press, publishing twelve editions of the works of Luther and his Wittenberg supporters. This included two small partial editions of Luther's New Testament translation, editions of the Epistle to the Romans and the Galatians.[28] Published here as short pamphlets, they made the text of Scripture accessible to the most marginal purchaser of Reformation *Flugschriften*. In 1523 Widemar moved on to Eilenburg, where a further thirty-five works of a similar character were turned off the press.

Widemar's press seems to have been sponsored by a Leipzig publisher, desperate not to lose a share of the buoyant market for evangelical texts when printing in Leipzig became impossible.[29] In the first years of the Reformation the city had played an important role in the publication of Luther's writings. Close commercial connections, however, could not insulate Leipzig from the bitter rivalry between the two collateral branches of the Saxon ruling house. In 1522, Duke George, ruler of Ducal Saxony, decided definitely against the

Reformation, and prohibited the production or sale of Lutheran texts in his territories. For the publishers of Leipzig this was a dreadful blow. In 1524 a deputation petitioned the Duke, asking to be allowed to publish Luther's writings once again. The books they were now required to print, written by Luther's Catholic opponents, were simply unsaleable, they claimed. Figures for the production of books in Leipzig support their complaints. Between 1515 and 1522 over 1,100 editions were published in Leipzig, an average of 140 titles a year. Following the ban on publishing Lutheran works this fell precipitously, to 43 titles in 1523 and 25 in 1524.[30] To add insult to injury these were the years when printing in Germany reached its zenith, a previously unimaginable output of almost 1,500 editions per year. There was no doubt that Leipzig's printers breathed a sigh of relief when, following the conversion of the Duchy to Lutheranism after the death of Duke George they were able to resume publishing Protestant works.

The impact on German publishing of the new market in Reformation pamphlets was very profound. We can identify at least thirty-four places where the Reformation controversies were responsible for the first introduction of printing, or the restoration of a print tradition that had lain dormant since the fifteenth century. These places were scattered through the Empire from Ingolstadt and Regensburg, to Kiel, Königsberg (1524) and Berlin (1540).[31] The late date of establishment of a number of these presses, long after the first fury of the Reformation controversies had died down, demonstrates that the impact of the Reformation on German print was long lasting. In the second decade of the Reformation, and particularly after the trauma of the German Peasants' War, Luther began to redirect his energies from controversy towards church building. The next thirty years would see the publication of an enormous range of pastoral and instructional literature for the new Protestant congregations: church orders, catechisms, hymn-books and sermons, for the use both of the new Protestant clergy and their congregations. The establishment of Protestant churches in cities and princely states around Germany in the later 1520s and 1530s provided new work for the printers, as each new church promoted its own regulations and the works of its local pastors and preceptors.

The fires of controversy were not entirely dampened. Among the evangelical works published in such numbers in places like Strasbourg and Basel were writings by many who either misunderstood Luther's teaching, or came to reject his leadership. A number of printers specialised in the publication of radical or spiritualist authors, and of their emerging counter-churches; some clearly sympathised with their views. Luther seldom failed to respond to any direct attack on his doctrine. Even in an increasingly domestic old age, he could still be stirred to action by some challenge to his teaching or other great event.

Luther's death in 1546 brought forth a new wave of commemorative publication, as loyal lieutenants and followers reflected on a pious life and momentous career.[32] The Protestant churches honoured a founder who had, certainly against his initial intention, established an enduring separate tradition in Western Christendom. He had also decisively changed the nature of the book in Germany. Luther's success as a writer was surprising considering that his conventional church background provided no training for the exceptional skill he would show as a vernacular writer. The rapidity with which Luther established such a commanding presence was all the more remarkable when one considers that the previous eighty years since the establishment of print had provided so few examples of any contemporary writer gaining a following among the reading public. Savonarola and Erasmus were both widely read in their own lifetime, but achieved nothing like Luther's success.[33] Luther could certainly have made a considerable fortune from his writing, had he chosen to do so. On one occasion the publishers of Wittenberg offered the reformer a retainer of 400 gulden a year for the assurance that they would have the right to publish his newly written works. This would have doubled Luther's income. The reformer refused, preferring not to compromise what he saw as a core part of his religious vocation. The fruits of his industry would continue to fall to others in the German publishing industry.

Luther's death occurred at a moment of crisis for the Reformation. As Luther lay dying, the Emperor Charles V was making preparations for a last great effort to impose his will on the Empire. In January 1547 the military alliance of the Protestant states, the Schmalkaldic League, suffered a crushing defeat at his hands at the battle of Mühlberg. With the leaders of the League his prisoners, Charles seemed poised to enforce a new conservative church settlement and roll back the achievements of the Reformation. The isolated and demoralised Protestant states had little choice but to accept the first phase of this, the Augsburg Interim, in 1548. Now the printing press came once more into its own. Deprived of the princely leadership that had defined Protestantism in the 1530s, the initiative now fell to a group of ministers determined not to compromise the Lutheran heritage. Printing presses established in the rebel city of Magdeburg poured forth a torrent of defiance and vitriol against the Emperor and those who had abandoned the cause.[34] Deprived of the rapid victory that had seemed within his grasp, Charles was forced to give ground. The Peace of Augsburg of 1555 would secure the Lutheran heritage and the future of the churches of the Reformation.

CHAPTER 6

LUTHER'S LEGACY

Not everyone in sixteenth-century Europe fell under Luther's spell. In France the most popular religious writer of the era was Pierre Doré, a Franciscan monk who utterly repudiated Luther's attack on the established Church.[1] In England none of Luther's admirers had the standing of Bishop John Fisher, whose elegant scholarly books in defence of the Catholic Church found a wide international audience.[2] In Italy the interest in Luther never matched the surge of pamphlets that had accompanied the preaching of Savonorola, another turbulent priest whose calls for repentance created good business for the booksellers. Perhaps Italy's publishers had learned the lessons of that traumatic event.

The Reformation's impact on the European book market was very patchy. Sometimes it brought new energy to a local market as it had in Germany; in other places, particularly in southern Europe, it did little to disrupt the normal patterns of production. The parts of Europe most affected were those that enjoyed the closest cultural connections with the German Empire, such as Switzerland and the Netherlands. Luther's movement also had a profound impact on the relatively small book worlds of the lands geographically closest to Wittenberg, in Scandinavia and eastern Europe. In these places the Reformation itself provided a decisive impulse for the development of a previously somewhat muted engagement with print.

Eating sausage and selling books

The Swiss Reformation is largely the story of the Reformation in Zurich. But there was nothing in the early history of Zurich typography to hint at the crucial role it would play in the leadership of the Swiss Reformation. A press established in the city in 1479 had printed a few small works for local distribution, but then, like so many in the fifteenth century, stuttered and failed. The dominance in the region of the great publishing centre of Basel made it difficult to establish a successful press in the other cities of the Confederation. In the years immediately before the Reformation neither Zurich nor Bern had a printing press. An attempt was made to re-establish printing in Zurich by one Hans Ruegger, but little had been achieved when he died in March 1517. His equipment was taken over by his apprentice, Christopher Froschauer, who in time-honoured fashion then married the widow Ruegger. The following year he published his first book, a small volume of devotions to the Virgin Mary. This would be Froschauer's last conventional religious publication. Henceforth, and beginning with two reprints of Luther's sermons in 1519, his press would be devoted entirely to the service of the Reformation.[3]

The moving spirit of the Zurich Reformation was Ulrich Zwingli, who had been appointed to the key position of people's priest in Zurich in this same year, 1519. Froschauer quickly became one of Zwingli's collaborators, committed to promoting reform within the city. Indeed it was at Froschauer's workshop that the critical incident at the beginning of the Zurich Reformation took place. In 1522 Froschauer's men were working long hours to have books ready for the Frankfurt Fair. The printer decided that the Lenten diet of vegetables would not be sufficiently sustaining for the arduous work ahead so the workmen cut and ate a sausage. This, at least, was Froschauer's explanation when he was reported to the council for breach of the Lenten fast. From what we have seen of the pressure on printers in the run up to the fair, the excuse was plausible, even if the challenge to Catholic orthodoxy was carefully contrived. When Froschauer was admonished and fined, Zwingli, who had been present but had not eaten, defended the breach of Lenten regulations from the pulpit. The sermon was then published, in the local vernacular, on the press of the unrepentant Froschauer.[4]

From this point on printer and reformer worked closely in the service of the Reformation. Each carefully choreographed stage of the Zurich Reformation was recorded on Froschauer's press: Zwingli's attack on papal mercenary service in 1522, the theses for the crucial public debate of 1523; all of his subsequent theological writings. In 1524 Froschauer published one of many reprints of Luther's New Testament. When the Wittenberg translation of the whole Bible was delayed by Luther's other commitments, the Zurich reformers embarked on their own. The result, published in 1529 and some years in advance of the Luther text, was a complete Bible, together with the Apocrypha.

The appearance of this book in three separate editions over the next two years, including a fine folio, signalled how far Froschauer's press had come.

Fig. 19 Zwingli's sermon on fasting. Like many Reformation printers, Christopher Froschauer was also an active participant in the movement. His press was an invaluable asset for Ulrich Zwingli as he sought to move Zurich's citizens and magistrates towards adopting the Reformation. *Von Erkiesen und Freiheit der Speisen*, 1522.

With the stimulus provided by the Reformation, and secure in the confidence of the reformed town council, Froschauer and his heirs were able to build a business of considerable size. The family firm published over 1,300 editions which included all of the key works of the Zurich church settlement, as well as twenty-eight editions of the Bible. The firm published over 80 per cent of the books, pamphlets and broadsheets that appeared in Zurich during the course of the sixteenth century. In terms of vernacular print this was an output that came close to matching that of Basel, though the established centre continued to hold an undisputed mastery in the scholarly languages.

Elsewhere in the German-speaking cities of the Confederation, there was nothing to match the emergence of Zurich, or the later spectacular growth of Genevan print in the Francophone world.[5] Bern had no printing press until 1537: the magistrates relied on the nearby presses of Basel or Zurich to print the orders and mandates that marked the tentative development of the Bern Reformation.[6]

The series of mandates commissioned by the Bern Council provide an interesting example of how the use of different media could signal subtle shifts in the balance of power. The major milestones of the Protestant advance in Bern were proclaimed in printed broadsheets, ordered from Froschauer in editions of 400. Often there was also a Latin edition, for international distribution. Yet official orders of 1524, that represented a conservative turn in events, were distributed only in manuscript, in between 35 and 39 copies. In this way the authorities could shape a debate even when they proclaimed official neutrality.

North and east

In marked contrast to the Swiss Confederation, the sparsely populated lands of the Scandinavian kingdoms lay on the outer rim of the medieval book world. The number of books printed here was extremely modest. Only twenty-six editions printed in Denmark during the fifteenth century are known, and just sixteen books in Sweden.[7] There was no printing in either Norway or Finland. But as was often the case, those who needed books were able to obtain them. In May 1493 the Archbishop of Uppsala had one chest and twelve barrels of books shipped from Lübeck to Sweden, a very considerable library.[8] Here, as in the manuscript age, Lübeck acted as the transit port for books manufactured in the major German centres of Mainz, Cologne, Strasbourg and Basel. Most of the customers were churchmen. Among the handful of books published in Denmark and Sweden in the fifteenth century were missals and breviaries for Uppsala, Odense and Strängnäs, and a psalter and manual for Uppsala.

This situation continued into the first decades of the sixteenth century. There was no printing press operating in Denmark between 1523 and 1528. The turbulent and decisive events of the Danish Reformation, the deposition of Christian II (1523) and the repudiation of Rome by his successor Frederik I (1526), thus all occurred without domestic print. The first Reformation tracts published in Danish were printed abroad, in Germany or in the Netherlands. The first Danish New Testament was published in Leipzig, by Melchior Lotter.[9] In 1531 the exiled Canon of Lund, Christiern Pedersen, translated and edited a number of Protestant works, which were printed in Antwerp by Willem Vorsterman, along with further editions of the New Testament.[10] When Pedersen returned to Denmark in 1532 he established a printing house in Malmö. In its first years this would be managed by another experienced printer from Antwerp, Johannes Hillenius von Hoochstraten.[11]

Assured of royal support, the printing presses of Denmark gradually expanded their productive capacity.[12] A reformed Danish liturgy was published in Malmö in 1528, and the following decade witnessed a significant flowering of religious and polemical writing in support of reform. Hans Mikkelsen, the mayor of Malmö, and Peder Laurensen, a former Carmelite, published important works in support of the evangelical cause. Yet when in 1548 it was decided to sponsor an official Danish translation of the Bible, a German printer, Ludwig Dietz, was summoned from Rostock to supervise this more complex task. The Bible was published in a print run of 3,000, and paid for by a levy on the Church.

Printing in Sweden was even more closely attuned to the needs of the official Church. From 1510 to 1519 a press had functioned in Uppsala, but few books were published in the Swedish language before the Reformation. In 1523 the Bishop of Linköping, Hans Brask, established a press in nearby Söderköping in an effort to support traditional doctrines. In this same year, however, a noble revolt against Danish rule established Sweden as an independent state. In 1526 the new king Gustav Vasa closed the press in Söderköping and seized its materials. The press was brought to Stockholm to operate under royal supervision. Henceforth this royal press would be the only one permitted and this royal monopoly of printing continued until the seventeenth century. This restraint on independent enterprise was unique in Europe. As Gustav Vasa converted his kingdom to Protestantism it ensured that the press would be entirely at the disposal of the new faith.[13]

With the exception of broadsheet royal ordinances, the publications of this press were overwhelmingly religious in character.[14] In 1526 the new press published a translation of the New Testament into Swedish; a complete Bible followed in 1541. During a productive period under the management of Georg Richolff the press turned out all the books needed in the new Church: liturgies, catechisms, prayer books, works of instruction and sermons. In contrast to Denmark, the quantity of polemical writing was negligible. The smooth progress of reform under Gustav Vasa stifled debate. The work of reform was pushed forward by Olaus Petri and Laurentius Andrae, both of whom combined the work of church reform with significant activity as authors. Many of their works drew heavily on German models, and the Swedish industry also relied heavily on German expertise. Richolff, the publisher of the Swedish Bible, was summoned back from Lübeck specifically to accomplish this task. The year 1543 also witnessed the beginnings of publishing in Finnish: a primer and short catechism written by the instigator of the reformation in Finland, Michael Agricola.

In eastern Europe the Reformation faced a different challenge. Here a patchwork quilt of ethnic communities cut across shifting political boundaries. Hungary, Poland and Bohemia had all to some extent embraced the Renaissance, and scholars eagerly sought out the latest humanist texts. The boldest of them dispatched letters to Erasmus, who would sometimes, but not always, favour them with a reply. These intellectual contacts ensured a healthy market for Latin and scholarly books. But the universities and towns of the region were widely dispersed. Individual vernacular communities were small, and the number who could read smaller still. This was difficult terrain for print.

For Luther, Bohemia (now the Czech Republic) represented a particular challenge. Intellectual and economic connections between Bohemia and neighbouring Saxony were close. The exploitation of the mineral resources of the Sudeten Mountains had depended wholly on German capital, and largely on an immigrant German workforce. Bohemia had already, in the fifteenth century, experienced its own patriotic Reformation, with the Hussite revolt of 1415. Even so the Wittenberg reformers had to proceed with some care, particularly as Luther was initially not keen to embrace the comparison with Hus made by his Catholic opponents. Debates about church order and liturgical customs led to quarrels between admirers of Luther and conservative Hussites. Nevertheless, the religious controversies of the sixteenth century brought new energy to printing in Bohemia. In the first half of the century presses were established in several provincial towns dispersed through the kingdom. Around fifteen printers worked more or less permanently in Prague, which became a significant centre of the printed book.[15] The largest proportion of these printed books were in Czech: around 2,800 of the 4,400 printed works published in Bohemia and Moravia during the sixteenth century.[16] The presence of a significant minority of Latin publications, many of them small works of humanist poetry, is a reminder that Prague was also, in these years, a significant cultural capital.

A number of the German reformers, including Luther, Melanchthon and Martin Bucer, were translated into Czech. Melanchthon was particularly admired, not least as the author of a Czech–Latin grammar which went through many editions. Polemics between the different churches were less prominent than editions of sermons, prayer books and works of consolation. All the churches could agree on the value of vernacular Scripture. The first translation of the Bible into Czech was achieved as early as 1488. This initiated a remarkable series of scriptural works, influenced increasingly by the Lutheran Bible, and especially by its illustrative tradition. The Czech Reformation also made a distinguished contribution to the development of the printed hymnal. Lay singing in the vernacular was an established part of the worship of the first Czech Reformation, and the tradition was stoutly upheld, especially by the Unity of Brethren.

The diversity and lack of dogmatism of the Czech Reformation assisted the printing industry, and there was little attempt to exercise restraint by

Bohemia's rulers. In Poland-Lithuania Lutheranism faced a more obdurate opponent in King Sigismund I Jagellion. During the 1520s he introduced a series of decrees which menaced any who introduced or distributed Luther's writings into the kingdom. These were, however, seldom rigorously enforced. Even in Cracow, the centre of the Polish monarchy, as well as its cultural and print centre, those arraigned for possession of heretical books usually escaped with a reprimand. When in 1544 a Cracow bookseller, Jan Schnitzer, was found in possession of a German bible, his explanation that he kept it for the magnificent illustrations rather than the text was accepted without demur. Although the church authorities strove to enforce edicts of censorship they received little help from the Polish nobility. A more substantial barrier to the early acceptance of Luther's teachings may have been the profound and far-reaching commitment to Erasmus. Between 1518 and 1550 some forty editions of his works were published in Cracow.[17]

The Polish authorities could, however, do little to restrain the spread of Lutheranism in their German-speaking territory: the vassal state of Brandenburg. These lands, originally the territories of the Teutonic Knights, were in 1525 secularised by the last Grand Master of the Order, Albert of Hohenzollern, as a princely state (the core of the later state of Prussia). While swearing an oath of fealty to the Polish crown Albert swiftly introduced a Lutheran Reformation. His capital, Königsberg (now Kaliningrad), became an important eastern outpost of Lutheran printing. The 500 works published in the city, mostly in German but some in Polish, were naturally disseminated widely through this large, sprawling and ethnically complex corner of Europe. Danzig, Breslau (in Silesia, now Wrocław in Poland) and Posen (Poznań) also provided avenues of access for Lutheran literature.

To the south, in Hungary, the progress of the Reformation was complicated by the political turmoil stemming from the relentless advance of the Turks. Their crushing victory at Mohács in 1526 led to the occupation of central Hungary, and its partition into three. The Habsburgs, asserting the right of succession to King Louis, killed at Mohács, established control in the north and west; in the east Transylvania was ruled as an independent principality. No books were printed in parts of the country under Turkish rule, which from 1541 included Buda. Even in the Habsburg territories printing scarcely flourished, with such books as were required being supplied from Vienna or Cracow. The future of Hungarian printing seemed for the time being to lie in Transylvania, and more specifically in Braşov, where in 1539 a print shop was established by the humanist Johannes Honter.[18] The fall of Buda in 1541 stimulated the attempt to introduce a formal Reformation in Hungary, orchestrated by Honter and strongly encouraged by Luther from Wittenberg. The Reformation in Hungary received strong support especially from the settled German enclave of the Siebenbürgen (Transylvania), which consisted largely of migrants from Saxony.[19] These gave the Transylvanian Reformation a strongly Lutheran character until the arrival of competing religious groups in the second half of the century.

The Bible of Alcalá

Although printing was introduced into Spain at an early date, the new art did not develop with the same vigour as in Europe's major markets. The rocky terrain of the central plateau created difficulties for the development of an effective, integrated market. While this encouraged the creation of a number of dispersed centres of printing, it discouraged printers from undertaking complex projects which required access to a large market. Spain produced less than 3 per cent of the books published in the fifteenth century, and books published in Spain made little impact on the wider European market. In the sixteenth century, and despite the vast wealth that would flow into the kingdom from Atlantic silver, domestic production of books remained relatively meagre. Castile, Aragon and Portugal were, throughout this period, major net importers of books. Much of this trade was organised through Venice, Lyon and, in the second half of the century, Antwerp.

Despite this, Spain's cities and universities could boast a lively intellectual culture, epitomised in the first decades of the sixteenth century by the new university established in Alcalá de Henares by Cardinal Ximénez de Cisneros, Archbishop of Toledo. The scholars gathered by Cisneros were the leading force behind Spain's enthusiasm for humanism, and especially the works of Erasmus, which circulated widely in Spain, and in Spanish translation.[20] Cisneros planned to cap his intellectual ventures with a work of textual brilliance to outshine Erasmus's New Testament. The fate of this venture would illustrate both the ambition and limitations of Iberian print culture.

The Polyglot Bible was intended to be the definitive work of textual scholarship, with texts and translations of the Old and New Testament in the ancient languages, together with a Latin translation. The scholars gathered at the university provided the expertise. The boldness of the scheme was exceeded only by its sheer impracticality as a publishing venture. Alcalá was not a major centre of printing: there is no evidence of the existence of a press before the foundation of the university in 1499. The necessary typefaces had to be laboriously imported and mastered by inexperienced pressmen. When published in 1522 the print run of 600 copies far exceeded the evident demand for so expensive a book, particularly as there was no established way of exporting them from Spain to other parts of Europe. Fernando Colón was able to pick up a heavily discounted copy in Alcalá itself, and the edition never sold out.

The failure of Cisneros's great project reinforced a number of stark lessons about the Spanish role in print. The Iberian peninsula was not well placed to contribute to the international book market. Spanish printers would do well to concentrate on supplying local needs: liturgies for local churches or devotional books for pious lay people. Even successful publishers like Juan Cromberger of Seville turned out tried and tested favourites for the vernacular market rather than attempting to compete in more challenging markets. This, indeed, was why his business was so successful. He was also able to cut his overheads by employing slaves as pressmen.[21]

More complex books were imported, mostly from France and Italy. The connections with Germany, Luther's homeland, were far more distant. The character of the choleric German reformer was in any case deeply unsympathetic to the Spanish temperament. Only thirty years earlier, Aragon and Castile had celebrated the subjugation of the last Moorish outpost, the kingdom of Granada. The Catholic Church had played a critical role in this heroic struggle; it was an admired symbol of national unity. The German heresies, to those who knew of them, evoked disgust and outrage.

This then was a very hostile climate for the distribution of overtly Protestant literature. The hostility to heresy, and the increasingly confident investigative activities of the Spanish Inquisition, ensnared many who had shown only a very non-confessional interest in reformist thought.[22] In the early part of the sixteenth century Erasmus's works had enjoyed great popularity in Castile; now, even that became too dangerous. The clamp-down on unorthodoxy reached its terrifying denouement in 1557–59, when a number of heretical cells were discovered in Valladolid and Seville. Arrests followed the capture of one Julián Hernández, caught attempting to smuggle Protestant books into Seville. Many thousands of books joined the condemned prisoners burned alive in a series of ceremonial *autos de fe*.

The scandalous events of 1557–59 had a further depressing effect on the press. Restrictions and controls were multiplied. In what was already a decade of economic crisis in Spain these cut deep into the core market in devotional books. Uncertain what was now considered orthodox, many printers were reluctant to risk new editions of once popular texts, even bestsellers of Catholic spirituality. This accelerated Spain's collapse into a dependent market. By the latter half of the century even liturgical texts were being supplied from abroad.[23]

Idle chatter and inappropriate books

The troubled reputation of Martin Luther also had a significant impact on the reaction to the Reformation in Italy. This, of course, had been one of the heartlands of print production since the first years, and a major net exporter of books. The German controversies initially excited considerable interest. Some members of the Italian church hierarchy were sympathetically disposed to aspects of Luther's theological agenda. The most notable representative of this tendency was the Venetian Gasparo Contarini, a humanist patrician who rose high in the Church during the pontificate of Paul III. Contarini, like many humanists, was strongly attracted to Luther's notion of the primacy of grace in the process of salvation. Charged by the Pope with preparing a programme of reform in advance of the Council of Trent, Contarini developed a bold vision of pastoral improvement that was unflinching in its analysis of the Church's institutional failings. Contarini and his allies represented an influential voice in the reform debate into the 1540s.

Despite this sympathy for the theological concepts of the Reformation, there was relatively little overtly evangelical printing in the Italian peninsula; a striking absence given the strength and diversity of the local printing industry. Although there was widespread interest in theological debate, and in church reform, the different strands of evangelical sympathisers never congealed into a recognisable movement. The salon evangelism that provided men like the Spanish refugee Juan de Valdés with a congenial home was essentially an elite movement, and its influence was therefore limited.[24] After a period in Rome, Valdés settled ultimately in Naples, where he gathered around him a circle of sympathisers that included the prominent noblewomen Vittoria Colonna and Giulia Gonzaga. Valdés published a number of books, including the *Alphabet of Christianity*, but his was a refined, inward spirituality that had little in common with the comprehensive institutional reform proposed by Contarini.

Italy presented significant cultural barriers to the success of the German movement. If intellectuals in all parts of Europe found Luther's tempestuous immoderation indigestible, this was particularly so in the Italian peninsula, where humanists were more used to setting the agenda than responding to events emanating from a distant corner of northern Germany. The strong streak of anti-Italianism in the German movement also contributed to the relatively unsympathetic reception for Luther's charismatic personality. Only one book was published in Italy that named Luther on the title-page as author. This was an edition of Luther's Latin *Appeal to the Council* published in Venice in 1518; that is, before Luther's decisive condemnation by the church authorities.[25] Thereafter such works of the German reformers as were published in Italy or in Italian translation abroad were seldom advertised as such. Luther's *Declaration on the Ten Commandments*, translated into Italian in 1525, was attributed to Erasmus. Philip Melanchthon was effectively disguised in an unrecognisable Italian transliteration as 'Ippofilo da Terra Negra'; the Strasbourg reformer Martin Bucer became 'Aretius Felinus'.[26] A number of Protestant texts circulated as part of compilations. The two most famous were the *Summary of the Sacred Scripture*, a text that enjoyed considerable currency in several vernacular languages, and the *Benefice of Christ*, published in Venice in 1543. This text was an enormous success, selling in large numbers and well received by many leading churchmen. They would have been unlikely to have approved had they known that the text included verbatim translations of parts of Calvin's *Institutes*.

Despite the success of these texts the quantity of evangelical writing smuggled into Italian vernacular reading in this way was relatively modest: a total of around forty editions were published before 1560.[27] Italian intellectuals maintained contact with the northern theological debate mostly by importing Protestant books in their Latin originals. Despite papal condemnation it was possible to find Luther's books for sale in Milan in the early 1520s. In the following decades citizens of the Italian towns were able to put together impressive libraries of reformed theology through purchase of imported titles. A key figure in this trade was the expatriate Lucca merchant Pietro Perna, who settled in Basel, where he operated as an agent for the publisher Johannes Oporinus, supplying books to clients in Venice, Bologna, Bergamo, Padua, Milan and his home town of Lucca.[28]

These sales demonstrated the extent to which the Reformation had impacted on the Italian urban bourgeoisie. A consciousness of the danger of this seeping influence caused increasing alarm among the church hierarchy. The danger was dramatically illustrated in 1542 by the sensational defection of two leading figures in the church hierarchy, Peter Martyr Vermigli and Bernardino Ochino. The flight of Ochino, head of the Capuchin preaching order, was a devastating blow to reformists like Contarini who clung to hopes of reform from within the Church. It also helped stir the orthodox to new vigour in defence of the Church.

Here defenders of traditional religion also made effective use of the press. This can be well illustrated in the career of the Veronese bishop Luigi Lippomano, a man convinced of the creeping influence of Lutheranism among his flock. He fretted that the 'plebeians and lower classes' of the city 'became more corrupted every day from idle chatter and inappropriate books'.[29] His response was to sponsor a series of books of his own to counter Protestant influences, notably his robust refutation of Lutheranism, *Confirmatione et stabilimento di tutti li dogmi catholici* (Confirmation and establishment of all Catholic dogma).[30]

Lippomano's writings offer an interesting window on a moment in Italian history when the threat from Protestantism was seen as very real. According to Lippomano Protestant books were circulating freely even in the decade after the door had been finally closed to the inner church reform sponsored by the *spirituali*. Lippomano envisaged the salvation of the Church in the creation of a preaching clergy, and he promoted the cause actively in print, publishing collections of his own sermons and a series of model sermons or homilies to guide secular clergy engaging in the unfamiliar activity of preaching for the first time. It was a clear indication that important figures within the Catholic Church recognised the role that could be played by print in the defence of orthodox belief.

The Affair of the Placards

The loyalty of the church hierarchy in Spain and Italy to traditional religion ultimately comes as no surprise. It created a significant barrier to the adoption of the Reformation in southern Europe. The populous lands of north-west Europe seemed more promising terrain. France was one of the centres of the new world of print; the densely populated urban communities of the Netherlands also seemed a fertile environment. Yet in both places Luther's movement would be thwarted and turned back. It was a crucial setback.

From the first days of Luther's notoriety the German controversies were closely followed in France, and especially in the capital, Paris. The German assault on papal authority could count upon some sympathy among the theologians of the fiercely independent Gallican tradition. But conservatives were also powerful; it was they who won the upper hand in the Sorbonne. The Sorbonne formed a powerful northern triumvirate with the equally conservative universities of Louvain in the Netherlands and Cologne in Germany. These universities swiftly published the Pope's condemnation of Luther. In 1526 the Sorbonne went a step further, combining with the Parlement of Paris to enforce another significant limitation on evangelical publishing: a ban on the publication within France of the Scripture text in the French language.[31]

For the printers of Paris this was an especially heavy blow. At this point Paris publishers dominated the market not only in France, but also of quality Latin editions exported to England and the Low Countries. This identification of vernacular Scripture with heresy was a new departure; plenty of French Bibles had been published before the Reformation. Luther had poisoned an established and lucrative trade. The ban on vernacular Scripture cut the well-capitalised Paris industry out of the market.

Frustrated they might be, but the Paris printers had little choice but to comply. Seated close to the major institutions of state, there was little scope for publishing books of which these official bodies did not approve. The production of the Bible in French passed first to Antwerp, and then to Lyon and Geneva.[32] The value of this trade contributed greatly to the growth of printing in these rival centres.

The next ten years were characterised by a dogged battle between conservatives and those who sought, notwithstanding these reverses, to promote reform in France. Reformers could count on the influential support of the king's sister, Marguerite. They hoped that the king's evident enthusiasm for humanist letters would also ultimately incline him to their cause. The disastrous climax of this contest was the Affair of the Placards of 1534, a radical demonstration of the polarising power of print. Broadsheets, printed in Neuchâtel and smuggled back into France, were posted up in the capital at night.[33] They denounced the Mass and Catholic priesthood with a vulgar ribaldry that appalled even many reformers. The posting of broadsheets was a routine way of conveying official instructions: the scandal of these placards' contents was exacerbated by this cheeky poaching of government prerogatives. It said much for the confidence and organisation of evangelicals that they could pull off such a coup; but the retribution was severe.

The outraged king initiated a severe persecution, and the small circle of reformist scholars in the capital, which included the young John Calvin, were forced to flee for their lives. While Calvin rebuilt French Protestantism in Geneva, others embedded within the French Church continued to circulate texts, in manuscripts and print, that kept the reform agenda alive.[34] This included a surprising amount of Luther in French translation, though such works never acknowledged Luther's authorship. But these small works, though interesting in themselves, were not typical of the religious works published in France in these years. Rather the challenge to church authority had stimulated a powerful defence of orthodoxy in a range of lucid French vernacular writings.[35] In contrast to the situation in Germany, French Catholic theologians did not find it difficult to articulate in print their opposition to reform, and their fealty to traditional teaching. The first generation of the Reformation had left French Catholicism more securely entrenched, and more eloquently defended, than before.

Fig. 20 French Bible (Lyon, Jan de Tournes, 1561). The ban on the publication of vernacular Bibles was a severe blow to the Parisian publishing industry. Production passed instead to printers in Antwerp, Geneva and Lyon, who were all too eager to seize the opportunity to publish large, often lavishly illustrated editions.

Heretic heartland

If the Emperor Charles V had had his way, the prospects for evangelical print in the Netherlands would have been every bit as dismal. Thwarted in his attempts to put an end to Luther's heresy in Germany, Charles V was determined that the evangelical doctrines would put down no roots in the Low

Countries: the land of his birth, and his patrimonial inheritance through his father, Philip the Fair of Burgundy. Starting in 1521 Charles V put in place a formidable array of punitive measures and controls to inhibit the publication, reading or circulation of evangelical books. Those who openly affirmed the German heresies trod a dangerous path. In 1523 two members of the Antwerp house of the Augustinians were executed in Brussels, the first executions for Lutheran heresies anywhere in Europe. From 1530 even the possession of a Protestant text was punishable by death.

The severity of these measures was a pragmatic response to the extent of the problem. Luther's Latin publications were easily available on the active Antwerp book market. Many of his works were swiftly translated into Dutch: a total of eighty in Luther's lifetime.[36] There were a number of reasons why the production of unorthodox texts proved so difficult to suppress. The sheer geographical diversity of the industry, as in Germany, afforded a measure of protection against the close control that was possible in, for instance, Paris or London. In the early 1520s Latin editions of Luther's writings were published in Leiden, Deventer and Zwolle, all remote from the centres of Imperial authority in Brabant. Nor was it easy for the authorities to identify heretical texts. Most of the writings of Luther translated into Dutch did not acknowledge his authorship on the title-page, and it was by no means clear from the title alone that what was for sale was not a far more orthodox work. The Leiden printer Jan Seversz published several of Luther's pastoral works, meditations on the Ten Commandments or the Lord's Prayer that from the outside seem very uncontentious.[37] These writings blended with a long-standing and deeply rooted tradition of devotional vernacular publishing that seems to have been especially strong in the Netherlands.[38] They treated themes that were of central concern to evangelicals, but that nevertheless had an impeccable Catholic heritage.

The greatest opportunity for evangelicals lay in a stubborn reluctance to follow the example of the Paris Sorbonne and condemn vernacular translation of the Bible. There was no inherent reason why the text of Scripture should be regarded as evangelical property, and in the Netherlands it was not. During the course of the sixteenth century printers in the Low Countries turned out over 1,600 editions of whole or partial editions of the Scripture texts, almost 200 of them published before 1520 and unimpeachably orthodox. Editions of the Psalms, individual books of the Old and New Testament, and of course Erasmus's milestone New Testament translations, continued to be published, unimpeded, throughout the period. But inevitably this complaisant attitude created space for more overtly Protestant translations, such as the Liesvelt Bible, a relatively faithful Dutch translation of Luther's text.[39]

All of these factors together, in a busy, buoyant and diverse print world, created far more space for the production and circulation of evangelical texts than Charles V would have wished. Nevertheless, the official condemnation and steadily mounting tariff of penalties did begin to have its effect. In 1526 the Antwerp printer Adriaen van Berghen had been put to death for printing Protestant books, an exemplary punishment that no doubt sent shock waves through the whole industry. The output of heretical books began to tail off.

The trade experienced a further decisive blow following the destruction of the Anabaptist kingdom of Münster in 1535. The scandal of Münster, where in 1534 Anabaptist radicals had established a visionary theocratic regime, had a powerful impact in the Netherlands. Many of those induced to leave their homes and join the New Jerusalem came from the northern Netherlands. Outlandish reports of the conduct of the new rulers of Münster, and the brutality of its eventual subjugation, had a profound effect on attitudes to heresy in the Netherlands.[40] In particular municipal authorities in Holland, who until this point had been inclined to treat the heresy laws with a degree of detachment, now learned the error of their ways. The destruction of the Anabaptist kingdom was followed by a sharp crackdown. This was particularly severe in Amsterdam, where the eschatological excitement raised by Münster had led to a clumsy attempt at an Anabaptist take-over of the city. Anyone suspected of sympathy for the radicals was rounded up, and several hundred were executed.

The assault on unorthodox religion was a mortal blow to a regional print industry already fading in the face of competition from Antwerp. By the 1520s Antwerp was coming to play an increasingly dominant role in the publishing world of the Low Countries. In the first years of print the printing culture of the Low Countries had been characterised by diversity, and well into the sixteenth century places like Deventer, Zwolle and Louvain retained a robust production of books.[41] Gradually though, this began to wilt in the face of the magnetic power of the southern metropolis. This had consequences for the control of heresy. As Antwerp began to take a more central role in the industry, the concentration of printing in one location made it far easier to regulate. Printers had to be mindful not only of official inspection, but also that they might be denounced by rivals wishing to steal a march in a competitive market. Prominent figures in the Antwerp industry became reluctant to risk their position by taking on work that might lead them into difficulties.

Evangelical printing was not altogether extinguished by persecution. In the early 1540s new evangelical cells were planted in several of the largest towns of Flanders and Brabant. A new generation of Antwerp printers, with less established business to place at risk, once again became heavily involved with evangelical publishing. The greater daring of this new evangelical generation led in due course to another wave of repression. It was this that embroiled the Louvain bookseller, Hieronymus Cloet, and the young cartographer Gerard Mercator, who were both among those imprisoned and interrogated. Cloet and Mercator successfully pleaded their innocence. The Antwerp printer Jacob van Liesvelt was not so lucky: he was arrested and executed. The evangelical gatherings were broken up, and those heavily compromised took flight abroad, amongst them Matthaeus Crom and Steven Mierdman, responsible between them for many of the evangelical works published in Antwerp in the early 1540s.[42] Both men went to England. From this point on the future of Dutch Protestant publishing lay mostly abroad, part of an increasingly important trade in exile literature, destined to be smuggled back to sustain embattled co-religionists living 'under the Cross'. Charles V had had his way, but at a price. The very severity of the persecution, forcing abroad many whose commitment to Protestantism was by no means fully developed, swelled the ranks of those who would become thoroughly radicalised in exile. The Emperor had sown the seeds of the brutal ideological conflict of the second half of the century.

Caxton's heirs

We have not heard much of English printing since marking Caxton's notable achievements for English literature and typography in the first age of print. In truth, there had been little since to build on Caxton's legacy. From the point when Wynkyn de Worde moved Caxton's shop from Westminster to London, printing in England was entirely concentrated in the capital. Even in London the industry remained small and, despite Caxton's precocious achievements, limited in range.

There were two main reasons why the print industry in England had not fulfilled its early promise. In the first instance the vernacular reading community was small. Whereas printers in France, Italy and Germany could each rely on a pool of vernacular readers extending over a significant part of Europe's populated heartland, the population of England and Wales at this time was only about two million (as compared, for instance, to fifteen million for France). Caxton had been able to put into print key works of English literature and translations of continental literary works thanks to the interest (and financial support) of high-placed patrons. But the market was simply not large enough to encourage his successors in the early sixteenth century to publish further editions of this sort.

The lyf of faynt Thomas of Caunterburye .· folio C v

Fig. 21 An example of Caxton's early work: the choice of title reflected the courtly tastes of a largely aristocratic clientele. This copy was loyally defaced by its owner during the Reformation, when the cult of Becket was prohibited. The markings are not enough to disguise the crudity of the original artwork.

London provided a market of significant size, but even here the range of texts published was, by the standards of the main continental centres, very limited. The crucial factor was the failure of London's print industry to capture a significant part of the Latin market. Notwithstanding the development of vernacular reading communities, the Latin market continued to form the bedrock of the book trade, in school-books, works of theology, and scholarly and technical literature. England was unique in contributing little to this Latin output. Through to the end of the sixteenth century only about 10 per cent of the books published in England were in languages other than English.

This was not because English readers had any less need of these books than students, scholars and churchmen elsewhere in Europe. England, and particularly London, had a healthy book market. Many continental publishers established an office there, and London bookshops were well supplied with books from all the major European centres of production. In the first years of print Amerbach dispatched from Basel significant consignments of books to

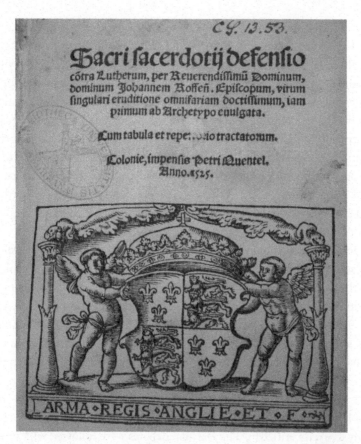

Fig. 22 Bishop John Fisher's defence of orthodox doctrine became an international bestseller, with editions in France, the Netherlands and (as here) in Germany. For English authors in search of an international audience publishing abroad was a logical choice.

London, and when Fernando Colón visited London in 1522 he was able to make extensive purchases of works published on the continent.[43] The problem for London's small number of publishers was that these commercial connections were so well established that it made it difficult to establish a foothold in production. Even the supply of books required in the universities was handled exclusively from the continent via London.[44] The first press established in Oxford in 1483 had failed within two years, and an attempt to set up a press for the university in Cambridge in 1520 was equally short-lived.

English scholars were not in any way impoverished by this dependence on imports, but for the print industry the consequences were significant. To be cut out of the Latin trade was to be excluded from a large part of the most dependable and lucrative part of the market. This severely restricted the growth of London's printing industry, hence of their capital resources, and for this reason severely limited the projects they felt able to undertake. Even liturgical works used exclusively in England, such as missals according to the Rite of Salisbury (used throughout the southern province of the English Church) were very often printed on the continent: in Paris, Rouen or Antwerp, and sometimes even in Venice.

So while the Church, the university and the population of London offered a lively market in books, much of this market was supplied by imports. For printers working in London, the residual market in English vernacular publishing offered limited opportunities for profit. In the first two decades of the sixteenth century the market was effectively shared between two printers, Wynkyn de Worde and Richard Pynson.[45] Both men relied on established niche markets: de Worde cultivated Caxton's old connections, while Pynson concentrated on official publications, proclamations and legal texts. When English authors wished to publish substantial works of theology or scholarship they very often looked to publish them abroad. John Fisher was the first English author to make a notable contribution to the Reformation debates, as an eloquent and pungent critic of Luther. His Latin treatises in defence of the true faith went through numerous editions in the 1520s, but they were usually published first in Paris or Antwerp and then republished in other continental locations.[46] Here they found a far wider audience than if they had been published in London.

There is little evidence that Luther's criticisms of the Church met a favourable reception in England. There was little scandal in the English church hierarchy to excite criticism. The German debates were followed with interest, but active commitment was confined to a small band of educated men who imbibed Luther's theology, often during travels on the continent. Even if Luther's followers had been more numerous, there was little incentive for any London printers to publish such works. The established firms were too dependent on official work to risk incurring the king's displeasure; and the industry was too small for there to be much chance that a clandestine press would pass undetected. In consequence many of the English Protestant publications of the first two decades of the Reformation were printed abroad: mostly in Antwerp. Even when the twists and turns of Henry's marital politics made him intermittently more sympathetic to a reformist agenda (or at least more prepared to bully the Church), the limited capacities of the London printers placed a significant restriction on the range of Protestant literature that could quickly be made available.

All of this creates an interesting context in which to re-examine the familiar story of the struggle for the first printed English translation of the Bible. Given what we now know of the small, intimate nature of the London print industry, it is inconceivable that such a project could be undertaken in England without permission. With a work of this size, the length of time the completed sheets would be hanging around the shop, exciting comment, and thus liable to inspection and confiscation, meant no printer would take it on, even if the paper could be found and paid for. Recognising this, William Tyndale sought first to obtain official support for an English Bible from Cuthbert Tunstall, Bishop of London.[47] It was only after Tunstall, mindful of the king's hostility, declined to help, that Tyndale began to look abroad. Here at first his innocence of the continental print world brought further disappointment. Tyndale began work with a printer in Cologne, a major centre of sophisticated typography, but conservative. Halfway through the printing a local theologian, Cochlaeus, intervened to have the work banned. Tyndale was lucky to be able to salvage the portion of the work already printed, which he hauled off to Worms, where the work was finally completed. It was only when Tyndale found his way to Antwerp that his fortunes turned for the better. Here, in this large metropolitan print centre, Tyndale finished not only his translation of the Pentateuch, but several of his most famous polemical works: the *Obedience of a Christian Man* and the *Practyce of Prelates*. Even after the shift in royal policy in the 1530s finally made it safe to print evangelical texts in London, Protestants continued to use continental presses for longer, more complex projects. Both the Coverdale Bible of 1535 and the Matthew Bible of 1537 were published abroad.[48] Even Paris, rather bizarrely, became involved in the business of English Bible publication. When the English authorities took in hand their own translation (the so-called Great Bible) the work of printing this large folio was put out to a printer in Paris, François Regnault. Given that Paris printers were not allowed to publish the text of Scripture in their own language, the outrage of Regnault's industry colleagues in the French capital was all too predictable. Regnault's shop was raided, and the sheets confiscated. The chastened publishers, Grafton and Whitchurch, were able to recover the work so far accomplished from a Paris waste-paper merchant, and eventually the task was completed in London.[49]

The Great Bible was scarcely completed when the death of Henry VIII signalled a change in policy. The new government of Edward VI gave unambiguous support to a programme of evangelical publications. The resulting deluge of printed texts transformed both the range of Protestant books available in English and the London printing industry. With the government standing so firmly behind the promotion of an evangelical church settlement, new men were tempted to set up business to explore the opportunities of a suddenly expanded market. The volume of books published in London doubled between 1546 and 1548, and increased again in 1550. Most of this new trade was in religious books: church orders, polemical works, and translations into English of works by the continental reformers. The reign of Edward also saw the only concerted effort to establish a functioning press outside the capital. Between 1548 and 1553 presses were established in four locations: Ipswich, Canterbury, Worcester and Dublin.[50] The strategic choice of these locations suggests a measure of official sponsorship, as does the nature of the business undertaken. The presses were put to work publishing reprints of small religious texts likely to find a market in the English county towns. When the Ipswich press proved not to be viable (it was easy enough to supply East Anglia from London, in any case), the Worcester press was given exclusive rights to a number of titles, so that London printers did not spoil their chance of profit. It was an imaginative part of the attempt to spread the Gospel to the English counties, and came to an end only with Edward's death in 1553.

The reign of Edward VI represents a brief interval of relatively unconstrained growth in the English print industry, before the accession of Mary brought the return to a more cautious and restricted canvas. A number of prominent printers either gave up work, or retired abroad; Protestant printing continued, but from the safety of sympathetic continental towns.[51] The reign of Edward VI though had demonstrated the potential for a lively market in England if market and political conditions were favourably aligned; it was a harbinger of what might be achieved when the accession of Elizabeth in 1558 brought the return of a Protestant government, and of some familiar names to the London printing industry.

Luther's legacy

Luther's legacy to the European book world was profound. The scandal, drama and excitement of Luther's assault on papal power attracted attention throughout Europe. The controversies ignited genuine concerns about the issues of redemption and salvation that preoccupied all Christians: the search for answers to these troubling questions allowed the market for religious books to grow exponentially. Printers and booksellers eagerly embraced the opportunity to reach a new book-buying public. The fact that so many of the new texts were short was a further incentive to men of little experience to try their hand in a buoyant market. The result was a flood of new books.

But this trade was not without its dangers. The impact of the Protestant attack on accepted teaching pointed up as never before the dangers of unrestricted access to print. Throughout Europe governments were stirred to establish mechanisms for managing the trade. These attempted to prevent publication and sale of forbidden texts, and to punish those who produced or bought them. Once such regulations were promulgated, governments found they were not difficult to enforce. Printers were businessmen, and books were a commercial venture. However much they resented the restrictions on their freedom to trade, they valued their livelihoods more. In some parts of Europe the publication of Catholic theology, and works against Luther, was a plausible alternative market. Otherwise printers drawn into the market by the Reformation controversies could try their hand with other types of publication to tempt the growing buying public. These new markets also offered rich pickings.

CHAPTER 7

FIRST WITH THE NEWS

L̲ᴜᴛʜᴇʀ's ᴄᴀʟʟ for reform did not succeed everywhere in Europe. But the fury of publishing activity, for and against his teachings, had demonstrated the extent of popular appetite for the printed word. Reporting from Augsburg in 1520, the agent of Charles V was immediately struck by the close connection between the evident popular excitement and the outpouring of printed works. In the process of engaging a wider public with Luther's movement, the *Flugschriften* had themselves become part of the phenomenon. No longer merely agents of information, they were now a newsworthy event in their own right.

The Reformation brought about a vast increase in the volume of publication at the cheaper end of the market. *Flugschriften* were short, cheap and instantly recognisable. If these were the first books that many urban readers purchased, they were certainly very different from the books that had until this moment dominated the publication strategy of most printers, which were by and large serious, bulky and expensive. As the Reformation controversies receded, publishers looked for other ways to engage this new appetite for cheap print. Books for entertainment, literature, ballads and plays became much more common. Publishers also began to exploit more systematically the evident appetite for news. The market in news had existed since the first days of print, but at first largely as an extension of traditional methods of communication between governments and the wider public. Now it began to expand beyond these modest beginnings.

Beginnings

The first printers were not oblivious to the potential of cheap print. Single-sheet publications, especially indulgences, were among the earliest publications of the Mainz proto-typographers. Such commissions brought in welcome income, and did not occupy much press time. It was seldom necessary to interrupt production of substantial projects for more than a day or two to finish the job. These were usually commissions undertaken and delivered to a single customer, who might either distribute them free, or sell them on. The printer would be paid for a job lot, usually on delivery.

Much of the cheap print of the incunabula age was of this character. Indulgences alone account for 30 per cent of surviving single-sheet items from the fifteenth century.[1] Printers were happy to undertake these, for what was a lively and profitable market. They printed other types of small devotional items too, prayers and pilgrimage tokens, or small collections of devotional material, very often for local religious communities. Printers also printed a number of broadsheets and pamphlets at the behest of the local town council: ordinances, proclamations and the like. These were intended either to be posted up, or made available in pamphlet form to merchants and traders.

Almost all of this was commissioned work, rather than books published for a general readership in the hope of profit. Publishers and booksellers in the fifteenth century were surprisingly slow to realise the potential of this aspect of print culture. Pamphlets, and small format works with a current affairs interest, remained in these early days under the shadow of officialdom. Almost all news pamphlets were, in some way or other, official works, commissioned to convey information to a defined public. Here a number of Europe's rulers gradually began to make more innovative use of print.

By some way the most creative in this respect was Maximilian I, ruler of the Burgundian inheritance in the Low Countries and from 1493 Holy Roman Emperor. Often impecunious and frequently worsted in the volatile alliance politics of the era, Maximilian nevertheless presents an engaging figure, irrepressible in his search for dynastic advantage to consolidate his disparate and rancorous territories. As a passionate patron of the arts Maximilian was quick to see the potential of the printing press. In the last years of his life he engaged many of Germany's leading artists in designing a series of elaborate woodcut programmes to immortalise the achievements of his reign.[2] He was not unaware of the more mundane uses of the new technology. From an early stage in the lifetime of print Maximilian made a regular practice of communicating his orders by printed proclamation, rather than the process he had inherited from his predecessor, Frederick III, which was to send manuscript letters under seal to designated recipients. These announcements, mandates and prescriptions could now be printed in three or four hundred copies, to be posted up and read out from the pulpits in the towns of his territories.[3]

Such broadsheets had a clear propagandistic as well as a legal function, explaining why Maximilian needed to raise troops or taxes. More overtly, propaganda broadsheets and pamphlets extolled Maximilian's virtues and celebrated his victories. Among the writers engaged in this work was the distinguished humanist Sebastian Brant, author of the *Ship of Fools*. Maximilian's restless desire to harness the new medium to his service led on one occasion to the imaginative device of commissioning pamphlets in Italian, intended to be distributed among the Venetian population urging them to rise up against their masters – then the Emperor's foes. The suggestion that these pamphlets were carried over the city by balloons, and released when the balloons were shot down by Maximilian's archers seems far-fetched. More likely they were distributed by Maximilian's agents in the city.[4] The leaflets themselves were well written and contain a well-judged appeal to any citizens restless under the rule of the Venetian oligarchs.

This increasingly imaginative use of print remained, however, largely at the disposal of the ruling powers. Printers worked to commission, and under their instructions. The news content was largely incidental to the primary purpose of raising money, explaining policy, or rallying support. It required great events to break this pattern. Towards the end of the fifteenth century the discoveries in the New World aroused a degree of public interest. A letter written by Christopher Columbus describing his voyage was swiftly distributed as a printed text. The original publication in Spanish (at Barcelona) was followed by a rapid sequence of reprints in Latin, and, after an interval of years, a single German translation. The New York Public Library has a wonderful collection of these rare and precious pamphlets.[5]

This communication, as it turned out, was of ideal length for what became a typical news format: four leaves in quarto. The published pamphlets made no attempt at adornment of the text, allowing the drama of the narrative to speak for itself. Through these pamphlets Columbus reached several thousand readers in influential places: Spain, Rome, Paris, and the merchant community of southern Germany.

Even more successful was the pamphlet penned a decade later by Amerigo Vespucci to celebrate the New World discoveries. Vespucci's letters quickly made their way around the major European centres of commerce, first in Latin and Italian, but were also swiftly translated into German. In Germany, anticipating the later transmission of the Lutheran controversies, Vespucci's letters were published in all the major centres of print, in Strasbourg, Basel, Leipzig, Augsburg and Nuremberg, as well as in Munich, Magdeburg and Rostock.[6]

As this example suggests, the market for news seems to have been particularly lively in the bustling commercial cities of the German Empire, which were closely connected by an intricate network of trading routes. Information was already freely exchanged between merchants and bankers whose livelihood might depend on the news of events that impacted on the safety of routes to distant markets. Markets and fairs were centres for the

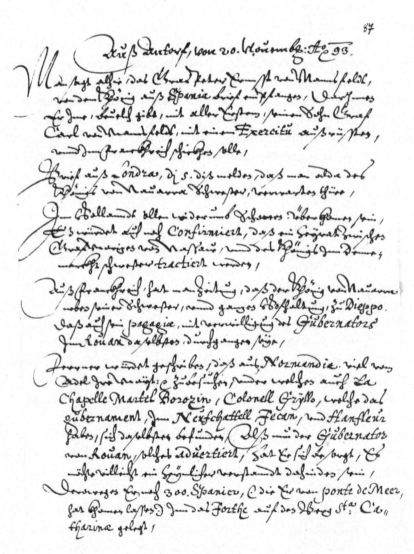

Fig. 23 The manuscript newsletter was a commercial service offered to those who needed regular access to up to date news. This digest of events from 1593 comes from the famous Fugger Newsletter in Germany.

exchange of intelligence, gossip and rumours. The posts carried news of great events as well as commercial transactions and bills of exchange. The wealthiest merchant and banking families maintained networks of agents and couriers. The Fuggers of Augsburg promoted a regular series of newsletters, circulated in manuscript. These manuscript newsletters were an innovation of the Italian commercial world, and date back to the fourteenth century. By the late fifteenth century the production of such *avvisi* was a well-developed commercial practice. Firms produced regular handwritten bulletins, which were then distributed to subscribers.[7]

It was not long before the printers began to recognise the potential of a wider audience for such news bulletins, now in printed, pamphlet form and freely available to any that chose to purchase them. These pamphlets are often given the generic title *Zeitung* or *Neue Zeitung*, a word that in due course gave its name to a new form of publication, the newspaper.[8] But for the earliest examples this can be rather misleading, for these were not serial publications on the model of the Fugger Newsletters (which in fact continued to flourish in manuscript for a century before any such serial publications were printed). The earliest *Zeitungen* were occasional, special pamphlets, stimulated by great events.

Although such pamphlets were published throughout Germany, Augsburg soon emerged as a precocious centre of newsprint. There were several reasons for this. As Germany's major banking centre the city had an acute need for accurate newsgathering. It was also well placed on the major transalpine roads to act as a conduit of intelligence between Italy and the Orient and the lands of northern Europe. Augsburg had been an early centre of vernacular printing. As we have seen, it was one of the few cities in Europe where more was printed in the vernacular than in Latin, even in the fifteenth century. Augsburg's first printers published vernacular books of great quality. The industry did however suffer a serious recession at the turn of the century, as the Franco-Imperial wars closed access to Augsburg's major markets and cut off supplies of Italian paper. Augsburg's depleted bands of printers were therefore very happy to associate themselves with Maximilian's propagandist ventures, initiating a tradition of pamphlet publication that flourished in the following decades.

The publication of news engaged some of the leading figures in the Augsburg printing industry.[9] This might be rather against expectations. The Reformation *Flugschriften* had demonstrated that cheap print did offer a real opportunity for more transitory and less capitalised ventures to find a place in the market. Short works quickly produced and with rapid turnover were the

Fig. 24 An early news pamphlet brings news of faraway battles. The generic woodcut could be re-used for any number of different titles.

ideal products for small businesses. But this did not mean that the more established publishing firms would despise such ventures: a small pamphlet run off in a day could ease cash flow while more complex works were in production. In the specific case of news pamphlets the larger presses enjoyed a further crucial advantage, that of access. Many news pamphlets were published as eyewitness accounts of great events, a dispatch written from the scene of a battle, ceremony or royal entry. The authors were often city officials, ambassadors or officers in the army. Such men were far more likely to convey their work to the city's leading publishers, who moved in their social circles, than to their grubbier backstreet neighbours.

The less well connected were forced to scavenge for what they could. They might not obtain the ambassadorial dispatches, but they could publish reprints. They also specialised in works that recycled the news in the language of the streets: poems of celebration or satirical songs. Such ballads, issued as broadsheets or pamphlets, played their part in the market for news, even if this most ephemeral of all print seldom survives. Ballad and news sheets of this sort were often sold by street merchants, who hawked their goods around the inns, taverns and marketplaces. Such hawkers were known in German as *Zeitungssänger* or *Gassensänger*, because they sang out the ballads they were offering for sale. Such travelling salesmen were often almost indistinguishable from the beggars and vagabonds that municipal authorities were keen to run out of town, but this could be a profitable business. In 1566 a travelling pedlar had a printer in Overijssel in the eastern Netherlands run off 1,000 copies of a sheet with three popular political songs. He paid one guilder for the whole job: if he sold each for the smallest coin in circulation then he would have made a handsome profit.[10]

Habsburg and Valois

Away from Germany a major stimulus for the development of news culture was the long conflict between the Habsburgs and the Valois kings of France. This was fought first in the struggle for supremacy in Italy, and then in a series of increasingly bloody campaigns in northern Europe. In addition to the military effort, both sides went to some trouble to persuade their respective citizenries that they had acted with honour, and that eventual victory would be theirs. The result was an impressive range of news publications relating the twists and turns of the conflict: sieges, battles and towns conquered, and the fragile friendships and attempts at peace that punctuated the wars.

The conflict between the two princely houses engaged two of Europe's most advanced print industries, France on the one side, and the active book world of the Habsburg Low Countries on the other. In France, the first surviving examples of printed news date from 1488, with two pamphlets recording the resolution of war with Brittany.[11] But it is with the Italian campaign of Charles VIII in 1494–95 that the genre begins to take on its definitive shape. Charles VIII's descent into Italy produced a flurry of pamphlets recording his

Fig. 25 Two songs from the time of the Dutch Revolt. These small broadsheets were among the most ephemeral of all forms of print. But they could be incredibly profitable, and a potent vehicle for the dissemination of political opinion.

triumphant progress through the peninsula: the battle of Rapallo and his reception at the court of Savoy; his entry into Florence and then into Rome; finally, the capture of Naples and the submission of the Pope bring forth a new flurry of celebratory texts.[12]

It is easy to imagine why news of these faraway events would have been eagerly awaited in the French capital. The publication of multiple editions of texts suggests that they did indeed find an extensive reading public. The pamphlets are cast in a style intended to emphasise their authenticity and urgent topicality, frequently in the form of a letter or dispatch from an eyewitness at the scene of the action. They are suffused by a tone of optimism that will be the prevailing spirit of news pamphlets for the next seventy years. They laud the ease with which French armies overwhelmed their enemies; they stress the warmth of their welcome; and they paint enthusiastically the many pleasures of the invested territories: the fine wines, the beautiful women, and their beguiling susceptibility to French charm.

These pamphlets are short, and almost invariably in quarto format (the same size as the German *Flugschriften*). They are by and large published by respectable Parisian printing houses. Consequently, although there is some evidence of haste in the production, the general quality of the workmanship is high: they show signs of typographical sophistication and are often illustrated, either with a single title-page woodcut, or with several text illustrations. But these are not woodcuts specially created for these pamphlets: they seem generally to have been re-employed from earlier, larger books. Sometimes the illustrations bear no relation at all to the subject matter of the pamphlet; sometimes the same woodcut is used again and again in a whole series of news prints. One large woodcut of the king surrounded by courtiers is found successively in an account of the beginning of the Italian campaign, a dispatch recording the fall of Naples, and two other pamphlets.[13]

The first war established a pattern where the Parisian public were eager to hear news, and the French crown was keen to feed this demand. Louis XII demonstrated a shrewd awareness of the power of the press, and the Italian campaigns of 1507 and 1509 saw a new peak of pamphlet production.[14] In the war of the League of Cambrai (1508–10) some of the leading literary figures of the capital were enrolled to heap praise on the king and abuse on his enemies, the Genoese, the Venetians and, more controversially, Pope Julius II.[15] Some of these works were in verse, and may have been intended for a largely courtly audience. Others found resonance with a wider public.

The pamphlet literature was always most dense when the tide of war was flowing in France's favour. The catastrophe of Pavia (1525) which left French Italian policy in tatters and the king a prisoner in Imperial hands, were met with deafening silence from the Parisian publishers. The initiative now switched to publishers in the Low Countries. Here the victory of the Imperial forces was reported and celebrated in a wave of triumphalist pamphleteering.

Especially noteworthy is the speed with which news of these events reached the Netherlands. The battle of Pavia took place on 24 February; the Antwerp publisher Willem Vorsterman had his account of the battle in print and on the streets within three weeks. Five years later the Emperor's ceremonial entry into Munich on 15–16 July 1530 was described in a pamphlet account published on 18 July.[16] Here Antwerp undoubtedly benefited from its place at the heart of a hub of information exchange developed to serve its cosmopolitan merchant community. Most of Antwerp's printers involved themselves in this news publishing. The surviving news pamphlets identified from this period can be attributed to around twenty different printers. It was a market from which none would have wished to be excluded.

The production of news pamphlets reached a crescendo in the years 1538–1544, when the conflict between Charles V and Francis I moved towards its climax and the ebb and flow of the war produced a huge volume of pamphlets. These great pamphlet salvoes were for the most part issued from the two leading centres of print, Paris and Antwerp. There was little sign of a significant market for news in major centres of provincial print culture in France, such as Lyon, Poitiers and Toulouse.

So at least I thought until, at the end of the end of an extended research trip in the magnificent Bibliothèque Méjanes in Aix, I made one of the most remarkable discoveries of my time working with early printed books. A volume in the library's reserve turned out to contain thirty-three individual works, most of them small pamphlets printed in Rouen between 1538 and 1544.[17] Closer examination revealed them to be news pamphlets: short, cheap, and rather crudely produced. This was evidence of a robust provincial market for news print.

Rouen in the 1540s was a bustling, mercantile city of around 70,000 inhabitants. But its local printing industry was small. Rouen was too much in the shadow of Paris; Lyon, strategically situated close to the major European markets of central Europe, was a crucial 200 kilometres more distant from the magnetic pull of the capital. Rouen printers produced nothing to compare with the magnificent scholarly volumes published in Lyon.

Any capable workman, however, could turn out pamphlets like these. In fact pamphlets in this collection are mostly the work of two printers, Jean L'Homme and Guillaume de La Motte. Neither man had a long career: they are scarcely known except for these small topical works. Yet together they kept the local population informed through all the twists and turns of this complex conflict. The pamphlets celebrated the early hopes of reconciliation, symbolised by the Emperor's progress through France on his return to his Netherlandish

Fig. 26 News of royal victories was shared with an anxious public: as in this crude pamphlet printed by Jean L'Homme in Rouen.

dominions. They reported the ominous alliance between Charles and Henry of England, leading to a final climactic invasion of French territory that saw Imperial forces at one point camped within miles of the capital.

These pamphlets clearly found an eager local readership. In a number of cases, where a second copy survives, it turns out to be a separate edition. When L'Homme published an account of the Emperor's ceremonial reception in Valenciennes at the end of his progress through France, it sold out within five days, and a second printing was necessary.[18] But the events shared with Rouen's reading public are extremely carefully chosen. L'Homme's pamphlets carry news only of French success: Rouen's merchants, anxious for their cargoes and consignments, would learn of defeats only by word of mouth. No French press, in Paris or the provinces, would provide a written account. In the news publication of the day, the imparting of information was inevitably constrained by the need to identify with the patriotic cause. It may indeed be that L'Homme's press was established by the Rouen authorities for precisely this purpose. A number of his books contain explicit reference to official encouragement, noting that a book was published 'by the command of the magistrates' or 'with the authority and consent of the magistrates'. Could it be that L'Homme's press was in effect the mouthpiece of the council, charged with maintaining morale in time of conflict?

This suggestion gains credence if we consider the numerous pamphlet celebrations that accompanied the final resolution of the long Franco-Imperial conflict, the Peace of Câteau Cambrésis in 1559. This was a bad peace for France, forced to abandon the aspiration to territory in Italy; on a permanent basis, as it turned out. It was a difficult outcome to present to the French political nation, and so the most distinguished court poets, including Pierre de Ronsard, were enlisted in the cause. In 1559 Ronsard was already emerging as one of the leading poets of the Pléiade, a poet of notable clarity and beauty of composition. He now embarked on a less heralded role as the principal literary apologist of royal policy.[19] But even in 1559 there was a sting in the tail, for the praise of peace was balanced by published peals of triumph for the victory of Calais, snatched from the English by the bold leadership of the emerging hero of militant Catholicism, the duc de Guise. It was an ominous reminder that if the French monarchy did not retain the confidence of the political nation, the printed resources used to rally support could easily be turned against it.

The Turk

Aside from the endless contests of Europe's warring dynasties, by far the greatest stimulus to the growth of a European news industry was the relentless encroachment of the Ottoman Empire. The invention of printing coincided almost exactly with one of the most cataclysmic events of the fifteenth century: the fall of Constantinople, capital of the Eastern Christian state of Byzantium (1453). One of the first works published by the Gutenberg press was a six-page pamphlet, 'A warning to Christendom against the Turk'. In the ingenious guise of a calendar for the year 1455, the verses arranged as twelve months of the year exhorted the Emperor, Europe's princes and the whole German nation to unite against the Turk.[20] The press also printed the indulgence proclaimed to raise funds for the relief of Cyprus against a threatened Turkish attack.[21]

Such exhortations became commonplace as the Ottoman forces continued their advance through the Balkans and the Mediterranean. Despite the epic victory outside Belgrade that propelled Matthias Corvinus to the throne of Hungary, the Turks swiftly absorbed the Serbian territories, the largest geographical buffer between the Ottoman Empire and the West. In the following decades the Turkish advance enveloped the rest of the Greek peninsula (1458–61), followed by Herzegovina and Albania. Meanwhile Venice was progressively driven back in the struggle for the Aegean Islands and the Dalmatian coast. Two epic sieges in 1480 and 1521 finally resulted in the Turkish capture of Rhodes. In 1520 the Turkish host seized Belgrade, reversing the defeat of sixty years before; six years later the catastrophe of Mohács resulted in the loss of much of Hungary, as well as the death of King Louis Jagiello and much of his nobility. This relentless sequence of campaigns, reverses and the occasional victory continued through the century with its well-known landmarks: the siege of Vienna (1529), the war in Hungary, the assault on Tunis (1535), the disaster of Djerba (1560) and the miracle of Malta (1565).

These events were accompanied by an increasingly diverse printed literature. In the first age of print, current affairs publications had a formal, official character. They consisted largely of papal bulls, orations and indulgences granted to those providing financial support. Indulgences in support of the Turkish war effort make up the single largest group of printed indulgences published during the fifteenth century. A pamphlet published in support of the campaign by Bernardus Justinianus was printed in at least ten editions in the years following its first publication in 1471. The treatise was published in four separate towns on the Italian peninsula, and in a wide variety of formats: folio, quarto and octavo. More striking still is the geographical range achieved by the indulgence proclaimed for the defence of Rhodes in 1480. This was reprinted all over Europe: in Italy at Florence, Venice, Ferrara, Mantua and Bologna; in Germany at Augsburg, Speyer, Basel and Reutlingen; at Zaragoza in Spain; in the Low Countries at Louvain and Oudenaarde; at Westminster and London in England.[22]

The sixteenth century witnessed the emergence of a more diverse literature, mixing breathless news of shocking events with more sober analysis and exhortation. The volume of pamphlets published followed closely the rhythms of the conflict. The second siege of Rhodes produced a flurry of publications in 1522 and 1523.[23] A desperate plea for help to the crowned heads of Europe placed in the mouth of the Grand Master of Rhodes went through no fewer than ten Italian editions, making it the most popular of these topical verse *lamenti* published during the century. On this occasion Rhodes was not to be saved. The echoes of this defeat were still reverberating through the press in 1525 when Jacques de Bourbon, a survivor of the siege, published his French eyewitness account. This went through at least five editions.[24] The following year, 1526, Christian Europe faced a new catastrophe, when the armies of King

Louis Jagiello of Hungary were annihilated at Mohács. News of the disaster reached the European public first through the German news market in a series of pamphlets relating the bare narrative of events. These pamphlets were subsequently reissued in Italian, French and Dutch.[25]

The tumultuous events in Hungary were also commemorated in a rash of newly written songs.[26] News ballads represent an important if often frustratingly elusive part of the news market: they seem to have been particularly important when the reading public was trying to absorb or understand bad news, such as the death of Louis or the fall of Rhodes. This may also have been because it was safer in these circumstances for a publisher to print a ballad than a bald prose account of military disaster.

The occasional success for Christian armies was naturally widely celebrated. The triumph of the Emperor Charles V over Barbarossa's corsairs at Tunis in 1535 was greeted with a surge of publications. But the profit derived from this victory was largely undone by the destruction of the Imperial fleet at Algiers in 1541, and an attempt by the new Spanish king Philip II to retrieve the situation led only to the débâcle of Djerba in 1560. These signal reverses made much less impact on the public prints than the earlier victory, especially in areas under Imperial influence. Charles V tried to minimise the impact of Algiers: among the casualties, he commented, 'there was not one man of substance'.[27] But the loss of the fleet, repeated at Djerba, left the western Mediterranean badly exposed, and there was little cause for optimism when, in April 1565, the main Ottoman host descended on the small island of Malta.

Malta was a strategic prize that could not be conceded, but relieving the beleaguered garrison of the Knights of St John seemed as if it would be beyond the divided Christian nations. In the event the Knights held out against all odds for the time necessary for a relieving force to be assembled at Naples. The brutal, bloody and on both sides heroic siege became one of the epic confrontations of the century. It was also one of its great news events. From the first landfall of the Ottoman fleet, through the assaults, repulses and reduction of the outlying fortifications to the final miraculous rescue, events in Malta were closely followed in all of Europe's major news markets.[28] For the first time, the interested public was assisted by a remarkable series of typographical maps illustrating the disposition of the island's defences and the attacking forces. A close study of a sequence of surviving copies demonstrates that these maps were copied and reprinted around Europe, the original Italian texts being substituted, where appropriate, with a new text and key in German, French and Dutch.[29] The copperplate or woodcut was also adjusted or re-engraved to show the progress of the siege. The advances made in technical cartography were among the most noticeable features of the sixteenth century, and of course of print culture, but it was only with the siege of Malta that their potential for news prints was fully recognised. Thereafter such maps became a frequent aspect of news publications relating the battles, campaigns and conflicts of the second half of the century.

The eventual lifting of the siege was also the subject of more conventional celebration in verse and prose, as the Knights of Malta, and their heroic captain Jean de la Valette, were fêted as heroes. Medals were struck to commemorate the events, and examples buried in the foundations of the new city of Valletta, established in the wake of the Christian victory.

Malta proved to be a respite rather than a decisive turning-point. In the years after the city's relief the Turkish host quickly recouped its losses and turned its attention to other targets in the eastern Mediterranean. Repeated attacks on Venetian outposts on the Adriatic coast at last persuaded the city to respond to the urgings of the new Pope, Pius V, for a Holy League. But the fleet laboriously assembled for the relief of Cyprus in 1570 turned back ignominiously before reaching Rhodes, losing much of its strength in a series of storms. For Bragadin, the Christian governor of Famagusta, there was to be no repeat of the miracle of Malta. The capitulation of the last Christian outpost on Cyprus was followed by the brutal execution of Bragadin and his officers, who had surrendered to spare the local population, with the assurance that their own lives would also be spared. Bragadin's ritual torture in the city square was recorded by an eyewitness, Nestor Martinengo, whose graphic account of Turkish perfidy and cruelty rapidly went through several printed editions.[30]

Lepanto

The disaster of Cyprus and persistence of Pius V finally induced Venice and Spain to overcome their cynicism and mutual suspicion and agree to the establishment of a joint fleet to confront the enemy. On 7 October 1571 the two great fleets met in the Gulf of Lepanto: here 208 Christian warships were ranged against 230 of the Turkish side. The result was a crushing victory for the Holy League. The Turks lost 30,000 men and all but thirty of their galleys. The Christian fleet lost a mere ten ships.

First news of this stunning victory arrived in Venice twelve days later, on 19 October.[31] It was brought by a returning galley, the *Angelo Gabriele*, its jubilant crew dressed ironically in Turkish garb. The discharge of celebratory cannon confirmed that the ship brought good news. Those who witnessed its docking carried the news through the city, with shouts of 'Victory, victory!' The streets soon filled with cheering crowds; bells were rung, and a great host gathered at

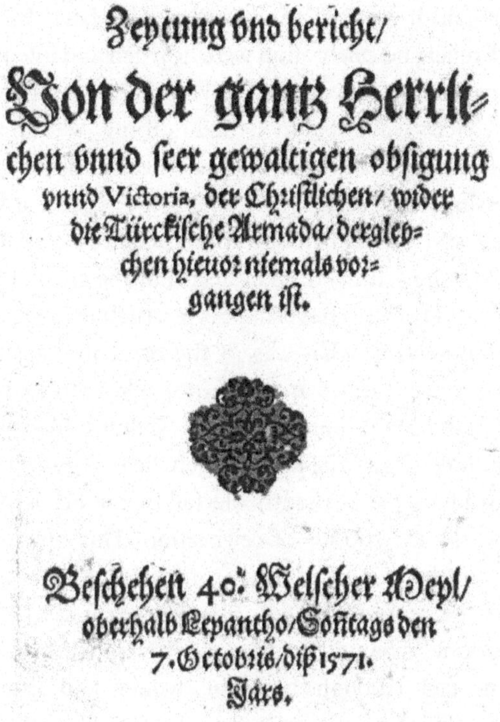

Zeytung vnd bericht/

Von der gantz Herrli=

chen vnnd seer gewaltigen obsigung
vnnd Victoria, der Christlichen/ wider
die Türckische Armada/ dergley=
chen hieuor niemals vor=
gangen ist.

Beschehen 40: Welscher Meyl/
oberhalb Lepantho/Sontags den
7.Octobris/diß 1571.
Jars.

Fig. 27 News of the victory at Lepanto flashed around the news markets of Europe. Here a German *Zeitung* shares the glad tidings: note how the critical word 'Victory' is emphasised by the use of Roman type.

the Piazza San Marco to see the Venetian commander's official account of the action presented to the Doge. Public celebration, bell ringing and fireworks continued for three days. On the first Sunday after news of the victory a celebratory Mass in the basilica was followed by a formal procession. Over the following days and weeks different parts of the community provided their own celebrations. These festivities continued into the New Year, when an elaborately costumed procession (the *mascherata*) was staged on Carnival Sunday.

All of these events were recorded in a host of celebratory pamphlets, turned off the press and instantly reprinted first in Venice, already one of Europe's principal centres of news publication, then throughout the Italian peninsula and all over Europe. The two years 1571 and 1572 witnessed a quite phenomenal output: a total of at least 300 editions.[32] As in Venice, first news of the Christian victory arrived by word of mouth, as couriers from Venice, and reports dispatched by foreign ambassadors stationed there, fanned out across the continent. The news had reached Lyon by 25 October, six days after the *Angelo*

Gabriele made landfall. It reached Brussels five days later. Everywhere, from London to Madrid, relief and celebration were heartfelt and intense. Bell ringing, prayers, processions and services of thanksgiving were the order of the day.

In the event, the victory at Lepanto settled nothing. Within a year a frantic programme of rebuilding had restored the Turkish fleet. In 1573 Venice vindicated the pessimistic cynicism of Philip II by signing a separate peace. The conflict flared and ebbed in the various theatres until the end of the century. In the 1590s the campaign in eastern Europe created a further lively burst of pamphlet activity.[33] It is nevertheless instructive to have considered in some detail how the news of what was, at the time, thought to have been a decisive turning-point was carried around Europe. We can see that the printed word, though it played an important role in shaping interpretation of the Christian triumph, was seldom the primary vehicle for conveying first news of events. People heard by word of mouth, alerted by the noise in the streets, by the ringing of bells, by the sounds of celebration. This must have been true of other of the century's most dramatic happenings – the Massacre of St Bartholomew, the defeat of the Spanish Armada. If people then subsequently bought news pamphlets they did this for a number of reasons: to sort rumour from fact (though here the wilder and more opportunist pamphlets might not help), to add extra detail, or simply to share again in the communal sense of joy unleashed by the first news.

Many of those who bought pamphlet accounts of the Venetian commemoration of Lepanto must themselves have been participants. Throughout the century it was far easier to sell pamphlets that spoke of joyful victories than those that described defeat. A careful study of the printed news *avvisi* published in Rome in the sixteenth century documents large groups devoted to Charles V's conquest of Tunis in 1535, the Peace of Câteau Cambrésis, and the battle of Lepanto. There are none recording the débâcle of Algiers, the concessions accorded the Lutherans in the Peace of Augsburg, or the defeat of the Spanish Armada (an expedition in which the Pope had invested very heavily).[34] Overall a study of the news pamphlets of the sixteenth century confirms that Europe had an active news community, hungry for information of great events. But the *Zeitungen* and *avvisi* turned out in such profusion by Europe's publishers certainly did not provide the dispassionate reporting that would have allowed readers to arrive at a judicious assessment of likely consequences. This applied even to the digests of news from different parts of Europe that began, in the latter part of the century, to offer a glimpse of the serial publication that would lead in due course to the birth of the newspaper. In the sixteenth century this still lay some way in the future.

Prodigies

Not all news pamphlets dealt with battles, sieges and the doings of the great. Europe's pamphlet readers also had an appetite for news of natural phenomena and other astounding prodigies of nature. An early exponent of literature of this sort was the German humanist Sebastian Brant. When in 1492 a substantial meteorite fell to earth near Ensisheim in Alsace, Brant supplied the definitive description of the event, and drew the appropriate morals.[35] This is an especially interesting text, because although the broadsheet publication may initially suggest an ephemeral quality, the text is clearly aimed at an educated readership.[36] Beneath a woodcut illustration of the meteorite descending to the astonishment of a watching ploughman is Brant's extended verse description, in two parallel versions, Latin and German. As a good servant of the Imperial cause Brant had no doubt that the evil portents were aimed at the French and Burgundians. A separate 22-line poem addressed Maximilian directly, urging him to seize the moment and put his enemies to confusion.

Brant developed something of a reputation as a specialist in this genre. Some twenty-three broadsheets can be attributed to his pen, describing a variety of floods, hailstorms and astrological events, including an early observation of a solar eclipse.[37] Such natural phenomena, especially those that involved significant loss of life, became staples of the developing news market. Most surviving sixteenth-century examples are pamphlets, rather than broadsheets, and the importance of illustrative material receded. Whereas the meteorite of Ensisheim relies for its impact on a well-drawn woodcut specially executed for the occasion, most pamphlets of this type have no more than a crude, generic title-page woodcut, often repeated and reused from pamphlet to pamphlet. The text was seldom provided by a writer of Brant's gifts; nevertheless, within the constraints of the medium they strove for accuracy and verisimilitude. Many pamphlet accounts of earthquakes recorded in the period offer highly specific accounts of local consequences and the violence of the eruption. For specialists these pamphlets are important sources on the seismicity of earlier times.[38]

A specific and interesting sub-genre of this literature is provided by the many published accounts of the birth of misshapen animals or children.[39] Such occurrences were always interpreted allegorically, as divine punishments or as portents of impending disaster. These publications were routinely accompanied by vivid woodcut illustrations, often the responsibility of one of Europe's leading artists. The interpretative freight placed on these events should not blind us to the fact that most described actually reported or observed events.

Fig. 28 This early representation of a set of conjoined twins depicts thoracopagus twins, that is, twins joined at the chest. Jacob Locher, *Carmen heroicum de partu monstrifero* (Ingolstadt, 1499).

Clinical examination of the pamphlets reveals that most of the illustrations correspond to known birth defects. Representations of conjoined twins, for instance, correspond reasonably well to modern clinical experience.[40] However macabre or unsympathetic the early modern fascination with the misshapen, these cases were not fantastical.

Accounts of prodigies and sensations – accidents, extreme weather, celestial signs, murders and unnatural births – flourished during the sixteenth century. Along with other types of news pamphlets describing battles, sieges, treaties and joyous entries, they made up a very considerable market. The pamphlets were affordable for those with a limited disposable income, but clearly they were also bought by those who bought more expensive books. As the market developed during the course of the century it seems to have been refined in three specific ways. Firstly, in the period from 1560 onwards, news pamphlets more frequently record local events rather than sensational occurrences in faraway lands. This applies most obviously to the pamphlet literature relating sieges and battles, but also to hazards and disasters, such as the Grossmünster fire at Zurich in 1571, or the Lucerne earthquake of 1601. The exhortatory power of such events, and indeed of murders and executions, seems to have been more powerful if the events happened in or close to the reading community.

The second half of the century also witnessed the emergence of a class of publisher who specialised extensively in literature of this sort. In the first half of the century, as we have observed in all the major centres of pamphlet production, news pamphlet publication was widely dispersed. Many of the leading printers in a major centre such as Antwerp or Augsburg played a role in the market, sometimes because publishers of this sort had privileged access to the original accounts. In the second half of the century news and sensations were the stock in trade for a growing category of pamphlet specialists. The Lyon publisher Benoist Rigaud published more than a thousand editions, almost exclusively pamphlets in small format, and most no more than eight or sixteen pages long.[41] Lyon was well placed as a conduit between the major centres of newsgathering in Italy and Germany (Venice, Rome, Augsburg and Nuremberg) and northern Europe. Rigaud exploited this enviable situation to turn out large numbers of news pamphlets, many of them descriptions of the battles and treaties of the French Wars of Religion, but also news from the Mediterranean, the conflict with the Turk on the eastern front, floods and catastrophes. Although they were short, the production quality of the pamphlets was very high, characterised by a clean, economic arrangement of type and easy legibility. These are books which, arranged and bound into thematic or chronological collections, would not have disgraced the library of a wealthy bourgeois or aristocratic collector: which is precisely why so many of them have survived.

The habit of bundling pamphlets together as *ad hoc* collections, which we first observed with Reformation *Flugschriften*, provides an intermediary step towards the publication of whole books of prodigious events, collected and described from previously known examples. This was a tradition that flourished especially in France and Germany. In France the best-known example is the *Histoires prodigieuses* of Pierre Boaistuau, first published in 1560 and a steady bestseller. More than forty issues of the French text included, most unusually, bilingual editions published in Cologne and Würzburg.[42] Boaistuau's book was also published in English, German and Dutch translation. The German print world read Boaistuau, but it had its own indigenous tradition of prodigy collections too. Although no single text established the market domination of Boaistuau, some thirty-two book collections of this type are known. Some, in Latin rather than German, and in folio, were clearly intended for a scholarly public (presumably of medical professionals). Most collections were published in German and in small format for a more mixed audience.[43]

With these publications the market for news had begun to blend with a broader market in recreational literature that encompassed poetry and prose fiction, as well as history. The moral context provided for prodigy tales was echoed in the world of fiction, but this should not disguise the fact that these were books bought as much for entertainment as edification. With these larger volumes, as with news pamphlets and broadsheets, we see the emergence of a reading public increasingly prepared to invest in books beyond the functional tools of their trade or devotional lives. It was a shift that opened up important new avenues for the book trade.

CHAPTER 8

POLITE RECREATIONS

Martin Crusius was a shining example of what could be achieved in the new Protestant intellectual elite of sixteenth-century Europe. The son of an evangelical minister, Crusius studied in Ulm and Strasbourg before in 1559 he was appointed Professor of Greek and Latin Literature at the University of Tübingen. In 1564 he took additional responsibility for the teaching of rhetoric, but it was as a scholar of Greek that he earned the greatest renown. Reputedly his lectures were so well attended that it was necessary to build a new lecture theatre to accommodate them. Crusius published a number of literary and academic works, and corresponded widely with fellow scholars and leading figures in the Church, most notably the orthodox patriarch of Constantinople. When Crusius died in 1607, his books were bequeathed to the University of Tübingen. The syndics were delighted to receive such a valuable bequest, but among the scholarly and academic works were some surprises.

For Crusius was an avid reader of romances. Over a number of years he had meticulously collected an extensive series of the adventures of *Amadis de Gaule*, a traditional tale of Spanish origin that enjoyed a huge vogue in the sixteenth century. Crusius read *Amadis* in French. He bought the various volumes of the chronicles as they became available in the late 1550s in a special compact edition, published in Paris for the export market. He read these books carefully and probably more than once. The endpapers of his richly bound copies are filled with manuscript notes in which he meticulously records the characters and episodes of each volume.[1]

Amadis de Gaule is now a little-known text, but it was one of the most popular literary works published in the sixteenth century. It was translated into almost every major vernacular language. From a Spanish original it made its way into Italian and French, and thence into German, Dutch and English.[2] It was the most successful of a large number of medieval chivalric fables that enjoyed an enormous vogue in the sixteenth century and entertained a vast and diverse public: of gentlemen and merchants, of bourgeois wives and aristocratic ladies; even, as we have seen, the occasional university professor. These books formed part of the growing market in recreational literature. As books became more commonplace and affordable, print gradually extended its reach beyond the technical, practical, scholarly and theological texts that had dominated output in the fifteenth century, when a book was still a very serious and carefully considered investment, and could only usually be undertaken for purely functional reasons. As the sixteenth century wore on, more readers of books could contemplate laying out funds on books that had no immediate practical or professional purpose. A new market in recreational literature was gradually able to develop.

Chivalric values

In the year 778 the Emperor Charlemagne led his Frankish host across the Pyrenees and into the Iberian peninsula. While besieging Zaragoza word reached him of a Saxon uprising in the north. Charlemagne lifted the siege, and made his way back to France. His rearguard, led by his nephew Roland, was ambushed and destroyed at the pass of Roncesvalles; Roland perished, along with many of Charlemagne's followers. From these events flowed one of the greatest narratives of the chivalric tradition. The sacrifice of Roland, the loyal service of the four sons of Aymon, the treachery of the jealous Ganelon, the hesitations and vengeance of the king: all these became staples of the troubadour ballads. As the centuries wore on these tales became fused and intertwined with a second major narrative strand, the Arthurian legend emanating first from the Celtic lands of the British Isles, but soon endemic in Europe. The experience of prolonged conflict with the Saracens during the Crusades added a third significant strand to the mix. By the time the great *Chanson de Roland* was written at the end of the eleventh century the victors of Roncesvalles were not the Basque irregulars who engaged Charlemagne's rearguard but the Saracen host.

Together these interwoven strands of history and fable provided materials for the two great storytelling traditions of the three centuries before print: the epic poem (*chanson de geste*) and the chivalric romance. The epic poem was particularly appropriate to an era when storytelling took place in communal settings. The poetic form not only allowed for dramatic performance (often sung) but also made it easier to memorise large parts of works that sometimes stretched to hundreds of stanzas. Over a hundred separate narrative epics survive from this period; they were still being composed up to the end of the fourteenth century. This and a more haltingly emerging prose tradition created a natural repertoire for the ambitious authors of the new age of print, many of whom were attached in one way or another to aristocratic households. Keen to show off their stylistic virtuosity they reached naturally for the characters and narratives that had thrilled their forebears. These tales also offered an excellent opportunity for the display of the virtues and vices that animated these quasi-aristocratic societies: virtue, honour, courage and fidelity, and their antitheses, treachery, dissembling and cowardice.

The tenacious appeal of these literary traditions can be observed in the careers of three of the most inventive authors of the first age of print: Matteo Maria Boiardo, Ludovico Ariosto and Torquato Tasso. All worked in Italian cities or aristocratic households; all took their inspiration from the epic poetic tradition. Matteo Maria Boiardo was a leading representative of that generation of authors and poets who combined literary endeavour with a career of public service. Boiardo, who was of noble lineage, prospered as a servant of the Este Dukes of Ferrara. In 1478 he was appointed governor of Reggio, an office he held until his death, with only a brief interval when he served the Duke as governor of Modena. In a long life Boiardo devoted much of his leisure time to composition. His master-work is undoubtedly the *Orlando innamorato*, a long (and sadly unfinished) epic tale of chivalry and romance. Taking his cue from the *Morgante maggiore* of Luigi Pulci (1482), a poet in the Florentine circle of Lorenzo de' Medici, Boiardo wove around the familiar tale of Roland/Orlando a complex and inventive epic. Its centrepiece is a magnificent tournament in Paris, attended by thousands of Christian and Saracen champions. When these are lured away by the erotic charms of Angelica, Princess of Cathay, the action follows the princess and her suitors to the Orient, before Saracen and Christian meet in a climactic struggle at Bordeaux. On Boiardo's death in 1494 only two of the three planned parts had been completed. The poem was nevertheless printed, to great acclaim, thanks in part to the financial investment in a Venetian edition by Boiardo's widow.[3]

Boiardo had many imitators, including one, the Venetian Niccolò degli Agostini, who ventured a continuation of the unfinished masterpiece. But Boiardo's true heir was Ludovico Ariosto, author of one of the most successful narrative works of the sixteenth century, the *Orlando furioso*. Ariosto was another who was obliged to combine his literary interests with public service, again in the household of the Este: first Cardinal Ippolito d'Este, whom he represented intermittently at the Papal Court, and later the Duk'e, Alfonso.

For three years he toiled as governor of the wild Apennine province of Garfagnana, before returning, with evident relief, to the more predictable pleasure of the Este court. Inspired by Boiardo's epic, Ariosto was hard at work on his interpretation of the tale of Roland from at least 1506. The first version of *Orlando furioso* was published in 1516, dedicated to Cardinal Ippolito. A second appeared in 1521, shortly after the break with the Cardinal, and the third, definitive edition a few months before Ariosto's death in 1533.[4] This magnificent, swirling epic, comprising forty-six cantos each of many hundreds of lines, is in its essence faithful to Boiardo's model. The essential parts of Boiardo's narrative all reappear: there is scarcely a new character introduced. Where Ariosto excelled his predecessor was in the quality of the poetry and the psychological depth with which he invests his characters.

Ariosto's apparently effortless virtuosity has all the easy confidence of its age. The epic feats of chivalry, the age-old conflict between Christianity and Islam, well matched and chivalrous opponents, are celebrated in tales infused with the knowing sophistication of the age of humanism. Torquato Tasso's *Jerusalem Delivered* (*Gerusalemme liberata*) is the product of a darker age, and a darker, more troubled mind. Tasso compiled his epic of the First Crusade at a time of great political and personal turmoil. He was the son of a poet whose own career had been shaped, and almost ruined, by attachment to the fortunes of an Italian prince, Ferrante of Salerno, whose inopportune defection from Spanish to French service had brought the loss of his family lands. The fortunes of the family improved only when the father, Bernardo, transferred to the service of Urbino. The young Torquato was subsequently placed in the service of the Este of Ferrara.

Settled employment finally provided Tasso with the opportunity to work on his epic celebration of medieval crusading. The work was complete in manuscript by 1574, but not published until 1581. The intervening years witnessed the collapse of both Tasso's public career and his health. The author had foolishly presented this manuscript for comment to numerous friends, whose conflicting recommendations for change could not be accommodated. The final published text, dense and complex, is not improved by the revisions of an increasingly troubled author, who, after quarrelling with his patrons, was eventually incarcerated for his own protection in the asylum at Ferrara on the instructions of Duke Alfonso. The changed climate of the times at the end of the sixteenth century also had an impact. Two generations of confessional conflict in Europe had taken its toll on the optimistic literary culture of the early years of the century. In post-Tridentine Italy, and after Malta, Cyprus and Lepanto, the traditional tale of the great clash of civilisations between

Christianity and Islam had a darker hue. *Jerusalem Delivered* is the least accessible of the great works in the romantic epic tradition emanating from Italy in this period.[5] Its success despite this is a tribute to the enduring appeal of the form as well as a witness to its protean malleability.

Reading and imagination

The works of Boiardo, Ariosto and Tasso offer a vivid demonstration of how the poetic epic evolved during the course of the first age of print. But it is also pertinent to point out some common features. All of these works are very long: they are vast and sprawling texts, highly episodic in character. This gives a clue to the way they were read. These were not books intended primarily for private consecutive reading: they were texts to which one would return, to enjoy a segment or sequence of stanzas, often within a communal setting.

Sixteenth-century Europe had not yet developed a strong sense of private space for reading, either in the sense of an allocated portion of the day, or a private place in the home to which one could retreat with books. Only princely households could contemplate separate space for a library, and libraries tended to be noisy, convivial places, designed as much for conversation and display as for concentrated attention to texts. A study was a place of business for men of affairs, a place to store ledgers and business correspondence. Montaigne's description of his study (in his case a tower) as a place of private philosophical contemplation was influential precisely because it represented an idealised vision, and an agenda. In reality few would have combined Montaigne's bookish inclinations and freedom from financial concerns.

For the most part the recreational reading of the sixteenth century, and especially these epic poetical works, fitted into an older tradition where precious leisure hours were spent in the company of others. A book could be read from, admired and served up as a conversation point, as an alternative or counterpoint to music or storytelling. Thus half-familiar tales, recast and refreshed with the artistry of the new age, met the expectations of readers and listeners who valued stylistic virtuosity above tightly organised narrative plotting. They admired particularly the evocation, and sometimes artful subversion, of conventional morality, and the discussion within fictional settings of the timeless preoccupations of those lucky enough to enjoy some measure of leisure for contemplation: love, marriage, loyalty, loss, trust and courage.

A striking feature of these sixteenth-century works of imaginative writing is their expansive geographical canvas. Ariosto's *Orlando furioso* led its protagonists (and readers) on a journey to all parts of Europe and beyond. Those who followed the hectic exploits of Ruggiero and his companions would travel from Paris to Jerusalem. They would sail north to Scotland and view the assembled hosts of the English nobility arrayed by the Thames. The frozen wastes of Iceland are contrasted with the sweltering heat of the famed Ethiopian kingdom of Prester John; the gift of a hippogriff, a winged steed with a griffon's head, even permits Ruggiero a lightning tour that sweeps him from India to Pomerania.[6]

This expansive, and at times vividly realized, imaginative geography is all the more appealing in an age when few even of the educated and courtly circles that made up Ariosto's readership travelled widely. This was an age when the outside world was often experienced vicariously, through the reports of those who did brave Europe's hazardous roads and waterways: adventures that often grew in the telling. Journeys were planned with great care, and attended with great uncertainty. The fragile comprehension of a world experienced through fragmentary and often contradictory accounts necessarily blurred the distinction between fact and fable, between news, history and epic fiction. In consequence Europeans had both a complex and a richly imagined view of the world even before the first reports of the New World discoveries added new strands of storytelling and fable.

The books themselves were of course seasoned, hardy travellers. Boiardo's *Orlando innamorato* enjoyed a considerable posthumous reputation in France after its translation into French in 1549.[7] Ariosto, too, was a favourite with French readers. *Orlando furioso* went through fifteen editions after its translation into French in 1545, and there was also a Spanish translation to introduce the text to readers in the Iberian Peninsula.[8] None of these authors could match the international appeal of Boccaccio, whose works spun around Europe in a blaze of translations.[9] Boccaccio is almost exclusively known to modern readers as the author of the *Decameron*, but sixteenth-century readers also appreciated the Latin works of his later years, especially *De mulieribus claris* (Of Famous Women). This collection of exemplary lives, consciously modelled on Petrarch's *Lives of Famous Men*, inspired many imitators, among them Jacopo Filippo Foresti, Alonso of Cartagena and Thomas Elyot's *Defence of Good Women*.

The episodic quality of a sequence of tales made it particularly suited for communal reading or discussion. This was a large part of the appeal of the *Decameron*, a collection of 100 moral, uplifting and humorous stories told, in Boccaccio's imaginative setting, by a group of young Florentine aristocrats sheltering from the plague. In the age of print Boccaccio's tales enjoyed enormous success after their first publication in Mantua in 1472. French, German and Spanish translations followed before the end of the fifteenth

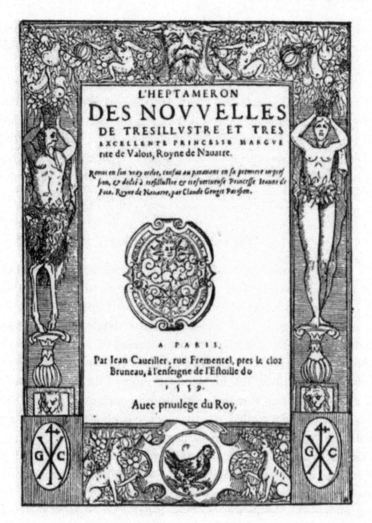

Fig. 29 The *Heptameron* of Marguerite de Navarre. One of the most popular of the episodic narratives cycles inspired by Boccaccio's *Decameron*, this was also one of the most successful works published by a female author in the whole century.

century; there would be editions in Czech, Low German, English and Portuguese before 1541. The fame of the *Decameron* spawned a considerable literature in this novella form, most notably the *Heptameron* of Marguerite de Navarre, and Bandello's *Novelle*. The *Heptameron* kept close to Boccaccio's original by preserving the conceit of a group of well-born travellers forced to take refuge together: in this case the travellers are a mixed group, five men and five women, and they take refuge from bandits and bears in a Pyrenean abbey. Here they exchange tales of celibacy, marriage, trust and infidelity. Perhaps the most remarkable variation of the genre was that provided by Geoffrey Chaucer in his *Canterbury Tales*. The setting of the pilgrimage provided the opportunity to place the tales in the mouths of a far more socially disparate group, and the stories too have an earthy rumbustiousness. In the age of print this has a somewhat paradoxical effect. For whereas in continental Europe a socially diverse reading public was diverted by the aristocratic storytellers of the *Decameron* and *Heptameron*, Caxton's edition of the *Canterbury Tales* was destined for the upper echelons of English society. Chaucer had produced the most bourgeois setting for a collection enjoyed by Europe's least bourgeois book culture.

The rise of the vernacular

For all their differences, the newly composed literary masterpieces of the first age of print shared one striking characteristic. Almost without exception, they were composed in vernacular languages: Italian, Spanish, French or, in Chaucer's case, English. This was a significant development. Scholars had welcomed print because it allowed them access to the great writers of the Roman and Greek worlds. Throughout Europe Latin remained the language of schools and universities. Yet the literary authors of the period, all educated men, also created a new vernacular literature, in poetry and prose.

This was a literature that simultaneously celebrated and enlarged the capacities of the common tongue. Authors recognised that in writing in their own languages they were doing something different, and quite radical. This in itself sparked a considerable literature, as authors and scholars debated the comparative merits of Latin and vernacular. In Italy the most influential contribution to this debate was the *Prose della volgar lingua* of Pietro Bembo (1525). This is a highly technical work, discussing in some detail matters of verse composition, rhythm, stress and cadence. Bembo was influential in a number of respects. His book greatly enhanced the popularity of his two models of correct style, Petrarch and Boccaccio, and helped accelerate the great flood of sixteenth-century editions of both writers. Bembo's choice of models also contributed to the comparative eclipse of Dante. The theoretical discussion of rhyme and metre proved highly influential in the development of the Italian madrigal, a cornerstone of Italian musical poetry in the sixteenth century.

Bembo's influential book is sometimes given credit for the establishment of Tuscan as the dominant medium in Italian literary publication. This is to overstate the case. In reality this had already occurred when the printers of

Fig. 30 Pietro Bembo by Titian. His treatise on the Italian language was a milestone in establishing the vernacular as a reputable alternative to Latin.

Venice decided to adopt the dialect of Tuscany as a common language of literature. Bembo canonised a change that had already taken place.[10] The practice of the printing press had played the vital role. Likewise in Germany, the vast success of Luther's Bible was crucial in giving general currency to a common form of written High German. Here Luther's conscious decision to avoid the dialect usage of Saxony, and his skill in executing this plan over a sustained programme of publishing, was instrumental in the development of a common literary language.[11]

The most developed and prolonged debate regarding the literary merits of the vernacular occurred in the third major centre of the European print world, France. Here printing and government policy combined to establish a common French tongue throughout this large realm of fifteen million inhabitants. Francis I's instruction, in the Edict of Villers-Cotterêts (1539), that henceforth French should be the exclusive language of official legal documents and statutes was an important landmark. Banishing both Latin and provincial dialects from legal proceedings, the edict established the French of the Île de France as the exclusive language of written documents even in provinces where the distinctive French of the south, the *langue d'oc*, was spoken, or quite separate languages such as Breton or Basque. The dominance of Paris and Lyon in the French print world ensured that the victory of French was even more complete than the supremacy of Tuscan in Italy. Printing in dialect was restricted to a mere handful of publications in Breton and Provençal, by and large vanity projects of local noblemen with antiquarian interests. Publishing in Basque was restricted to church orders in the independent Protestant kingdom of Béarn.[12]

French authors took their cue from their royal patron, and gradually shifted their composition from Latin. Jean Le Maire de Belges and Geoffroy Tory both wrote strongly in favour of the vernacular. The influential political philosopher Claude de Seyssel made the comparison between linguistic and political hegemony explicit.[13] Thomas Sebillet's *Art póetique françois* demonstrated how classical and Italian models could be absorbed into a refined French vernacular, anticipating the arguments (if not the influence) of du Bellay's *Défense et illustration de la langue française*. Du Bellay's work was an inspiration to a rising generation of poets who, with Pierre de Ronsard as their guiding star, explored the full poetic range of the new classicised French.

Du Bellay and his disciples would have been less willing to acknowledge the part played in the development of the language by another talented young French scholar, the Protestant reformer and church leader John Calvin. Calvin was remarkably innovative in his use of language, perfecting a terse economy of style and clarity of exposition that contrasted markedly with the rambling, repetitive tradition of much religious polemic.[14] Confined for the moment to a minority cause, the impact of Calvin's stylistic originality was easy to overlook. It would be felt far more profoundly in the second half of the century. For the moment authors celebrated the new confidence in the vernacular by making available an ever greater quantity of the inherited canon in translation: from Latin, Greek and other European languages. Texts moved swiftly around the European book world, finding new readers in every part of the continent. The publications of these years, especially of the two decades between 1540 and 1560, created a new type of literary man: the translator.[15]

Authors and patrons

Despite this, a career as a professional writer remained an elusive goal for aspiring men of letters for much of the sixteenth century. Many of those honoured by posterity as the most original and creative literary talents of the period lived difficult and turbulent lives, dependent on patronage and the fickle favour of great men. Hopes that literary fame would make it possible for them to sever such ties and establish social and financial independence proved largely illusory. Of the three Italian authors examined earlier only Ariosto reaped significant financial benefit from his masterpiece, and he too ended his life reflecting bitterly on the perfidy of princes and publishers.

The complexities of the author's situation derived partly from the fact that the production of a text required him to manage two separate sets of relationship, with patrons and publishers. These demanded quite different and sometimes contradictory skills. The great literary works of the fifteenth century emanated from the court. It was not only in their subject material that these authors were deeply influenced by the inherited canon. They were also immersed in the traditions of a world where literature was produced for a small circle of readers with shared interests and social values. A text would enjoy a limited circulation as a manuscript. In the fifteenth century few authors could aspire to a print edition of several hundred copies. Such parameters encouraged a certain rhetorical disdain for print and, of course, for the inky artisans who were routinely accused of having mangled their fine verse. 'Ignorant printers of various sorts,' fumed the poet Cassio da Narni in a verse inserted at the end of a popular romance, *La morte del Danese*, in 1521, 'have several times made one so angry with their errors that I have longed for death.' There is no evil more hard to bear, he concluded, 'than to see one's verses torn to pieces by printers steeped in ignorance.'[16]

Such attitudes left poets ill-equipped for a commercial world where, in truth, publishers held most of the cards. The publication of an extended verse epic such as Boiardo's *Orlando innamorato* required as substantial an investment as any major scholarly work, and the return was if anything more uncertain. A work in the vernacular language had less potential than the large books in Latin that were major publishers' stock in trade. The publication of an original literary composition therefore usually required a considerable subvention before a printer would take it on. Either the author (or his heirs) must provide the money, or enter into the equivalent of a joint stock partnership to raise the cash and share the risk. Even when the book was published few authors could expect a cash reward. At most they could hope for a number of copies that they could dispose of, either for money, or as gifts to impress potential patrons.

From the first decades of print, publishers were accustomed to making use of scholars and literary men to perform the mundane but vital editorial tasks of the print shop, as translators, copy-editors, or to write a dedication or verses for the preliminary pages. Such a relationship scarcely encouraged them to treat writers' literary sensibilities with especial care. At the beginning of the sixteenth century a Paris court heard a complaint from the author Jean Bouchet against the bookseller and publisher Antoine Vérard. Vérard had effectively cornered the market as purveyor of vernacular texts and recreational literature to the Paris elite.[17] Bouchet, then at the beginning of his career, offered Vérard his first great work, the *Regnars traversans les voyes perilleuses*. Vérard agreed to publish it, but chose to attribute it to Sebastian Brant, the celebrated author of the *Ship of Fools*, which was already a bestseller in French. Bouchet protested not against this effacement of his authorial identity, but about the fact that Vérard had joined to his text a series of additional works by neither Brant nor Bouchet. According to Bouchet these works were of an inferior quality likely to damage by association the reception of the *Regnars traversans*. In a careful judgment the court found for Bouchet, but did not insist that his authorship be acknowledged. Rather the court specified that a manuscript should not be altered without the author's permission.[18]

Faced with a marketplace that attached so little value to modern concepts of intellectual property, authors had little choice but to engage themselves in the production process. The early success of *Orlando furioso* may have something to do with Ariosto's willingness to play an active role promoting it. The author personally arranged for the importation of the 200 reams of paper necessary to see it through the press in Ferrara. When this was achieved he set off to Mantua with a chest full of copies, some of which he presented to the marquis, Francesco Gonzaga; others he sold. When the first edition proved a success, Ariosto raised a personal loan to finance a second. Of this he sold 100 copies to a local bookseller, and exploited court connections and commercial relationships to oversee sales in Genoa and elsewhere. For the third definitive edition of what was by now an established bestseller, Ariosto purchased the

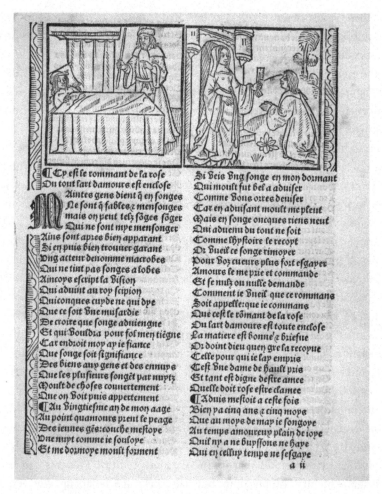

Fig. 31 *Roman de la Rose* (1505). The French romances so popular in the manuscript era made an easy transition to print. Antoine Vérard dominated the market in Paris, as he had the supply of manuscripts to the Parisian elite.

paper and took charge of sales. He also obtained privileges to protect the book from unauthorised reproduction in a number of Italian jurisdictions, from the Pope, the Emperor, Venice and Milan.

Soliciting privileges to protect investment in new and original work against unauthorised reprints was an area where authors could make themselves especially useful, since they could often exploit established relationships at court. The grant of a privilege was also a way in which the prince could reward service at no financial cost. Despite this, the privilege was far more frequently granted to the printer or publisher than to the author. The publisher also swallowed most of any profit. The best that the author could hope for was that the publication would enhance his career. This seems to have been precisely what occurred when Pietro Andrea Mattioli sought a privilege for his edition of the writings of the Greek botanist Dioscorides. This was one of the great publishing successes of the age, but the profits went to the bookseller/printer Vincenzo Valgrisi, the actual holder of the privilege. This was a book that required many detailed woodcuts which the publisher presumably paid for. Even so, the eventual profits were very large, since during his lifetime Valgrisi was able to dispose of 32,000 copies of his various editions of this large folio.[19]

Bemused and battered in a commercial environment foreign to their nature, it is no wonder that many authors looked to profit from their artistry through more traditional means: through the rewards of generous patrons. The favour of the rich was notoriously fickle. Many authors were disappointed in their hopes of preferment or financial gain, but others did receive tangible reward for their service. The Piedmontese Matteo Bandello was appointed Bishop of Agen. Bandello's collection of short *novelle* in the tradition of Boccaccio later found an enormous following in France in the popular translations of Pierre Boiastuau and François de Belleforest.[20] Jacques Amyot, whose French translation of Plutarch was a stunning literary success, was the tutor to the sons of Henry II of France. He was later promoted to Bishop of Auxerre.

For authors hungry for recognition the best hope lay in the liberal distribution of presentation copies, often accompanied by prefatory dedications lauding the achievements of the great. Such dedications – sometimes short poems, but often extended encomia or philosophical essays – were an established feature of publishing by the middle years of the sixteenth century. This was true not only of original literary compositions, but also works of scholarship, new editions of the classics, history books and medical texts. All were accompanied by a dedicatory letter to the noble, bishop or mentor by whom the author hoped to be rewarded. These outpourings bear witness to an extraordinary complexity of relationships between authors, editors and translators and their dedicatee. A large proportion acknowledged an established relationship of dependence and obligation. An author honoured the support of an employer, patron, or those who had financed publication.

Other writers used a dedication to associate their work with a distinguished figure, sometimes a better known scholar in the same field, without particular expectation of pecuniary reward. The intention here was to assume the lustre of the more famous individual (sometimes to the dedicatee's intense irritation). A third category again was those who used dedications as a means to influence public policy. This was a particular feature of writings by leading

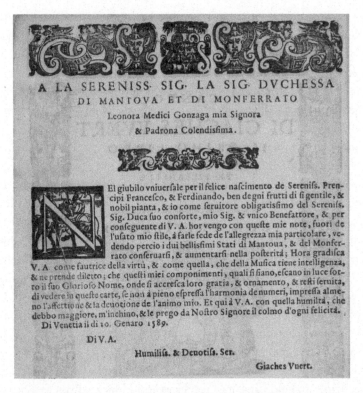

El giubilo vniuerfale per il felice nafcimento de Serenifs. Pren-
cipi Francefco, & Ferdinando, ben degni frutti di fi gentile, &
nobil pianta, & io come feruitore obligatisfimo del Serenifs.
Sig. Duca fuo conforte, mio Sig. & vnico Benefattore, & per
confeguente di V. A. hor vengo con quefte mie note, fuori de
l'ufato mio ftile, à farle fede de l'allegrezza mia particolare, ve-
dendo percio i dui bellisfimi Stati di Mantoua, & del Monfer-
rato conferuarfi, & aumentarfi nella pofterità; Hora gradifca
V. A. come fautrice della virtù, & come quella, che della Mufica tiene intelligenza,
& ne prende diletto; che quefti miei componimenti, quali fi fiano, efcano in luce for-
to il fuo Gloriofo Nome, onde fi accrefca loro gratia, & ornamento, & refti feruita,
di vedere in quefte carte, fe non à pieno efpreffa l'harmonia de numeri, impreffa alme-
no l'affettione & la deuotione de l'animo mio. Et qui à V.A. con quella humiltà, che
debbo maggiore, m'inchino, & le prego da Noftro Signore il colmo d'ogni felicità.
   Di Venetia il di 10. Genaro 1589.

      Di V. A.

         Humilifs. & Deuotifs. Ser.

                  Giaches Vuert.

Fig. 32 The dedications in volumes of music were usually mercifully short, acknowledging an established relationship between composer and patron/employer. When an author was striving for favour dedications could be both wordy and unctuous. Giaches de Wert, *Il primo libro delle canzonette villanelle à cinque voci* (Venice, 1589).

Protestant authors such as John Calvin and Heinrich Bullinger, whose dedications were employed to flatter, ingratiate and instruct the rulers and statesmen of the Protestant states. But of course many dedications were the work of hungrier men who hoped that literary virtuosity and extravagant praise would loosen the purse strings or open the doors of the great. Many of the leading figures of European society could expect to be honoured often, and by a large number of authors. In France, a notable feature of these dedications is the frequency with which books are dedicated to noblewomen. They offer telling evidence of the powerful and growing influence of women in the sixteenth-century book world as sponsors and patrons of texts.

In Italy, the existence of multiple courts and divergent centres of print presented rich opportunities for those with the wit and confidence to exploit them. None were so brazenly cynical in their manipulation of patronage opportunities as the flamboyant and extravagantly talented Pietro Aretino.

Perhaps because he came from a humble background (he was the son of a cobbler) Aretino was far less reticent in acknowledging the mercenary aspect of literary activity. Throughout his career he was careful to follow the advice he shared frankly with Bembo: that if one wished to win crowns of gold and not merely crowns of laurel, it was necessary 'to foster the pride of the great with great praise, holding them ever aloft with the wings of hyperbole.'[21]

Aretino, like Ariosto, lavished great care on the preparation of dedication copies. Having invested in rich illumination he did not scruple to remind the dedicatee, through a secretary, that a present was anticipated in return. Aretino's most innovative technique was to document these gifts, with exact specification of the sums he had received, in the letters he prepared for publication. Six books of this collected correspondence were published between 1538 and 1557.[22] Through this public medium his benefactors received praise for their generosity; those who had been less forthcoming had their meanness exposed. It is hard not to admire the nerve of a man who lived by his wits and to some degree managed to tilt the balance between writer and patron. Aretino, characteristically, was his own greatest admirer. 'Before I began to attack the reputation of patrons,' he reflected in 1537, 'men of talent had to beg for the basic necessities of life.' Now, thanks to him, talent wears brocade, drinks in gold cups, has necklaces and money.[23] Even as a boast this was overdrawn; but Aretino had at least demonstrated one way to prise open the purses of the rich.

The life of the poet was hard and uncertain: living on his wits, depending on the fickle favour of the great and the vagaries of taste. Nevertheless, the creative genius of a notable generation of authors and the shrewd commercial pragmatism of their publishers had by the middle decades of the sixteenth century begun to effect a discernible change in the author's status. By this point the prestige of a book was becoming ever more intricately linked with authorial identity. A decree published in Venice in 1545 forbade the publication of a book without the author's permission.[24] With the emergence of literary lions like Ariosto and Aretino, for the first time the name of a living author became a book's principal selling point.

The books of the brave

Early in the sixteenth century authors of new texts were beginning to make an impact on the market in recreational literature. But they still found it hard going in a marketplace of conservative tastes dominated by the inherited literature of previous generations. Tales of love, valour and noble virtue dominated not only the poetic canon adapted with such brilliance by Ariosto, but also the increasingly popular vogue for fictional works in prose. Nothing is as eloquent in this regard as the tenacious popularity of the chivalric romance. The roots of this literary genre lie in Spain and the long conflict to recover the territories of the Iberian peninsula from the Moorish invader. This great clash of civilisations was resolved only with the capitulation of the last Moorish outpost, the kingdom of Granada, in 1492. This signal event, coinciding with the unification of the Spanish kingdoms and the opening of the New World, elevated the military values of the chivalric literary tradition to a new place in Spanish society. The popularity of the genre was reflected in a huge wave of publications of printed texts, most adapted or translated from the inherited medieval canon. None of these compositions enjoyed the sustained popularity of the extended series of texts known collectively by the name of their leading figure: Amadis de Gaule.

This extremely successful narrative fable tells the story of Amadis and his love for Oriana, daughter of the king of Great Britain. Amadis is the unacknowledged son of Périon, king of Gaul. His obscure lineage leaves him little choice but to win Oriana's hand by feats of great bravery. The reader follows Amadis through extended travels and adventures, as Amadis confronts monsters and enchanted islands, defeats armies and triumphs in single combat to win the hand of his lady love. The four volumes of this odyssey were the work of Garci-Rodríguez de Montalvo, a courtier in the service of Queen Isabella. Their astonishing success prompted Montalvo to embark on a sequel that would follow the exploits of Amadis's sons and other descendants. Eventually the series extended to a bloated eighteen volumes. The popularity of Amadis inspired the creation of a rival dynasty which followed the adventures of Palmarín de Oliva and his son Primaleón; further popular works drew on the cast of characters familiar from the Arthurian legends and the songs of Roland.[25]

The romances of chivalry reached the peak of their popularity in the first half of the sixteenth century, at precisely the time when printers across Europe were exploring the full potential of the market for recreational literature. The astute (and wealthy) Seville publisher Juan Cromberger published a wide range of titles, all in a lavish folio intended for a moneyed audience. But the appeal of the deeds of Amadis and his companions crossed all social boundaries. The Emperor Charles V was a devotee, and took several chivalric romances with him to his retirement at Yuste. St Teresa of Avila had, as a young woman, read romances: she explained in her spiritual autobiography that she had caught the contagion from her mother. 'I became so utterly absorbed by this that if I did not have a new book, I did not feel that I could be happy.'[26] Novels of chivalry filled valuable space in the knapsacks of diplomats, and accompanied the conquistadores in the perilous voyages of discovery and conquest.

Here the lurid tales of military valour take on a darker hue. The feats of arms achieved by Cortés, Pizarro and their small bands of adventurers almost beggar belief; the utter devastation they wrought on the indigenous civilisations of the Aztecs and Incas cast them in a less heroic light. But if we are to ask what inspired them to these unlikely victories, what shaped their hopes of fabulous wealth and steeled them for endless treks into the unknown, then the valorous deeds of their fictional heroes undoubtedly played their part. For Primaleón, Palmerin and Amadis also faced impenetrable jungle, towering mountain ranges and exotic adversaries. Some tangible evidence of the inspiration the Iberian warrior class drew from these tales comes from a Portuguese account of a common soldier whose bravery in battle astonished his mess-mates. When questioned about his foolhardy behaviour he spoke of the tales shared by his literate companions: 'I didn't do the half of what any of the knights did in the book that you fellows read to me every night.'[27] Far from the hearths of their native lands, these cherished narratives really were 'the books of the brave.'

Lying histories

The chivalric novel was not without its critics. Moralists and educational theorists across the continent fulminated against the dangers of these alluring worlds of the imagination, and the dissipation of time that could better be spent on more worthy tasks. To Juan Luis Vives, contemporary of Erasmus and a distinguished writer of school texts, these were books 'devoid of culture and full of vices and filth.'[28] To Antonio de Guevara, another distinguished and popular author, they were deceitful tales, a lure to the credulous who believed them literally to be true. This conceit was encouraged by the use of history in many of the titles of the books. Both men called for legislation to inhibit the circulation of these dangerous fictions. The call was partly answered when in 1531 Queen Eleanor, acting as regent for the absent Emperor, banned the export of works of fiction to the Indies. The ban was renewed by further orders of 1536 and 1543, all citing the dangers that such books might pose to the indigenous population.

> Much harm results from taking to the Indies books in the vernacular of profane and imaginative character such as those about Amadis and others of this type of lying histories, because the Indians able to read turn to them,

forsaking works of proper and sound doctrine.[29]

If this really was the reason for the ban, then nobody took much notice. The Crombergers, who had secured the monopoly of export of books to the Americas, continued to ship large consignments to their readers overseas. Two inventories, compiled on the death of Juan Cromberger in 1528 and his son in 1540, reveal large stockpiles of Amadis and other titles.[30] In 1555 the authorities issued further regulations, requiring that a detailed docket listed the titles of all books consigned for export to the Indies. A number of these lists survive, and they demonstrate the persistent popularity of light recreational literature in cargoes otherwise dominated by liturgies and prayer books for the new churches overseas.[31] The lists also document the rapid success of Cervantes's *Don Quixote*, copies of which were included in consignments of books destined for the Indies even in 1605, the year of publication of its first volume. Cervantes's masterpiece

Fig. 33 *Amadis de Gaule*. An early Spanish edition, published in Venice. Despite official disapproval, these books made their way to the Americas in vast numbers, and conquered Europe in a wave of translations. That this was published in Venice hints at the early penetration of the Iberian market by Europe's leading centres of print.

is often credited with having sounded the death knell of the chivalric romance. Certainly the pathos of the eponymous hero's ponderous adherence to the honour code is a sea change from the solemn celebration of the implausible feats of Amadis and his compeers. But if Cervantes's gentle mockery drove the chivalric knights out of the salons, they found a new appreciative audience in the streets. Already in the late sixteenth century Paris printers were experimenting with cheap pamphlet versions of the chivalric tales, a tradition continued with the cheap mass-produced editions of the *Bibliothèque bleue* in the seventeenth century.[32]

For, ironically, just as the chivalric vogue was losing momentum in Spain, Amadis and his companions had found a new audience in northern Europe. The critical event that propelled *Amadis* to the status of international bestseller was the preparation of an outstanding French translation, published in eight volumes between 1540 and 1548. This was the work of the courtier and soldier Nicolas de Herberay, seigneur des Essarts. It is thought that Herberay acquired his knowledge of Spanish and love of Spanish literature as a prisoner, with Francis I, after the battle of Pavia. King Francis certainly encouraged Herberay's literary endeavours and provided a privilege that assured the translator of all rights in his work. Thus protected, Herberay could drive a hard bargain with the Parisian printers. Three leading booksellers, Janot, Longis and Sertenas, formed a partnership to publish the work, for which Herberay received generous cash payments. Anticipating a popular success, the publishers commissioned a series of new woodcut illustrations: the text was published in a striking Roman type in a lavish folio edition.[33] This again was a departure from tradition: until this point recreational texts would have been published in Gothic black-letter type rather than the Roman type associated with scholarly texts.

The publishers were not disappointed. Each edition quickly sold out. When Herberay abandoned the Amadis translation after eight volumes, others came forward to continue the sequence. The first Paris edition was clearly conceived for an elite, moneyed audience, but other publishers recognised the wider public appeal. To cater for these new readers publishers swiftly moved to the publication of editions in smaller, cheaper formats.[34]

While *Amadis* was conquering France, it also continued its triumphal progress across Europe. In Italy Mambrino Roseo da Fabriano added six books of his own devising to those translated from the Spanish, bringing the total in the Italian cycle to eighteen. When *Amadis* mania reached its height in France, French editors turned to this Italian continuation to feed an eager public. Between 1576 and 1581 Books XV to XXI appeared in French translations from the Italian – though some of the title-pages continued, misleadingly, to assert Spanish antecedents. In Germany the local popularity of the work stimulated the creation of three further books – which brought the total number of books in the German *Amadis* cycle to a bloated twenty-four. This left only England without a translation of *Amadis*: it was not until the last decade of the sixteenth century that a partial English version was eventually published.[35] This is an interesting text none the less, because it demonstrates that even in translation each culture created a slightly different book. The French version of Herberay is noticeably more explicit in its treatment of the erotic and sexual than the restrained Spanish original. The English translation, perhaps unconsciously, returned far closer to the Spanish original. Although translated from the French it adopts much more reticence and euphemism in its description of the sexual encounters.[36] Through translation each nation created its own vision of chivalric values.

Polite diversions

The sexual licence of the chivalric tales added to the fury of those who denounced the frivolity and immorality of books of this type. They feared, particularly, their appeal to female readers, well attested by the notes of ownership in surviving copies. But if such books were not suitable for young ladies, how should they occupy their leisure moments? One imaginative response came from a group of aristocratic ladies who gathered on the island of Ischia in the Gulf of Naples to converse, read and write poetry.

This was the first of a series of salons, formed and shaped by aristocratic ladies in the cities and states of the Italian peninsula in the middle decades of the sixteenth century. These were brutal years for the Italian people. The protracted conflicts between the Emperor, France and successive popes brought frequent incursions from undisciplined armies. After the Sack of Rome in 1527, Naples, Ferrara and Siena would also experience the horrors of war over the following decades. In these troubled times the salon provided a welcome refuge from the tumult of politics; it also harboured those whose theological views crept dangerously close to heresy. The Spaniard Juan de Valdés, already a refugee from Spain's austere religious climate, found sanctuary with Vittoria Colonna and her friends. He played an influential role in shaping the views of many of the salon devotees and of their literary culture.

The chief literary fruits of these salon discussions were a series of poetical anthologies published between 1545 and 1560.[37] Most were the work of the Venetian printer Gabriel Giolito. The poets published were not only the male authors patronised by Colonna and Giulia Gonzaga, but also women authors: Veronica Gambara, Laura Terracina and Colonna herself. For fifteen years Giolito put out a new volume every year, expanding his circle of authors to something over 500. The series reached its climax with a volume showcasing almost exclusively the work of female authors.

The popularity of the anthology is a striking feature of the literary culture of these years. It allowed the reader not only to enjoy the fruits of the literary craft, but to taste the atmosphere of the salon, where poets read and enjoyed each others' work. The genre had its prose cognate in the intimate literary dialogue, a genre that also flourished in these years. For the printer the anthology represented a safe haven in troubled times. In 1548 the Venetian Inquisition ordered the burning of over 1,400 allegedly heretical texts.[38] In the next ten years the published lists of forbidden books were expanded to encompass not only theological works, but also secular literature labelled immoral and lascivious. Among the authors singled out for condemnation were Rabelais, Boccaccio and Aretino. The anthology, because it had the name of no single author on the title-page, gave less provocation in the new climate of suspicion. Even so it is revealing that for his collection of female authors the editor chose not Giolito's well known Venice press, but the relative publishing backwater of Lucca, farther away from the prying eye of the Inquisition.

This was a major work, a powerful demonstration that women, long recognised as readers and patrons of print, were now making their way as authors. Vittoria Colonna led the way. The publication of her sonnets in 1538 was the first such publication attributed to a named female author. Colonna was already a literary celebrity, hymned by Ariosto in the *Orlando furioso*, praised by Tasso and an intimate of Castiglione. The sustained success of her published works was the inspiration for a whole host of other female authors. Among the most successful was Laura Terracina, whose poems, published by Giolito in 1546, were reissued at various times to the end of the century. By 1600, and despite a marked reduction in the market for secular poetry as the influence of the Tridentine reforms made themselves felt, more than 200 female authors had appeared in print in Italy.

Making music

In several respects the literature of the sixteenth century stood at the cusp of far larger developments. This was an age that had not quite invented the novel; just as the pamphlet publication of news and sensations had not quite invented the newspaper. But the printers of the age made possible one very significant shift in the cultural fabric of European society: the domestication of music-making. This is a part of the cultural heritage of the period that has received comparatively little attention, except among music specialists. But making music for private family pleasure played a major role in the domestic recreational culture of prosperous bourgeois households, and publishers turned out for their use literally thousands of collections of secular and spiritual songs.[39]

The creation of what was substantially a new aspect of European cultural life required the resolution of one of the most complex technical problems facing the new print technology: the printing of musical type. Once resolved, music publishing became an important sector of the European book trade.

In the age before print the choir was the exclusive preserve of the cathedral or the princely household, much like the garden, the menagerie of exotic beasts, or indeed the library. The musical repertoire conceived for the use of choirs in cathedrals and princely chapels was almost exclusively concentrated on the glorification of God through worship. By the end of the fifteenth century this included masses of great virtuosity and musical sophistication. The interest exhibited by these same patrons of learning in the new invention of printing led naturally to a desire to apply the new invention in the publication of music. How to do so was not, however, immediately apparent. The first experiments in musical printing were conducted with the same double impression technique employed in the Gutenberg era to render headings and decorative features. The first pull would lay down the five horizontal lines of the stave, on to which the notes, initially rendered as crude round figures, would then be imposed with the second impression. This required absolute precision: any slippage, or misalignment, and the notes would be placed half a tone askew. Thus although two-colour double impressions survive in musical printing into the sixteenth century, especially in large format decorated missals, it was not practical for mass-market musical printing. The solution to this technical problem lay in casting a whole new musical type, now with individual notes each with its own background of a tiny stretch of the five-bar stave. Once cast in sufficient numbers these pieces of musical notation could be set up in the same way as a normal row of type.

Although technically brilliant this still demanded the design and casting of an intricate new font of type. This was not something every printer could afford, even when the design principles were widely known. In the first years printers who invested in musical type therefore sought and received extended privileges to protect their capital outlay on casting the new type. The first successful experiments were pursued in Italy, with Venice at the forefront: in consequence the city was able to dominate the Italian production of music publications for much of the sixteenth century.[40] North of the Alps Paris established a leading role in the production of musical print, thanks in no small measure to the interest of King Francis I, who in this respect at least lived up to his self-image as the Renaissance prince. Francis awarded to the printer Pierre Attaingnant both an exclusive right to music printing, and the valued title of King's Printer of Music. Thus encouraged, Attaingnant turned out a distinguished series of musical editions, albeit in an awkward Gothic typeface.[41] These crude and inelegant designs were subsequently improved by his successors in Parisian musical publishing, notably the firm of Adrian Le Roy and Robert Ballard. Publishing music almost to the exclusion of all other work, Le Roy turned out some 700 separate printings in the second half of the century.[42] Yet phenomenal output was not enough to secure for this Paris firm

Fig. 34 An early example of German music printing. Here the melody is picked out in a single line; the densely packed text will not make it easy to follow until the user has learned the words.

Fig. 35 This second example of early music printing has four parts set out across two pages: the text is set out below the music. Later the four voices would normally be published in separate pamphlets.

total domination of the market. The same era witnessed the establishment of a number of firms in the Low Countries, at Louvain and Antwerp, which became significant forces in music publishing. Lyon also established a presence in music publishing.[43]

Between them around a dozen specialist firms in Venice, Paris, the Low Countries and Germany turned out about 6,000 separate printings of musical part books between about 1520 and 1600: approximately three million printed items.[44] Given that these were inevitably expensive books to publish and purchase, because of their technical complexity, this represents an impressive level of penetration into the limited share of the market available for purely recreational purchases. Yet all the indications are that the books were bought in large numbers, and heavily used. The evidence of this comes partly from a very unusual pattern of survival. On the whole expensive or complex books tend to survive in larger numbers than cheap, ephemeral books. Expensive books were purchased for reference, for consultation and for collection. In consequence they were carefully conserved. Yet this is not the case with musical part books. Many survive in only one copy, and sometimes in just one part, a tenor, bass or treble ('superius'). In fact for many of these rare books we know of their existence only because a single part survives in one of the small number of great collections of music, in Paris, Uppsala, Munich or Vienna. These are the copies that made their way into princely libraries; the rest of the edition seems, quite literally, to have been used to destruction.[45]

There were books created for parlour use. They were almost always printed in a convenient oblong format, one part to a voice. A few rare editions were printed with two parts opposite, upside down on the same page. Here presumably the singers were expected to congregate around a table, the alto opposite the bass. But this was too restrictive and the practice did not catch on. The single part per book became the standard format. In this format Europe's music printers over the course of fifty years made available a glorious range of music in four-part arrangements: love songs, traditional *chansons*, metrical psalms and adapted hymn melodies. The collections mingled songs from different musical traditions, and sometimes in different languages: French, Latin, Italian and German. The capital of this multilingual publishing was once again the Low Countries, which through a willingness and capacity to print in different languages succeeded in capturing a large part of this lucrative market.

The publication of musical part books was the final segment of a market for recreational literature that had enjoyed enormous growth since the first decades of the sixteenth century. This represented a sea change in the attitude both of those who bought books, and those who sought to make their living through them. Before the sixteenth century the book was the preserve of the wealthy. Books, manuscript or print, were prized objects bought for very specific purposes: as an adjunct to worship, as a scholarly resource, as a professional handbook. During the sixteenth century books became more affordable, and many more people aspired to own them. Personal collections became larger; many of Europe's citizens accumulated collections of twenty, fifty or even several hundred books. Amongst the books they gathered as the tools of their trade, a few crept in bought purely for pleasure or diversion: an *Amadis*, Boccaccio, or a collection of *chansons*. It was a crucial change for the sixteenth-century intellectual world.

CHAPTER 9

⋙ ✳ ⋘

AT SCHOOL

LIKE MANY of the sixteenth century's greatest authors Desiderius Erasmus was both prolific and versatile. He was a brilliant linguist, and a textual scholar of acknowledged genius. Even those who disapproved of his New Testament acknowledged the scholarly virtuosity of his edition of Jerome. His engagement with issues of contemporary politics revealed both a subtle intelligence and a fierce polemical skill. A peerless stylist, Erasmus mixed wit and wisdom to devastating effect.

So when Erasmus turned his attention to the debate on education his views could be sure of a hearing. His treatise *De ratione studii* (On the Method of Study) (1512) was an important milestone of the humanist programme, setting out Erasmian precepts for the cultivation of the young scholar. Yet there is a curious detachment from the everyday realities of schooling. The text is suffused with a tone of optimistic good will but specific prescriptions were surprisingly vague.[1] Erasmus recommends a large variety of authors and endorses the need for a broad general education without giving any indication of where admired texts should be placed in the curriculum. Erasmus had designed a programme for a private tutor working with a single gifted pupil: he was not seeking to develop a curriculum or syllabus for a system of mass education. This was the view of education of a man who had never had to teach a class.

Teaching the teachers

Erasmus's treatise brings home that the humanist programme had very specific goals. It prescribed liberal education for a social elite: those who followed it would be Latinate, cultivated and polished, fit for a life in public affairs. It was a reminder that the humanist educational programme was as much concerned with cultivating civility as teaching literacy. This is made explicit in the title of Erasmus's best known and most successful educational tract, *De civilitate morum puerorum* (On Good Manners for Boys) (1530).[2] In its French translation, *La Civilité puerile*, this text was so successful that it coined a generic name for a new stylised typeface, *civilité*, closely modelled on the cursive handwriting taught to school pupils.[3] Erasmus was undoubtedly a force for good. He insisted that knowledge of language was acquired by contact with the best authors and that fine style was taught by imitation. This made a strong case for the widest possible availability of the best books, for the use of the teachers as well as their students. In the humanist world this meant the classics of Roman and Greek letters. The demand for these texts in schools and colleges ensured that printers could turn out repeat editions of the most valued titles with the assurance of a robust market. But the vacuum at the heart of this agenda was the teaching of basic literacy. We learn little from Erasmus of how this precocious, idealised youth would have taken his first steps.

This is in many respects the most impenetrable aspect of sixteenth-century education. We see evidence at every turn of a vast increase in the number of active readers in European society. The appetite for learning brought a large increase in the numbers of students enrolled at universities, at grammar schools, and in the new academies. All of these new students required books. The young Nuremberg patrician Friederich Behaim enrolled at the Academy of Altdorf at the age of fourteen. His letters home make frequent mention of his urgent need for books, which he wanted either to be purchased for him in Nuremberg, furnished from the family library, or bound by the bookbinder who had lately set up business in Altdorf. But it is much more difficult to know how a young man like Friederich was qualified for a bracing tryst with Demosthenes (supplied by his obliging mother in a parallel Greek and Latin edition).[4] The books used in elementary education have by and large vanished altogether, used to destruction by their young, careless and often reluctant owners. We know that this too was an enormous and lucrative part of the market. The *ABC with Catechism* was one of the most valuable books for which the London printer John Daye held the exclusive licence, a privilege grimly defended by Daye and bitterly resented by others in the London trade. Yet scarcely any of this enormous production has survived. Some editions can be identified only from fragments recovered from the bindings of other books, where they had been used as printers' waste.[5]

This was an era when educational provision advanced dramatically. The new availability of printed books increased interest in reading. The increase in students fuelled the demand for books. This virtuous circle made the market in educational texts one of the most important parts of the publishing industry. It explains the continuing dominance of Latin in the print output of the period, despite the growing interest in vernacular texts, for Latin was the language of education throughout Europe. If we take into account the numbers engaged in teaching or providing lodging and accommodation for students, then education was one of the fastest growing industries of the sixteenth century. Printers made sure that they took their share of the profit. It was a long way from the high-mindedness of humanist theorists, though ultimately it all tended to the same purpose: to increase the number of Europe's citizens able to delve into the world of books.

Theory and practice

The years between 1450 and 1600 were a period of growth for Europe's universities, despite intermittent setbacks. The expansion of student numbers in the universities of northern Italy in the second half of the fifteenth century was a major stimulus for the development of printing in Venice, which monopolised provision of books for the three distinguished local universities, Bologna, Ferrara and Padua. The warfare that engulfed Italy in the first decades of the sixteenth century caused a precipitate decline, as students fled and courses closed. This was balanced by a rapid growth in student numbers north of the Alps, epitomised by new foundations such as the University of Wittenberg, established in 1502. This growth was in turn interrupted by the turbulence of the Reformation. Provision of education was seriously disrupted by the Reformation disputes in Germany between 1520 and 1550, and England between 1530 and 1550.[6] Hereafter the upward march resumed, with the foundation of a wave of new institutions in the Netherlands, Germany and the Swiss Confederation, and of new colleges at Oxford and Cambridge. These foundations often had explicitly religious motivation. Excluded from traditional places of study in towns loyal to the old religion, Protestant authorities established their own academies.[7] Since they could not obtain the necessary Papal Bull of foundation, these institutions could not formally be constituted as universities, but they were nevertheless soon recognised as distinguished centres of teaching, and an important part of Europe's network of educational provision. In the last part of the century colleges founded by Catholic religious orders, especially the Jesuits, added further to the rich tapestry of educational provision.

The growth in the size of Europe's student body, and in the diversity of educational institutions, was accompanied by a profound debate about syllabus and curriculum. The fundamental purpose of universities in the medieval period was training for the priesthood. In the sixteenth century it became routine to undertake a costly university training even when a career in the Church, or the law, was not the intended destination; a period at university became an accepted part of a good general education. This owed a great deal to humanism, a movement that challenged many of the ideological precepts of the medieval university. Humanism praised the art of rhetoric, in place of logic; it substituted the oration for the disputation. The most influential thinker of the fifteenth century, Guarino Guarini of Verona (1374–1460), articulated a vision of education based on the twin foundations of grammar and rhetoric.[8] It was an educational programme tailored to the needs of the active man of affairs rather than the professional scholar. Guarino's themes echo through much of the published scholarship that explicitly discussed educational reform, most notably in the early sixteenth-century works by Erasmus and Juan Luis Vives.

North of the Alps the impact of the new educational programme was most obvious in the foundation of a series of posts or institutions dedicated to the study of the scholarly languages. The attraction of the new linguistic scholarship was evident in the establishment by King Francis I of the Lecteurs Royaux for the study of Latin, Greek and Hebrew at the University of Paris. The foundation of the Collegium Trilingue at Louvain challenged the traditionalism of this ancient university, which like many prestigious northern centres had previously been a bastion of scholasticism. Both foundations were testimony to the influence of Erasmus, whose publications made a passionate case for the importance of philological purity. The foundation of Regius Chairs of Greek and Hebrew at Cambridge (1540) and Oxford (1546) further enhanced the prestige of the new learning. At Wittenberg and Marburg Luther's disciple Philip Melanchthon pursued a greatly expanded curriculum that laid more emphasis on Hebrew, Greek, history and poetry, as well as the quintessentially humanist discipline of eloquence. This diversification of the traditional order of study became a model for Protestant universities and newly created Protestant academies.

Erasmus's most profound influence on the university world was through the ubiquitous circulation of his works among the student body. We have striking evidence of this in a generous gift of books received by Alexander Nowell when his friend Thomas Bedel graduated from Oxford in 1539. The thirty-six volumes listed (an extensive collection for an undergraduate at this date) included at least ten works by Erasmus.[9] In much the same way the influence of the new learning would percolate down into the next layer of educational provision: the grammar schools.

Willingly to school

In Italy, civic schools had been established in most of the leading communes since at least the mid-fourteenth century. The need to provide a steady supply of well-trained notaries, officials and secretaries guaranteed a high level of support for these institutions among the city elites, who were careful to ensure that they were well run and adequately supplied with instructors. In 1528 the commune of Bologna supported between twenty and thirty teachers in both secondary and elementary schools. By this time many smaller communes had also undertaken the expense of hiring a schoolmaster. Typically, such communal masters taught about thirty students, often with very mixed levels of income. They were permitted to charge fees, at a level laid down by the municipality, to augment their salary.[10]

Many towns also boasted a variety of teachers offering instruction as independent masters. In the largest cities the vast majority of students were taught in establishments of this sort. Surviving notarial records from Venice record the names of around 850 teachers working in the city between 1300 and 1450, as many as fifty-five of them in a single year. Such independent teachers continued to dominate educational provision in the city through the sixteenth century. In 1587, responding to pressures to ensure that teachers were of demonstrable Catholic orthodoxy, the Republic questioned all teachers offering instruction at the elementary or secondary level. Of 245 teachers registered, 160 (65 per cent) were independent teachers offering the Latin curriculum. Between them they taught an estimated 1,650 pupils, easily surpassing the 200 pupils who could be accommodated by the five teachers of the communal school.[11]

Parents committing their boys to a master for a Latin education would have had a clear idea of what could be expected in terms of pedagogic method, and indeed, of what texts would be in use. The fifteenth century had witnessed a profound shift in the curriculum, as the medieval texts that had dominated the syllabus were progressively replaced by the rediscovered classics. The late medieval Latin curriculum had consisted of a limited range of very familiar texts. First steps in Latin and grammar were taken with three ubiquitous titles. The *Ars minor* attributed to Aelius Donatus was a limited syntax manual intended to be memorised. The *Disticha Catonis* was a collection of moral sayings attributed to Marcus Porcius Cato (234–149 BC) but with further medieval accretions. The fables of Aesop, the third of this triumvirate of primers, enjoyed a lasting influence and popularity throughout Europe well into the age of print, as the numerous printed editions testify. From these, students would move on to a group of grammars, often in verse, such as the *Graecismus* and the *Catholicon*, a large glossary. Medieval teachers also taught a few classical authors, notably Virgil and Ovid.

The fourteenth- and fifteenth-century rediscovery of classical texts of rhetoric, and particularly major texts of Cicero, permitted the articulation of a radically new school curriculum. The student should use the letters of Cicero to capture an easy writing style. Virgil's poetry should be learned by heart. The student should study Horace, Plautus, Ovid's *Metamorphoses*, the *Tragedies* of Seneca, Terence's plays and the *Satires* of Juvenal. This educational agenda, articulated most clearly in Battista Guarini's *De ordine docendi ac studendi* (The manner of teaching and studying) of 1459, rapidly became the universal practice of education. The admirably detailed survey of pedagogic practice conducted by the Venice authorities in 1587 confirmed Cicero as the universal author of choice, followed by Virgil, Terence and (at some distance) Horace.[12] Of Cicero's works the most widely used was the *Letters to Friends*, but teachers also valued the variety of his works available, both singly and in composite editions. Printers in Italy and northern Europe were only too happy to publish multiple editions to satisfy a demand which, for many, was central to their trade.

Editions of Cicero were a hardy perennial in the first age of print, published and republished in all the main print zones of Europe, their popularity undiminished with the passage of time. A survey of surviving copies reveals a substantial 300 editions for the incunabula age, and a further 1,500 for the sixteenth century.[13] There may have been more since many of the more ephemeral school-books survive in only one copy, and it is to be assumed that others have disappeared altogether. Repeat editions served a steady demand for texts used throughout the schoolrooms of Europe: printers and booksellers had good reason to bless the prolific Roman statesman. All told, printers must have turned out something like two million copies of the various Ciceronian texts in the first century and a half of print. It was a barometer of the success of the new humanist curriculum incubated in the schoolrooms of the Italian peninsula.

Northern lights

France was a land of many provincial towns, many of them cathedral cities of the kingdom's numerous small dioceses. Cathedral schools were the natural focus of Latin education in the fifteenth century, but this monopoly was increasingly challenged in the age of print by municipal authorities. The city fathers were unwilling to stand idly by when, as in Amiens, the agents of the diocesan officer in charge of schooling raided unlicensed schools, 'grabbing the children's books and taking them away, without any legal right to do so as collateral for the fees they claimed were due to them from the children'.[14] Many municipalities responded by appointing their own schoolmaster.

Such schools may have been founded mostly to provide instruction in basic literacy for the sons of the citizenry but from the sixteenth century towns also began to interest themselves in the study of the liberal arts. In this period many French cities erected a public school, established in a building provided by the municipality, sustained by a combination of public funds and donations or bequests from local notables.

Such institutions became the focus of considerable local pride. A local grammar school enabled the citizenry to educate their children without sending them away from home. In Bordeaux, it was argued, a new *collège* would 'increase the profit and honour of the city' with a school patterned on the *collège* at Paris. In Toulouse the city received permission from the king to liquidate the assets of old clerical establishments to endow a new school, allowing them to erect an imposing new building. These new schools expressed both a growing municipal pride and self-confidence, and an edgy, ambiguous relationship with the distant capital. Citizens were happy that their children could be educated without being sent away, but they were keen that this education should be 'in the Parisian style'. This was a phrase that implied both a broad approach to education (a humanistic orientation and a concern for good Latin) and certain common organisational features, in reality not necessarily based on any very obvious Parisian precepts. The new schools were divided into forms for instruction carefully gradated to suit the capacities of the students as they moved through the classes. This highly structured training regime was powerfully influenced by Erasmian precepts, widely disseminated both in his own Latin writings and in French translation.[15]

The six-class structure is helpfully set out in a contract between Master Massé, schoolmaster, and the city fathers of Auch in 1565. The lowest class, the *seizième*, offered basic literacy: the children were to be taught their letters in Greek and in Latin. In the next class they were introduced to further textbooks (Cato, Donatus and the grammar of Despauterius), and began reading Cicero and Terence. These two authors also dominated the curriculum in the *quatrième*, with Virgil and Ovid added to the reading list. The *troisième* introduced the study of eloquence, with Cicero again, Virgil's *Georgics* and Ovid's *Metamorphoses*. The *seconde* introduced Cicero's *De officiis* and Virgil's *Aeneid*. The highest class was devoted to the study of rhetoric, with more Cicero, Horace, and the addition of Quintilian, Sallust and Livy.[16]

Sylua.
Frutetum.
Collis.

CVM PRIVILEGIO.

PARISIIS
Apud Franciscum Stephanum.
1 5 3 8

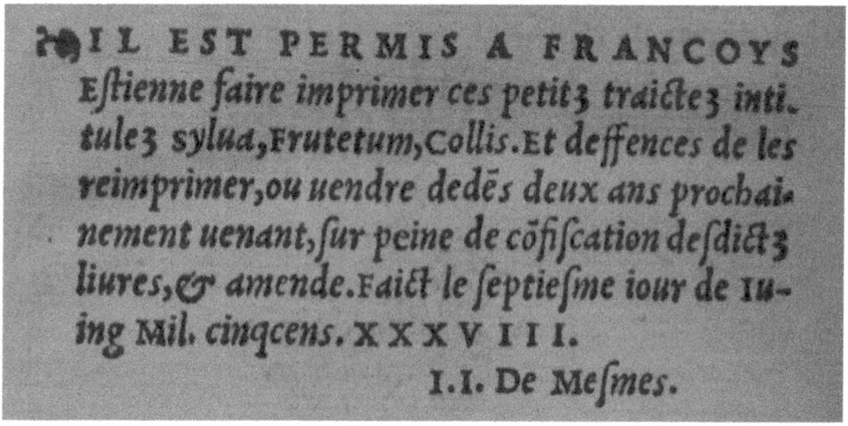

IL EST PERMIS A FRANCOYS Estienne faire imprimer ces petitʒ traicteʒ inti- tuleʒ sylua, Frutetum, Collis. Et deffences de les reimprimer, ou uendre dedēs deux ans prochai- nement uenant, sur peine de cōfiscation desdictʒ liures, ⁊ amende. Faict le septiesme iour de Iu- ing Mil. cinqcens. X X X V I I I.

I. I. De Mesmes.

Fig. 36 a & b Charles Estienne, *Sylva*, 1538. This was one of a series of short manuals designed to help students widen their vocabulary and understanding of Latin. This dates from Estienne's early career as tutor to the children of the writer Lazare de Baïf. He later went on to be Regius Professor of Medicine in Paris. The privilege was to the printer, François Estienne.

The establishment of what came close to being a standard curriculum in the new municipal schools had distinct advantages. As teachers moved from one school to another they knew exactly what to expect. They could fit easily into the fourth class or sixth without interruption to their students' progress. They were unlikely to deviate from the established order, partly because textbooks were sometimes, as in Auch, prescribed in the local regulations. In any case the local booksellers would have the customary books in stock. In this way the new humanist curriculum soon gained some of the fixity of the old medieval order.

Competition for the best teachers was intense. A notable preceptor like Mathurin Cordier was regarded as a civic adornment, and the city fathers of Nevers went out of their way to provide him with living accommodation of some grandeur. Even with much less distinguished individuals it could be costly to lure a teacher from the excitement and bookstores of the Latin Quarter in Paris to the more sedate life of a small provincial town. Master Gilles du Quemeneur made clear he would not move to Lectoure for less than 100 *ecus*. After consulting local notables (a total of forty-three persons) the town agreed to meet his price.[17]

Some towns sought to protect the position of the new school in much the same way as the old cathedral establishment, by cracking down on unlicensed teaching. When the new *collège* was set up in Toulouse all private teaching was abruptly forbidden. The attempt to draw all municipal education into a single institution seems to have been unique to France, and certainly contrasts with the variety of establishments available in Italy, or in Germany and the Netherlands.

In England, the wholesale confiscation of monastic property by Henry VIII and the subsequent abolition of urban chantries seemed to open the way for a rapid expansion of grammar school provision. In reality the vacant properties and endowments were also coveted by local notables and aristocratic patrons, and the seemingly inexhaustible supply of former ecclesiastical properties was soon grossly depleted. The new Tudor foundations were far less numerous than the more idealistic reformers had hoped, and their early years were dominated more by wrangles over property and securing promised endowment than by earnest discussions of curriculum.[18] Many of the great names of English schooling were founded in the period, and some in towns of relatively modest size, such as Oundle (1556), the Northamptonshire town that benefited from the will of a prosperous member of the London Grocers' Company, local boy William Laxton. The will of Robert Johnston led to the establishment of two schools in his county of Rutland, at Uppingham and Oakham. But we know far

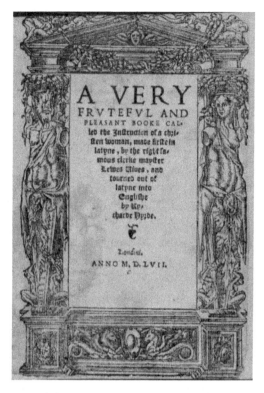

Fig. 37 *A very fruitful and pleasant book called the instruction of a Christian woman,* 1557. Juan Luis Vives was one of the most influential of the humanist theorists on education. This text, dedicated to Catherine of Aragon, was written to guide the education of the Princess Mary, daughter of Catherine and Henry VIII. Fittingly this English translation was published after Mary had become Queen.

less of what was taught than one might hope. Some foundations, like that at Saffron Walden in Essex, stipulated enigmatically that the school should follow 'the order and use of teaching grammar in the schools of Winchester and Eton', both of course medieval foundations.

In other cases we can be more certain that the foundation was animated by the spirit of humanist educational reform, if not precisely what was taught. The new school founded by John Colet at St Paul's Cathedral in London stipulated there should be 153 pupils, divided into forms, each presided over by a senior pupil. Children were to attend school from seven in the morning until eleven, and from one until five. Unlike in Italy no distinction was made between summer and winter hours. The daily round was punctuated by prayers, prescribed to be said three times: morning, noon and evening.[19] The school at Berkhamsted (1541) was also founded by a dean of St Paul's; here there were to be 144 pupils. Most of these schools were not particularly well endowed with books. At Boston, in Lincolnshire, it was decided in 1578 to buy a dictionary, 'to be tied on a chain and set upon a desk in the school, whereunto any scholar may have access as occasion shall serve'. Four years later at Cheltenham School, money was provided for 'such Latin and Greek books as shall be most necessary for public use of the said scholars, to be tied fast with little chains of iron'.[20] In 1601 Felsted invested in seven books, including works by Livy, Xenophon and Erasmus, as well as a dictionary. The exception was Guildford school, almost embarrassingly well supplied with books thanks to a bequest of John Parkhurst, Bishop of Norwich. In 1586 a gallery was converted to create a library to house them, the earliest known example of a school library. It is not certain what use the scholars would have made of a collection made up largely of Protestant biblical commentaries.[21]

One very tangible aspect of the new educational agenda of the Renaissance was a sharp increase in the prestige of history. Indeed, the teaching of history was in many respects the most original curricular innovation of the period. History was not taught in the classroom in classical times, and medieval educators showed, if anything, even less interest. The revival of history was initiated by Petrarch, whose sequence of biographies, *De viris illustribus* (*Lives of Famous men*), became an extremely popular genre in the fifteenth and sixteenth centuries, and was widely imitated. The humanist pedagogues of the fifteenth century repeatedly emphasised the value of the study of history, and particularly the ancient historians. Propelled by these endorsements, Livy, Sallust, Tacitus and Caesar all found favour as models of style and tutors in the arts of virtue. Caesar, Sallust and Valerius Maximus, author of the *Facta et dicta memorabilia*, were soon firmly embedded in the school curriculum throughout Europe. The ordinances of the grammar school at Norwich placed all three on a list of recommended authors. The timetable laid out for the free school at Leicester ordained Caesar's *Commentaries* to be studied in the seventh (top) form on Monday and Wednesday mornings. Valerius Maximus was prescribed for Monday and Tuesday afternoons.[22]

The outstanding example of municipal enterprise, as opposed to private beneficence, was the school at Shrewsbury, established in 1552. By 1562 the school had 266 boys, divided into seven forms. By 1581 the number had risen to around 600.[23] Camden described it as the largest school in England. But even with outstandingly successful initiatives such as this, stimulated and sustained by the local citizenry, it is unlikely that the total number of boys enrolled in the new Tudor foundations exceeded three or four thousand at any point in the reign of Elizabeth. The grammar schools broadened the stream of qualified entrants for the two English universities at Oxford and Cambridge. But they were far from monopolising educational provision in England.

First steps

In England, as elsewhere in Europe, the burden of providing first instruction in reading and writing fell on a separate stratum of the educational system, the elementary schools. The separation between the Latin curriculum of the grammar schools and the prosaic tasks of teaching reading, writing and arithmetic was not absolute, or clearly maintained. Some students obviously entered the grammar schools without mastering the art of reading and writing. In Italy it was common, as was the case with the young Niccolò Machiavelli, to intermit a grammar school education to master the art of mathematics.[24] In England, grammar schools made no formal provision for teaching writing; few classrooms in this era had desks. English pupils were forced to perfect their calligraphy in school vacations, or employ a writing master.

The intermingling of methods was reinforced by the fact that first instruction in reading was given, even in the elementary schools, from texts largely in Latin. These ABC books are among the most ephemeral of all the products of the book trade and surviving examples are rare. Only just enough survive to give us a flavour of how elementary education was conducted. The printed primer derived from the horn book, in Italian *tavola*, used in the manuscript era: literally a small board into which letters had been carved, or on to which a paper sheet with the letters of the alphabet had been pinned. A thin piece of translucent horn was used to protect the surface, hence the name.[25] The printed primer followed this tradition, adding to the alphabet various texts to be learned by heart. A surviving school primer from Perugia gives an idea of the content in a Catholic context. An edition of 1578 is a small octavo of twelve printed pages. There is no title-page – the first sheet begins with the alphabet, then common consonants with each of the vowels: la, le li, lo, lu. Then, still on the first page, comes the Paternoster in Latin, followed by the Ave Maria, a grace, a few psalms, the Magnificat, Nunc Dimittis and other prayers.[26]

This organisation of material seems to have been common to elementary education in most European countries, although inevitably the content shifted to reflect confessional change during the century. Some very rare surviving examples are single printed sheets like the *Tabulae abcdariae pueriles* (ABC for children) printed in Germany in the sixteenth century and now in the Morgan Library and Museum in New York, but most surviving examples are small pamphlets.[27] In Elizabethan England the two officially approved reading primers were the *ABC with Catechism* and the longer *Primer with Catechism*. The *ABC* consisted of alphabets in upper and lower case in three typefaces. This was followed by the Prayer Book catechism, and a small collection of prayers and graces. The longer *Primer with Catechism* contained all of the above, along with a calendar and almanac, the order of morning and evening prayer and a wider selection of prayers. The *ABC with Catechism* was the text for which John Daye held a controversial monopoly, and it was clearly immensely lucrative. So few copies have survived that it is impossible to reconstruct its publishing history with any certainty. But even judging from those alleged to have been published in pirated editions (including 35,000 copies in a single decade of the 1580s) the numbers involved must have been huge. A total estimated output of 200,000 copies of the two basic texts is probably towards the lower end of likelihood.

Schools made use of other catechismal texts too, such as Calvin's catechism. This was the first book given to Philip Sidney when he went to Shrewsbury School in 1564.[28] Elementary classes also continued to make use of other grammars including the perennial medieval favourite, the *Donatus*. So popular was this text in the first age of print, and so erratic its survival, that early bibliographies list each surviving fragment rather than attempting to identify to which of the numerous printings (mostly anonymous) these fragments belong.[29] This book scarcely survives as a complete text, though it was clearly ubiquitous in fifteenth- and early sixteenth-century elementary teaching. To add to the confusion the *Donatus* most used in Italy was not the same work, but a separately derived medieval grammatical text, the *Janua*. Library catalogues frequently confuse the two, as did most early users.[30]

After the first steps had been taken in establishing basic literacy, educational pathways diverged. In Italy those intended for a purely vernacular education would follow a different regime. The vernacular curriculum had its own distinctive features, and commonly used texts. It did not, however, have the coherence of the Latin curriculum and instead developed without the articulation of an overall pedagogic theory or curricular recommendations: educational theorists ignored the vernacular schools. Schoolmasters made use of texts that were their own favourites, or books the pupils brought with them from home. These tended to be texts written for an adult audience and which their parents had enjoyed or thought properly edifying. Boys were introduced to a variety of pious literature: catechisms such as the *Christian Doctrine*, the scriptural text *Epistles and Gospels*, hagiographical lives of saints. A particular favourite was the *Fior di virtù* (*The Flower of Virtue*), a medieval handbook of vices and virtues.

Vernacular classes also made use of a surprising variety of secular texts including chivalric romances. Ariosto's *Orlando furioso* was a favourite in

Venetian schoolrooms, no doubt for its combination of soaring imaginative narrative and fine poetic style. Schoolmasters also used the fictional life of Marcus Aurelius by the Spanish courtly author, Antonio de Guevara. A loosely organised work of moral philosophy penned in a highly rhetorical style, the *Vita di Marco Aurelio* placed advice on good conduct and personal morality within an ingenious, imagined Roman setting. Vividly written and full of easily assimilated anecdotes, Guevara's book became a European bestseller, a favourite inside the classroom and out.[31]

The choice of texts gives the clue to the purpose of vernacular education: to prepare pupils for the world of work through the inculcation of good moral values and conventional piety. Students would learn to read and write but also, within their appointed order, to be good citizens. The vernacular schools taught practical skills, such as *abbaco*, practical mathematics. From basic counting, multiplication and division (taught in the ageless fashion with tables), pupils were moved on to more complex problems of the sort they would face in their everyday lives: calculation of prices, the correct interest to charge on loans, payments due on bills of exchange in different currencies.

The dominant role of independent masters in the Italian system made it reasonably easy to offer these different educational pathways. The tradition of a separate vernacular curriculum was far more developed here than in other parts of Europe, where the distinctions were more blurred.[32] We have seen that in France mastering basic literacy was undertaken in the lowest class of the *collège*. Here, apart from their alphabet, children would be taught 'to form syllables with letters and the practice of writing with a pen until they know how to read and pronounce words and begin to write them in Greek as well as Latin'.[33] This, from the contract made at Auch quoted earlier, clearly implies that the pupils would be taking their first steps in literacy within the context of a grammar school education. The insistence in French municipalities that the *collège* should enjoy a monopoly of educational provision inhibited opportunities to gain the basics of literacy in the small schools that seem to have been ubiquitous elsewhere in Europe. France was unusual in this respect, but even in England grammar schools were often under pressure to teach basic literacy, particularly in small towns where the recently founded grammar school might employ the only teacher in the town. The detailed syllabus drawn up for the free school in Leicester offered the full Latin curriculum, but in the first class pupils were to study catechism and English grammar throughout the week, with two hours of daily writing lessons; the second form was to progress to the *Sententiae pueriles* (Maxims for children) with more English grammar.[34]

A mission to educate

For places too small to sustain a grammar school, finding a competent master was always a struggle. It would be interesting to know whether the tiny town of Le Buis did indeed employ Raymond Chaussenc, who in 1593 wrote the following disarmingly frank letter of self-recommendation:

> I write to let you know that I am willing to serve you and teach your children good manners, reading in Latin and in French, and all sorts of letters. As for grammar, I don't know too much about it, except some simple conjugating and some of Pellisson's rules. If you find my handwriting acceptable, of which this letter may serve as a sample, although I can do better, you will find that I will serve you as loyally as any man of letters could, without tormenting your children.[35]

Just in case the village elders were still inclined to proceed, Chaussenc felt duty bound to add: 'I happen to be a Protestant. But I beg you to fear nothing, because I am used to teaching Catholic children in such a way that you will never know that I am a Protestant.'

It was inevitable that in the inflamed atmosphere of the second half of the sixteenth century religious issues would loom large in the management of schooling. Schoolmasters had to be trusted not to poison young minds. But the religious convulsions of the period produced one further and immensely valuable addition to elementary educational provision: the catechism school. These schools, though charged with a narrow and specific purpose, offered an important service, particularly for those for whom the fees demanded by the schoolmaster or dame school were an insuperable obstacle. Catechism schools were free. They followed basically the same educational method as other schools, inculcating religious principles and basic literacy through rote learning. As we have seen, the catechism was in any case a frequent feature of the standard ABC books. The catechism schools met for one or two hours on Sundays and religious festivals. Through regular attendance the scholar could pick up important rudiments of literacy.

Catechism schools were a common feature of all religious cultures. Inculcation of the catechism was an essential feature of the pedagogic scheme in the new Lutheran states of Germany, where the minister was sometimes expected to double as pedagogue. In Italy after the Council of Trent, the schools of Christian doctrine enrolled large numbers of children, who might or might not have access to secular education. In Milan in 1564, 2,000 students were taught in classes of ten in some twenty-eight separate establishments. In Bologna in 1568 Sunday enrolment reached 4,900.[36] These catechism schools also provided important educational opportunities for students excluded from much conventional schooling: the children of the working poor, and girls.

Educating women

The statistical evidence for women's education in the sixteenth century makes grim reading. In the Venice survey of 1587 only 0.2 per cent of the pupils registered were female.[37] This barren landscape cannot tell the whole story. During the course of this survey of the European book world we have met with widespread evidence of female engagement with the printed word, as patrons, dedicatees, authors, master printers and especially as readers. All of these roles imply a high level of female literacy, for all that it is often invisible in the type of evidence frequently cited in scholarship on the subject. Scholars have traditionally assessed literacy rates by calculating the proportions able to sign their name on legal documents. Women were seldom able to hold property in their own right, and so were far less likely to be the signatories. They were also far less likely to be listed as the owner of the books in the household. Yet a close reading of testamentary evidence shows that husbands at the point of death were very likely to pass management of their business to their widow, a role the woman could only perform if she could read or write. Women played an especially important role in the printing industry, often proudly advertising their responsibility for the press as 'the widow of François Regnault' or under their own names.[38] Again, such a female proprietor could hardly have managed a printing press without being able to read or write. Where did women gain such skills, if they were not able to go to school?

The absence of girls from the schools of Venice reflects partly the reluctance of citizens to have their daughters venturing forth alone in public, rather than hostility to women's education. Humanist commentators strongly supported the principle of female education. The principal beneficiaries were of course a small number of well-known figures who received a diverse and thorough classical education. Marguerite de Navarre and Elizabeth I of England were being educated for a special social role. But many other young women from the upper and middle echelons of European society also received the benefits of a diverse education at home from private tutors. These tutors followed a curriculum close to that of the vernacular schools, though with more emphasis on practical training in music. None of the books used in the Venetian

Fig. 38 Jeanne Rivière, wife of Christophe Plantin. She successfully ran the business for several years after her husband's death, working with her son-in-law, Jan Moretus.

vernacular schools would have been thought inappropriate for female readers. Devotional texts and small collections of moral precepts such as the *Flowers of Virtue* were thought particularly suitable for female readers, who were known to be avid readers of chivalric romances.

These were opportunities available mostly to women from the genteel, leisured classes. Elsewhere, the catechism school provided an important new avenue of female education. Whereas for boys who attended school catechismal instruction might have been an unwelcome intrusion into precious leisure time, for many girls, and boys from poorer homes, it was an educational lifeline. Many girls will have received their only formal reading instruction in the catechism schools. The value of such institutions should not be doubted; Protestant churches and post-Tridentine Catholic institutions invested considerable energy in them. Both traditions believed strongly in the beneficial influence of female piety. Women were believed both to have a natural propensity towards religious observance, and to exercise a strong and positive influence on the men of their families. The Protestant emphasis on the home as a school of religion encouraged the transfer of the religious instruction offered in church into a domestic setting, where the Bible would be read in the presence of children and servants, and the lessons of the catechism reinforced and tested. Generalisation of such household devotion provided further educational opportunities for the daughters of the house and, to a lesser extent, female servants.

The most profound articulation of Reformation principles in the area of female education was found in Germany.[39] Although Luther is more often quoted for the offhand and chauvinistic remarks on women that litter his *Table Talk*, he was a firm proponent of female education. In his *Address to the Christian Nobility of the German Nation* (1520) he lamented that convents had forsaken their educational vocation, and called for the establishment of schools for women. Four years later he urged city magistrates to provide the best possible schools both for boys and girls in every locality. He believed that girls as well as boys should be offered a broad curriculum, rather than simple religious instruction. Girls, too, should learn history, literature, music and mathematics. Luther's exhortations were given body and shape by Philip Melanchthon, the principal educational theorist of the Lutheran Reformation, and by Johannes Bugenhagen, responsible for formulating a range of church orders for churches across northern Germany and in Scandinavia. One of the earliest examples was the church order for Braunschweig in 1528. This provided for two Latin schools and six German schools, two for boys and four for girls. These were to teach Scripture, the catechism and Christian songs. The four girls' schools were also to teach history. In Strasbourg, where the late medieval decline of monasticism had left a weak educational inheritance, Martin Bucer pressed for the establishment of a new generation of schools, six for boys and six for girls.

There is plentiful evidence that prescriptions of this nature were put into practice. The new church order at Wittenberg made provision for a separate schoolmaster to be put in charge of a new girls' school. Even in the very small town of Mölln located between Lübeck and Hamburg there was scope for a separate girls' school, run by the schoolmaster's wife. The interest in pursuing this education programme is reflected in the increasing number of texts published specifically for the use of girls' schools. A pioneer in this field was Johann Agricola, whose *One Hundred and Thirty Common Questions* for the young children in the German girls' school at Eisleben was published in 1537.[40] Other authors who wrote with the needs of girls in mind included

Johann Spangenberg of Nordhausen, Nikolaus Herman, the noted hymn writer of Joachimsthal, and Johann Jhan, the girls' schoolmaster at Torgau.

A leading contribution to this literature was the *Jungfrauschulordnung* (School Ordinance for Girls, 1574) published by the reformer of Württemberg, Andreas Musculus.[41] The Württemberg church order of 1573 had made provision for the establishment of girls' schools, where the daughters of the community should be taught reading, writing, the art of prayer and Christian songs. This emphasis on singing was further elucidated in the *Jungfrauschulordnung*, and seems to have been a common theme of Lutheran church orders. It built on the prominent role accorded to hymn singing in the Lutheran churches, and in the pedagogic process.[42] This reflected the recognition that hymn singing employed the same process of rote learning and repetition used in all classes of school education. In this the liturgical order was the school of Christ, and the hymns sung and memorised moved easily into the home and workplace, where the texts could be shared with new generations of future pupils.

The overall impact of two generations of pedagogic planning in the Lutheran German states can be tested in the returns of the comprehensive visitation records compiled in the last quarter of the sixteenth century. Here the vast improvement in available educational opportunities emerges very clearly. In Ducal Württemberg at the time of the Reformation there were fifty known schools. Twenty-five years later there were sixty-one Latin schools and 180 vernacular schools; by 1581 there were 270 schools, and 401 at the end of the century. Only the tiniest village would have been utterly bereft of educational provision. It is not clear how many made provision to accept girls, but in Brandenburg, where there were only four girls' schools before the Reformation, by 1600 there were forty-five; this compares with an increase from fifty-five to one hundred in the number of boys' schools. Albertine Saxony adopted the Reformation only in 1539, but within twenty years sixteen of the larger towns had functioning girls' schools.[43] The scale and effectiveness of this investment in female education is in marked contrast to the far less extensive institutional provision in other parts of Europe. It is one of the most impressive, if not often observed, achievements of the Lutheran Reformation.

Circles of readers

The impact of this very varied and extensive educational provision is not easy to quantify. The measurement of literacy in sixteenth-century societies is not an exact science. Most studies of literacy rates assume that those who can sign a document were also able to read. This reflects an understanding that reading and writing were taught sequentially; even the most rudimentary writing ability is then acceptable evidence that the signatory had learned to read.[44] Of course this measure makes us wholly dependent on the written record of documents compiled for quite different purposes: specific surveys of literacy are unknown for this period, and even surveys of educational provision, such as we have cited for Venice and Germany, are very rare. We rely on creating a general sense of the contemporary situation from diverse scraps of local information.

Most of the surviving data relates to that which can be most easily measured: that is, urban male literacy. It is generally acknowledged that literacy rates were far lower in the countryside. Even here the chasm may not be as large as is sometimes implied. Many country people moved to the towns, and sometimes back again. Many townspeople passed through or lingered in villages. Places where visitors were most likely to congregate were also places where reading matter was posted or displayed, in the marketplace or the tavern. In this way occasional visitors made an important contribution in increasing the circle of those who had access to print in rural areas beyond permanently settled readers, the priest, the schoolmaster, the squire and his steward.

We must also accept that female literacy is not susceptible to the normal means of measurement. Many female readers were unlikely to leave a documentary record. They were under-represented among those who required literacy as part of their working lives, or social dignity. Some professions, such as the law or academic medicine, were closed to them altogether. Many women read and enjoyed books, though they were far less likely to be recorded as owners of these books. Books in the household would usually enter the documentary record, and be recorded in wills or inventories, as male possessions.

With all these provisos the evidence is still highly suggestive. Some cities already recorded an impressive level of literacy before the age of print. In Florence in 1480, 28 per cent of boys aged between ten and thirteen were in school. By the end of the sixteenth century Venice had a male literacy rate estimated at 33–34 per cent. To put these figures in perspective, the Italian census of 1871 revealed a literacy rate of 57 per cent (for both sexes) for Rome, considerably higher than the figure of 31 per cent for Italy as a whole.[45] Sixteenth-century literacy rates in highly urbanised areas were therefore already approaching those registered in systematic surveys three hundred years later.

In England, the diocese of York in 1530 had an estimated male literacy rate of around 20–25 per cent in 1530. This had improved to 41 per cent by the end of the century. In Languedoc (southern France) almost all merchants were

E'λληνικόν.	Latinum.	Duytſch.	François.	Eſpañol.	Italiano.	Engliſh.	Hochteutſh.
ἀοιδός	cantator	een fangher	chantre	cantor	cantore	a fynger	eyn finger
φωνή	vox	die ſtemme	la voix	vox	voce	the voyce	die ſtym
σάρξ	caro	dat vleeſch	la chair	carne	carne	fleſh	vleyſch
δέρκ	pellis, cutis	die huyt, vel	la peau	pelleia	pelle (me theſkynne haue	lether	leder
δέρμα	corium	leer	le cuyr	cuero, corā-	cnoio, coia-	lether	leder
βυσσάω	tufsire	hoeſten	touſsir	toſser (me	teſsire	to cough	huoſten
βήξ	tufsis	den horſt	la toux	tos	la toſsa	the cough	der hueſt
ἐκτός	ruptus	gheſcoert	rompu	rompido	ilrutto	toren	zeriſſen
φόφος πεσίξος	crepitus	een enverſt	vn pet	pedo	ilpetto	a fart	furtz
πέρδομ	pedere (tris	vieſten	peter	peer	pettegiare	to fatte	furtzen
πέρδω ἅπαξ	pede femel	vuſt eens	pette vne fois	pea vna vez	tra vn petto	fartoneſcēyp	furtz ryn mae
κόλπος	faliua	ſteeſel	crachat	eſcupetiua	ſputo	ſpatle	ſpeychel
σίαλον	finus	den ſchoot	le fein	falda	ilſeno	a boſome	der buoſz
ἐγκύλπᾳ	in finu	inden ſchoot	au fein	en la falda	inſeno	in the boſo	der ſchoſz
χειρίς	manica	die mouwe	la manche	manga	manica	the fleue	eyn ermel
ἐν χειρίδι	in manica	in die mouwve	en la manche	en la manga	in manica	in the fleue	im ermel
περιτράχεω	collarium	die colliere	collier	collar	collare	the collate	eyn goller
κόλπωμα	gremium	den ſchoot	le geron	gremio	grembo	the lappe	die ſchoſz
πίλιον	pileus	een hoet	chappeau	zombrero	ilcapello	an hat	eyn huot
πίλιον καρφ-	pileus ſtrami	eet ſtreyen	chappeau de eſtrain	ſobrero de pa-	capello di pa-	a ſtrayve	eyn ſtrowern
δις	neus	hoet	eſtrain	paia	glia	hat	huot
δεσμός	nodus	een knoop	vn neu	nudos	nodi	a knotte	eyn kneff
θλμξ	funiculus	een cordeken	corde	cucida	el dordel	a corde	eyn ſchnuerli
ζωης	corrigia	een gordel	courroye	torrea	la cintha	latchettes	eyn gurtel
ζώνη	zona	eenem riem	ceinčture	vna cinta	el veneriero	a gyrdle	eyn gurtel
πόρπη	fibula	een doré, haet	boucle	eſpina	la ſibbia	a buckle	eyn haft
πρόνη	acicula	een ſtelle	vne eſpingle	craquido	lardion	a pynne	eyn gyſen

Fig. 39 Dictionary in eight languages, Paris, 1552. One of thousands of dictionaries published in the sixteenth century, this was intended primarily for the use of merchants and travellers. Words were therefore arranged by theme, rather than alphabetically.

literate. Two-thirds of artisans could sign a lease, compared to one in ten farmers and only 3 per cent of labourers. Here one has to remember that more could probably read than write. The precise place of signing one's name on the intersection between the two is difficult to determine.

Areas of high urbanisation had the highest levels of literacy. In the Low Countries by 1549 there were 150 schools in Antwerp (which boasted a separate schoolmasters' guild); Ghent had forty, and Breda fourteen. A survey of 141 rural parishes in Tournai in 1569 found only three entirely without some basic school provision. There were eight Latin schools and two catechism schools, teaching those who had no time to come to school on working days.[46] It was understandable that an aristocratic Spanish visitor to the Low Countries at this time formed the impression that 'almost everyone' could read and write, even women.

These places had developed substantial circles of potential readers; yet not all who read possessed books. The growth of literacy required the industry to adapt its output to produce printed works that would tempt these new circles of readers to part with the very limited part of their income that would not be spent on the necessities of life. That this could be achieved was demonstrated by the early rash of printed certificates of indulgence. Here the promise of salvation could be seen as a necessity, and worth the investment, even if it meant going hungry. When the prestige of indulgences was damaged by the Reformation it was more difficult to persuade less literate purchasers to invest in books, whether devotional, or purely for information or recreation. These were nevertheless important and growing markets, though we must not make the mistake of assuming that cheap print was published exclusively with the less prosperous or less fully literate in mind. The evidence suggests, rather to the contrary, that most cheap print was bought by readers who also bought more expensive books. Rather than owning a very small number of books, they bought both increasing numbers of large books and a variety of pamphlets and small texts.

The study of the school curriculum of the sixteenth century suggests one further important reflection about the reading public. We must not assume that the Latin book trade and vernacular publications served two distinct audiences. Clearly those who read Latin also bought vernacular books. These mingled together in their book chests, sometimes even bound together in the same volumes. Many who ostensibly had a Latin education in later years read more comfortably in their native tongue. This helps explain the large number of scholarly, academic and technical books that were translated into French, German or Italian. But even those who received what was described as a vernacular education were exposed to a great deal of Latin. The ABC books and primers were, as we have seen, made up largely of Latin prayers. Latin grammars like the *Donatus* featured in most schemes of elementary education. Exposure to the Latin languages continued, through the liturgy, which would, to many who had been to school, have been something more than the mumbo-jumbo often claimed in reformist sermons or satirical theatre. This is not to say that those with a more rudimentary education would have been comfortable readers; simply that Latin on the printed page would not have been wholly foreign or impenetrable.

Among the most successful books were those that enjoyed currency both for classroom use and recreational reading. History books were used extensively in the classroom: the prestige of the Roman authors also stimulated renewed interest in contemporary history. This was already very evident in the fifteenth century, when a new generation of chronicles emerged from the environs of the court, in France, Italy, England and the Burgundian Low Countries. Works like Froissart's *Chronicles* and their continuation by Enguerrand de Monstrelet enjoyed a wide circulation in manuscript, and made an easy transition to print.[47] The turbulent political and religious events of the sixteenth century called for a new generation of historians, though now with a rather more complex political agenda than that which faced the fifteenth-century chroniclers. Protestant authors like Johannes Sleidanus developed their own, highly particular view of the historical past.[48] The appeal of history in a wide range of contexts is evident from the large number of vernacular translations of the Roman historians: Caesar's *De bello gallico* and other works went through at least sixty separate printings in French translation.[49] This was an expensive book, which readers might have met for the first time in their Latin schools and then returned to for enjoyment as adults. A less costly investment was an edition of one of the many collections of moral, witty or apposite sayings, such as the *Disticha* of Cato or the *Adages* of Erasmus. These too went through numerous editions both in Latin and in vernacular translation. Remembered from the classroom, they were much used by adults to fashion a witty retort or an elegant tag in correspondence. Books of this type were a great boon to the self-educated, who could also draw on manuals of style and courtly behaviour such as the *Treasures of Amadis*.[50] Another hardy perennial was Aesop's *Fables*, which was published throughout Europe in Latin and in virtually every European vernacular.[51] This was the classic everyman book, used to brighten the schoolroom, read and retold at home. These and other texts of trans-national appeal demonstrate that the sixteenth-century school was not a sealed and separate place, but a partner in a lurch towards literacy that had many settings, formal and informal, in the sixteenth-century book world.

By the middle of the sixteenth century two centuries of investment in a vastly increased range of educational provision had expanded Europe's reading public, in ways both clearly measurable and some less evident. This brought huge opportunities for the entrepreneurs of the publishing world. For Europe's rulers it also brought some obvious dangers. As Europe's readers had access to an ever greater range of books, some readily affordable, so they gained the means to engage in new ways with the great controversies that had now engulfed European society. It was a combustible combination.

PART III

CONFLICT

CHAPTER 10

THE LITERATURE OF CONFLICT

FEW EVENTS in the sixteenth century would have the symbolic resonance of a small ceremony performed outside Wittenberg on 10 December 1520. Four months previously the Pope had condemned Luther and ordered him to recant. The Papal Bull of excommunication, *Exsurge Domine*, was spread around Germany by the Pope's agents. Luther was given sixty days to respond. Instead he led a small band of followers to a spot in the town ditch where he burned the Bull, along with a copy of Canon Law and some pamphlets of his principal opponents, Emser and Eck.[1] With this Luther passed a personal point of no return with the institutional Church. He also helped usher in a new phase in the conflict of ideas: where books would be victims as well as protagonists.

In the first seventy years of print controls on the publication of disapproved materials had developed very slowly. The medieval Church had occasionally added texts to the fires that burned condemned heretics. In Florence Savonarola had dramatised his attack on the licentiousness of Renaissance Italy with a bonfire of lascivious texts (which included Boccaccio and as much Ovid as he could lay his hands on). But these tended to be isolated incidents. It was only with the Reformation that the authorities grasped the new scale of the threat posed by the circulation of books.

The response from Europe's governing powers was of a new order from anything that had gone before. The Papal Bull against Luther ordered that his books also be destroyed: small ceremonies of public conflagration followed wherever the Pope's decrees were obeyed.[2] But after this spasm the fires cooled. Few in the book world favoured the punishment of inanimate objects. Books were expensive. Luther's plans to kindle his fire in Wittenberg with the works of the scholastic theologians Duns Scotus and Thomas Aquinas had to be abandoned because no Wittenberg scholar would sacrifice their copy.[3]

The burning of books returned with a vengeance in the third decade of the Reformation. In 1548 at Venice over 1,400 forbidden Protestant texts were consigned to the flames. The execution of heretics in Spain in 1559 was accompanied by a huge bonfire of books, as was the expulsion of Huguenots from Paris the following decade. In 1567 cheering crowds in Lyon watched as many thousands of books were ferreted out of the warehouses and hurled into the flames.

The scale of this destruction was a sign of a new hostility in the Reformation conflicts. In the second half of the century the battle between Catholic and Protestant took on a murderous intensity. Luther and his Catholic opponents had swapped insults, but in Paris in 1572 the Catholic population hunted their Huguenot neighbours through the streets. The return of religious enthusiasm led to conflicts of a previously unimaginable bitterness. The disputes over religion had sowed the seeds of a genocidal rage in which whole populations were at risk.

In the polarised societies of this era governments exercised new care over what their subjects read. And in this they were right, because much of the toxic energy of the conflict came from the printed page. These pamphlet wars brought a new pungency and partisanship to the European book world. For bookmen it presented both opportunity and danger.

Defining orthodoxy

The increased number of books in circulation after the invention of printing inevitably focused minds on the need for controls. But the first attempts at censorship concentrated mostly on individual texts, and did little to inhibit the relatively unregulated flow of books to the marketplace. Even after Luther's attacks on the Papacy the multiplicity of jurisdictions in the German Empire diluted the impact of measures taken to control the publication of disapproved texts. If a printer was deterred from printing, the same book could usually be turned off a press a few miles away. The decisive stage in the development of censorship came with systematic efforts to compile comprehensive lists of forbidden texts in the third generation of the Reformation, the 1540s.

These new codes of censorship were of a different order from the fitful and largely local regulations previously promulgated. A crucial trigger was the disintegration of the Italian *spirituali*, the group of Catholic theologians committed to a negotiated end to the Reformation controversies through reconciliation with German Protestantism. This policy was utterly discredited when the leading *spirituali* fled Italy and became Protestants; the outrage to Italian opinion provoked a sharp conservative reaction. Across the peninsula

Fig. 40 *Quaestiones in quattuor libros sententiarum* (Venice, 1477). An early printed edition of Duns Scotus. It is easy to see why no Wittenberg scholar was prepared to surrender their copy of so precious a book for Luther to burn.

new measures were put in place to inhibit the sale of heretical books: and for the first time authorities began to publish comprehensive lists of titles. Here the Italians could follow the lead of the two bastions of northern Catholicism, the universities of Paris and Louvain, both of which had also recently drawn up a first listing of forbidden texts.[4]

The development of the Index of Forbidden Books represented a crucial shift in the regulation of the book trade. Instead of concentrating purely on controlling production, the Index anticipated a comprehensive regulation of the trade at the point of sale. This was very significant. From the 1520s onwards most states with a local book industry had taken measures to regulate production. In theory the controls were stringent and comprehensive: publishers wishing to print a new text were required to submit their manuscript for prior approval to a designated local official, usually a leading pastor or cleric. But pre-publication censorship was clumsy and time-consuming. The local censor might sit on texts for some time; fees had to be paid. In practice most printers ignored the regulations, knowing they would only get into trouble if a text they had printed subsequently caused a scandal. Pre-publication authorisation was seldom enforced.

The publication of the first indexes of forbidden books created a problem of a different order of magnitude for the book industry. It signalled that the conflict of ideas had entered a new phase: mere possession of a forbidden text became evidence of heresy. Booksellers faced denunciation by their customers, and confiscation of their stock; printers faced the loss of their press. Each new edition of the Index seemed to draw the boundaries of orthodoxy more narrowly. The 1554 Venetian Index included not only titles of forbidden works, but a long list of Protestant authors and scholars whose works were subject to a blanket ban. The 1559 Roman Index added for good measure a number of Protestant printers: any works printed by these heretical presses were forbidden, whatever their subject matter.[5]

The impact on the print world was profound. The battle of ideas became increasingly polarised. For those out of sympathy with the local orthodoxy the print world had become a dangerous place. Those who were committed to dissident publishing tried various strategies of dissimulation. Sometimes they printed a book with a false place of printing, or simply left their name off the title-page. But the cloak of anonymity seldom succeeded in drawing the authorities off the scent. When a heretical title appeared on the market, the authorities often attempted to identify the printer by taking a copy round the print shops and asking if anyone recognised the type. This generally succeeded in finding the culprit. Most print communities were very close knit; they comprised a relatively small group of artisans, who would be in and out of each others' workshops, often loaning types and ornamental initials. It was hard to disguise a text when your working style was so well known, leaving a distinctive, largely unconscious fingerprint. Even when a printer deliberately printed in the plainest text, a unique feature of the font – a distinctive capital or broken type – could easily give them away.

Why did printers denounce each other in this way? Some, no doubt, acted from conviction. Most Parisian printers shared the Catholic convictions of their compatriots, and were as outraged as other citizens by heretical Protestant publishing. But there was also an economic motive. If regulations prohibited the publication of Protestant or Catholic works, then printers did not want to see others profit from a part of the market from which they were excluded.

Printers soon learned that even if they trusted their workmen, it was virtually impossible to mix disapproved works in with their normal production. Few wished to take the risk. Dangerous work could be undertaken only far away from their normal place of work. For those who put faith ahead of an established livelihood, the only choice was to leave their home, and face an uncertain future abroad.

Nests of heresy

The religious conflicts of the sixteenth century stimulated a massive movement of people, as believers sought a safe place for worship according to their consciences. This had an impact on the European geography of print. Exile radicalised those who went abroad; they became eager consumers of the most violent religious polemic. It also provided an opportunity for printers to make a new career elsewhere.

The refugee diaspora led to the establishment of a number of significant new centres of printing. English Protestant exiles during the reign of Mary Tudor printed in a variety of places in Germany, including the Rhineland towns of Wesel and Strasbourg. Dutch Calvinist exiles established a vibrant press at Emden in northern Germany.[6] By far the most important and influential of these exile printing centres was Geneva. For Geneva possessed an incomparable asset that set it apart: like Wittenberg before it, it could boast a church leader, preacher and author of the first rank, in John Calvin. Just as Luther had in Wittenberg, Calvin made possible the emergence of Geneva as a pre-eminent centre of print culture.

The history of printing in Geneva before Calvin's arrival is the by now familiar story of early promise and rapid decline. In the fifteenth century Geneva established a lively and relatively substantial production of printed books. But in the harsher climate at the end of the century Geneva, like cities elsewhere, found it difficult to compete with the emerging major centres. Such books as were required could just as easily be supplied from Basel, only 50 miles away. For thirty years before the Reformation there was no printer working in the city for much of the time. All this changed with the arrival of

Calvin, who was first appointed to the ministry in 1536; he was permanently settled in Geneva from 1541 to his death in 1564.

Calvin revealed himself to be an author of rare talent and versatility.[7] For any leaders of the Reformation the basis of ministry was preaching. In this Calvin was a master, preaching a continuous sequence of courses on the major books of the Bible with such clarity and force that a relay of scribes was established to take them down verbatim for subsequent publication.[8] His lectures on Scripture to trainee ministers and later students in the new Academy were published in a separate Latin series of biblical commentaries. Most unexpected was that Calvin, until this point a somewhat withdrawn and ascetic figure, revealed himself to be a polemical writer of some talent. A stream of pungent French pamphlets kept the printers busy.

It was the range of these publications that made Calvin so potent a force for the printing industry. When Calvin first arrived in the city, the underdeveloped state of Geneva's publishing industry made it impracticable to produce larger and more scholarly works locally. Until 1548 Calvin sent his larger Latin works to Strasbourg for publication and only his shorter polemical works were given to local Genevan printers. This was an arrangement that suited all parties. Calvin could be assured of high quality and accurate work for his most substantial writings, and access, through Strasbourg, to the large market in the Empire. Meanwhile the Geneva press received the profits generated by the rapid turnover of a sequence of popular vernacular tracts.

As Calvin's reputation grew, the print industry in Geneva was able to put down solid foundations. A critical moment came in 1551, with the arrival of a number of printers with experience of printing elsewhere, including Robert Estienne, scion of the famous Paris printing dynasty. Calvin kept the printers supplied with a steady stream of new works and began to entrust local printers with the serious scholarly works he had previously sent to Strasbourg. Throughout the 1550s and until the year of his death, Calvin's output of original writing for the press never fell below 100,000 words a year.[9] This was despite all his other duties, and persistent, sometimes crippling, ill health. When one takes into account the numbers attracted by Calvin's teaching to study in Geneva, he was undoubtedly the major motor of the Genevan economy by the end of this decade. The city grew in population, wealth and influence.

The Protestant underground

This mass of published works began to have its effect, particularly in Calvin's French homeland. In the 1540s and 1550s the French crown, deeply committed to the maintenance of a Catholic state, observed the birth of a new, more robust dissent. The new king, Henry II, had little doubt of the cause. The Edict of Châteaubriant of 1551 clearly identified Geneva as the source of the infection. French citizens were forbidden all contact with Calvin's city.[10] Despite this, the output of the Genevan presses grew steadily through the 1550s as did their influence in France. The books were carried over the mountains by a small army of travelling salesmen (colporteurs), who risked their lives in this hazardous trade.[11] Other books reached France through Lyon or the Low Countries. Here they were eagerly read by members of the small evangelical communities which now, in defiance of the law, began meeting in cities around the kingdom. The crown seemed powerless to prevent this, particularly after the sudden death of the persecuting king, Henry II. Over the next three years, as France descended into crisis, the French evangelical movement grew exponentially until by 1561 there were reported to be over a thousand congregations, and almost half the nobility had adopted the new faith.

These were heady days for French Protestantism. In 1561 the Genevan ministers brought to a conclusion their translation of the metrical psalms, the communal rite that had become the centre of the Calvinist worship service. The timing was providential, but it was now necessary to bring this book to the new congregations in France, and this posed a considerable challenge. The publication of the psalms was not a simple business, since all editions had to be printed with musical notation. This required special typefaces and expertise. Elsewhere in Europe musical printing tended to be the preserve of a small number of specialists.

To bring the psalms to the fast-growing churches in France the authorities in Geneva orchestrated one of the most remarkable publishing operations of the sixteenth century. The publisher Antoine Vincent was vested with the exclusive rights of the edition, and charged with ensuring the publication of some 30,000 copies.[12] This he achieved by dividing the work among all of Geneva's major printing houses, but also subcontracting a part of the edition to printers within France: in Lyon, Caen, Orléans and even in Paris itself. Vincent achieved his target. The 30,000 copies were brought to the press and shipped to their congregations. Further editions would be printed in the following years.

The publication of the metrical psalms was a monument to the capacities of the Genevan industry. But the involvement of presses within France also signalled a significant shift, and an end to Geneva's position as monopoly provider to the French Huguenot movement. The crisis of authority made it for the first time possible to publish Protestant works within the kingdom in reasonable safety, and of course in much greater proximity to the new market.

Fig. 41 The Huguenot Psalter. The simultaneous publication of the Huguenot Psalter in multiple locations in 1562 was one of the most complex publishing ventures of the century. It remained a steady bestseller to the end of the century, and beyond, although still a specialist task for those printing houses that possessed the necessary special type for musical notation.

The Protestant presses established in Normandy and Lyon were a natural response to this evolving market opportunity.

The new presses in Caen, Lyon and Orléans were soon turning out hundreds of books: catechisms and church orders for the new churches, but also more polemical works, sharply critical of the Roman Church and its clergy.[13] In Lyon there developed a powerful tradition of satirical verse writing, which drew on the congregations' growing familiarity with the metrical psalms. Political poems were published with the instruction that they should be sung 'to the tune of Psalm 62'. Musical notation was not considered necessary with these small pamphlets, for the tunes would by now have been familiar enough. The Psalms were no longer merely the core of the worship service, but the cultural badge of identity of the new Church, sung on all occasions: in the church, at the workplace or home, or on the streets.

The speed with which these new songs were composed was often quite extraordinary. At the zenith of the French Calvinist movement in 1562, the congregations mounted a bold coup that gave them temporary control of Lyon, second city of France. A pamphlet celebrating this triumph was on the streets of Lyon the same day. A rare surviving copy of this pamphlet, recently discovered in Aix-en-Provence, shows evidence of the haste of composition, with smudging and a very basic unitary typeface.[14] But it is not crude, either in poetical form or vocabulary. These were pamphlets written by and for a bourgeois church membership. They represent a confident assertion of right by a movement that expected to carry all before it.

The vocabulary of hate

The Protestant onslaught on Catholic orthodoxy in France was frantic and intense but it was not uncontested. As authority drained away from the royal government, Catholic authors found their voice, warning against compromise and denouncing those of the new religion; or as they put it 'of the so-called reformed religion' (*religion pretendue reformée*). These books too found an eager public. For the first time the Reformation conflicts were pursued by both sides with equal passion.

In this respect the religious conflicts of the second half of the century deviate sharply from the situation of the press in Germany in the first Reformation era. Although Catholic opponents of Luther eventually found a voice, there is no denying that evangelicals commanded overwhelming advantage in terms of published output: building on the enormous popularity of Luther's own writings they out-published their opponents by a margin of nine to one.[15] In this they were undoubtedly assisted by orthodox doubts about whether theological debate should be shared with a lay vernacular audience. In France there seems to have been no such doubt. Even in the first generation French Catholic authors presented themselves for service, with brusque denunciations of the German heresy and eloquent defences of Catholic belief.[16] When the Huguenot threat became most potent they were primed and ready to combat heresy anew.

The murderous intensity of the conflicts that erupted in France after 1562 finds its echo in the violence of these pamphlet exchanges. The doctors of the Sorbonne who took to the pulpits and then to print to combat the new heresies ranged far beyond the confutation of disputed points of doctrine. For them the Calvinist insurgency struck at the heart of French society, its values, its integrity and the authority of French sacral monarchy.

Catholic authors directly confronted the Protestant claim to be the purveyors of true doctrine.[17] The Huguenot challenge to the established Church was an attack on the social order itself: they saw the establishment of separate Protestant congregations as an attack on the fundamental unity of French society. This would have struck a chord with many who saw neighbours who had once been friends now absenting themselves from church, or worse, parading the streets singing psalms. Divisions cut deep as individuals made the painful decision to abandon or uphold traditional allegiances. Catholic authors addressed these fears. The Protestants were to blame for the fissures that had opened up in French society. Their doctrines encouraged disobedience, and disorder within families. They set wife against husband, children against parents. Such disorders were a reflection of the great threat to the unity of the kingdom:

> It will come to pass that the husband will be of one opinion and his wife of another, the children and the servants will be of another, so that there will be nothing but disagreement and rebellion. Finally it will follow that the son will want to kill the father, the brother his brother . . . because heresy is such that as soon as it makes its way into a house, city or kingdom, it brings such division and discord that the husband disagrees with his own wife, the servants and citizens with one another, and the subjects with their lord.[18]

By breaking away from the Church Protestants committed spiritual adultery. If the true Church was the bride of Christ, then heresy was a whore. Catholic preachers promoted the darkest suspicions about what occurred in private Protestant gatherings. Catholic propagandists evoked ancient nightmares of heretics conducting a parody of the Mass, drinking the blood and eating the flesh of a murdered infant conceived during their dark nocturnal orgies. Such charges, incredible to the modern ear, draw on a rich heritage of stereotypes, reaching back to the persecutions of the early Christian

Church but also invoking the despised and outcasts of the medieval era. The accusations of ritual sacrifice were a sinister echo of the medieval blood libel against the Jews. Protestantism was seen as a spiritual leprosy, from which good Christians must be isolated. Most tellingly and persistently, the Huguenots were compared to the medieval heretics, the Albigensians, who had challenged the unity of the Church in France. The Albigensians had been put down with great brutality in a long military campaign. As in those days now long past, so the modern heretic must be exterminated.

Elimination, amputation – the language was unambiguous. Catholic preachers begged the crown to confront heresy and root it out. To compromise was to sacrifice the Christian unity that was essential to faith. The articulation of these views, by men who commanded the pulpits of Paris as well as the Parisian print shops, undermined the crown's attempts to promote reconciliation. Only when the crown embraced a policy of uncompromising opposition to heresy did Paris show its support: by turning their knives on the neighbours they had been taught to believe no longer shared the common attributes of humanity.

The St Bartholomew's Day massacre in Paris was wildly celebrated throughout Catholic Europe as a turning-point in the fight against heresy. The news of the destruction of the flower of the Huguenot nobility and the rampage through Paris evoked stunned horror in Protestant Europe. But if the scale of the ferocity was unprecedented, the event itself was long prepared in the preaching and pamphleteering of the Parisian clergy.

It is hard to deny that with the pamphlet exchanges of these years the religious controversies of the sixteenth century took on a new and poisonous intensity. Modern scholars of this literature see, with justice, many of the characteristics of modern propaganda: the endless repetition of the same baleful message about the adversary, who is discredited by crude smears and parodies; the reduction of complex social change to a simple confrontation between good and evil.[19] But the Catholic writings (and their antithesis in the anti-clerical satires of the Huguenots) were not crude, nor were their authors unsophisticated. Rather they offered explanations and solutions to a disorder that the inhabitants of France could observe all too clearly in their own communities, neighbourhoods and families. They did so by evoking shared Christian values and a shared patriotic heritage that offered a healing balm and the promise of a more ordered future. It was not difficult to understand why angry and bewildered citizens, resenting a stubborn minority who proclaimed virtue while promoting disorder, might think their Christian duty lay in helping to rid society of this pollution; and why they rejoiced when this was achieved.

War and the marketplace

The conflicts in France soon found their counterpoint elsewhere in western Europe, particularly in the seventeen provinces of the Low Countries, the restless northern outpost of the empire of Philip II, King of Spain. For a time events here moved on a strange parallel with France. The crisis came in 1566 when Margaret of Parma, regent for the absentee Philip of Spain, was coerced into proclaiming a limited toleration. The Low Countries erupted in a summer of demonstrative public preaching, orchestrated by Calvinist ministers and eagerly abetted by many hundreds who hurried back from exile. Through July and August in the fields outside the urban centres great crowds gathered to hear the sermons and sing together the Calvinist metrical psalms. Fascinated Catholic observers, who had journeyed out to observe these unprecedented public gatherings, noted carts parked on the edge of the crowds doing a brisk trade in cheap editions of the catechism, church orders and books of psalms.[20] Some were supplied from Emden, the established centre of Dutch exile printing, and others by local printers who had joined the trade in this moment of maximum demand. One alert if unscrupulous entrepreneur had decorated his books with a re-cut version of the elegant and distinctive printer's device of the leading Emden printer, Gellius Ctematius. Ctematius had been responsible for the first quasi-official editions of the Dutch Reformed Confessions, and his *Schat in der Acker* device was an easily recognised seal of quality. Here it was appropriated by an altogether less prestigious firm.[21]

The heady moment of evangelical freedom proved short-lived. By the end of the year the government was back in control, and an army *en route* from Spain to punish the guilty. Many thousands who had joined the new churches fled abroad. The new governor, the Duke of Alva, took brutal retribution against those who remained. The presses of Antwerp, once again obedient, returned nervously to their normal trade. Their first task for Alva's regime was to publish a new Index of Forbidden Books, carefully listing the evangelical texts that had circulated so abundantly in recent years.[22]

These measures did not succeed in stifling dissent. By 1572, a new invasion, this time led by Prince William of Orange, reignited the conflict. It would be forty years before the fighting was brought to a close by the foundation of a new free state and the permanent partition of the provinces: the southern part (now Belgium) remained under Spanish control.

All of this, the ebb and flow of the military conflict, and the frantic turmoil of the battle of ideas, had a powerful impact on the Netherlandish publishing industry. In the years immediately before the Dutch Revolt Antwerp had been

Fig. 42 A short account of the siege of Alkmaar, 1573. The twists and turns of the religious wars in northern Europe were eagerly followed by the public. This text was published in Delft, on one of the first presses to be established in the rebellious Northern Provinces. Later they would completely eclipse the previously dominant metropolis, Antwerp.

one of Europe's most cosmopolitan printing towns. Between 1520 and 1576 the city's printers were responsible for well over half the books published in the Low Countries. The demand for devotional texts, almanacs, news books and bibles generated large profits, which printers were able to reinvest in more ambitious projects. By the second half of the century Antwerp had also become a major centre of scholarly publishing.

All of this was put at risk by the Dutch Revolt. Even for printers who attempted to avoid partisan involvement, it was not easy to remain above the fray. The difficulties of the times can be well illustrated by the trouble that beset one of the most successful publishers of the sixteenth century: Christophe Plantin.[23] Plantin, a native of France, had moved to Antwerp at a young age to take advantage of the business opportunities opening up in the vibrant city. Early in his career he received a salutary lesson in the dangers of the times. In 1562 a text of doubtful orthodoxy was found to have been printed with his types and Plantin was accused of heresy. He escaped serious punishment only by claiming, rather discreditably, that the book had been printed by his workmen without his knowledge while he was out of Antwerp.[24] The excuse was accepted, if not believed; in the following years, with the help of wealthy business partners, he gradually rebuilt his business. But Plantin had learned his lesson. Whatever his own personal religious views, he was careful to cleave to the prevailing local orthodoxy. The standing orders of his print shop forbade the discussion of religion.

By a combination of outstanding technical skill and business flair Plantin built one of the largest publishing enterprises in Europe. His output developed from the small literary and religious works that had been an early speciality to embrace every aspect of scholarly print, along with the new discipline of cartography. Plantin was a regular visitor to the Frankfurt Fair, where he routinely shifted several thousand copies of his newest titles. His firm built a commanding role in the supply of imported scholarly works for the English market.[25]

But even a firm like Plantin's was not immune to the consequences of the military struggle. By 1576, after four years of attritional fighting, the Spanish treasury was exhausted. A large force of Spanish troops descended on Antwerp to extract from the commercial metropolis the wages they were owed. The result was the Sack of Antwerp, an orgy of violence that lasted three days and left 10,000 dead: more than the victims of the St Bartholomew's Day massacre.

Plantin's business was brought to the brink of collapse. With Spanish mutineers roaming the streets in search of loot, he was forced to pay ransom money on nine occasions to prevent his premises being set ablaze. When the dust settled, a business which at its peak operated twenty-four presses had only one still functioning. Plantin now embarked on a long winter journey, to Liège, Paris and finally Frankfurt, to raise money to pay back the friend who had advanced him cash for the ransom.[26]

The Plantin press had the resources to survive and rebuild; but Plantin was too astute a businessman not to take precautions for the future. Over the

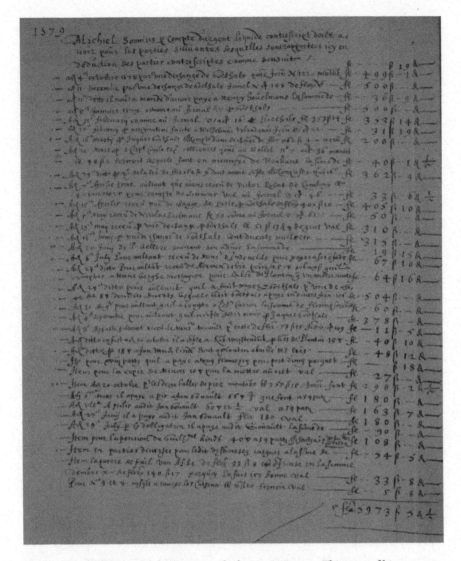

Fig. 43 Christophe Plantin's business was the largest in Europe. This page of his account book represents half the transactions with a single Paris bookseller, Michael Sonnius, in one year. His meticulous bookkeeping also makes this archive an indispensable treasure trove for historians.

following years an increasing proportion of the scholarly publishing of the Plantin press was transferred to a branch business in the rebel provinces, in the new university town of Leiden, in the province of Holland.[27] This was the harbinger of a more general reorientation of Low Countries printing from south to north, a movement that gathered pace after Antwerp was restored to

Spanish rule in 1585. Many printers were among those who moved north, to Leiden, Amsterdam, Dordrecht, Delft and Rotterdam. Antwerp's output of books fell precipitously, to around 25 per cent of the total Low Countries production. The age of Antwerp as a printing metropolis was over. In the new century much of this economic vitality would pass to the new commercial giant, Amsterdam.

A church in England

Warfare could have a traumatic impact upon a mature print culture. Against this, as we have seen in relation to Luther's lifetime, religious controversy could be a considerable stimulus to the activities of the printing press. This seems to have been the case with both England and Germany in the second half of the century.

During the reign of Elizabeth the English printing industry took great steps towards the maturity and independence that had eluded it in the first century of print. The industry remained small, and largely confined to the capital, London. But the second half of the sixteenth century saw a significant enlargement of its capacities. In the initial period of Elizabeth's reign output recovered strongly after the doldrums of the latter half of Mary's reign, and London printers took on some notably ambitious projects (such as Foxe's Book of Martyrs, the *Actes and Monuments*). Thereafter the industry exhibited steady growth through the middle years of the reign, with an increase in output of 30 per cent in the 1570s, and a further 30 per cent in the 1580s. By the last decade of the century the average yearly output was double that of the first year of Elizabeth's reign.[28]

The bedrock of this growth was the market for religious books. At the beginning of the reign the creation of a new settlement of religion involved a range of pressing tasks. It was necessary to establish a new national church order; to inculcate the principles of the Protestant faith among the wider population; and to defend the Elizabethan Church against both foreign enemies and domestic critics. All of these tasks were pursued through the medium of print.

The defence of the new church order occupied many of the most able minds of the Elizabethan settlement. John Jewel's *Apology of the Church of England* was an officially sponsored work. Published in 1562, first in Latin for an international readership, then in an English translation by Anne Bacon, wife of Lord Chancellor Sir Nicolas Bacon, the *Apology* provided the intellectual justification for England's separation from the Church of Rome. It also provided the spur for an energetic counter-argument by dispossessed Catholic prelates who had withdrawn to the continent rather than accept the new Church. Thomas Harding's *Answer* (to Jewel's Paul Cross Sermon of 1559) and his *Confutation* of Jewel's *Apology*, were both published, as was so much of the English Catholic literature of this period, in the Low Countries.[29] Most of the English Catholic polemicists made use of one of a small number of presses in either Louvain or Antwerp run by sympathetic printers: Jan de Laet, Jan Fouler, Aegidius van Diest and Jean Bogard. From here the English writings found their way back across the Channel, as had the writings of Protestant exiles in the first half of the century.

Harding's *Answer* set off a brisk exchange which continued until the death of Harding and Jewel within a year of each other, in 1571 and 1572. The close attention with which they had followed each other's works suggests a mutual intellectual respect which was not typical of this literature as a whole. When during these years exiled Catholic authors returned again and again to the central issues of authority and legitimacy, the representatives of the Elizabethan establishment were often slow to respond. Public interest seems to have been muted. Few of the controversial writings, on either side of the debate, merited more than a single edition. Throughout the controversies of the 1560s the greater urgency lay on the Catholic side, fuelled by a sense of injustice and dispossession.

The English authorities were concerned most with the impact of Catholic writing on international opinion. Latin works written for an international audience did not go unanswered. In 1573 they commissioned two separate responses to Nicholas Sanders's masterly *De visibili monarchia ecclesiae* (The visible monarchy of the church), a work that won widespread acclaim in the international Catholic community.[30] Sanders was Professor of Theology at the University of Louvain, and his views carried weight. The Catholic controversialists were often men of considerable intellectual stature. Those who took up their pen against the Elizabethan Settlement included Richard Smith, previously one of the leading theologians of Marian Oxford, Thomas Stapleton and William Allen. Nicholas Harpsfield contrived to write his *Dialogi sex* against Jewel's *Apology* while incarcerated in the Tower of London.

While the leaders of the new Church recognised the need to engage with Catholic criticisms, the impact of this controversial energy is hard to measure. The Protestant authors had much else to do in building their new Church; answering the criticism from abroad was but one of the many calls on their time. Aside from the multiple problems of creating an adequate preaching ministry they also had to fend off criticism from within – from men they might have thought of as allies in the struggle to create a new evangelical nation.

Unforgiving friends

The outrage of deposed Catholic prelates was to be expected. Few in the Elizabethan hierarchy could have anticipated the speed with which disenchantment would spread among Protestant zealots, many of them former colleagues of the Marian exiles. The first confrontation, over clerical dress, found only a faint echo in print.[31] Although the Vestment Controversy led to the dismissal of a significant portion of the London preaching ministry, no press in London could be found to publish the opinions of the dissident ministers.[32] This would be a recurrent theme of the confrontations between the Anglican establishment and their increasingly embittered opponents. The *Admonition to Parliament*, the literary highlight of the Presbyterian Parliamentary campaign of 1572, was published on a specially established press in Hemel Hempstead (Hertfordshire), 40 miles out of London.[33] This press, like all subsequent similar ventures, proved short-lived. In 1573 a royal proclamation ordered the suppression of this and Cartwright's *Second Admonition* and the author fled abroad. Cartwright's further answer to Archbishop Whitgift was put to the press in two parts at Basel and Heidelberg. The Hemel Hempstead press was dismantled.

This case illustrates very well the uneven struggle facing critics of the Elizabethan regime in bringing their views to a wider public. If it was difficult to persuade a London printer to take on projects critical of the regime, it was almost impossible to maintain a press outside London and escape detection. In 1580 and 1581 a fugitive Catholic press was briefly operating at East Ham in Essex. This managed only five small tracts.[34] The overwhelming proportion of Catholic polemic, in both Latin and English, was published abroad.

The most audacious attempt to publish books critical of the regime in England was the work of a dissident London printer, Robert Waldegrave, publisher of the Marprelate tracts. These irreverent, malicious and often very funny diatribes against the establishment were printed on a press that Waldegrave set up first at East Molesey near Kingston upon Thames. As the authorities closed in, Waldegrave moved first to the home of a sympathetic Puritan in Northamptonshire, and thence to Coventry. The final Marprelate tracts were printed at yet another location, at Wolston in Warwickshire.[35] Yet this was a strategy always destined to fail. The more rural the location, the more certain it was that a printing press would attract attention and the greater the difficulty of securing necessary supplies of paper and ink.

Waldegrave abandoned Marprelate just in time; his collaborators were not so fortunate. Criticism and ridicule had touched a sensitive nerve, and several of those taken in the search for culprits suffered exemplary punishment. The separatist critics of the Elizabethan Church that emerged in the last decade of the reign, the supporters of Henry Barrow and the Brownists, wisely did not repeat the doomed experiment of the fugitive press. Instead they looked once more abroad, and particularly to the newly established print centres of the free northern Netherlands. Here during the 1590s a sizeable number of tracts were published, for the use of the nascent separatist exile communities and their adepts in England. At least seventy separate works were published during these years, at Amsterdam, Leiden and Dordrecht, and especially at Middelburg, where the press of Richard Schilders became the principal voice of English dissent.[36] The English works of adherents of the Family of Love were published in Cologne.[37]

Building a church

Most of the major London printers, from John Daye to Henry Bynneman, played their part in publishing controversial literature. But they seem to have done so mainly out of a sense of duty. In England controversy was not a main driver of the trade in religious literature. Controversial works make up only a tiny proportion of the avalanche of religious publications that were the bulwark of the book industry. The real bestsellers were bibles (and subsidiary partial editions of the Scripture, such as psalters), catechisms and sermons.[38]

The quantities of this literature published were very impressive. Catechisms and primers catered for every level of theological instruction, from the youngest child to the curious adult.[39] More complex theological questions were taken up in a broad range of treatises and in sermons. The massive demand for religious publications generated a number of palpable bestsellers, books reprinted in many editions and often published over a long time span. These books were those most prized in the trade, and jealously guarded against industry competitors.

The steady profits they generated gradually enlarged the capacities and ambitions of the London print trade. This remained, by European standards, small and rather conservative. Even at the end of the century the needs of the market could be served by twenty-five London firms operating a total of fifty-three presses, and even those would not have worked at full capacity.[40] The development of a provincial press was inhibited by the fierce defence of the London monopoly. The alliance between the English government and the London Stationers' Company was self-serving: both believed they benefited from retaining tight control of an industry more heavily concentrated on a limited range of literature than in any other part of Europe. But despite this, religious publications made a major contribution to building a body of believers that, by the end of the sixteenth century, identified with increasing intensity with the Church established in England.

Luther's legacy

In Germany the passing of the great reformer in 1546 found the Protestant churches in contemplative mood. At least they were able to reassure their congregations that Luther had died well. He had not, as had been gleefully predicted by Catholic critics, been dragged by the Devil, roaring and lamenting, to his place in hell. His friend Lucas Cranach, who had done more than anyone to fix the iconic image of Luther, journeyed to Eisenach to make one last representation of Luther, his features in death in calm repose. The story of Luther's passing was preached from the pulpit, and then circulated in print.[41]

Those who marked Luther's death were not to know that the greatest test of German Protestantism was imminent. As Luther's obsequies were celebrated, the Emperor Charles V was assembling an army to confront German Lutheranism. In April 1547 the Protestant army was shattered at the battle of Mühlberg and Charles was able to enforce a settlement of religion that had eluded him during Luther's lifetime. The Augsburg Interim of 1548 commanded the restoration of Catholic ceremonies, while permitting the continuation of communion in both kinds. Many Protestant cities conformed; even Philip Melanchthon, Luther's spiritual heir at Wittenberg, was able to satisfy himself that the Emperor's prescriptions, though unpalatable, could be tolerated.

Others did not agree. Lutheranism found a more resolute standard-bearer in Matthias Flaccius Illyricus, a former colleague of Melanchthon who now left Wittenberg and settled in the independent city of Magdeburg. For the next three years Magdeburg would be the symbol of defiance for Lutherans determined to resist the Emperor's settlement, sustained by a torrent of pamphlets from the city's presses.[42] The eventual resolution of the conflict, the Peace of Augsburg of 1555, was a triumphant vindication of those who had upheld the defence of the Church.

The conflicts of these years would define the character of German Lutheranism for a generation. Tried in the fire of the Schmalkaldic War, German Lutherans saw little scope for doctrinal equivocation. In the second half of the century the articulation and defence of orthodoxy became a pressing, defining characteristic of Lutheran identity. This became an urgent public issue when, in 1563, the Elector Palatine, one of the principal princes of the Empire, orchestrated the adoption in his dominions of the Reformed faith. The inevitable collision of Calvinist and Lutheran forces within the Empire was made more volatile by the obvious appeal of Calvinist theology to Lutherans in the more irenic and intellectually flexible tradition of Philip Melanchthon, a figure now despised and distrusted by the orthodox.

The prolonged struggle for the soul of Luther's Church generated a huge controversial literature. Its impact on the mass of the church population is however uncertain. Theological exposition and controversy generated around 1,300 titles: an impressive quantity, but a small portion of the total output of religious works from the German presses in this era. The bedrock of religious print remained the same categories of book that had fuelled the German press since the first polemical fires had dimmed in the late 1520s: bibles, psalters, catechisms and prayer books. To this agenda, largely similar to the published output of the English presses, the German tradition added certain distinctive features of its own. The greater number of urban communities and diversity of print centres spawned a large market for published sermons. Preaching lay at the heart of the pastoral mission, and many ministers preached incessantly; pastoral routines often required up to four sermons a week, that is 200 a year. To guide the less experienced there were postils or epitomes to lead the minister through the ordered regimen of scriptural lessons that formed the basis of sermons.

This preaching activity leaves a considerable footprint in published texts. Between 1542 and 1565 the minister of Joachimstal, Johannes Mathesius, is reckoned to have preached 5,000 sermons; of these, some 1,500 were published.[43] In addition to the regular round of congregational preaching, German Lutheranism discovered a particular taste for funeral sermons, preached at the graveside and subsequently published, often paid for by the grieving family. The genre reached its peak of popularity in the seventeenth century, generating a scarcely credible 200,000 examples.

This tells its own story. The ultimate success of Lutheran and Anglican churches in building religious consciousness relied less on treatises and controversy than on catechisms, domestic religious observance, and the patient ordered regularity of congregational worship. Nothing demonstrates this more emphatically than the quintessential innovation of the Lutheran worship tradition, the hymnal. Luther was an enthusiastic writer of hymns, firmly believing that music played a crucial role in inculcating the principles of religion.[44] The popularity of congregational singing in Germany was a vindication of this confidence. Among the litany of complaints recorded by the exhaustive Lutheran church visitations at the end of the sixteenth century, weakness of congregational singing was seldom mentioned.[45] The Lutheran people were eager to sing. Hymn writing remained a popular activity for musically inclined pastors throughout the century. None, even Catholic composers, could escape Luther's legacy. Of 249 hymns in one Catholic hymnal of 1567, a third were adopted from Protestant texts. All told, Germany's printing presses published around 2,000 hymn editions between 1520 and 1600, a total of some two million copies.[46] Overwhelmingly these were for congregational and domestic use, almost invariably in the small octavo format. Some contained text specially prepared for use at home. A striking testimony to the value of this domestic hymn singing comes in Paul Eber's preface to Herman's *Sonntags-Evangelia*. According to Eber, singing hymns at home, combined with patient explanation, could do more good than 'a lengthy and carefully prepared sermon'; an astonishing statement from one of the Lutheran Church's indefatigable preaching ministers.[47]

Domestic piety, congregational worship and bitter controversy: all combined to ensure a continuing healthy trade in religious books through the second half of the sixteenth century. To a quite unprecedented extent this expansive publishing world remained centred on the writings of the German Church's first founder, and his contested legacy. Martin Luther – pastor, preceptor and theological lodestar – sailed untarnished through the squalls of successive generations, his works reprinted in substantial numbers in every decade to the end of the century. His physical features were recalled in numerous illustrated broadsheets; his hymns were sung in every church. This reverence for the Reformer on occasion took unusual forms, such as the tradition of the incombustible Luther: a portrait of the Reformer said to have been recovered undamaged from the ashes of a house destroyed by fire.[48] Reverend commemoration reached its climax with the great ceremonial that attended the hundredth anniversary of the Reformation in 1617. For this anniversary year many commemorative works were published, along with medals and special ceremonies of thanksgiving.[49] It was a strange Indian summer of the German Reformation, and of the German print industry, played out amidst the gathering storms of the Habsburg succession crisis that would shortly ignite the Thirty Years' War.

Testing times

The second half of the sixteenth century was a testing time for the European print world. For publishers prepared to enter the market for religious instruction, there were rich pickings. But for those engaged in the international book trade, war, conflict and the new climate of regulation created incalculable difficulties. Moving books from place to place inevitably meant that consignments passed through different jurisdictions, some Protestant, some Catholic. Everywhere they were subject to scrutiny and confiscation. Publishers and booksellers active in the international scholarly trade particularly resented the blanket ban on all books written by an author who happened to be a known heretic. This meant that they could neither publish nor sell a variety of established legal texts, medical books, grammars or dictionaries because their author (Melanchthon, for instance) was tainted. The problem became acute when dealing with anthologies or compendia that included works by many authors. Bookmen grumbled, but not too loudly. Publishers knew that if they associated too closely with dissent they risked being added to the list of those whose works were subject to a blanket prohibition.

These complexities made for troubling times. The canny publishers adapted. Both printers and authors began to trim their sails, adopting a form of self-censorship in anticipation of a more stringent examination. The Italian publisher Giolito, innovative publisher of poetry anthologies in the 1550s, now abandoned his most provocative texts. Instead of the works of Aretino he turned out multiple editions of the devotional texts of the Spanish author Luis de Granada.[50] In this way it was possible to survive and even prosper. But nothing could insulate publishers from disruption to international trade by war or roving bands of soldiers, as Plantin and the suffering printers of Paris in the 1590s could testify. Most of all the print world yearned for stability. Government efforts to promote order could rely on their enthusiastic support.

CHAPTER 11

>~~ ✳ ~~<

THE SEARCH FOR ORDER

In January 1576, and for three years thereafter, King Henry III of France would retire to his study twice weekly after lunch to hear specially arranged lectures. Those who spoke, and others present, included the leading poets, writers and philosophers then attending the French court.[1] Some of the king's advisers questioned whether at a time of national crisis the monarch should devote such time to philosophical debate. But the much-travelled monarch was determined to complete his political education with lectures on ambition, honour and anger. This, admittedly, was a quality not in short supply four years after the massacre of St Bartholomew's Day.

The new king was a man whom the French political nation found perplexingly difficult to read. As heir to the throne he had been the great hope of Catholicism, a titan in the military campaign against the Huguenots, and a hero of St Bartholomew's Day. Henry's election as King of Poland capped a glittering career. But when Charles IX died in 1574 Henry abandoned Poland with indecent haste. Having ridden hard and fast to make it to the Polish border before the court discovered his disappearance, Henry then occupied a further three months in an indulgent perambulation around northern Italy. His reception, in a series of lavish ceremonial entries, was reported to an increasingly anxious French public in a sequence of printed accounts.[2] The pressing affairs of the kingdom were meanwhile left in the hands of the queen mother. When Henry finally returned to his capital it was to a restless and distrustful political nation. Was this the man to solve the problems of a divided country?

This was the context for Henry's innovative attempt to devise an active political philosophy through conversation with the French capital's greatest minds. There could be no doubt that after a decade of civil war France was in a very perilous position. A restless nobility, urban communities traumatised by riots and massacre, an alienated and heavily armed Protestant minority: all of these problems pressed upon the king, along with a welter of conflicting advice. For observers of the sixteenth-century book world what is fascinating is that in trying to come to grips with the urgent need for peace and reconciliation, France's leaders reached for nostrums and strategies derived from the common corpus of their classical learning. After years of discord and open warfare, almost the only thing that united France's political classes was a common political vocabulary, derived from a shared tradition of education and reading. It remained to be seen what hope this offered for finding tangible solutions to the nation's intractable problems.

Rights and obligations

Henry's initial attempts to promote harmony achieved little success. A meeting of the Estates-General produced no resolution of the critical question of the moment: whether peace could be restored by reasserting Catholic unity, or by continued accommodation of the Huguenot minority. The only way forward lay in persuading the political nation to accept the king's authority through a series of separate local negotiations. In 1578 the king's commissioners fanned out across France to undertake this daunting task. It required all of their rhetorical skills: in time of need they reached for the classics.

At the Estates of Normandy Jacques de Bauquemaure cited Isocrates: the whole office of a king consisted in ensuring the well-being of his subjects. Henry III was no Lycurgus, enforcing peace by military means (Lycurgus was the law-giver of Sparta, and the example was drawn from Plutarch). Switching metaphors Bauquemaure then compared the passions of a state to the four elements: they must be balanced just as fire and earth were kept in measure by air and water. Returning in 1579 the king's representative expanded this frame of reference further, citing Plato and then, turning once more to Plutarch, examples of kings who had raised false hopes by promising to abolish taxes.

Bauquemaure was here drawing upon a range of texts that would have been familiar to his audience in French translation. Most widely disseminated were Jacques Amyot's magnificent French Plutarch, first published in 1559. French printers turned out over 250 editions of Plutarch's writings in various combinations during the sixteenth century.[3] Also highly influential was the collection of the writings of Isocrates and Xenophon published by Louis Le Roy, *Enseignements pour bien regner en paix et en guerre*.[4]

Bauquemaure's eloquence, though widely admired, did not achieve its immediate objective of securing compliance with the king's command. The same repertoire of classical examples was freely available to those who urged different policy choices, and indeed they were liberally employed by representatives of the provincial Estates to make their case. In an audience before the king Nicolas Boucheret, representing the Estates of Burgundy, drew on both Tacitus and Plutarch to remind Henry of the king's duty to his subjects. Rather courageously Boucheret also evoked both Tiberius, whose harsh rule had caused civil war, and Alexander of Macedon, as an absolute ruler who had surrounded himself with favourites. Those urging that lasting peace could follow only from the erasure of past offences could call on Seneca: 'Optima civilis belli defensio, oblivio est' ('the best defence against civil war is to forget'). The text was printed on the title-page of Antoine Loisel's discourse to the *chambre de justice* at Agen in 1582.[5] Perhaps recognising the ultimate futility of such classical ping-pong, another of the king's representatives, the veteran Jean de Montluc, tried a different tack, promising simple plain speaking. He would not, he said, beguile them with 'beautiful speeches, enriched with examples from Plato, Aristotle and Plutarch'.[6]

These exchanges, at a time when the French political nation was groping its way towards solutions to bitter, apparently intractable conflicts, demonstrate, if not the democratisation of learning, then at least the ubiquity of learned reference. By this point a fairly comprehensive range of the major political and historical writings of the ancients had been rendered into French, many of them during the great burst of literary creativity of the 1540s and 1550s. The king, Francis I, had been an active patron of such endeavours, persuading Jacques de Vintimille to undertake a translation of Xenophon's *Cyropaedia*.[7] De Vintimille also translated Herodian and Machiavelli. A number of translators mixed in this manner milestones of classical learning and modern Italian works. Others, like Louis Le Roy, undertook translation alongside their own original writings. Le Roy's influential survey of the fall of empires, *De la Vicissitude ou variete des choses*, was informed by his success as a translator and editor of a number of important texts by Aristotle and Xenophon, as well as Plato's *Symposium*. Aristotle in particular enjoyed something of a vogue, the attention to his political writings in some measure compensating for the gradual erosion of his influence on the natural sciences. For those too busy to immerse themselves fully in the classical authorities there were helpful short cuts, compendia of extracts for particular occasions. Cicero, of course, was ubiquitous. The advice proffered to Henry III included the suggestion that he should commission a new translation of *De officiis*, to be read to him a chapter a day. This is somewhat puzzling, as French translations of this work had been freely available in print since the fifteenth century.[8] Perhaps it reflected a sense that, even a century into the age of print, only a fine manuscript was fit to read to a king.

Warnings from Scripture

There is little doubt that in the second half of the sixteenth century, classical authors, especially Seneca, Cicero and Plutarch, provided the starting point for the discussion of virtue in public life. But in troubled times orators drew with equal facility on another ubiquitous repertoire of political and moral precepts: the Bible. To Protestant audiences King Henry's representatives quoted Isaiah blessing the feet of those who brought peace to Jerusalem. Catholics were served up Jeremiah. But this was a contest in which the king's men were easily outgunned, for Protestants had long appropriated the text of vernacular Scripture. In desperate times it was here that they turned to justify violations of the accepted political norms.

Kings and rulers were compared with King David. Virtuous queens were Deborah and youthful princes exhorted to godly rule inevitably Josiah. In moments of conflict other less flattering archetypes sprang to mind. David could easily become Saul, the jealous, unjust persecutor. Deborah might be Jezebel, whose gruesome fate was a warning to all who flouted God's law. The self-righteous selectivity of the Protestant use of Scripture goaded some Catholic authors beyond endurance. Arnaud Sorbin was not alone in pointing up the hypocrisy that when the Huguenot armies pillaged and burned, they claimed to be chastising the Amorites and Canaanites; when royal armies responded, the king was Pharaoh, Nebuchadnezzar or Holofernes.[9]

Though the point was well made, Protestants were not in any way deterred. The use of Scripture to justify resistance and acts of violence against the established political authority was now a central part of the political vocabulary.

The revolutionary potential of the Protestant Reformation was obvious from the moment of Luther's defiant repudiation of papal authority. It took political form at the Diet of Speyer in 1529, when the evangelical states were forced to articulate their refusal to accept the majority position. The doctrine articulated here, that 'in matters touching divine honour and the salvation of our souls, each man must stand alone before God' was one that clearly carried its own dangers. The Peasants' War of 1525 and the horrors of the Anabaptist take-over of Münster a decade later demonstrated the awful consequence of the unrestrained application of Divine Law to political affairs. Luther had learned his lesson. When asked by groups outside Germany whether they should abandon the local Catholic church, Luther invariably counselled political obedience. This was the beginning of an instinctive loyalism to the state power that lasted through to the twentieth century.

For German Lutheranism this became uncomfortable only when Protestants who had tasted the experience of living in a godly state felt once more embattled and under threat. The growing alienation of the Emperor Charles V from the German Protestant princes forced Lutheran theologians to explore cautiously the theoretical grounds for armed defence of their new religious freedoms. The Emperor, Lutheran jurists reminded their readers, was elected under conditions which circumscribed his rights and duties.[10] The defeat of the Protestant army in the Schmalkaldic War of 1547 and the Emperor's determination to impose his own religious settlement led to the development of a new doctrine of German resistance. For four years the city of Magdeburg was the symbol of a defiance expressed in a sudden torrent of printed manifestos. Most acknowledged the authority of the Emperor in worldly matters, while defending the right to uphold the cause of true religion. The city, it was promised, would cease resistance in return for a guarantee of religious freedom and traditional religious prerogatives.

Here the juristic argument and Scripture came together in a reasoned claim of right. But such calm, measured statements were given spice by pamphlets that were far more incendiary in tone. The Magdeburg presses, until then negligible, turned out over 400 editions in the space of four years. These pamphlets identified the forces ranged against the city as the agents of the papal Antichrist. They called down ridicule and contempt upon their opponents as hypocrites and trimmers.

The presence in Magdeburg of the unreconciled Lutheran theologian Matthias Flaccius Illyricus gave this press campaign intellectual coherence, but the pamphlets were marked by a great deal of stylistic variety. The texts include songs, prayers, bawdy satirical verse, news prints and historical reflections as well as more sophisticated theological treatises. Flaccius could call upon a considerable network of sympathisers in other cities who supplied the Magdeburg authors with documents and information. This permitted the pamphleteers to put into the public domain a number of private documents that their original authors would have preferred to remain secret. A notable example was a letter of Philip Melanchthon sharply critical of the Augsburg Interim on theological grounds.[11] Its publication made Melanchthon's later acceptance of the Interim seem self-serving and hypocritical. The greatest coup was the exposure of a letter from Pope Paul III to the Swiss Cantons expressing his desire for a military solution to the German question. This pamphlet was rapidly reprinted all around Germany, and its patent authenticity gave it added force.[12] By identifying the papal machinations at the root of the Schmalkaldic War, Magdeburg's authors provided the intellectual framework for justifying resistance as godly obligation against the power of Antichrist, side-stepping uncomfortable issues of temporal authority.

A few years later the bruised and embittered remnant of English Protestantism, the Marian exiles, were sheltering in Europe from the restored Catholic regime in their homeland. Traumatised by the defeat, they too began to toy with radical ideas. Christopher Goodman's *How Superior Powers Ought to be Obeyed* based its repudiation of crown authority on entirely scriptural grounds. As John Ponet argued in his *Short Treatise of Politic Power*, obedience to the unfaithful magistrate might require disobedience to God, and that could not be contemplated.[13] Here was an echo of the Magdeburg principle that the true confession of God must, in moments of crisis, be a public confession. It articulated the most consistent strand of Protestant thought in times of adversity: a denunciation of those who preferred the comfort of silent compliance ('Nicodemism') to the painful witness to truth.

Goodman and Ponet were the radical thinkers of the Marian exile, but it was John Knox, with his virulent blast *Against the Monstrous Regiment of Women*, who almost stole the show and wrecked the whole enterprise. Published just as Mary's reign was coming to an end, Knox's trumpet call achieved little except turning the new Protestant queen against the exiles. The substitution of Deborah for Jezebel did little to assuage her anger. The new reign found John Calvin struggling to dissociate himself from a text published, with unprovidential poor timing, in Geneva only a year before.

Machiavellian moments

Ten years later the same repertoire of arguments found new currency in France as a Protestant movement shattered by the St Bartholomew's Day massacre struggled with a sense of desolation and abandonment. The trauma of these years produced some of the most fundamental expressions of a radical political philosophy of resistance ever written in the sixteenth century. How far they exercised a real influence on contemporary opinion is questionable.

Among the many works published in these years, three in particular have enjoyed the admiration of posterity: François Hotman's *Francogallia*, *The Rights of Magistrates* by Théodore de Bèze, and the anonymous *Vindiciae contra tyrannos*.[14] Each has a slightly different genesis. Hotman had been working on the *Francogallia* for some years before 1572. It is a weighty work of constitutional history, which places the rights and responsibilities of the political nation within a historical context reaching back to the earliest times.[15]

It was left to de Bèze to make more directly the case of resistance to an unjust ruler: a responsibility *The Rights of Magistrates* placed firmly in the hands of the inferior magistrate, in the specific case of France the princely leadership of the Huguenot cause. The *Vindiciae* dealt at greater length with the dangers of tyrannical rule and its remedies in political action.[16]

Yet by the time the *Vindiciae* was published in 1579 the moment of greatest danger was past. Of the three works only that of de Bèze seems to have enjoyed wide contemporary currency.[17] The anger, alienation and desire for vengeance that animated the Huguenot movement in these years touched a more popular nerve in far less philosophical works of polemic, such as the vituperative *Reveille-matin des François* of 1574. This and other works of the same genre tapped into a rich vein of anti-Italianism focused on the person of the queen mother, Catherine de' Medici, and on the reputed influence of Machiavellian principles on French politics.

Machiavelli was certainly a much-read author in French, and until this point, much admired. *The Prince*, the *Discourses* and the *Art of War* had all been rendered into French during the great burst of literary creativity in the 1540s and 1550s, sometimes more than once.[18] Interestingly, the long series of editions published in French was scarcely impeded by the addition of Machiavelli's name to the list of authors banned by the Roman Index of 1559.[19] Though no Italian press could risk a new edition, the French Machiavelli sailed on undisturbed, assisted by the fact that the French translation had prudently removed some of the more direct criticism of the Papacy.[20]

In the wake of St Bartholomew the reputations of Machiavelli and Catherine de' Medici became fatally intertwined (*The Prince* had been dedicated to Catherine's father). Two works proved especially popular: the *Discours de la vie de Catherine de Medici*, a vituperative and wilfully defamatory life of Catherine, and Innocent Gentillet's magisterial assault on Machiavellian principles, the *Discours sur les moyens de bien gouverner*.[21] Both went through multiple editions in the years immediately after publication. Gentillet, in particular, found a popularity with contemporary readers that has not been echoed by modern intellectual historians, who find him shallow, crude and derivative. Certainly his advice to readers gave a hostage to fortune in its cheerfully frank description of his working method. In every science, he proclaimed, 'it seems to be the best (that men may well employ their time, which is dear and short) to read few books, to make good choice of them, and well to understand them'. But the authorities he listed were in fact the common corpus of almost all contemporary authors: Sallust, Tacitus, Suetonius, Herodian, Livy, Thucydides and Xenophon. Gentillet was not the only one taking short cuts.[22]

The success of Gentillet and the scurrilous *Life of Catherine* should warn against overestimating the importance of the texts most studied and admired today. The three famous 'monarchomach' treatises have received more attention because of a double posthumous resonance: firstly when they were rediscovered by the opponents of the crown in the English Civil War; later because of the precocious modernity of their evocation of citizen rights. The danger of reading these texts through this lens is that it uproots them from the particular historical and especially religious crisis in which they were born. With these texts, as with Protestant resistance theory in general, it is important to realise that arguments for resistance are posited in a strongly theological context, in a dialectic moment when the Antichrist was abroad and the faith in deadly danger. They are highly time specific; when the crisis passed, so did the sense of eschatological urgency. The doctrine of tyrannicide was no longer of relevance. As the threat to the survival of French Protestantism receded, the search for security was pursued, and obtained, through entirely traditional channels of political influence and established social structures.[23] Protestants turned once more to traditional leaders of society, the nobility and the princes, especially once Henry of Navarre was miraculously propelled to the position of heir, then king. The dire warnings of the retribution to be visited on unjust rulers were swiftly forgotten.

Much the same can be said of the parallel process of resistance and opposition in the rebellious Dutch provinces.[24] During the first stage of the conflict Calvinists concentrated on demands for (their own) freedom of religion, but this did not develop into a fully articulated doctrine of toleration. When Calvinists were placed intermittently in a position of supremacy they were just as keen to establish a monopoly of official religion for their view of divine truth. The issue of political sovereignty was even more difficult to resolve. It gradually became evident that continued obedience to Spanish rule would not be compatible even with limited freedom of religion. But the development of a new concept of local sovereignty was painfully slow and hesitant. Even as the tide of war turned against Philip of Spain the rebellious provinces for many years expressed their opposition within an essentially conservative framework, appealing to traditional rights and liberties which, it was alleged, the king had infringed. Only when the search for an alternative ruler had twice ended in fiasco would the Dutch finally accept the pragmatic reality of pooled sovereignty, and do without a monarch altogether.

The search for reassurance in troubled times is best captured in the runaway contemporary success of a very different work of political philosophy, Jean Bodin's *Six Books of the Commonwealth*. Bodin's unambiguous reassertion of

Fig. 44 Jean Bodin, *Six Books of the Commonwealth*. Bodin's soothing view of an ordered society found an eager audience in troubled times.

monarchical power has been viewed by modern commentators as a precursor of seventeenth-century absolutism, and the attention it has received has been largely unsympathetic.[25] Yet in its own time Bodin's text was extremely popular. After its publication in 1576 the *Six Books* was reissued almost annually in French.[26] It was published in a Latin edition in 1586, and by the end of the century translated into Italian, German and Spanish.[27] Bodin's work, too, must not be divorced from its historical context. It was conceived as an answer to the tortured politics of a divided French nation, and its emphatic restatement of monarchical sovereignty was an explicit response to the challenge of rebellion. It struck a deeper chord because its assertion of lordship was accompanied by a sense that power must be tempered with justice and a concern for the common good. This resonated with a powerful tradition in sixteenth-century writing, represented most magisterially in the *Grand Monarchy* of Claude de Seyssel, and by the extended series of writings in the 'mirrors for princes' tradition. These were texts written ostensibly to guide young rulers in training for kingship, urging them to temper might with mercy, justice and wisdom. In contrast to the wild urgency of the resistance tracts, Bodin put forward a political philosophy that offered a restoration of more ordered times and a confidence in existing social hierarchies. In this he spoke for most contemporaries, for whom the desperate remedies of the Protestant theorists had fleeting appeal.

The king's command

Bodin, of course, had his critics. The first result of his publications was an increase in the welter of passionate controversy discharged by the press. In any case the crown could scarcely wait for Bodin's earnest arguments to carry the day in order to effect the pacification of the kingdom. Nor would it have been wise to rely on the classical eloquence of its emissaries to the provincial estates. Political debate was therefore necessarily accompanied by a parallel attempt at peacemaking: an effort to restore the rule of law and promote royal authority through the normal practice of administration and justice.

In the long term this undramatic pursuit of the everyday tasks of government was the most critical aspect of the search for order in Europe's troubled nations. It was a task pursued at every level of administration; and it was a task, crucially, that made full use of the capacities of the press. This aspect of the sixteenth century's print output has seldom been considered in the context of political philosophy. It plays no part in any handbook or survey of early modern political thought. Yet it provided the most articulate demonstration of the power of the state, and the virtues and benefits of peace.

The search for peace in France began immediately after the furious bloodletting of 1562–63 had brought the first hostilities to a tenuous ceasefire. After negotiating a grudging end to hostilities, the queen mother, Catherine de' Medici, embarked on a long tour of France to show the young King Charles to his people. At each stop the royal party proclaimed edicts of pacification. The tour culminated at Moulins in 1566 in a concerted effort to settle outstanding issues raised by the violence of the fighting and the difficulties of accommodating rival religious faiths. The notables gathered at Moulins also agreed a comprehensive edict of reform, an ordinance of eighty-six provisions for the legal and financial restoration of the kingdom. This was immediately printed in Paris by the royal printers, and then in six provincial locations around the kingdom: Lyon (the local printing centre proximate to Moulins), Dijon, Poitiers, Caen, Rennes and Toulouse.

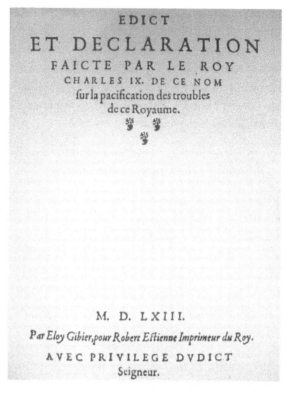

Fig. 45 The French crown's peacemaking efforts were relayed to local populations through a network of provincial printers: here at Orléans.

This set a pattern that was repeated at each stage of the conflict. The Peace of Longjumeau (1568) was printed in Paris and nine provincial locations; the Peace of Saint-Germain (1570) in twelve cities. The ordinances of Blois, promulgated in 1579, were again printed in twelve places around France.

These edicts of reform were in fact only the most widely disseminated examples of a buoyant trade in government documents. In the last forty years of the sixteenth century France's printers published over 4,000 editions of French royal acts and edicts: an average of over 100 printings each year. Many edicts were printed and reprinted many times over, often several times in the same year.[28]

Who were the likely purchasers of pamphlet copies of royal acts? Among the most widely circulated were ordinances on fiscal matters, listing the coins in circulation (often with woodcut illustrations). These were useful handbooks for merchants and tax officials.[29] Merchants and traders also bought edicts detailing tolls on the Loire, France's major navigable river, and regulations for the production and wearing of cloth.[30] Other edicts dealt with tax levies, local

EDICT ET
DECLARATION
FAICTE PAR LE ROY CHARLES
neufieme de ce nom, fur la pacification des
troubles de ce Royaume, le XIX.
iour de Mars, mil' cinq cens
foixante deux.

A TROYS
Par Iean Damian, fur la copie imprimée à Paris
M. D. LXVIII.
AVEC PRIVILEGE.

Fig. 46 Announcement of the Peace of Longjumeau, published at Troyes. Despite its crudity, this pamphlet proudly displays a primitive version of the royal arms.

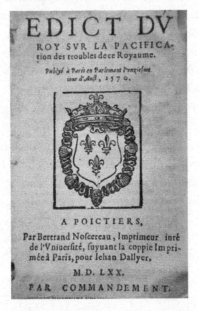

EDICT DV
ROY SVR LA PACIFICA-
tion des troubles de ce Royaume.

Publyé à Paris en Parlement l'ynziefme
iour d'Aust, 1570.

A POICTIERS,
Par Bertrand Noscereau, Imprimeur iuré
de l'Vniuerfité, fuyuant la coppie Impri-
mée à Paris, pour Iehan Dallyer,
M. D. LXX.
PAR COMMANDEMENT.

Fig. 47 The Peace of Saint-Germain. Poitiers was a crucial relay station for royal edicts to the south and west of the kingdom, and its printers profited accordingly.

settlements of the rights of worship, the preservation of the royal domain and the raising of troops, and these were purchased by a wide range of magistrates and interested citizens.

This was a very lucrative trade. Consequently the right to print royal edicts was keenly sought after by members of the French publishing fraternity. In 1561 the crown appointed for the first time an official printer of royal edicts in Paris.[31] The royal printer was obliged to print any document requested by the king, and in return enjoyed the privilege of printing a commercial edition of any newly published edict for which they anticipated demand. Other printers could print their own edition after the expiry of the allotted monopoly period (usually three months), and any edicts for which the royal printer did not see a market. It says a great deal for the extent of this market that at some point over a hundred Paris printers printed royal edicts.

Such work was also eagerly sought after by printers in French provincial cities. When an edict was proclaimed it was sent around France by a network of royal couriers. Town councils were sent a copy (normally the version published by the royal printer) along with written instructions to make the edict known locally. The town council would have it proclaimed on the marketplace; sometimes they would also ask a local printer to print up an edition for further distribution.[32] This was the sort of work these small provincial printers loved. The opportunity to print a simple pamphlet or broadsheet and deliver the whole edition to a single client (in this case the city magistrates) was an ideal commission for a jobbing printer, particularly as they would be promptly paid. The small number of surviving examples of these local broadsheets must be the tip of a very considerable iceberg: a comprehensive search of archives would no doubt reveal more.

With the passage of years many provincial printers began to branch out and print their own local editions of edicts emanating from the Paris courts, along with pamphlet accounts of the local wars. This became a mainstay of the provincial press: indeed, it contributed very materially to the revival of printing around France in the second half of the sixteenth century. The crown was quick to recognise that these local reprints suited their interests by reinforcing royal authority around the kingdom, so in a number of towns they followed the example of the capital and named an authorised local royal printer.

Mastering the press

The French crown faced its greatest challenge with the succession crisis of 1588–89, after the assassination of Henry of Guise and the last Valois king,

Henry III. The new king, the former Henry of Navarre, had received an inkling of the difficulties he would face when Henry III had surrendered to the League's demands and banned Protestant worship. The two edicts encapsulating these decrees, in 1585 and 1588, were reprinted more widely across France (and abroad) than any other edicts: in a total of eighteen French and foreign locations. When Henry became king he faced a Catholic backlash all the more intense because virtually every significant printing centre in France, with the exception of Protestant La Rochelle, was in the hands of his opponents, the Catholic League. Even the royal printer Féderic Morel elected to remain in Paris and throw in his lot with Henry's opponents. He printed no royal acts until 1593.

The king responded by establishing new presses in loyalist towns, in Châlons and Chartres, in Caen, Langres, Nevers and Tours. The major centre of loyalist propaganda was Tours, where newly appointed royal printers set about publishing a stream of royal exhortations to obedience, protestations of good will, and hints of Henry's readiness to embrace Catholicism.

One by one the towns of France made their peace. This process produced a new type of royal edict, as the king used the press to publicise widely the terms under which each town had accepted royal authority. Starting with Chartres in 1591, Henry published an account of these acts of reconciliation in some thirty different places, both in the city newly reduced to royal obedience, and elsewhere around France. The biggest prize of all was the submission of Paris, celebrated in thirty-four editions, and that of the League's leader, the Duke of Mayenne.[33] Mayenne's agreement with Henry to a general truce was published in fifteen locations around France.

In an age that valued the public display of the attributes of kingship Henry IV had an exceptionally vivid presence. Decisive and ebullient, he ceaselessly toured his troubled dominions, hatching schemes and making promises. Not the least of his attributes was his exceptional shrewdness in exploiting the capacities of the printing press. In Henry's active pursuit of royal power through print we see the convergence of two tendencies growing in potency through the century: the ambitions of Europe's rulers to extend the scope of their authority, and the urgent demand for information among their subjects. In France this climaxed in a dogged campaign to promote royal authority and make Henry of Navarre, against all obstacles, the focus of patriotic loyalty. The French crown did much to stimulate the restoration of French regional print. In return, the presses made a case for the new king even when his own capital city was closed against him.

Municipal duties

The development of a provincial press in France was the response to a very specific set of circumstances. But the output of these new presses also reflected a trend visible throughout Europe, as governments sought to bring order and regulation to the lives of the peoples under their jurisdiction. The increasing scope of government activity has been widely noted by historians of sixteenth-century politics. At all levels of social organisation the authority of the state was expanded to take in an ever greater range of responsibilities. In many parts of Europe the printing press played an important role in the articulation of these ambitions.

The use of print in the mundane everyday functions of government is not at all easy to reconstruct. Most pieces are ephemeral so have disappeared altogether: they were never intended to be stored for posterity. They were posted up in the markets and on public buildings and wind and the weather did the rest. But we get a hint of how it must have been throughout Europe thanks to one extraordinary collection, in Antwerp. That this survived was entirely due to the meticulous archiving practice of the great Antwerp printer, Christophe Plantin. Plantin kept one copy of everything he printed, including broadsheet acts and ordinances: even labels and receipts. After his early bruising entanglement with heresy, he steered clear of politics. Plantin's press served the local ruling power, whoever that might be. For Philip II he published not only a lavish series of liturgical texts, but an edict of 1569 announcing the new Antwerp Index of forbidden Protestant texts. In the period that Antwerp was ruled by the rebel forces, Plantin printed the mandates of the Estates-General, including the edict declaring Philip II deposed.

Throughout this period he also placed his press at the disposal of the Antwerp city council to print their orders and regulations. Between 1583 and 1589 he was the city's official printer. In this time he printed around 450 official mandates, an average of six a month.[34] They offer us a unique insight into the preoccupations of a city administration in sixteenth-century Europe attempting to regulate the multiple affairs of a teeming mercantile city in a period of great political turbulence.

The edicts issued by the Antwerp city authorities addressed three main issues: the regulation of trade, public order and public sanitation. They also made provision for the local taxation necessary to fund city administration and the programme of public works necessary to maintain the infrastructure of the city. Excise duties were raised on grain, beer, salt and a whole host of staples. The city also collected tax on property, and separate duties on cellars and sewers. A great

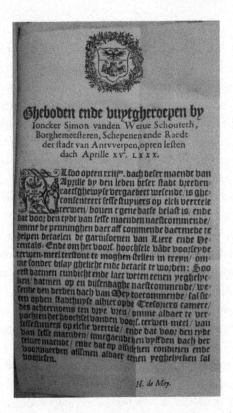

Fig. 48 Ordinance of the city of Antwerp, 1580. These broadsheet orders were printed either in large format, to be posted in public places or (as in this case) as hand bills to be distributed. This example deals with a tax levy to pay for the garrison at Lier in 1580.

deal of attention was accorded to the orderly conduct of business, the provision of goods, the regulation of prices, shop hours, and the working hours of tradesmen. Antwerp's international trade brought enormous wealth, but commensurate issues of public order. The council intervened repeatedly to ensure that the unloading of goods was properly regulated, and to control ship traffic. Antwerp was accustomed to a large transient population of temporary residents, and during the 1580s their numbers were greatly increased by the dislocation caused by warfare. The city fathers ordered on several occasions that the names of strangers lodged in the city should be registered, a form of targeted census undertaken in several major European cities at this time. Where these records survive, as in London, they provide exceptionally rich documentation of the human consequences of religious discord.

The conflicts of these years have left their imprint on the legislative records of the Antwerp council in several respects. In July 1581 the council issued an order forbidding the exercise of the Catholic religion in the city.[35] The Protestant ascendancy of this period is reflected in orders for repeated days of prayer and fasting and a ban on dancing in the streets.[36] In 1585 the city was forced to capitulate to the forces of the Duke of Parma, and passed into Catholic hands. The days of prayer were replaced by orders for processions, and a reminder that no meat should be eaten in Lent.[37] Interestingly, the ban on dancing was maintained: perhaps this reflected a wish to limit potentially explosive public gatherings at a time when the city's population was still divided and troubled.[38]

A constant concern in so large a city was the battle against epidemic disease. In the second half of the sixteenth century this stimulated in many of Europe's major conurbations a new concern to put in place practical measures to improve urban sanitation. Antwerp's city council issued a sequence of orders mandating the disposal of garbage, the clearing of cesspits and the cleaning of streets. A public officer was appointed to kill stray dogs.[39] In 1583 the city embarked on a long and rather quixotic campaign to prevent the keeping of pigs.[40] This may reflect the impact of a large influx of country folk who had taken refuge in the city from marauding troops, and who apparently let their pigs loose on the public thoroughfares. This went beyond normal measures taken to ensure the prompt removal of human and animal waste, and to ensure that the slaughter of the vast number of animals required to feed the city population did not pollute the water supply. The regulation of the food supply posed daunting problems to city administrations throughout Europe. It was an essential part of the maintenance of public order in normal times; in these troubled years it became a constant preoccupation.

The problems faced by the Antwerp council were magnified in scale by the sheer size of the city and its place at the heart of Dutch political controversies. But the more mundane issues the council addressed reflected the challenges of public administration in most of Europe's towns and cities. The municipal archive at Troyes has, very unusually, preserved several boxes of broadsheet ordinances from the sixteenth century.[41] They cover a range of matters from the regulation of bread prices to responses to local developments in the French civil wars: the raising of troops, and the disorders caused by marauding soldiers. All these broadsheets were published on presses newly established in the town from the 1570s. They make up, indeed, quite a large proportion of the total known output of these presses.

In the same way work for the municipal authorities was an absolute mainstay of the business of many printing houses in Germany. Reconstructing this business is not easy; not every printer was as meticulous in retaining file

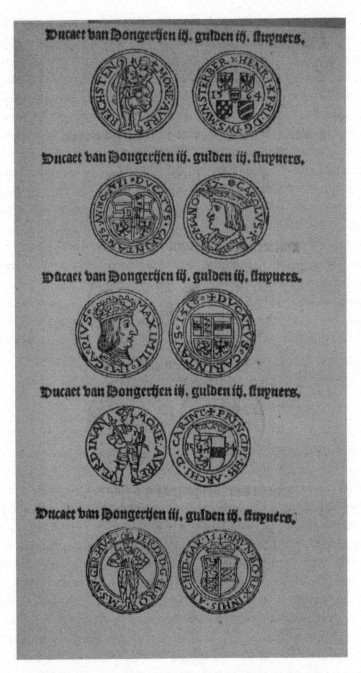

Fig. 49 One of the most important uses of woodcut illustrations was to allow merchants to recognise coins in legal circulation. In the sixteenth century silver coins were accepted for transactions throughout Europe irrespective of the issuing jurisdiction. The scope for forgery was obvious, making such handbooks an indispensable tool of business.

copies as Plantin, and ephemeral printing of this type seldom found a home in libraries.[42] Our best-documented case in the Germanic print world comes from the Swiss city of Zurich, where the government made extensive use of the press to regulate its territory.[43] Most of these items emanated from the publishing house established at the time of the Reformation by Christopher Froschauer, and continued through the century by his heirs. The Froschauers were responsible for most of the publications of the Zurich Reformation; but they also gladly undertook the jobbing work necessary to local administration. Froschauer printed for the Zurich council the range of orders and mandates familiar from Plantin's Antwerp production, but also, on his own account, a large number of more popular broadsheets, news prints and sensations, monstrous births and the like. His involvement in this trade brings into relief one other aspect of this ephemeral production: that it was often extremely lucrative. The records of the town council at Bourges in central France record a series of payments to the printer Jacques Garnier for printing ordinances and proclamations.[44] Without this work his press would not have been viable: indeed, these manuscript references are the only reason we know such a press existed, as not a single copy of any of his imprints has survived. Work for the municipality was the mainstay of Garnier's business. It would most likely have been a similar story for printers in many of Europe's smaller towns.

Emblems of peace

Religious dissent and the poisonous passions it unleashed brought many parts of European society to the brink of catastrophe. In the last decades of the sixteenth century Europe's nation states were locked in a climactic struggle for supremacy, a struggle that drained resources and left communities shattered. Yet even while they pursued these conflicts Europe's rulers knew that peace would ultimately require efforts to repair the body politic and restore social harmony. These concerns were shared by city magistrates faced with the task of limiting the impact of war. They were also shared by many private citizens, especially members of the scholarly community who wondered that intellectual speculation and theological disputes had brought society to such a pass. Temperamentally they shared a visceral hostility to the crude confessional hatreds unleashed by the religious wars of the late sixteenth century. Intellectually they chafed at the obstacles war and religious conflict placed in the path of scholarly investigation.

A sense of critical distance from the most heated passions of the day could be expressed in a number of ways. Many scholars continued to correspond

Fig. 50 Hadrianus Junius, *Emblemata*, 1565. The pelican feeds her young by pecking her own breast. This frequent encapsulation of parental devotion was also used as a title-page device by the Paris printers of the Marnef family.

with friends across the confessional divide. They bought for their libraries works of scholarship written by authors of a different confessional perspective, and not just to have these works on their shelves for purposes of refutation. The republic of letters offered a moment of release from the angry polemic of religious discord.

Distaste for the fixed confessional divisions of the sixteenth century found its most eloquent expression in a new genre of literature that achieved enormous popularity in the sixteenth century, the emblem book.[45] This was a refined literary form only possible in the developed international book market that had evolved by the middle of the sixteenth century. An emblem book consisted of a series of pictures, woodcuts or engravings, sometimes taken from the Bible but usually of a classical subject and accompanied by a motto (*inscriptio*) and a poetic epigram (*subscriptio*). The epigrammatic poem would explore the meaning of the picture in a deliberately elliptical fashion. The pleasure lay in unwrapping the mystery or uncovering layers of ambiguity. It was a playful, artful genre that flattered readers by inviting them into a lettered, knowing community of learning and sophistication.

Emblem books were purposefully non-confessional in their evocation of shared, timeless virtues and values. They mirror the humanist agenda both in their assumption of a shared context of learned reference, and in their promotion of a shared intellectual spirituality. Comment on contemporary events, while guarded, also reflects an intellectual distaste for fanaticism, disorder or unguarded passions. An emblem of Joannes Sambucus, *Sacro ne violato* (Do not violate what is sacred) applied an anecdote of the Greek geographer Pausanias to the contemporary issue of iconoclasm.

The heavenly creatures are propitious and God hears one's prayers the moment one feels regret and shame. But when by chance you see an offering which once had the most sincere functions, made piously and with pure intentions, why should you want to violate it? Why eagerly molest and lay your sacrilegious hands on what is forbidden?[46]

Writers of emblem books emerge from both Catholic and Protestant traditions. The first, and by far the most successful sixteenth-century collection was the *Emblematum libellus* of the Italian jurist Andrea Alciato. Published in 1531, Alciato's collection was republished in more than a hundred editions over the next century, including translations into every major vernacular language.[47] Although the emblem vogue began as a fashion among the international scholarly community, the popularity of these collections soon spread to the wider reading public. The French translation of Alciato went through more than thirty editions; all told, a recent survey of French emblem books lists around 200 editions of more than twenty separate collections from the sixteenth century.[48] Alciato's career epitomises the sort of scholar drawn to the new genre. A peripatetic and highly respected jurist,

Alciato taught at the University of Bourges in France, and acted as a consultant on legal questions to the Council of Trent. Erasmus spoke highly of his learning. But he was also an exponent of reform, and a vehement critic of monasticism. Like Erasmus he had little sympathy for the vulgar theatricality of Luther, and he came to regret allowing Erasmus to see his manuscript criticising monastic life. Desperate to prevent it being printed, he appealed to friends to help him get it back. Alciato's visceral aversion to controversy became axiomatic to the writers (and publishers) of emblem books. It is no surprise that a man such as Christophe Plantin, who had built his career around the avoidance of religious controversy, should have been responsible for two of the most popular collections of the second half of the century, those of Joannes Sambucus and Hadrianus Junius.[49]

The trade in emblem books became, in the second half of the sixteenth century, an important part of the international book trade. New titles were advertised in almost every catalogue of the Frankfurt Fair. Publishers embraced the genre precisely because these books were sold and collected by scholars of all religious persuasions. Emblem books also played an important part in the vogue for *Alba amicorum*, the manuscript equivalent of the emblem book and a distinctive feature of international scholarly culture during this period.[50] As young scholars travelled around Europe in the course of their education, it became the custom to solicit inscriptions in an autograph book, from friends, fellow students and distinguished local scholars. Each contributor would be allocated a page in which to pen an epigram and often furnish an illustration. Some manuscript albums contain illustrations of considerable artistic merit. For the less gifted a printed emblem book provided an appropriate alternative; copies could be sold with interleaved blank pages to be inscribed with an appropriate verse. Of the 1,535 albums listed in a comprehensive survey of surviving examples from the sixteenth century, over 300 are printed books adapted in this way. The most popular archetypes are the collections of Alciato, Sambucus and Junius; Alciato accounts for a third of the total.[51]

The emblem book, which reached into every major part of the European book market, could not remain entirely aloof from religious controversy. Théodore de Bèze, Calvin's successor at Geneva and a considerable scholar, designed a set of emblems explicitly to provide a model of Protestant poetic spirituality. But this was very much the exception. For the most part, the emblem tradition continued to breathe the spirit of Alciato, its first begetter. For the scholarly community of late sixteenth-century Europe the tradition offered a moment of tranquillity in the darker perspectives of societies riven by violence and discord. It was a powerful evocation of the spirit that had inspired the first humanist engagement with the world of print, and of the classical learning that provided a shared point of reference in otherwise divided societies. It provided respite, but not refuge. These same readers of emblems were often public men whose affairs necessarily embroiled them in the turbulent events of the day. By the second half of the sixteenth century all aspects of their lives – the conflicts of faith, the search for peace, the administration of justice and good order, the welcome moments of literary respite – were expressed in print. The interior dialogues of troubled times were played out in print shops and bookstalls throughout Europe.

CHAPTER 12

MARKET FORCES

T HERE WAS every reason why publishers should enthusiastically support the elusive search for political stability in the second half of the sixteenth century. Governments were the sources of privileges, patronage and power. The political turmoil of this era was extremely traumatic for publishers, not least because it threatened what had been one of the fundamental cornerstones of the trade: the smooth functioning of the international market. There were years when Plantin could not move new stock to the Frankfurt Fair. Paris printers were sometimes totally absent.

Economic activity was also extremely vulnerable to intermittent, purely local events. The savage plague epidemic in Venice between 1575 and 1577 cut publishing activity to around a third of normal capacity; the famine of 1591 brought another precipitous fall. But publishing had an exceptional vitality and resilience. New print shops sprang up, old ones re-formed. Emerging tastes in the market were smoothly catered for. Through all of this the European geography of print was refined and consolidated. Print spread across the whole of Europe; but it retained its centre of gravity in the largest centres of print, in Europe's major central marketplace.

European heartlands

In times of crisis the health of the European print trade revolved around the three largest markets: Germany, Italy and France. Together with the distribution centres in the Low Countries and the Swiss Confederation, these markets were responsible for four out of every five books published on the continent. The Swiss print centres in Geneva and Basel were essentially satellites of the larger French and German markets. In this era the Genevan industry successfully adjusted its production from the purely partisan works of Calvinist theology to a broader scholarly and more Latinate output. Basel flourished, as before, as a centre of scholarly publishing.[1]

In the Low Countries the middle years of the century witnessed a remarkable concentration of production in Antwerp, the commercial metropolis. For three decades the city engrossed over 70 per cent of the total of an increasingly confident trade.[2] Antwerp's printers published books in a wide range of genres and languages and the volume of publishing relative to the size of the local population was larger here than anywhere else in Europe: a large part of the books published in the Low Countries were destined for export. The decline of Antwerp after 1580 led to a rapid northward shift of printing activity to the new free states. In the seventeenth century Holland would take over Antwerp's role as a universal emporium.

While print in the Low Countries emerged largely unscathed from the political crisis of the late sixteenth century, France was very different. In the

Fig. 51 War disrupted the international book trade but it also created another new class of literature: military handbooks. Vegetius' discourse on Roman military tactics was of great interest in the Renaissance, not least for its insights into recruitment, discipline and morale. Flavius Vegetius, *Du fait de guerre et fleur de chevalerie* (Paris, 1536).

first half of the century the story of French print was essentially the story of Paris and Lyon. Together they dominated the French print world, with over 90 per cent of all books published in France between 1500 and 1555 emanating from these two cities. The traumatic impact of the French civil wars totally transformed this geography. The establishment of Protestant printing abroad, and then in Normandy, Lyon and La Rochelle, presaged a prolonged pamphlet conflict, latterly between different camps within Catholicism: Leaguer and Royalist. These developments revitalised French provincial printing. Small printing presses sprang up in over forty different cities; larger centres of provincial printing were established in Bordeaux, Toulouse, Rouen, Orléans and Poitiers.[3] The domination of Paris was significantly weakened. A robust provincial printing industry would be an enduring feature of French culture well into the seventeenth century.

This was not without cost. Between 1500 and 1560 Paris and Lyon had built one of the most sophisticated book markets in all of Europe. Well-capitalised, long-established firms published scholarly and literary works for the local and international market. These were beautiful books: lavish folios for the scholarly and legal texts, quartos and octavos for theological works.[4] By mid-century printers had expanded this market to incorporate new veins of vernacular literature and poetry, along with translations of major works of Italian and Spanish literature. It was the great age of French literary publishing.

The French wars greatly disrupted this market. As Paris printers redirected their efforts to the production of Catholic religious polemic, religious and political pamphlets soaked up a larger proportion of readers' disposable income. Marauding soldiers and the ravages of war caused further damage to the business infrastructure. In the last stages of the conflict, the outpouring of bilious pamphlets disguised a precipitous fall in the overall volume of print.[5] Starved of paper, Paris printers had little choice but to reduce activity.

Lyon fared rather better: it was better situated to retain its connections to the main markets in Germany, and more distant from the main fighting, so its share in the international trade in religious and scholarly books held up well. All of this adjusted the balance of power in the French print world away from the capital and towards Lyon and the rising provincial markets. This shift can be followed in stock lists compiled at different points in the century for French printers or booksellers. Paris in its pomp is represented by the inventory of the stock of the Parisian merchant publisher Jean Janot. When Janot died in 1522 he left remaining stock of 159 different works, a total of 53,000 copies, mostly unbound in sheets.[6] Janot specialised in the vernacular trade and, judging from the amount of property and goods he bequeathed, this trade had been

Fig. 52 Italian literature in translation from the glory days of French typography. The title-page deftly conveys a mass of information while preserving a perfect elegance and balance. Bandello's short tales found a ready audience in France; this edition dates from the period immediately before the wars of religion convulsed the Paris book world. The red ruling on the title-page was common in a presentation copy.

extremely lucrative – and diverse. He had published a large number of songs and carols (*chansons* and *Noëls*) and he also left almost the complete stock of a simple mathematical textbook, *The Art and Science of Arithmetic*. He had a healthy market in local legal codes. His stock included copies of the customs of Paris, Sens, Chaumont, Orléans and Vitry. These were towns that in later years would have had their own printers but at this stage relied on books sent down from Paris.

The two largest sectors of the market, judging from Janot's stock, were popular devotional texts and vernacular literature. The market for literary texts was shared between recent French authors (Gringore and Meschinot) and more traditional fare. Janot published both the *Pathelin*, a popular verse work, and the more courtly *Roman de la Rose*. In addition he offered his clients an extensive range of prose chivalric tales. He had stock of at least eight: *Ponthus, Merlin, Mélusine, Aymon, Ogier le Danois, Artus de Bretagne* and

Huon de Bordeaux. These were the texts that dominated the market for the twenty years before publication of the French *Amadis*.

For more contemplative moments Janot offered a range of vernacular devotional texts: the *Mirror of Consolation*, the *Mirror of the Sinful Soul*, lives of the Virgin Mary and a narrative of the Passion. A number of these smaller texts were illustrated. The two genres of literature and devotional religion overlapped in the numerous saints' lives, another Janot speciality. Many of these were in fact play texts (*The Mystery of St Peter and Paul in characters*), or, more accurately, synopses from which the performers were expected to extemporise a longer performance. Surviving copies of such texts are incredibly rare, so it is interesting to see what an important part they play in Janot's trade.[7] The individual cost of these little vernacular texts was very modest. Janot clearly expected to sell substantial numbers to the Parisian book-buying public, and he grew rich doing so.

A different picture comes from inventories compiled later in the century. Here the corrosive impact of religious dispute is all too evident. The inventory of the stock of the Paris bookseller Richard Breton revealed a business orientated wholly towards supplying the book needs of the residual Protestant population of Paris. In 1569 angry Parisians had ransacked the bookshops of known Protestant sympathisers, and Breton had lost a considerable portion of stock. But he swiftly resumed trading. The inventory completed two years later (by carefully chosen fellow Huguenot members of the book trade) reveals a stock in which the devotional texts of Janot's day were replaced by psalters, New Testaments, and a fair range of the vernacular works of Calvin and other leading French Protestant authors.[8]

It may seem astonishing that Protestant books could still be sold so easily in the French capital at this date, when the general political climate was so hostile, but this relative freedom to trade is confirmed by another inventory compiled in the same year at the other end of the kingdom, in Bordeaux, traditionally regarded as an outpost of the Lyon publishing world. The stock of the bookseller Estienne Thoulouze, compiled in 1552, reveals that it was heavily dependent on Lyon publishers. Thoulouze had some 665 titles, mostly of an academic nature. He was described in the inventory as 'master bookseller of the University of Bordeaux'; for his customers he stocked mostly classical works, treatises on rhetoric, works of law and medicine. There was very little theology beyond a few vernacular devotional tracts.

The Bordeaux stock left by Vincent Réal in 1571 was much larger and very different in character.[9] This was clearly an enormous business with over 2,000 titles including a comprehensive range of classical literature. The Bordeaux masters and their students could still rely on Réal to provide them with law books, works of the Church Fathers and modern Catholic authors. Réal also stocked a surprising range of Protestant texts, supplied from Lyon, Geneva and Zurich. This was not a narrowly Calvinist selection, though the Genevan Fathers certainly predominated. Purchasers could also buy a number of German authors, such as Johannes Brenz. Réal's stock paints an intriguing picture of the book world in a city normally seen as a reliable beacon of Catholicism in the Protestant south.

Pride of Italy

The political and religious crises that afflicted Italy were less sustained than the civil wars in France. Nevertheless the impact on the print culture was profound. The early supremacy of Italian print was first arrested and then reversed by the long economic crisis unleashed by the Franco-Imperial wars. As German print found new confidence, Italian print culture fell further into the shadows.

The engine of recovery was inevitably Venice, trade emporium and motor of the southern European economy. The vogue for literature in mid-century seemed to offer the means of revitalising print, only for the Inquisition to impose severe restrictions on the industry's freedom of manoeuvre: no Luther, obviously, but also no Machiavelli, Boccaccio or Aretino. Venice was best equipped to weather the storm, as the sheer size of the market made regulation and control logistically more complicated. The ruling elite of the Republic were only intermittently sympathetic to the new Puritanism. As smaller centres of production found the market more difficult to negotiate, Venice took an ever larger role in what had previously been a diverse print industry.

In the sixteenth century Venice published three times as many books as Rome, and five times as many as Florence. In fact the dominant printing house in Florence for much of the century, the Giunti, was a branch office of the family's Venice business.[10] Luc' Antonio Giunti, who took over the Venetian business in 1564, maintained agents in every major city in Italy, from Turin to Palermo. This was not unusual. Many of Venice's leading publishers spread their operations through the peninsula. Gabriel Giolito had bookstores in Ferrara, Bologna and Naples in 1565. Vincenzo Valgrisi had shops in Padua, Bologna, Macerata, Foligno, Recanati and Lanciano (and also in Frankfurt and Lyon).[11] The full extent of Venetian domination can be illustrated from the catalogues of the Frankfurt Fair. From 1564 until the end of the century an enterprising German bookseller issued a catalogue of all the new books available at each fair: a cumulative total of 20,000 titles. Venice accounted for three-quarters of the titles sent to Frankfurt by Italian publishers.[12]

The resilience of the Venetian market was impressive. But proportional to total output the Frankfurt data still shows that Venice was losing ground to the major northern centres of the international trade: Antwerp, Lyon, Paris, Basel and Geneva. In this respect the new climate of restriction in Italy had a profound impact. The wholesale international trade in books was conducted largely by exchange. The restrictions imposed on the Venice market made this trade far more complicated, since many of the books offered in exchange for Venetian imprints by northern dealers could not be sold openly in the city. Venetian publishers were forced to resort to subterfuge, disguising their more dubious purchases on the inventories they provided for customs officials. Sometimes this worked, but not always. In 1581 a bookseller was fined for bringing back from Frankfurt copies of the New Testament and other forbidden books. His defiant defence, that prohibited books like this were sold in Venice all the time, only served to increase the size of his fine.[13]

Despite these difficulties the Venice book fraternity enjoyed significant advantages. One was relative proximity to the northern markets. Another was the fact that Venetian bookmen seem by and large not to have denounced each other. Many concluded that the restrictions, particularly on scientific books by northern authors, were too broad to be upheld. They also suspected that the apparatus of control was designed to assist Rome publishers, favoured with papal privileges, against Venetians. In the mental tussle between religious orthodoxy and economic opportunity parochial patriotic considerations made sure that economic pragmatism won the day.

Print's engine room

Of the great print cultures Germany was the least damaged by the conflicts of the sixteenth century. The central landmass of Europe was not untouched by warfare, but there was nothing to compare with the civil wars in France, or even the Italian wars. With the vast increase in demand for books that followed the Reformation, German print entered on a period of sustained growth that lasted to the end of the century.

The Reformation also effected a gradual shift in the centre of gravity of German print. The first decade of the Lutheran controversies brought new energy to all Germany's presses: traditional centres such as Nuremberg and Augsburg benefited as much as those close to Wittenberg. In the longer term the Reformation shifted production towards the major theological

Fig. 53 Ariosto's *Orlando Furioso*, Venice, 1558. The popularity of Italian literature was one of the cornerstones of the Italian book trade – although even here, the progressive expansion of the register of forbidden books posed a challenge for printers.

centres of Lutheranism, particularly the nexus of Wittenberg, Jena and Leipzig in the north-east. In the last decade of the sixteenth century these three places out-published Augsburg, Nuremberg and Basel by a margin of two to one.[14]

But the real strength of German print lay in its diversity. Production of books was dispersed between around eighty places, including twenty that boasted a publishing industry of some size.[15] To the established centres from the first age of print the later sixteenth century added a number of newly important locations: Heidelberg and Tübingen serving the Protestant academic market; Ingolstadt, Munich and Vienna on the Catholic side; Frankfurt serving the book market. Germany participated fully in the international book trade, and at the same time produced a rich and varied vernacular literature. Certain larger publishing centres developed a distinct market niche. For scholarly theological books and Catholic liturgies, Cologne was the market leader; for Catholic pastoral works and theology, booksellers looked to Ingolstadt or Munich. Nuremberg led Europe in the production of scientific texts, while Augsburg was the acknowledged centre of news print. Basel was a leading centre of medical publishing. Wittenberg and Jena retained the primacy in the production of Protestant bibles and theology.

All these texts were traded through the biannual fairs at Frankfurt. The fair has attracted most interest for its role in the international market, but it was important for the local German trade too: 70 per cent of the titles offered for sale at Frankfurt were published in Germany. Many were scholarly Latin tomes, but Frankfurt also did a roaring trade in less serious literature.

The volume of books traded at Frankfurt was quite staggering. One can get a sense of this from the account book of Michael Harder of Augsburg, a regular visitor to the fair.[16] Harder was not one of the great figures of the trade. He took no part in the international trade in scholarly books. He sold mostly retail, and almost exclusively vernacular texts. Nevertheless at this single fair he disposed of over 5,000 books. Two of his bestsellers were literary works: *The Seven Wise Masters*, of which he sold 233 copies, and *Schimpff and Ernst*, of which he sold 202. Other popular literary works were *Mélusine*, *Ritter Ponthus*, *Eulenspiegel* and *Florio and Biancefiore*.[17] The inevitable Aesop also sold well, as did various books of practical husbandry. A household medicine book, *The Little Handbook of Apollinaris*, sold 227 copies, and there were decent sales for manuals of medicinal plants and a book on distilling. Harder also made something of a speciality of small books inveighing against vices. Here drunkenness narrowly outsold profanity and gambling.

Supplying the periphery

Outside the central heartland of print the environment was far more challenging. Places like Spain, Portugal, England and Poland each had a considerable reading community, served by a lively print fraternity. But it was more difficult for printers in these places to play a part in the production of books for the international trade. None had a large export market, and this imposed significant limitations on the total size of domestic production.

The markets to the north and east were essentially tributaries of the gigantic German trade. Denmark and Sweden were Europe's least diverse print trades. The royal press in Stockholm was exclusively directed towards the production of necessary texts for the Church and crown. All other books were imported. The press in Denmark was also very restricted, heavily dependent on Lutheran literature and official publications.

The three largest markets in eastern Europe were Poland, Bohemia and Hungary. The production, transportation and marketing of books in eastern Europe posed daunting problems as the vernacular reading community was large, but often widely dispersed. Multiple, shifting political jurisdictions and a patchwork of ethnic groups added to the complexities. Despite this, the desire to participate in print culture was strong. However daunting the commercial logistics, a number of significant intellectual trends powerfully assisted the growth of print. The regional influence of distinguished medieval universities at Vienna, Prague and Cracow provided a bridgehead for scholarly print. The difficulties of linguistic fragmentation were ameliorated by the persistence of Latin, and the ubiquity of German, which functioned as a language of trade around the Baltic and through much of eastern Europe. Many towns in Hungary and Bohemia, or under the jurisdiction of the Polish crown, had a substantial German population. The Baltic, like the Rhine or the North Sea, functioned as a sort of trade super-highway through northern Europe, making it easier to print books many hundreds of miles away from their eventual purchasers.

Around 4,000 books were published in Poland during the sixteenth century; the print output of Bohemia was about the same, the Hungarian print world rather smaller. In all of these places the needs of the local Church, or churches, continued to play a predominant role. Catholic priests required missals and breviaries; Lutheran and other Protestant churches, vernacular church orders. But for more serious works of scholarship, and German-language literature, the nearby German market remained dominant. The Leipzig Fair acted as a major distribution centre for eastward trade, though the market for scholarly books was sufficiently large for Venetian publishers to retain a close interest.

Luc' Antonio Giunti sold books to the value of 1,000 ducats in Cracow every year.[18] In cities like this the demand for books far outstripped local production. The international market was smoothly organised to supply the deficiency.

Rebel spirits

England was in many respects Europe's most unusual book market. A population of between two and three million created a considerable vernacular reading community. This was a mature nation state with a smoothly functioning government apparatus. London was one of Europe's great cities, Oxford and Cambridge two of its oldest universities. But the print industry remained small: its total output of around 15,000 books during the century was half that of the Low Countries.[19] Printing in England was almost wholly confined to London, and the books published were almost all in English. London publishers printed fewer Latin books than even those of Poland or Bohemia.

These singular characteristics of the English industry were closely connected. Because the English trade was confined to London, the seat of government, it was closely controlled. It was not difficult to regulate output, partly because the industry was happy to co-operate. The English print industry was ruled by the Stationers' Company of London (a unique example of a local trade guild performing such a national regulatory function).[20] The small number of print shops operating in London made a relatively secure living; so it was in the Stationers' interest to assist the government in stamping out unauthorised enterprises, in London or elsewhere. This was a conservative industry, content to bank the profits of multiple editions of reliable sellers. Buyers could not object, because the other titles they wanted were easily available, imported from Antwerp, France or Germany. Through this international book trade English readers could build large and impressive collections of scholarly books.[21] But English publishers played little part in this lucrative trade.

A few men did try to challenge this cosy consensus and disrupt the comfortable, enervating Elizabethan book world. One such was Roger Ward, the bad boy of Elizabethan print and a persistent thorn in the flesh of the Stationers' Company. At least three times Ward set up an unauthorised press, only to have it raided and closed down. So in 1580 he changed tack, and set up a bookshop in the provincial town of Shrewsbury.[22] The concept was sound. Shrewsbury was home to what was rapidly becoming the largest school in England, and Ward could expect also to sell his books to a string of market towns in the English marches from Chester to Hereford. The business was underwritten by a loan of £240 from a local Shrewsbury draper. The failure to repay this loan led to legal proceedings, resulting in a carefully itemised inventory of the books Ward had for sale.

The inventory lists 500 titles, mostly in small quantities. Ward stocked large quantities of popular school-books, and multiple copies of the staples of congregational worship, the Psalms, and a large variety of catechisms and sermons. He also kept in stock an impressive range of anti-Catholic pamphlets. A visitor to Ward's shop could pick up both Christopher Carlile's splendidly titled *Discourse wherin is plainly proved that Peter was never at Rome*, one of Ward's own London publications, and the recent translation of Philip Marnix's popular *Beehive of the Roman Church*. This was part of an extensive range of controversial Protestant writings available in translation.[23]

For members of the county community Ward stocked legal, medical and recreational texts. Aesop's *Fables* were there, of course, but also chivalric romances such as *Palmerin, Valentine and Orson* and the *Mirror of Knighthood*. Members of the Shropshire bench would have been able to supply themselves with copies of the Statutes, Littleton's *Tenures* and even the Magna Carta. Popular medical compendia are a strong feature of the list, but Ward also offered a range of imported Latin texts, medical texts especially.

Ward's selection of stock seems well balanced but extremely ambitious in its size and range. As an indication of the reading preferences of provincial England it must of course be used with caution. Ward's venture ended in failure and bankruptcy: that was why the inventory was compiled. It represents a list of books an ambitious tradesman hoped to sell, rather than those he had disposed of in the market.

Spain

The Iberian peninsula presented a difficult challenge to an indigenous publishing industry. Castile was a well populated land of ancient towns, but these were widely spread across a central plain with difficult road communications and few navigable rivers. There was no great metropolis to act as the central focus of the publishing industry; indeed until the emergence of Madrid late in the century there was no fixed capital. Barcelona in Aragon and Lisbon in Portugal enjoyed a more favourable geographical situation, and better communications with the outside world. But for publishing purposes they were locked into small vernacular reading communities (Catalan and Portuguese) and this inevitably restricted their ability to develop a broad range of vernacular publications. In consequence no single city emerged as a dominant force in Spanish publishing, though several, including Salamanca, Seville, and later Madrid, developed a significant industry.

Around 18,000 editions were printed in Spain in the course of the sixteenth century.[24] Despite this the book-reading communities of Spain remained heavily dependent on imports for works in scholarly languages. In the first century of print Venice and Rome both built up healthy markets in the Iberian peninsula. Luc' Antonio Giunti owned shops in both Salamanca and Medina del Campo,[25] but by the middle of the sixteenth century the Venetian ascendancy was being challenged by publishers from northern Europe, and particularly France.[26] The Spanish print world seems to have suffered from a distinct skills shortage, with Spanish printers often relying on French print workers to operate their presses. This provided an opportunity for skilled but impecunious pressmen who having worked in Lyon or Paris decided to try their luck further south: some were even able to set up their own press. Naturally they brought with them the typographical habits of their home towns. The design features, typographical layout and working practice of the books they produced in Spain are often indistinguishable from contemporary Lyon work.[27] This, in turn, helped prepare the market for imports from Lyon and Paris.

The penetration of the Spanish book world by imports from northern Europe can be documented from a number of sources: library lists, of course, but also booksellers' accounts and correspondence between merchants. A most unusual case involves the complex legal proceedings that followed the murder of the Lyon publisher Symphorien Beraud.[28] The motive and the culprit were never discovered, though it seems Beraud died the day after he had broken off a commercial association with another Lyon publisher, Etienne Michel. In 1580 Beraud had inherited massive stock in Lyon and considerable business interests in Spain and Italy from his former commercial partner, Filippo Tinghi. In settling the estate he had to collect debts from booksellers in Florence, Naples, Siena, Turin, Venice, Piacenza and Milan. This was a powerful demonstration of the extent to which Lyon had colonised this southern market.

Beraud also inherited interests in Barcelona, Zaragoza and Medina del Campo, the Spanish fair town where many Lyon publishers kept stock. Tinghi had maintained relationships with two local agents, including a nephew of Benôit Boyer, the largest bookseller in the city. Another member of the same clan, Jacques Boyer, was a bookseller in Salamanca. The Boyers settled their debt to the Beraud estate for 4,000 *écus*, but the stock of books held in Medina del Campo was obviously far larger. In 1589 an action was undertaken to recover from Beraud's other local agent the sum of 18,000 *écus*. Beraud's Lyon stock had been sold to his erstwhile partner Etienne Michel for 23,500 *écus*. Michel had had to raise his offer to outbid another Salamanca bookseller, Claude Curlet. We can deduce from these transactions that the Lyon stock was of approximately equivalent size to that held in Spain. When inventorised it amounted to 545 bales of books or 2.8 million printed sheets.

This was an enormous stock: it is highly significant that a Spanish bookseller had attempted to secure it for sale in Spain. The Lyon stock consists very largely of weighty learned tomes, mainly of Roman and Canon Law, along with their glosses and commentaries. There is a great deal of Catholic pastoral theology, and standard works by Aristotle and Aquinas. Some of the stock was very old, and for this reason was given a lower value. It included 565 reams of books published between 1520 and 1560, 10 per cent of the total stock. Scholarly publishers had to be prepared to hold stock for many years, but the lower valuation suggests diminishing expectations of sale.

The volume of trade between Lyon and Spain revealed by these transactions is striking, and has to be seen in the context of the oft-quoted decision of the leading Spanish merchant active in the book trade, Simon Ruiz of Valladolid, to sever his connections with France. In 1572 Ruiz had declared that he would no longer deal in books imported from France, because 'so much corruption comes from that country that they are rightly examined very carefully before being allowed in'.[29] Certainly immigrant print workers were frequently suspected of being secret Lutherans. The arrest and interrogation of a French print worker in 1569 led to a string of denunciations and some executions.

Much of the book trade from Lyon to the Iberian peninsula was conducted through Bordeaux and Toulouse, or by transhipment through the Mediterranean. Other books followed a northern route, overland to Orléans, down the Loire to Nantes, and then by ship through the Bay of Biscay to northern Spain. This had the advantage that mixed consignments of Paris and Lyon materials could be assembled in the warehouses of Nantes. This became a substantial business in a French Atlantic port not otherwise known as a major force in the book trade.[30]

In the last third of the sixteenth century France's hold on the Iberian trade was challenged by the new power of Antwerp. Netherlandish publishers were sufficiently confident of their market to challenge native Spanish firms even in the vernacular trade. In the course of the second half of the century printers in Brussels, Louvain and Antwerp published over 500 editions of books in Spanish.[31] The higher wages and transport costs they faced in bringing these books to the market were outweighed by the superior quality of workmanship they were able to offer their customers. The most notable example was Plantin's contract to provide liturgical books for use in Spanish churches. For Plantin this may have been a way of demonstrating his Catholic faith and personal loyalty to Philip II. If so it was a costly gesture, for Plantin never received the payments specified in his contract. Nevertheless over the course of several years Plantin supplied over 52,000 missals, breviaries and Books of Hours.[32] It was a remarkable example of the extent to which the book market in one of Europe's proudest and most powerful nation states had been colonised by the more confident and economically sophisticated books markets of northern Europe.

Outriders

Although small in relative terms, each of the markets away from the centre of European print developed its own, smaller satellites. Together these outriders spread the experience of print to the farthest reaches of the European landmass – and beyond. The small Scandinavian book world was behind the establishment of printing in Iceland. A breviary published for Bishop Jon Arason of Hólar in 1534 may have been the work of a Danish press, but in the last decades of the century Jon Jonsson created a native printing shop in Hólar. Between 1575 and the end of the century it turned out at least thirty works, mostly church handbooks and devotional texts.[33]

Printing in Scotland was closely linked to the larger markets to the south. When two Edinburgh tradesmen, Walter Chapman and Andrew Myller, undertook to bring print to the Scottish capital in 1508 they found the necessary equipment and technical expertise in Rouen in Normandy. This reflected the close cultural connections then existing between two traditional allies: it also hinted at the warm encouragement of the king, James IV, made explicit in a royal privilege. The principal purpose of the Myller/Chapman printing house was the publication of a breviary for the diocese of Aberdeen, and its bishop, William Elphinstone. The other smaller volumes turned off this press survive mostly as fragments. Once the breviary was accomplished, the press was closed down.[34]

It would be several decades before printing was securely established in Scotland, nurtured by religious reform and the increasingly close political ties with England.[35] The crown encouraged the development of a local press by establishing the office of King's Printer. Yet only in 1570, when both Thomas Bassandyne and Henry Charteris were active, did the number of books published in a single year reach double figures.

Connections with the larger London market were strengthened with the arrival, in 1583, of the Huguenot *émigré* Thomas Vautrollier, who had run a busy London shop since 1570. His wife, who remained in London, continued to run the London business, ensuring a smooth supply of texts not available locally. Vautrollier was followed to Scotland by Robert Waldegrave, another man who had his problems with the English political establishment. Both newcomers were cherished by James VI, who clearly appreciated the aesthetic

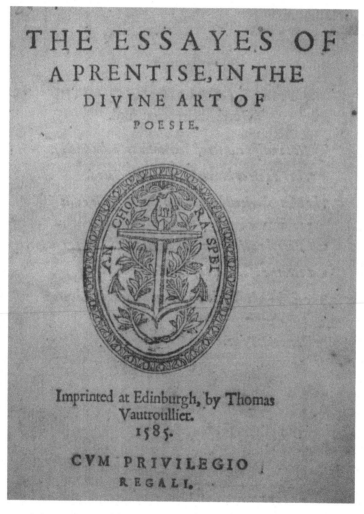

Fig. 54 London printers tempted north found an eager patron in the king, James VI. This translation of a work by the French Protestant poet Guillaume du Bartas was largely James's own work. *The Essayes of a Prentise, in the Divine Art of Poesie* (Edinburgh, Thomas Vautrollier, 1585).

sense they brought to the Edinburgh book world. But by any standards the Scottish book world remained small. In all, only around 350 books were printed in Scotland in the sixteenth century.[36] The growing connections with London functioned alongside a busy continental trade in Latin books. Here the Low Countries gradually replaced Rouen and Paris as the principal source of supply. The continued weakness of indigenous print was demonstrated by the large quantities of pirated English bibles imported from Holland throughout the seventeenth century.[37]

In eastern Europe print markets were always complex and intertwined. Königsberg, in East Prussia, developed a substantial production of printed books, almost exclusively German. This now seems a rather isolated outpost of the German print world, but Königsberg was a German settlement throughout its history. Its metamorphosis into Kaliningrad is entirely a product of twentieth-century politics. Breslau (Wrocław) was also German; Danzig (Gdansk) more ethnically mixed. Further east, cultural exchange finally seeded experiments with printing in Imperial Russia. In 1553 Tsar Ivan (the Terrible) had attempted to encourage the establishment of a native industry, but it would be another ten years before Ivan Federov finally succeeded in printing a number of texts in Church Slavonic. His efforts were not well rewarded. A conservative backlash, led by the Muscovite scribes, forced Federov to flee to Lithuania.

The conservatism of the Orthodox tradition was just one of the obstacles to the development of printing in Russia and the Balkans. A huge technical problem was the casting of Cyrillic type. Given the relatively low levels of literacy this involved an investment that could most easily be undertaken in the larger, better capitalised centres of printing. Most early printing for the south Slavic lands was undertaken in Venice. Particularly remarkable was a missal with Glagolitic type published for use in Croatia.[38] This was a cultural masterpiece, but a doubtful economic proposition. Other works in Cyrillic characters were printed in Cracow and Lvov, both then in Poland; print was established in Kiev, in the Ukraine, early in the seventeenth century.

After the Ottoman conquest of Hungary the independent kingdom of Transylvania was a lonely outpost of western Christian culture. The Siebenbürgen (seven towns) were the most substantial urban communities in what is now Romania. The establishment of a paper mill in Hermannstadt (Sibiu) permitted the growth of a modest print industry. By the end of the sixteenth century printers in Sibiu, Braşov and Cluj had published around 380 books, more than half of them in Latin. Around 120 editions were in Hungarian; only fifteen in Romanian.[39] Overall, printing in the Slavic languages is the most fragmented and disjointed of all the European print traditions: a tribute to the enduring interest in experimentation rather than a fundamental factor in the intellectual evolution of these lands.

The furthest eastern outpost of print was the cosmopolitan city of Constantinople, where Hebrew printing was established.[40] This owes its genesis to events in Spain. The first printer of Constantinople, David Nahmias, was one of many Sephardic Jews forced to leave the Iberian peninsula after the expulsions of 1492 and 1497; the works published in Constantinople were largely in this Sephardic tradition. After a period of intense activity in the first half of the sixteenth century the Constantinople presses declined, eclipsed by the more sustained Hebrew printing of Italy. Nevertheless, presses in Constantinople and Salonika between them contributed around 200 separate editions, including, quite unexpectedly, a Hebrew translation of the ubiquitous *Amadis de Gaule*.[41] Hebrew typography was a unique phenomenon in the Ottoman Empire, where print was otherwise scarcely known until the seventeenth century.

Atlantic crossings

By far the most important satellite of the Spanish print industry was in Spanish America where the printing press followed hard on the heels of the explorers as an essential part of the desire to plant European societies in the new territories. The first press set up in the Indies was a partnership between Diego de Merieta, Bishop of Mexico, and the Seville printer, Juan Cromberger.[42] Merieta was passionately committed to bringing Catholicism to the indigenous peoples of his new diocese, and believed that print would play an essential role in this. Cromberger was a logical partner: all goods exported to the Indies passed through Seville, and Cromberger was the city's largest publisher. He and his father each maintained a factor in Mexico City to handle the large quantity of books and other goods they shipped westward. The new branch office in Mexico was entrusted to Giovanni Paoli, an Italian from Brescia; the first books rolled off the press in 1540. All the raw materials – ink, type, instruments and paper – came from Spain.

The Mexico office produced books of great beauty. The most culturally significant were the grammars, catechisms and liturgies written in the local languages.[43] But these could just as easily have been printed in Spain (as Cromberger had demonstrated in 1538, before the establishment of the Mexico press). The volume of books produced in New Spain, and later in Lima, though significant, was easily swamped by the vast consignments of imported books that continued to the end of the century. It is hard to avoid the impression that Cromberger's investment in printing abroad was little more than a loss leader, designed to curry favour with the crown and local administrators in the new territories. The royal decree confirming the rights of the Cromberger press also granted the family a monopoly of all books exported from Spain. This privilege more than justified the modest investment in shipping a single press to Mexico. The grant of a stake in the new silver and gold mines opened the way to another fortune.

The total output of the print shops of Mexico and Peru was something in the region of 300 editions.[44] The overall volume is small, but they included books of real typographical sophistication. The quality of workmanship in this respect contrasts markedly with the later and puzzlingly halting development of print in colonial North America.[45] Although a print shop was established in Massachusetts by 1640 to serve the needs of the new Harvard College in Cambridge, print developed far less rapidly than other aspects of the material culture of the British colonies. For more than a hundred years, indeed right up to the war of independence, large quantities of books were imported from England. Local firms published mostly pamphlets or news print, a growing market in the eighteenth century and a telling barometer of the opening gulf of incomprehension between the homeland and colonial society.

Heart of Europe

The planting of print in the remotest corners of the European landmass, and beyond, was an extraordinary testament to the faith in books. The significance of these small and fitfully successful enterprises went far beyond the quantity of books produced: the number of books published in the Spanish Americas was insignificant compared to those shipped from Spain and it was certainly as easy to bring books from Denmark as to set up a press in Iceland. The purpose of these local presses was partly symbolic. Their existence expressed faith in literary culture as a part of the civilising process. For the kings of Scotland an indigenous printing industry, however small, was as important an attribute of the nation state as a crown or palace.

Nevertheless the capacities of the smaller centres of print remained limited. In the course of the sixteenth century iron laws of economics reinforced the domination of the largest and best-located centres of print, and the best-capitalised firms. Certain books could be undertaken only by firms with large capital resources and access to reliable credit. Large scholarly and technical volumes became an effective monopoly of these firms.

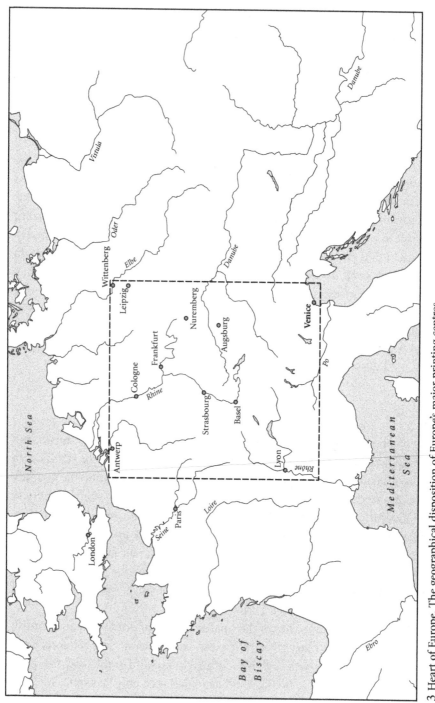

3 Heart of Europe. The geographical disposition of Europe's major printing centres.

The major print cultures closest to the heart of Europe dominated the output in scholarly and learned literature: around 92 per cent of all Latin books published in the sixteenth century emanated from these places. The market functioned efficiently to deliver these books to readers from Prague to Shrewsbury, from Stockholm to Zaragoza. But for printers in these smaller peripheral markets it was hard to envisage publishing the large folios or scholarly texts that have excited posterity. Plantin's Polyglot Bible, Münster's *Cosmography* or the anatomical treatises of Vesalius could only be undertaken by one of the largest firms. Most works of this type came from a handful of cities that between them shaped the market: Paris, Lyon and Antwerp; Venice, Basel, Frankfurt and Nuremberg. If print was to articulate the excitement that animated the age of discoveries – in science and medicine, technology and map-making – then it would be to these places that Europe's best minds would necessarily bend their steps.

PART IV

NEW WORLDS

CHAPTER 13

SCIENCE AND EXPLORATION

In 1539 a young mathematician, Georg Joachim Rheticus, embarked on a journey of momentous consequence for the history of science. Rheticus is not a name well known even to scholars. At this point in his life he had little to distinguish him from other graduates of Wittenberg University apart from a family scandal: his father, a medical doctor, had been convicted of embezzlement and beheaded. In 1538 Rheticus left Wittenberg and settled in Nuremberg. Here he fell in with Johann Schoener, the city's most distinguished astronomer; the following year he set off alone for Frauenberg, a small cathedral city on the Baltic coast beyond Danzig.

The purpose of this journey was to visit the renowned astronomer, Nicolas Copernicus. Although Copernicus had travelled in Europe earlier in his life, from 1510 he was permanently settled in his Polish-Prussian homeland, relatively remote from the major centres of European scholarship. To ingratiate himself with the older man Rheticus had been provided with three valuable scientific volumes for Copernicus's library. This was a gift with a purpose. The texts were the work of a Nuremberg printer, Johannes Petreius, who wanted Rheticus to persuade Copernicus to let him publish the master-work it was widely believed he would soon have ready for the press. The gift of the three texts was to demonstrate that only Germany's greatest centre of scientific publishing could do justice to Copernicus's work; and to help Rheticus prise the precious manuscript from the old man's hands.

Copernicus kept Rheticus guessing. He seems to have enjoyed the younger man's company, and it was 1541 before Rheticus could set off back to Wittenberg, clutching the manuscript of what would be Copernicus's major text, *De revolutionibus (Of the Revolution of the Heavenly Spheres)*. The following year he journeyed on to Nuremberg, where Petreius was waiting to set it on his press; it took until 1543 before the text, complete with its famous woodcut diagrams of Copernicus's heliocentric system, was ready for sale.[1]

It would be many years before Europe's community of astronomers and mathematicians finally assimilated the full importance of the discoveries revealed in this text. But its complex publication history already tells us something important about the printing of scientific books. For while books of mathematics, medicine, astronomy and technical manuals of many sorts had been appearing from the first decades of print, the publication of serious works of investigative scholarship required a particular sort of printer.[2] Most of the books that we think of as milestones of scientific investigation were large and complex. They were published in large formats, and usually in the scholarly languages, for a widely dispersed international readership. In other words they shared many characteristics with the works of textual scholarship, theology and law that had dominated the output of the largest printing firms since the development of an international trade. The same firms would play a critical role in the growing market in books of science.

Publishing science

The overwhelming proportion of scholarly, scientific books published in the sixteenth century emanated from the limited group of publishing houses that already dominated the book world at the top end of the market. It was a difficult part of the market, requiring a heavy investment of capital, both financial and intellectual. Even for the well-established publishers it was often necessary to share risk: with the author, or even with the supplier of the paper. Given the large quantities of paper required for large books, the paper merchant could sometimes be persuaded to advance supplies on credit in return for a share of the finished texts, which he could then sell on. Large, serious books had to be distributed over a wide area to reach a market that was potentially large, but widely dispersed. So centres of scientific publishing tended to be in places that were close to leading centres of scholarship and had good access to an established distribution network.

This happy confluence helps explain the emergence of Basel as a major centre of scholarly printing in precisely this period. A regional centre of some significance since the fifteenth century, the Basel printing industry expanded rapidly in the 1520s. In these years it profited from a combination of favourable circumstances, uniting the prestige in intellectual circles that came with the patronage of Erasmus with an active participation in the printing of the Protestant Reformation.[3] The heirs of the house of Froben, particularly

Fig. 55 The heliocentric cosmology. A dramatically simple representation of a revolutionary thesis.

Johannes Oporinus, were able to build on this foundation by creating a distinct market specialism in the publication of scholarly, especially medical, texts.[4] Basel was home to one of Europe's leading universities, and a reputation for a degree of religious toleration encouraged original and unconventional thinkers to settle in the city. It also profited from its position on some of Europe's major trade routes. With good connections to the fair at Frankfurt and the distinguished medical faculty of Montpellier, Basel acted as an effective conduit between the university faculties of Italy and the intellectual world of northern Europe.

Basel's close connections with the south German Imperial cities made it well placed to exploit the growing use of woodcuts as illustrative material in printed books. This feature of the middle decades of the sixteenth century impacted particularly on the production of large and expensive books in the fields of science and exploration and marked a quantum shift in the role that illustrations would play in printed books.

In the early years of print most books on scientific subjects were not illustrated, reflecting the scientific precepts of the ancients. In the fifteenth century woodcuts were used largely for adornment rather than instruction. As the market for scholarly books developed in the sixteenth century, perception of the utility of illustrations would change. The naturalistic rendition of plants, animals and the human body, architectural plans and geometric diagrams of the planets, became an essential part of the pedagogic scheme. From the middle years of the century an increasing number of books on scientific subjects were provided with woodcut illustrations, often in great profusion.

This came at a cost. The design and execution of such technical woodcuts (and later engravings) required great technical skill, and could be extremely expensive. Often the artists had to work closely with the author, in a way in which those who worked on woodcuts of the Virgin for a theological book did not. When the great encyclopaedic books of nature called for several hundred woodcuts, the costs could be prohibitive. In some complex projects illustrations made up around three-quarters of the capital cost, and this had to be recouped from the customer. The authors of one German herbal decided to publish their book without illustrations in the fifteenth-century fashion, specifically so as not to put purchase outside the range of their intended student readership.[5] But this was simply no longer conceivable in some classes of book where, from the mid-sixteenth century, anatomically correct illustration was central to the book's scientific purpose.

The development of the technical woodcut had important consequences, both philosophical and practical. In the first place it helped tip the balance of scholarly investigation towards a science of investigation. In all branches of scholarship, as we shall see, the tenets of the ancient authorities continued to exert a powerful hold: all scientific investigation was constructed within an intellectual framework created by Aristotle. Yet even while the classical authorities continued to be honoured, in repeated editions and commentaries, the contents of new scholarly writings permitted the dissemination of thoughtful, painstaking work that privileged a science of observation. It was an important transitional step towards the philosophical reordering of knowledge that followed in later centuries.

Dissemination was also assisted by certain practical aspects of the trade, not least the fact that illustration had an international currency not dependent on comprehension of the accompanying text. Thus it became possible to promote the distribution of illustrated scholarly books even when the text was in an unfamiliar vernacular language. It may be that some of the larger, more expensive vernacular editions were only viable because they tapped into an international market normally only available for books in Latin. Certainly a striking feature of the development of the market in scholarly, scientific books in several disciplines is the large number of vernacular editions; a sure indication of public interest in the science of observation that had spread far beyond the learned elite.

Disordered heavens

Modern scientific notions make a clear distinction between astronomy, the study of the number and nature of heavenly bodies, and cosmology, the study of the nature of the universe as an ordered structure. These are carefully distinguished from astrology, the interpretation of the influence of the heavenly bodies on earthly matters. Renaissance Europe, in truth, recognised no such tidy distinctions.

Those who searched for order in human existence scanned, searched and invoked the heavens. Heavenly bodies, and the restless march of the seasons, shaped the patterns of daily life and offered portents for the future. So it is not the case that one can distinguish a scholarly interest in cosmology and astronomy from a popular concern with astrology. Europe's citizens, educated or merely curious, spanned the entire spectrum from the most learned investigation to the most credulous reading of runes. Popular publications such as almanacs and calendars may seem a long way distant from learned works of scientific cosmology. But the two were closely linked, both by the intellectual framework of the leading practitioners, all urgently convinced of the relevance of celestial motions for understanding life on earth, and by the capacities of the printing press to present and articulate their discoveries.

Both astrologers and cosmographers made heavy use of ephemerides, printed volumes of mathematical tables computing planetary positions on a daily basis. These austere volumes made heavy demands on the competence and accuracy of a printer: they could only really be undertaken with the author or another competent astrologer at hand. Works of cosmography also demanded large numbers of specially drawn woodcuts.

As with so many branches of the scientific investigation, cosmology lived in the shadow of the ancients. In Aristotle's firmly geocentric system, earth was the fixed point around which the other celestial spheres moved. The Renaissance rediscovery of the Greeks enhanced and reinforced the prestige of the ancient wisdom, most specifically with the publication of the influential work of Ptolemy. The Ptolemaic revival owed much to two fifteenth-century German astronomers, Georg Peurbach and Johannes Müller von Königsberg, known as Regiomontanus. Their success helped establish Nuremberg as a leading centre of scientific publication, with important consequences for the sixteenth century.

The sixteenth-century astronomers also promoted the study of comets, which became an important stimulus to practical astronomy throughout the period. According to classic Aristotelian theory, comets consisted of terrestrial exhalations extracted from the earth by the heat of other celestial bodies. Their appearance in the sky, and passage through the stations of the zodiac and prominent constellations, provided the key to interpretations of their significance. Few in the sixteenth century doubted that the appearance of a comet was an event pregnant with meaning.

From antiquity to the Renaissance, blazing stars seemed to augur menacing, traumatic events, often in concert with other portents: unseasonable weather, hailstones that flattened crops, unnatural births. In the Reformation comets were often seen as harbingers of the end time. Such interpretations were encouraged by readings of the Book of Revelation, vividly illustrated in the new Protestant translations of the Bible. Preachers seized eagerly on this opportunity to reinforce calls for repentance. Thus Martin Luther, in a sermon on the Second Coming, preached in 1522:

> We see the Sun to be darkened and the Moon, the stars to fall, men to be distressed, all the winds and waters to make a noise, and whatever else is foretold of the Lord, all of them to come to pass as it were together. Besides, we have seen not a few comets, having the form of the cross, imprinted from heaven, both on the bodies and garments of men, new kinds of diseases, as the French pox, and some others. How many other signs also, and unusual impressions have we seen in the heavens, in the Sun, Moon, stars, rainbows and strange apparitions, in these last four years? Let us at least acknowledge these to be signs, and signs of some great and notable change.[6]

Luther and the scientifically minded Melanchthon led the Protestant tendency towards ever more specific interpretation of celestial apparitions.[7] Printed pamphlets injected monsters and celestial prodigies into the heart of the polemical debate. Numerous pamphlets and broadsheets offered accounts of the passage of comets and vivid interpretations of their significance. The careful plotting of their passage through the constellations provided data for learned cosmologists. Tycho Brahe, one of the most gifted and influential cosmologists of the day, drew up two detailed horoscopes of the comet of 1585.

Europe's rulers followed these events with interest: no wonder, since the great events foreshadowed by comets were usually believed to include the death of kings. In consequence the leading cosmographers were much cherished at court. Their tactful interpretation of celestial events for anxious royal patrons helped secure patronage and financial support for their scientific investigations. Tycho Brahe's observatory on an island in the Danish sound was established at the invitation of the King of Denmark. Petrus Apian's masterpiece, *Astronomicum Caesareum*, was, as the name suggests, crafted for the pleasure of his Imperial patron, Charles V.

This royal support was very welcome, because works of scientific cosmology were some of the most complex and expensive books of the era. Many were embellished not only with tables of mathematical observations and schematic geometric diagrams, but also with volvelles, printed discs layered one above the other, which could be rotated to indicate the position of the planets. Some cosmological publications included three or four such devices. Authors muttered darkly that these rotating paper instruments were often misplaced in the text, and they are frequently missing from copies that survive today. But it says much for the commitment and growing confidence of the publishing community that they were willing to take on such complex projects in the first place.

The book nobody read

Sixteenth-century scientists relied on a complex network of interlocking connections: with the small group of printers capable of publishing their books; with the royal patrons who underwrote their investigations; and with the small, dispersed community of fellow investigators. The circulation of printed books helped bring them together. But such men also kept in contact by other means: through the university system, through correspondence, and by exchanging and copying manuscripts. Given the complexities of rendering scientific diagrams into printed form, manuscripts would have an important continuing place in scientific discourse long into the age of print.

All of these elements came together in the long journey that brought Copernicus's great book to public notice. Copernicus's theory that the earth rotated around the sun was already quite well known thanks to a manuscript summary he had circulated among scholars as early as 1514. It was this that prompted Georg Joachim Rheticus to embark on his long trek north to Frauenberg twenty years later. Thanks to Rheticus's skilful diplomacy, the *De revolutionibus* was finally completed a few weeks before Copernicus's death in 1543. He had been incapacitated by a stroke the year before.

Yet how influential was the publication of this text? Copernicus's discovery did not win wide acceptance straight away. Even those who assisted in its publication were careful to distance themselves from its most daring, and potentially heretical, propositions. Only two generations later, with the more sustained published programme of Kepler, would the heliocentric hypothesis begin to dominate cosmographical science, leading to the notable denouement of the trial of Galileo. What does this tell us? Was Copernicus's text, as the author Arthur Koestler famously declared, 'the book nobody read'?

If Copernicus did not immediately radicalise cosmography, he was certainly not ignored. Forty years ago the American astronomer Owen

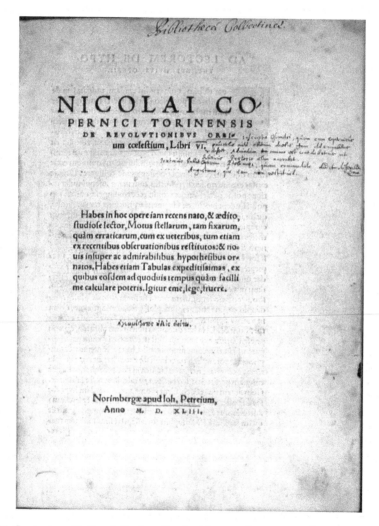

Fig. 56 Copernicus, *De Revolutionibus*. On the title-page the owner, Willebrord Snell, affirms his support for Copernicus's views, and his disapproval of the cautious preface inserted by Andreas Osiander (without the author's knowledge), to the extent that Copernicus's radical hypotheses 'need not be true nor even probable'.

Gingerich, goaded by Koestler's caustic aphorism, determined to examine the contemporary influence of Copernicus's book by compiling an exhaustive bibliography of surviving copies of the two sixteenth-century editions.[8] Spurred by his discovery (in the Royal Observatory in Edinburgh) of the copy of the first edition annotated by Erasmus Reinhold, Professor of Astrology at Wittenberg, Gingerich embarked on a remarkable odyssey, tracking down a total of some 600 copies: about half the estimated original print run of 500 copies in each edition. Many were richly annotated, suggesting a close engagement with the text, even by owners who were careful to signal their disagreement with the central heretical thesis of a rotating earth.

The spread of contemporary notes of ownership, in Germany, England and France, makes clear that this was a book that contemporaries regarded as important and were keen to own. The number of copies that are in relatively pristine condition suggests that some owners did not study the text very intensively: for them it was a prestige purchase rather than a text with which they engaged. But the scientists who owned this work did read it very carefully, and often filled the margins with detailed notes.[9] When a distinguished scientific author died other colleagues were very keen to buy his books, largely to have access to these manuscript notes. Such annotations were even sometimes transcribed from copy to copy: they became, in this sense, an important part of the research resource.[10] This was a small intimate world where manuscript and print converged and sometimes merged.

New worlds

Divining the secrets of the cosmos occupied many of Europe's greatest minds; terrestrial geography offered another potent challenge. There is no doubt that the voyages of discovery and exploration had a profound impact on Europe's intellectual culture, stimulating a new interest in divining and describing the secrets of the terrestrial world. Accounts of the early voyages were read and published around Europe. The potential of the unknown lands soon began to excite scholars, and, for rather different reasons, Europe's ruling powers.

The assimilation of these new discoveries into the European world view was neither easy nor straightforward. This was partly because the reading public had inherited from the fables and imagined narratives of the medieval period a perception of the non-European world so exotic that the reality could appear prosaic in comparison. The most popular of the medieval travelogues was the *Travels* of John de Mandeville, a mishmash of plagiarism and fiction that remained a steady bestseller long into the age of print. This beguiling book, which begins as a practical guidebook for pilgrims before launching into a more exotic description of the marvels of the East, went through multiple editions in almost every European language during the sixteenth century.[11]

The tenacious popularity of this fantastical narrative – and the marginally more sober Marco Polo – helps explain why Christopher Columbus's brief factual account of his new discoveries was soon eclipsed by the more sensational works of Amerigo Vespucci. Vespucci's narrative resonated with an audience ready to accept that the dark places of the earth housed monstrous and fantastic creatures. Thus while Columbus had only heard tell of cannibalism, Vespucci had met a man who had eaten 300 people – and there was much more in the same vein. Vespucci's *Mundus novus* of 1504 was swiftly republished in Augsburg, Nuremberg and Cologne.[12] His voyages found their greatest renown through the *Paesi novamente retrovati et novo mondo*, a retelling of Vespucci's narrative edited by Francanzio da Montalboddo. This enjoyed considerable popularity in Germany, thanks to a rapid German translation, and then, rather later, in France. Five editions of the French translation appeared between 1515 and 1517, with further reprints in 1521 and 1534.[13]

Interpretation of the newly discovered continents had also to negotiate and assimilate the established and still revered wisdom of the ancients. The influence of classical authority was, as in all areas of scholarship, powerful and pervasive. In the field of geography Ptolemy and Strabo, the two names that stand above all others, functioned as representatives of two broad approaches to recording and mapping knowledge of the world familiar from the ancients. Those inspired by Ptolemy would study cartography, applying mathematics and geometry to the task of fathoming the shape, size and relative proportions of lands and seas. Those who followed Strabo would adopt a more descriptive and anthropological approach, describing the land as experienced by man; its landscape but also the customs and institutions of its peoples. By the middle of the sixteenth century these two traditions would merge in the great works of universal cosmography.

The New World voyages were not the only inspiration for the development of geographical literature in the sixteenth century. Accounts of the New World discoveries had to compete with tumultuous events closer to home, events often with more immediate consequences: the wars in Italy, the relentless advance of Ottoman power through the Mediterranean and the Balkans. Many of those who pursued geography through description of place, landscape and natural world in the tradition of Strabo found their subjects closer to home. An extremely popular work in this genre was the *Omnium gentium mores* of

Johannes Boemus, an account of the peoples of the known continents of Europe, Africa and Asia. Where the customs and mores of distant peoples are described in these works it is often to contrast them with the cultured and civilised core of Christian Europe. In fact the descriptions of non-European peoples show a clear taste for the aberrant and monstrous that has not progressed far beyond Mandeville. Boemus was especially keen to celebrate German history and achievements, taking up the challenge laid down by Conrad Celtis, the prince of German humanists. This cultural nationalism was a distinct feature of many of the historio-topographical works of the sixteenth century. German readers fascinated by Boemus's descriptions of the dog-faced peoples of Asia's mountain ranges would also have enjoyed the contrast he made between the effete French preoccupation with dress and the robust masculinity of the German race.

So authors who sought to interest readers in the peoples of the New World faced formidable competition: small wonder that they dug deep into the well of inherited tropes to add sauce to their testimony. The dangers as well as the excitement of this new topographical literature are well illustrated by the career of its most controversial exponent, the French author André Thevet. Thevet was a man of relatively modest social origins, who owed his education and opportunities for travel to his upbringing in the Franciscan Order.[14] Three years in the Middle East, travelling between Jerusalem and Constantinople, provided the inspiration for his first geographical work, the *Cosmography of Levant*, though in truth this is a work that owed more to the compilations of humanist authors than to his own experiences.[15] Anthologies like the *Ancient Lessons* of Coelius Rhodiginus were frequently plundered by sixteenth-century geographical writers to give their works a lustre of learning, and Thevet used this text shamelessly.[16] In doing so he exhibited a borrowed humanism, recycling the digested learning of the early sixteenth century for a public with no knowledge of Greek, or even Latin.

The compositional techniques Thevet used in the *Cosmography* would be put to further use in his second and more famous work. In 1555 Thevet was among those who accompanied Nicolas Durand de Villegaignon on the ill-fated French expedition to Brazil. The expedition proved rancorous and ultimately unsuccessful, and Thevet's role was distinctly inglorious: falling ill shortly after disembarkation, he was sent back when the ship that had brought him returned to France. But from his short ten-week stay Thevet fashioned the work that would establish his reputation: *Les singularitez de la France antarctique*.[17] In this work Thevet created a Brazil that owed something to observation, but far more to a prolific use of ancient and modern learned authors. These borrowings were not without cost to Thevet. The copious citations of Greek and Latin authors were largely the contribution of Mathurin Héret, a learned doctor and classicist who had acted as Thevet's assistant. When the book was published, Héret contested Thevet's right to be named sole author. Thevet successfully defended his right of authorship, at the cost of surrendering to Héret the financial profit from the book.[18]

The solution, though squalid, was probably just, for Thevet's debt to ancient and modern authorities went far beyond Héret's decorative citations. Thevet's presentation of the indigenous peoples he can scarcely have experienced is in perfect conformity with the topos of the barbarous native emerging from the conflation of ancient historical writers with modern authors such as Polydore Vergil.[19] In his discovery of the fourth tribe of the Amazons, and a native king of Herculean powers and appetites, Thevet created a Brazil that was at one and the same time thrillingly exotic and yet reassuringly familiar; and this, indeed, may have been the basis of his success.

The search for the Amazons, located by the ancient Greeks in Asia Minor, and discussed in Mandeville, Marco Polo and other medieval travelogues, was a common theme of sixteenth-century travel literature from Columbus onwards. In the fictitious chronicles of *Amadis* this warlike tribe of women who lived without men are located on the island of 'California'; later Spanish authors sought them in the new lands of southern America.[20] For Thevet the temptation to claim them for Brazil was irresistible.

Thevet's work brought him welcome attention at the French court and, ultimately, appointment as Cosmographer Royal – a new post apparently created for him. This financial security allowed him to embark on his final great work, the *Universal Cosmography*, a work on a grand scale but with the American voyage still at its heart.[21] But Thevet was not without his critics, and it was this last work, published in 1575, that stirred his most powerful detractor, Jean de Léry, into action.[22] De Léry was another veteran of the Brazil expedition, though he arrived after Thevet had already left the colony. De Léry witnessed the voyage's failure, but survived to return to France and become a Protestant minister. The Huguenot role in the colonial venture became one of its most controversial aspects. When Thevet took the side of Villegaignon, who had blamed the Huguenots for the expedition's failure, de Léry was stirred into action. His *History of a Voyage to the Land of Brazil* is therefore in large part a work of justificatory religious polemic, but the detailed and acute observation of the local flora and fauna, and the life of the indigenous population, have ensured de Léry's work the admiration of posterity. The book was certainly an enduring bestseller, going through ten editions between its publication in 1578 and the end of the century.[23]

De Léry was merciless in his ridicule of Thevet's fictions, particularly his presentation of the Herculean king, Quoniambec. This was a myth that grew in precision with the passage of years, ending with his assimilation into the gallery of the great in Thevet's *Lives of Illustrious Men*, alongside Charlemagne and Julius Caesar.[24] De Léry's assault on Thevet, though powerful and telling, was not unprecedented. The limitations of the ancients as a guide to contemporary geography and topography were now increasingly acknowledged. Gonzalo Fernández de Oviedo, author of the *General and Natural History of the Indies* (1535), did not hesitate to criticise the ancient authorities, while stressing the importance of his own observation and experience. Amerigo Vespucci, for all his faults and exaggerations, recognised the significance of what was being achieved when he wrote to his patron Lorenzo de' Medici, 'by this voyage of mine the opinion of the majority of the philosophers is confuted . . . Rationally, let it be said in a whisper, experience is certainly worth more than theory.'[25]

Through the course of the century, as the books of description multiplied, the whisper became louder and more self-confident. An explicit affirmation of the superiority of knowledge derived by observation became a commonplace among writers who aimed, by their description, to encompass the world. But this was a development always hedged by qualifications. Oviedo, bold in his criticism of Ptolemy and Avicenna, was careful not to challenge the authority of the Church in the fields of sacred history and geography. At the very end of the century the Jesuit scholar José de Acosta would win the esteem of his contemporaries with the criticisms of Aristotle in his *Natural and Moral History of the Indies* (1590). His experience of the equatorial regions caused him 'to laugh and jeer at Aristotle's meteorological theories and his philosophy'. But Acosta's own methods were hardly those of the emancipated explorer/observer. Rather he pieced together a mosaic of evidence from diverse sources to show that other ancient writers were innocent of the errors of Aristotle. In other words, Acosta relied not on his own observations to defeat Aristotle, but on other ancients.[26]

Mapping the world

The impact of the New World voyages was most profound in the field of cartography. Maps became objects of fascination in the sixteenth century, amounting almost to a craze. Europe's publishers and booksellers found a new, lucrative market in the sale of maps; either maps bound into collections with other texts, or specially produced wall maps; sometimes made up of several printed sheets. The representation of the world, the outline of Europe's coastlines and the delineation of nations became familiar for the first time. By the end of the sixteenth century ownership of maps was widespread. Among the upper echelons of European society map ownership made possible the assimilation of a wholly new type of spatial awareness, and a vastly more ambitious sense of place.

The assault on the medieval concept of geography had taken a decisive step with the fifteenth-century rediscovery of Ptolemy. Ptolemy was revered by sixteenth-century geographers less for his maps, which were progressively rendered obsolete, than for his articulation of a method. In place of a theological

Fig. 57 *L'henry-metre*. The surveyor at work. It was common in scientific books to honour a patron or potential sponsor with a laudatory address. Henri de Suberville went one stage further and named his device after Henry IV. The name did not catch on.

geography that placed history and religion at the organisational core of the world (and Jerusalem at its centre), Ptolemy set out a system for the empirical analysis of data generated by the application of mathematics and geometry. His geography offered both a list of 8,000 located places and an explanation of the principles of latitude and longitude. The impact of this technical revolution helps explain the otherwise paradoxical fact that Ptolemy's *Geography* was revised and reissued throughout the sixteenth century even as his maps were increasingly shown to be inaccurate. The successive editions served to invoke his authority and protection for new maps redrawn to reflect the knowledge flooding into Europe as a result of Atlantic and Asian voyages.

The delineation of space, however, remained complex. The range of methods available to sixteenth-century mapmakers remained limited and imprecise. Surveying continued to rely on the tested method of measurement of height and distance between two visible points. In consequence only comparatively small areas of the European landmass could be mapped in this way. Surveyors (sometimes cartographers unwillingly pressed into service) could provide detailed maps of the disposition of towns, villages and geographical features in a relatively discrete area. The longer routes could be charted with the help of familiar itineraries, descriptions of pilgrim routes and post roads, but the delineation of larger landmasses beyond the well-known Mediterranean routes required the application of imagination and the careful sifting of often contradictory authorities. For most mapmakers recasting the Ptolomaic world view required a careful study of travel narratives, newly furnished information, and of course other maps.

Thus the correct delimitation of geographical space emerges slowly, and not without many setbacks and meandering down blind alleys. A major impulse to the resolution of remaining cartographical difficulties was provided by the growing popularity of globes. It had been acknowledged since the time of Strabo that the globe presented the best method of representing the whole world – people knew that the earth was round. Until the advent of printing the technical problems associated with constructing a globe limited the use that could be made of this knowledge. However, in the new age of print it was now possible to assemble a globe from printed oval segments of a map (known as gores) which would then be pasted on to a papier mâché core. It was a precise and intricate operation. The best globes were made from maps engraved on copperplate. This work engaged the expertise of some of Europe's leading cartographers, including Gemma Frisius, Oronce Fine and Gerard Mercator.[27]

A globe was intellectually more challenging than a flat map. With a flat map the unknown lands beyond the seas could be relegated to the map's borders, where *terra incognita* could be disguised with elaborate scrolls, texts or sea monsters. But a sphere has no periphery, so globe-making offered no opportunities to obfuscate difficult choices. It was an important stimulus to attempts to give concrete shape to far distant places.

The beginning of a relatively accurate representation of the world and its continents can be discerned in some very early cartographic books. The woodcuts of the hemispheres published in the *De orbis situ ac descriptione* (Geography and description of the world) of Franciscus Monachus (1527) show all the major continents of the known world in a broad outline that is easily recognisable.[28] Thanks to the coastal exploration and portolan charts of the Portuguese the continental landmass of Africa is confidently drawn, and Arabia, Persia and India are clearly identifiable. Even the newly discovered continents of the Americas are rendered in reasonable outline, with the Caribbean, the North American eastern seaboard, and even the Pacific coast of South America all shown.

These were not the only mysteries to be resolved. The outer periphery of the European landmass also required more precise delineation. Not all the decisions made by cartographers were well advised. When Gemma Frisius was constructing his new globe in 1536, he had access to a new representation of Scandinavia which showed Scotland accurately protruding northwards from England rather than, as in Ptolemy, bending at a right angle towards Denmark. But since Peter Apian and the German Waldseemüller had also presented the British Isles with this Ptolomaic kink, Frisius went with the consensus and retained a right-angled Scotland.

Some of the choices to be made were of a sensitivity that went beyond geographical accuracy. By the sixteenth century geographers were convinced that Ptolemy's projection awarded too much of the world's landmasses to the Mediterranean. But shrinking the Mediterranean meant shrinking Spain; not easy when Spain's ruler, Charles V, was a major sponsor of cartographical projects. Frisius, an Imperial client, felt it wise to remain with the traditional representation. Oronce Fine, working at the French court, had no particular need to heed Habsburg sensibilities. His map of 1531 presents a dramatically shrunken Spain.

Of course the whole development of map-making was politically charged in more ways than indicated by this rather comical episode. Rulers commissioned maps to facilitate campaigning or exploration, to lay claim to newly discovered territories, or, more prosaically, to survey more accurately the extent and disposition of their lands. For all of these reasons the engagement of Europe's rulers gave significant support to the development of cartography. Many of Europe's leading cartographers profited from the patronage of Europe's crowned heads: Apian and Frisius at the Imperial court, Oronce Fine in Paris. In England both Christopher Saxton and John Norden worked under the protection of the English crown; the county maps gathered together in Saxton's Atlas of 1579 made a material contribution to consolidating a sense of place in the English county community.[29]

The years between 1565 and 1580 witnessed a number of significant milestones in cartographical publishing. In 1569 Gerard Mercator published his famous world map, the result of a lifetime of methodological investigation, and the first to apply the representational principles that still bear his name: the Mercator projection. The world map was the first step towards the creation of an atlas to replace the outdated maps of Ptolemy, a project completed only after Mercator's death. Meanwhile Mercator would be overtaken by a former protégé, the more commercially minded Abraham Ortelius. In 1570 Ortelius published at Antwerp his *Theatrum orbis terrarum*, an atlas of fifty-three plates, the first atlas in the modern sense.[30] Ortelius was a less gifted cartographer than Mercator. He freely acknowledged that the maps in his collection were copied from the work of others, and the preface to the *Theatrum* named eighty-seven 'authors'. By orchestrating such a project in the printing metropolis of Antwerp Ortelius offered a compilation of the major advances in cartography in the previous century. The public response was immediate: a further twenty-four editions would be published before Ortelius's death in 1598.

Ortelius's *Theatrum* should be considered alongside another great work of cartographical compilation, the *Civitates orbis terrarum* of Georg Braun and Franz Hogenberg. This work was a collection of city views, and recalls the great success of Hartmann Schedel's *Nuremberg Chronicle* in the first print era. Schedel's cityscapes were uniform in style, showing a city in a profile that emphasised the grandeur of the major civic and ecclesiastical buildings crammed within the walls: this was the city as viewed by a traveller arriving on foot. The woodcuts were often representational, rather than accurate (Schedel sometimes used the same woodcut for completely different cities), but they did effectively convey the majesty and power of the urban community. During the sixteenth century the genre advanced. City plans, based on observation from clock towers or pacing with a compass, became more accurate. The panoramic profile in the style of the *Nuremberg Chronicle* remained popular, but to give a full impression of the layout of the city artists often preferred a diagonal or bird's eye view: the best example is Cornelis Anthonisz's (1544) view of Amsterdam.[31] A third option was the planimetric representation, as if seen directly from above, a style that revived classical Roman practice and presents an accurate rendering of distance, if a less pleasing image to the eye.

It was Georg Braun, a Catholic cleric from Cologne, who first proposed a compendious collection of such city plans that would mix representations of all types (and a large measure of textual description). To engrave the plates he engaged the Protestant artist Franz Hogenberg. The result of this collaboration was a collection of some 550 views, and a publishing triumph.[32] The collection went through many editions, in many languages, and found its way into prosperous homes throughout Europe. As a means of evoking the civilising achievement of European society what could be more effective than a teeming vision of Europe's most richly populated cities, all represented as discrete, usually walled communities, shorn of their suburbs (which, in reality, were a filthy and disorderly ordeal for any traveller to pass through)? All this was presented in a volume that was itself a monument to the technical capacities of print.

The organisation of knowledge

In due course the two traditions of geography, the descriptive and the cartographical, would diverge. Cartography would develop as a technical science, with ever more exact methods of measurement and ever more exacting standards. The tradition of descriptive geography would recede, until reborn in the age of mass tourism as the Baedeker and Rough Guides. But in the sixteenth century there was no sense that these two geographical traditions should separate. Rather authors pursued the goal of encyclopaedic geography, encapsulating the knowledge of the world and its peoples with maps and descriptive text.

This was the principle that lay behind the *Cosmography* of Sebastian Münster, one of the most ambitious scientific publications of the age.[33] But it also reflected a wider urge to capture, order and display knowledge of the world and its peoples, flora and fauna, a movement that was a distinctive feature of the intellectual culture of the period.[34] The quest for encyclopaediac knowledge was not new: we have seen that notions of this nature lay behind the construction of the greatest libraries, the desire of Cosimo de' Medici, Corvinus or Colón to create a collection that would encompass all of the world's learning. The achievement of such an ambition proved to be beyond even the richest collectors. Instead, scholars pursued other means to register, collate and order knowledge. This would prove to be one of the most significant intellectual imperatives of the sixteenth century.

The accumulation of material for Münster's great project began as early as 1528, sixteen years before publication of the first edition. Münster always conceived of it as a collaborative venture. He knew such a work could not be achieved without contributions from the dispersed scholarly community, to whom he now appealed for topographical information and financial support.

Münster was a cartographer of some note. In the course of accumulating data for his book he travelled widely, and the first part of his text offers a discourse on surveying techniques. In 1540 he published a distinguished edition of Ptolemy, which was repeatedly republished. The first edition of the *Cosmography* appeared in 1544, a work of 640 folio pages and 520 woodcuts, along with 24 large double-page maps. To Münster's relief, and that of the publisher Heinrich Petri, who had borne most of the cost, the work was an immediate success, with new editions in 1545, 1546 and 1548, all in German.[35] With each new edition the book expanded until by the definitive edition of 1550 it had reached 1,233 pages, with 910 woodcuts and 54 new maps. The expanded coverage corrected the Germanic bias of the first version and made it more suitable for an international audience. The 1550 edition was the first to be issued in Latin, and other vernacular translations followed: into French (1552), Czech (1554) and Italian (1558).[36] The pace of production was not slowed by Münster's death. An expanded posthumous edition was published in 1572, and this formed the basis for François de Belleforest's vast French *Cosmographie universelle* (1575). The provision of a large quantity of new material, including 600 pages on the geography and customs of France, brought the work to a massive 4,000 pages.[37]

Who were the intended users of such a book? Belleforest introduced many new topics, increasing the amount of space devoted to descriptions of different political systems. But he also abandoned many of Münster's maps, a considerable loss, since a striking feature of Münster's project is the cartographical diversity. The maps showed little of the visual austerity and high seriousness that came increasingly to characterise the cartography of the latter part of the century. The oceans are richly populated with fish and sea monsters and there are woodcuts of earthquakes and volcanoes, exotic beasts and monstrous races. This is a celebration of an expanding world in all its rich, and sometimes imagined, variety.

The natural world

Natural history was another field that profited greatly from the systematic scientific research of the era. Here illustrations played a crucial role in expanding knowledge. In medieval manuscripts plants were valued for their medical utility, and those of no immediate pharmaceutical use were largely ignored.[38] This was an area of scholarly investigation where the inherited intellectual framework was peculiarly unhelpful, since the medieval tradition largely followed Aristotle in his preoccupation with the soul of plants. A further problem with the traditional herbals was that when plants and their medicinal properties were described they were given local names that were not easy to translate into a form that would allow the same plant or herb to be recognised in another part of Europe. Without accurate pictorial representations it was difficult to establish from textual description alone whether the German and Arabic names described the same plant. For all of these reasons real progress in botanical description was possible only when scholars and medical practitioners had access to accurate realistic illustrations, reproduced and distributed as woodcuts or engravings. This also explains why so many of the fundamental botanical texts emanated from Germany, the acknowledged centre of sixteenth-century woodcut art.

The development of botanical illustration was deeply indebted to the path-breaking work of Albrecht Dürer, who had set new standards in the naturalistic representation of animals and plants. It was a student of Dürer, Hans Weiditz, who provided the illustrations for the *Herbarum vivae icones* (Living Portraits of Plants) of Otto Brunfels, published in 1530.[39] As the title suggests, the text, a pastiche of the Greek physician Dioscorides, was less important than the illustrations, 260 superbly executed woodcuts. Like his medieval forebears, Brunfels excluded any plants that had no obvious medical applicability. But his work was an important first step towards the enumeration and ordering of Europe's plant life. It would be continued by a host of talented naturalists, among them Leonhard Fuchs, the author of *De historia stirpium* (History of Plants) (1542).[40] This contained 500 illustrations of plants, arranged in alphabetical order. A version of these illustrations was later employed by William Turner for his *English Herbal.* Turner, realising that a major source of pharmacological confusion was the difficulty in recognising plants variously described in different languages, concentrated on matching plants with their names in five languages: Greek, Latin, English, German and French.[41] This became a standard feature of many of these encyclopaedic works.

In botany the principal classical archetype was the compendious *De materia medica* of Dioscorides, the foundational work of medical pharmacopoeia. One of the most influential of all sixteenth-century botanical works, the *Discorsi* of Pietro Andrea Mattioli, was ostensibly a commentary on Dioscorides: in practice it ranged much wider, with each successive edition incorporating new illustrations, including previously unknown plants brought back by travellers from the Near East and the newly discovered continents of the New World.[42]

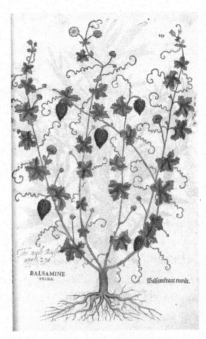

Fig. 58 a & b Leonhard Fuchs, *De Historia Stirpium,* depicting the illustrators at work. Meyer makes the likeness, which Füllmaurer then cuts into the woodblock, and *(right)* the completed woodblock.

Particularly important were the Levantine journeys of the French botanist Pierre Belon, and the groundbreaking enumeration of the flora of the New World by the Spanish physician, Nicolas Monardes. His *Historia medicinal de las cosas que se traen de nuestras Indias Occidentales,* published in parts from 1565 onwards, was quickly translated into Latin, French and English.[43] The Latin edition of 1574 was the work of Christophe Plantin, who by this date had built up in his print shop in Antwerp a considerable repertory of botanical woodcuts. These he used interchangeably to illustrate the botanical texts of Charles de l'Ecluse (Clusius), Rembert Dodoens and Matthias de l'Obel (Lobelius). Not all these great projects were brought to fruition. The Swiss scholar Conrad Gesner accumulated some 1,500 illustrations of plants but turned first to the animal kingdom, perhaps in imitation of Aristotle: when Aristotle embarked on his *Historia animalium* he left the plant world to his pupil, Theophrastus. Gesner's work of the same title appeared in four volumes between 1551 and 1558, a monumental work of around 1,200 illustrations. In the same year Guillaume Rondelet, regent in the medical faculty of Montpellier, published his study of fish, *Libri de piscibus marinis,* a book that enjoyed popular success especially in the French translation by Laurent Joubert.[44]

The encyclopaedia urge

Although Conrad Gesner would publish only a proportion of his researches on the natural world, his reputation as one of the great encyclopaedic authors of the sixteenth century was already secure. In 1545, aged just twenty-nine, Gesner published his *Bibliotheca universalis*, an alphabetical index of all known authors who had written in Greek, Latin or Hebrew. If the lost libraries of Alexandria and Byzantium could never be recovered, the names of the authors could at least be honoured. Gesner searched the catalogues of the great libraries of Italy; he enlisted the aid of printers and booksellers in Germany, Italy and France. The result was a list of some 3,000 authors and 10,000 titles, organised and divided by genre. Gesner's great work was the inspiration for a wave of similar projects in different parts of Europe. John Bale's careful enumeration of the Anglo-Saxon and Norman literary heritage of the British Isles was based on a personal examination of many monastic libraries before their dissolution. The French scholars La Croix du Maine and Antoine du Verdier documented the works of French authors.[45] Gesner also stimulated greater interest in the thematic classification of knowledge, an impulse reflected both in the published catalogues of the Frankfurt Fair and in schemes of library classification that reached their apogee in the work of Gerard Naudé in the seventeenth century.[46]

The search for order in the expanding world of knowledge had consequences for the design and presentation of scholarly books. The index, at first an occasional and somewhat haphazard feature of the printed book, became increasingly systematic, and a standard feature of scholarly texts.[47] While indexes were known in printed texts as early as the 1480s, and indeed even earlier in manuscripts, they remained for some time idiosyncratic in both their subject treatment and their organisation of material. The sixteenth century saw a progressive rationalisation of the principles of indexing: here Conrad Gesner was influential in his call for strict alphabetisation. An index was now characteristically printed as separate gatherings, which could be bound either with the preliminaries, as a guide to what followed, or, as is now the standard practice, at the end. An index could also be a useful feature in justifying or advertising a new edition. Many scholarly books advertised an index on the title-page as an inducement to purchase, often alongside more doubtful claims that an edition was 'completely revised'. These title-page advertisements also reveal the extent to which the development of a scholarly text represented an evolving conversation between printer, author and the reading public. The title-page of the Basel edition of Ptolemy's *Geography* of 1552 listed various additional features, including 'two indexes requested by many until now, through the use of which one can easily deduce the location of sites both ancient and modern'.[48]

Perhaps nothing encapsulates the passion for encyclopaedic knowledge that gripped this era better than the vast growth in the writing and publication of dictionaries. The middle years of the sixteenth century spawned an extraordinary number of dictionaries in every format and language, or combination of languages.[49] They served the needs of a wide variety of anticipated users, from the school pupil, student and scholar, to the merchant seeking equivalents for vocabulary essential to trade. Dictionaries of the ancient languages represented notable feats of scholarship, over which authors laboured for many years.

The heights that could be attained by these monumental works are epitomised in the legacy of the Bergamese lexicographer Ambrogio Calepino. The first edition of his dictionary, a glossary of Latin words with Greek equivalents, was already a work of mature scholarship. Calepino, born in 1440, had consulted and incorporated the best fruits of fifteenth-century Italian lexicography.[50] The dictionary was an immediate success, and through successive revisions took on an ever more cosmopolitan character; mostly, after Calepino's death in 1510, in the hands of editors. A Venetian edition of 1545 added Italian equivalences; an Antwerp edition of the same year, justly titled 'Pentaglossos', contained five languages, Latin, Greek, German, Dutch and French. As Calepino's text bounced around the major printing centres of Europe, new languages were added or subtracted to suit the anticipated local clientele, culminating in the prodigious eleven-language editions published in Basel from 1590.

This was from the beginning a large and complex book. The first edition of 1502 was already a folio of 400 leaves; the multilingual edition of 1590 sprawled over 2,000 pages, again in folio (the book was only rarely printed in a smaller format). Given the size and complexity of this project, it is not surprising that publication was monopolised by a small number of Europe's best-financed printing houses. Of the 166 editions published during the sixteenth century, more than 85 per cent were published in just four cities: Venice, Paris, Lyon and Basel. But if production was a highly specialised task, the book was certainly disseminated very widely. A huge number of copies survive in libraries all over Europe. The sheer expense of purchasing a copy ensured that it would be cherished; not least as a symbol of the seriousness of purpose of the library that possessed it.

Calepino's dictionary was a publishing project that can truly be said to have engaged a wide cross-section of Europe's scholarly elite: as editors, publishers and purchasers. The Venetian edition of 1520 claimed already to have introduced 7,000 corrections to Calepino's original text. By 1550 one of the sequence of distinguished editors, Sébastien Gryphius, acknowledged that there was little of the original text remaining. This was a collective intellectual accomplishment, a monument of scholarship in an age that put a high price on scholarly achievement.

Learning did not necessarily lead to enlightenment. It is as well to remember that despite the huge increase in scholarly publishing, in many fields the sixteenth century saw no significant advances in scientific understanding. Yet for all that, this was an age that revered learning, almost for its own sake. Scholars valued their membership of a society that crossed national, linguistic and religious boundaries. Through their published works even those without formal qualifications cherished their access to an expanding world of knowledge. Only when this knowledge faced the test of practical application was their faith tested, and never more so than in matters of life and death: when medical theory confronted the intractable challenge of human suffering, illness and disease. Here, too, the world of print was deeply engaged.

CHAPTER 14

HEALING

In 1508 Johann Amerbach faced a decision that would be the nightmare of any parent. By this point Amerbach was one of Germany's most successful printer-publishers. He was deeply engaged in the patristic editions that would make his reputation; his place in the industry, and among the business elite of Basel, was secure. But few would have envied him when his much-loved second son, Basilius, contracted kidney stones. The stone was a common affliction in sixteenth-century Europe, particularly among the well-to-do. It was a condition of prosperity, stimulated by an unbalanced diet with too much meat or fish. It was also painful and debilitating, to the extent that the afflicted might eventually be prepared to contemplate the danger of surgery.

Cutting for the stone was an established technique, one of the few surgical procedures that could be contemplated with a reasonable chance of success.[1] But the procedure was still invasive and uncertain, and, without anaesthetic, appallingly painful. Patients naturally explored any alternative therapy before subjecting themselves to the knife. The reformer, John Calvin, another sufferer, was advised to ride over bumpy roads in the hope that this would jolt the stones free and enable him to discharge them through urination.[2] But this too was horribly painful, and Calvin eventually desisted through exhaustion. So Basilius and his father prevaricated, while the pain increased. First to take the matter in hand was Conrad Leotorius, a family friend charged with looking after the Amerbach boys in Freiburg. He urged Basilius not to delay: modern surgeons, he said, had developed instruments that could probe for the stone with far less discomfort. But when Basilius was unpersuaded, and seemed minded to heed the advice of a physician who suggested that surgery could be avoided, Leotorius changed tack. The doctor, he advised sternly, was a charlatan.

If kidney stones could be cured without incision, then surely Cornelius Celsus, 'that eloquent doctor' would never have undertaken the procedure. Celsus was one of the many ancient writers whose works had been rediscovered in the Renaissance. First printed in 1478 his *De medicina* was now at the height of its influence.[3] Leotorius urged Bruno, the eldest son, to bring it to his brother's attention.

> If your father has Celsus in his library, read in volume seven, in the chapter about difficulty in urination and about the stone and its cures. If you don't have Celsus I will send it to you if you wish for your use and certainly for the benefit of your dear brother – a fine volume bound together with Pliny.[4]

The story ends happily. Basilius underwent the procedure, and survived. But it is revealing that, faced with this life and death decision, Amerbach and his friends reached instinctively for the wisdom of the ancients. Here it was Celsus; more usually it would be Galen or Hippocrates, the progenitors of the fundamental theories of human physiognomy that many centuries later still dominated Renaissance medicine. Galen and Hippocrates taught that the human body was made up of four basic substances, or humours, linked with the elements of earth, fire, water and air. Health depended on maintaining the four elements, blood, phlegm, yellow and black bile, in balance; any imbalance required therapeutic treatment to bring the body back into equilibrium.

The sixteenth century was an era of unremitting hardship for those who fell ill, as the normal pains of untreatable disease were compounded by new epidemics, repeated incursions of the plague, and the unfamiliar horrors of new battlefield injuries. The growth of cities created ideal conditions for great waves of mortality that could carry off a high proportion of the resident population. And through all of this, medical treatments were in thrall to the wisdom of a pair of Greek sages whose understanding of the human condition was based on philosophical premises that were wholly false.

The upsurge of medical writing did little to challenge the supremacy of Galenic medicine. Indeed, by enhancing the prestige of learned medicine at the expense of a more pragmatic, observation-based folk culture, it probably reinforced it. The tremendous growth in medical publishing during the course of the sixteenth century was a taxonomy of human anxiety and ingenuity. But overall it probably did little to relieve the pain and suffering of a society for which illness and sudden, unpredictable mortality were brutal facts of life.

Healing in print

In the field of scientific publication medical books formed a particular and specific category of the marketplace. From the first days of print medical texts were published in large numbers. Small wonder, for they spoke to some of the universals of the human condition: the desire to avoid pain, and to prolong life. A rich cross-section of those who bought books were prepared to invest in printed texts that promised relief from everyday aches or offered some hope of surviving one of the terrifying incursions of epidemic disease that blighted European society in this era. The first printed book on a medical subject was published as early as 1466; thereafter textbooks, compilations and cures for specific ailments followed in a steady profusion to the end of the fifteenth century. The thousand or so medical books published in this period represent a decent proportion of the total printed output of the incunabula era.[5] All the major centres of early printing, from Naples to Antwerp, played a healthy role in this production, with Augsburg, Strasbourg, Paris, Lyon and Rome emerging as early centres of medical publishing. As in so much else, Venice was by far the largest centre of production, with around 200 editions, a fifth of the total.

The field of medical publishing posed the dilemma at the heart of Renaissance intellectual culture: how to balance the rediscovered wisdom of the ancients with the disseminated, empirical knowledge of healers and healing handed down through the generations. In the field of medicine this dilemma was acute because so large a part of the inherited corpus of medical knowledge originated in the Islamic world and had been spread through medieval Europe in Latin translation. Twenty editions of the most popular Arabic text – the medical encyclopaedia of the Arab scholar Abu Ali al-Husayn ibn Sina (known in western Europe by his Latin name of Avicenna) – were published before the end of the fifteenth century. His major rival was Albertus Magnus, the thirteenth-century Dominican theologian whose encyclopaedic works in the field of medicine and natural science were wholly shaped by Aristotelian principles. The compilations of Arnoldus de Villanova (1235–1311) and Guy de Chauliac (1300–1368) also enjoyed considerable popularity. But in this, as in so many areas of scholarship, much energy was concentrated on recovering the great works of antiquity: in the field of medicine Hippocrates, and, towering above all others, Galen. In the first age of print their writings were frequently incorporated into the medical compendia popularised by the Venetian presses.

The first attempt to collect together Galen's writings into a coherent body was published in Venice in 1490; as a scholarly work of reference this was surpassed by the definitive five-volume edition published in Greek in 1525.[6]

This key work ushered in the great age of Galenic publishing: in all, over 600 editions of different texts by Galen were issued during the sixteenth century.[7] Authors who republished or translated the classical medical authorities shared the general humanist tendency to exaggerate the significance of the ancient writings and denigrate those of the medieval period. They were anxious to claim a Renaissance in medicine equivalent to that in the humanities. Martin Akakia casually overlooks the great popularity of the leading medieval authorities when he speaks of medicine in the Middle Ages as having been 'buried and overwhelmed in great gloom'. A dedicatory epistle to Francis I prefixed to a sixteenth-century Galen makes the inevitable contrast between that dismal past and the current era, wherein 'medicine has been raised from the dead'.[8]

A prominent feature of this medical writing was the extent to which these classical texts were also published in vernacular languages. A large part of the Galenic canon was made available in French in a great wave of translations between 1530 and 1550.[9] Galen could also be consulted in numerous Italian and German editions. This is all the more striking when one considers that there existed a strong body of opinion that deplored popularisation of the learned discipline of medicine. University-educated physicians, eager to distinguish themselves from the vulgar barber-surgeons, had no wish to see their learned arts debased by vernacular publication. The first lecturer in the University of Paris who attempted to offer expositions of Guy de Chauliac in French for the local surgeons, William Copp, was asked by his superiors to desist. This prejudice against practitioners with no formal Latin education dogged the career of even so distinguished a figure as Ambroise Paré, a pioneer in surgical techniques and much-admired author.

These attempts to defend the privileges of the practitioners of learned medicine did not prevent the development of a strong tradition of vernacular medical publication throughout Europe. This tells us a great deal about the strong desire of Europe's book-buying community for solutions, however implausible, to the overwhelming challenge of life, pain, illness and death. Some they found in the ancient classics newly translated. But the sixteenth century also brought new hazards, such as syphilis, the venereal scourge brought back from the Americas, known to contemporaries, somewhat unfairly, as the French disease: *morbus gallicus*. Modern warfare also brought a range of new and complex injuries caused by gunpowder weapons, muskets and cannon fire. But nothing impacted on contemporary consciousness with quite such force as the terrifying, unpredictable blight of epidemic disease.

Plague

Epidemic disease was a consuming preoccupation of the people of sixteenth-century Europe; unsurprisingly, it occupied a large role in published medical writing. The population of Europe's cities grew rapidly during the sixteenth century, and most of this growth took place within the medieval city walls. Although city councils occasionally decided to expand the city by rebuilding walls or fortifications, they invariably frowned on the unplanned growth of suburbs outside the walls. This had the self-defeating result that more and more people were crammed into the urban core. With no fundamental improvements in sanitation, increased mortality was the inevitable result.

The impact of plague on sixteenth-century society was profound. Plague epidemics returned with alarming frequency. In Holland outbreaks of plague were recorded in 107 of the 219 years between 1450 and 1668.[10] In some instances mortality reached 20, or even 40 per cent. In England plague returned to the major towns on average every sixteen years, with London suffering two crippling epidemics during the reign of Elizabeth (in 1563 and 1592–93).[11] In the period between 1494 and 1648 Europe-wide epidemics were recorded on seventeen occasions; it is probably true to say that outbreaks of the plague were recorded somewhere on the continent in every year.

The plague was one of the most terrifying of diseases: its onset unpredictable, its progress very rapid, the chances of survival bleak. Early modern societies lived in constant terror of its arrival. Plague was ubiquitous, but towns were particularly vulnerable. The larger the town, the greater the danger: rich and prosperous cities, likely to act as a magnet for immigrants, were especially at risk. Of course these were precisely the places also most likely to be centres of the printing industry, and indeed, to be the place of residence of the scholarly authors writing medical texts. Some, like the great Swiss botanist Conrad Gesner, would themselves succumb to the disease. Such personal concerns added urgency to the search for an explanation of plague.

Not surprisingly, then, the literature of plague was extensive: all over Europe the reading public had access to a large number of texts offering treatments and proffering explanations as to the cause.[12] Most medical authors regarded plague as a poison to be driven out of the body. The first remedy proposed was inevitably bleeding, as it was for any medical condition. Drawing blood was regarded as essential, to restore the balance of the humours; if this did not cause the plague buboes to discharge their poison then special dressings should be applied. The most popular internal medicines were theriac, commonly called treacle, and mithridate, the two most trusted remedies since the time of Galen.

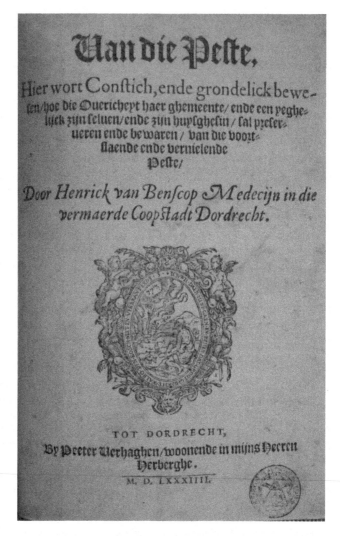

Fig. 59 The plague. Printers turned out hundreds of original compositions offering advice on combating or treating epidemics. None got to the root of the problem. This Dutch tract prescribes both treatment for individuals and advice to the council on public hygiene.

But sufferers were prepared to try anything. Many tracts offered a large variety of remedies, some reflecting the influence of the new Paracelsian science.

Some of the finest medical minds in Europe shared in the attempt to determine the causes of plague, alleviate its symptoms, and prevent its spread. Ambroise Paré, writing at the behest of Catherine de' Medici after a severe outbreak in France in 1565, agreed with most authorities in seeing plague as a poison. The hard, swollen buboes that caused such excruciating pain should be soothed by an ointment to draw the poison through the skin. For the higher echelons of society he described a more eccentric treatment. 'If any noble or gentlemen refuse to be anointed with this unguent, let them be enclosed in the body of a mule or horse that is newly killed, and when that is cold let them be laid in another, until the pustules and eruptions do break forth, being drawn by the natural heat' of the animal's corpse.[13] There was some recognition that bleeding, the traditional remedy, only served to weaken the patient. After consulting with other doctors Paré urged that bleeding be discontinued.

None of the prescribed treatments did much to relieve the swift agony of death; nor did writers on the plague make any significant progress in isolating its causes. Diagnostic clarity was impeded by the variable symptoms. This was one field in which Galenic medicine, with its concentration on the disposition of the individual patient, offered no helpful guidance. According to Galen each patient's condition reflected the healthy balance, or unhealthy imbalance, in the body's basis substance, the four humours. Therapeutic treatment concentrated on readjusting these conditions to restore balance and health. This led to a restorative emphasis on diet, good air and rest; and, less helpfully, to the sixteenth-century obsession with bleeding, to purge the evil humours. But because each patient's condition was unique the Galenic system could not adequately respond when many people fell ill with a similar condition at the same time. It had no clear answer to epidemic disease.

The most obviously relevant aspect of Galenic theory was the focus on the quality of the air. The stink of putrefaction as the epidemic wore on encouraged the theory that plague emanated from a miasma, and this explained its spread over large areas. To escape, many sought refuge in flight to a place where the air was pure. The advanced Italian cities instituted a system of quarantine, recognising implicitly that plague was contagious. Venice established its *lazzaretti* on two islands in the lagoon. A large part of the literature of plague, particularly in the Protestant north, debated the question whether flight was an appropriate Christian response. When plague came to Wittenberg in 1527 Martin Luther ignored instructions from the Elector to leave the city: the good shepherd, he argued in a published tract, cannot abandon his flock. John Calvin, in Geneva, volunteered his services in the plague hospital, but was forbidden by the town council: his life was felt too valuable to risk. Debating the question later in the century Théodore de Bèze was inclined to accept the argument that the true Christian owed it to God to take the sensible precaution of flight.

This debate was so pertinent because, in the search for medical causes, few in the sixteenth century doubted that plague was first and foremost a divine punishment. Ambroise Paré whose discourse on plague was observant and thoughtful, was nevertheless careful to emphasise:

> It is confirmed, constant and received opinion in all ages amongst Christians that the plague and other diseases which violently assail the life of man, are often sent by the just anger of God punishing our offences.[14]

The Dutch name for plague, *De Gave Gods*, 'God's gift', reflects this general sense of helplessness in the face of God's inscrutable purpose.[15] In contemporary art plague was often represented as an arrow sent from heaven (which naturally made St Sebastian the patron saint of plague victims). Some tracts abandoned hope of medical cure, and instead recommended patient resignation as the only proper response. A large part of the enormous literature of plague urged repentance as the proper, indeed only effectual response to epidemic disease. But such dire warnings, repeated from the pulpit, simply added to the pervasive terror. Many believed that astrological events, such as comets, could ignite epidemic disease; sometimes, it was even suggested, epidemics occurred because the infection had been spread deliberately by individuals with diabolic intent. Accusations of plague-spreading erupted from time to time in the febrile atmosphere of Europe's cities, most notably in Calvin's Geneva at the height of the political turbulence that followed his arrival in the city. Witnesses swore that the accused had been observed daubing the lintels of houses with a special noxious ointment. A number of those arrested were tortured into confession, and executed.[16]

If this could occur in Geneva it is no wonder that the desperate hope of relief provided ample room for charlatanism and opportunist profiteering. In Venice, during the great plague outbreak of 1575–77, the city authorities entertained several proposals from individuals who claimed to have a successful treatment for the disease. Such medical 'secrets' were a common feature of the period, and an important aspect of the medical marketplace. The most prized was the secret offered them by the *lazzaretti* doctor Ascanio Olivieri. In return for putting his secret at the Republic's disposal Olivieri requested 500 ducats and an income of 30 ducats a month for his lifetime and that of his children. The Health Office was keen to deal, because Olivieri was known to have inherited knowledge of the treatment pioneered by his father-in-law Nicolo Colochi, a doctor in the Venetian Health Office since 1528. The secret had been carefully preserved in the family, and passed to Olivieri as his dowry. The Health Office agreed to pay the requested monthly sum, along with a rather lower cash payment.[17]

The key to the success of this negotiation was precisely that the mysterious regime had *not* been published. After purchase Olivieri provided a shortened version for printing, but this was a greatly simplified essence to alert pharmacists to keep in stock the necessary ingredients for lotions and medicines: the real secret stayed in the family. When finally written down in 1598 the Olivieri regime turns out to be a complex recipe of common palliatives. But by this time it had sustained an entire family for the best part of a century.

At least the Olivieri mix of rhubarb and endives was less theatrical than the secret provided by the Flanders merchant Antonio Gualtiero, which required patients to be dosed with their own urine, while their sores were rubbed with hot faeces. To prove its efficacy Gualtiero visited the houses of the quarantined poor, where he swiftly contracted symptoms and succumbed to his own treatment. This was a relatively common fate for medical entrepreneurs. What is striking about this particular case is that when faced with the urgency of epidemic disease, experienced civic leaders were prepared to entertain proposals from virtually any source, whether medically qualified or not.

Despite this huge outpouring of creative energy, the sixteenth century made little fundamental progress in the treatment of plague. The Great Plague in London in 1665 called forth a familiar torrent of invocations of divine judgment and calls for repentance. In the event it was not medical science but another affliction, the Great Fire, that finally brought the plague bacillus under control.

The surgeon's knife

The struggle to unlock the mysteries of human physiognomy occupied some of Europe's most inquisitive minds. In the fields of anatomy and internal medicine men like Andreas Vesalius and Paracelsus made notable discoveries. The impact on the medical practice of their own time was, however, limited. Paracelsus's emphasis on chemical interventions was highly controversial, and if applied would probably have been of doubtful efficacy. His contentious nature and wild, self-destructive life style ensured that he would remain an outsider in the increasingly status-conscious world of academic medicine. The printer Johannes Oporinus, who had served as Paracelsus's assistant as a youth, leaves a devastating portrait of his master reeling drunk around a chaotic workshop.[18] It was only when Paracelsus's discoveries could be separated from his unedifying personality after his death that his insights could be refined and integrated into treatment.

Fig. 60 Paracelsus. A difficult and troubled man, his awkward and quarrelsome personality cast a shadow over his professional reputation, but did not prevent his works being published in large numbers.

Issues of status and dignity were also of relevance in the field of anatomy. When anatomy became recognised as part of medical training, this was a significant breakthrough. It meant that academic medicine recognised, at least implicitly, the role of observation and investigation alongside theoretical discourse. In practice, however, dissections were normally undertaken by assistants while the professor, seated in his high chair at some physical remove from the cadaver, read from a prescribed text. This meant that the professor could scarcely profit from observation of the opened corpse, and the

Fig. 61 Andreas Vesalius. The greatest anatomist of the sixteenth century, Vesalius also had a shrewd idea of the role that print could play in publicising his discoveries and building his reputation.

students were forced to draw their own conclusions as the internal organs were laid bare.

The most significant challenge to this distant desiccated practice came from the brilliant and innovative Andreas Vesalius.[19] Vesalius was born into a distinguished medical family. His grandfather had been Royal Physician to the Emperor, Maximilian I, and his father served as Imperial apothecary. It was natural that the young Andreas should be prepared to follow in these footsteps, first in the new University of Louvain, then in the most distinguished medical school north of the Alps, at Paris. Vesalius arrived in Paris when the vogue for the newly discovered texts of Galen was at its height. In 1514 Henri Estienne had published a small collection of Galen's writings translated by Niccolò Leoniceno, the first of a wave of publications that transformed the local medical environment. In 1526 the Paris Faculty purchased for its library a copy of the Aldine edition of the Greek texts of Galen. Given the linguistic capacities of Parisian physicians this was mainly a totemic gesture. In 1531 the publication of Galen's *Anatomical Procedures* in a local Latin edition made available the Greek master's full teaching on anatomy, including a detailed discussion of dissection. The suddenness of Galen's conquest of Parisian print produced in the Paris Faculty what has been described as an 'enslavement to Galen and a new Galenic conservatism'.[20] Shortly after, two professors in the University of Louvain were dismissed because they were held to be ignorant of the 'new' Galenic medicine.

With Paris a stronghold of Galenism it is perhaps just as well that the resumption of warfare between France and the Emperor in 1536 forced the young Vesalius to abandon the city. After defending his thesis in Louvain he moved to Italy where, at the age of twenty-three, he was appointed Professor of Surgery and Anatomy. Vesalius immediately introduced a revolution in practice, insisting that he conduct dissections personally, surrounded by his students, explaining and making copious sketches as he went. Vesalius's passion for dissection was pursued to the verge of illegality. He later had to reprove his students for raiding graves for new subjects. Fortunately in Padua and Venice he found co-operative magistrates prepared to ensure him a sufficient supply of corpses of executed felons; even timing the executions to suit the needs of pedagogy.

The sketches made at the dissection table became the basis for Vesalius's first major anatomical publication, the *Anatomical Tables* of 1537–38. This was a brief commentary on six 'tables' of anatomical woodcuts, three of internal organs and three skeletal figures. The internal diagrams were probably based on Vesalius's own sketches, and the skeletons the work of Johannes Stephanus (Calcar), a pupil of Titian. The quality of these representations of the human form has sometimes led them to be attributed to Titian himself. It was not the first time a human skeleton had been illustrated in a medical text (and it was a familiar topos in art); but the anatomical quality of these woodcuts represented a quantum leap forward for medical science. Their success and influence is evident in the extent to which they were copied and redrawn for other medical texts and unauthorised editions of the *Tables*. An outraged

Vesalius denounced unauthorised use of his artwork in editions published in Augsburg, Strasbourg, Frankfurt and Paris. Most can indeed be matched to surviving editions.[21]

This sense of injustice may partly explain why Vesalius decided to look away from Venice for the publication of his master-work, *De humani corporis fabrica* (On the Structure of the Human Body). This was an altogether more ambitious undertaking than the *Tables*. Here Vesalius offered both a defiant advocacy of his own practice of conducting dissections, and an unapologetic challenge to ancient wisdom where his own observation suggested different hypotheses. Vesalius even had the temerity to challenge Galen, pointing out that the Greek authority had never dissected a human cadaver, as this would have offended the Graeco-Roman sense of the inviolate nature of the human body. The lengthy text was accompanied by copious woodcut illustrations. In 1541 the woodcut blocks cut in Venice made a long and perilous journey across the St Gottard Pass to be printed in Basel.

By this date Johannes Oporinus, free of the incubus of Paracelsus, was proprietor of one of Basel's leading printing houses.[22] A scholar of some repute, Oporinus had been successively Professor of Latin and of Greek before turning his attention to scholarly printing. Naturally his printing shop was a magnet for serious scholarly projects of a theological and scientific nature. Oporinus also attracted the unusual and unorthodox. He championed Sebastian Castellio in his bitter dispute with Calvin, and published several of his works. His publication of Theodor Bibliander's Latin translation of the Koran caused further controversy, and resulted in Oporinus being briefly imprisoned. Vesalius, as the author of a text that challenged both scientific and pedagogic orthodoxy, may have felt a natural affinity with him. But Basel also made good sense on practical business grounds: its proximity to the northern markets made for easy distribution and discouraged pirate reprints.[23] This was important, because in addition to the substantial *Fabrica*, Vesalius also planned to publish a far shorter *Epitome*, essentially the woodcuts from the *Fabrica* with a brief textual explanation on the model of the earlier *Tables*. It was explicit recognition that the appeal of the work lay as much in the illustrations as in the learned text.

Vesalius secured a battery of privileges to protect his work: from Venice, from the Emperor and from the King of France. If he hoped in this way to maintain control over his images he was to be sadly disappointed. The illustrations of the *Fabrica* and *Epitome* were widely imitated and copied into numerous other medical texts. They became the foundation of anatomical illustration for the larger part of the century. In this respect the impact of

Vesalius's work is somewhat paradoxical. The monumental seven-volume edition of the *Fabrica* secured Vesalius's reputation as one of the leading medical authorities of the age. Shortly after publication he was appointed Imperial physician to Charles V, an appointment that required him to leave Italy and abandon academic medicine. But the publication of the book did little to disturb the prevailing Galenism. The criticisms of Galen were pointed enough to earn a furious published rebuke from Vesalius's former teacher and mentor Sylvius, who in 1551 published his *Vaesani cuiusdam calumniarum in Hippocratis Galenique rem anatomicam depulsio* (A Repudiation of the Calumnies of a Certain Madman concerning Hippocratic and Galenic Anatomy). The title might have been more temperate had *vaesanus*, madman, not offered an irresistible pun with Vesalius.

If to us Vesalius represents the visionary thinker, Sylvius found more sympathy among his professional colleagues. Medical science, concerned above all to preserve the dignity of academic medicine, was not ready to undertake a fundamental re-evaluation of the ancient texts that lay at the basis of medical practice. The humoral theories of Galen, with their confidence in the individuality of the human condition, reigned supreme, even in the anatomy theatre. An inadvertent witness to the persistence of Galenic modes of thought was the Italian author Ludovico Ariosto, whose embalmed heart was exhibited at the anatomy theatre of the University of Ferrara. Presumably the vital organ of the great epic writer was regarded as worthy of special study to discern the wellsprings of his inspiration.

The extent to which observational science could challenge orthodoxy was therefore limited. The greatest leap in understanding was made by a man whose discovery remained totally unremarked in the medical mainstream, the freethinking physician/theologian Michael Servetus. Servetus, who had trained (with Vesalius) as an assistant to the Paris surgeons, correctly observed, and described, the circulation of the blood. But his publication of this observation was buried deep in a theological work, *The Restitution of Christianity*, which was deeply unorthodox: fatally, Servetus denied the doctrine of the Trinity. The text was universally condemned, and copies ordered to be burned. When Servetus, now a homeless wanderer, strayed into Geneva, he was arrested and burned. Servetus is now remembered as a martyr for religious toleration rather than the medical pioneer he might have been. His text is almost completely lost, and the significance of his medical discovery went unobserved by contemporaries.[24] It would fall to William Harvey, early in the seventeenth century, successfully to establish and publish on pulmonary circulation.

Wounds of battle

The appointment of Vesalius as Charles V's physician gave the illustrious anatomist an opportunity to test the practical applicability of his new medical theories. The lifestyle of the Imperial patient, a notorious glutton engaged on a ceaseless round of frantic journeying around his multiple dominions, posed an obvious challenge to his hard-pressed doctors. Attending the Emperor on campaign they were also expected to treat other wounded, and Vesalius experienced a baptism of fire in the campaign of 1544. He badly botched an amputation, which had to be painfully completed by experienced field surgeons. It was a sobering demonstration of the limitations of the skills Vesalius had acquired during dissections.

Field medicine and military surgery promoted major advances in patient treatment and surgical procedure during this period. The new, unfamiliar injuries produced by gunshot, which shattered bone and caused widespread trauma, allowed experimentation with new and radical treatments. At Saint-Dizier in 1544 Vesalius was introduced to a technique of treating complex wounds without the agonising procedure of cauterising with pitch or fire. Such new techniques gradually became known through the published writings of a gifted French surgeon, Ambroise Paré.

Unlike Vesalius, Paré had received no university training, a circumstance frequently cited against him by outraged members of the medical establishment. As he never acquired Greek, or even Latin, his knowledge of Galen was necessarily derived from French translations. Paré was employed as a humble barber-surgeon, first in the Hôtel-Dieu, the chief public hospital of Paris, then as a military surgeon to the French army. It was here, through empirical observation, that Paré made his greatest contribution to surgery, first by the substitution of salves for cauterisation, and secondly through experiments with ligatures to reconnect blood vessels after amputations. Paré published these discoveries in French, in a bold break with tradition necessitated by his lack of formal education. His works owed much of their success to their vivid woodcut illustration of surgical instruments.[25]

Paré's growing reputation drew him to the attention of the king: in 1552 he was appointed one of the royal surgeons in ordinary. When Henry II was grievously wounded at a tournament in 1559, Paré was summoned to treat him. He probably felt an enormous relief that the great Vesalius was also brought from Flanders to consult on the king's wound (he had been pierced in the face by a lance) and so shared the responsibility for the failure to save Henry's life.

In 1561 Paré published his most ambitious work, his *Universal Anatomy*. This was followed by a battery of texts, on surgery, on diseases of the head and on plague.[26] In 1570 his treatise on monsters demonstrated that the fascination with freaks of nature was shared by members of the medical professions and the general reading public. This was one of his most successful books. In 1575, emboldened by conspicuous signs of royal favour and generous privilege for nine years, Paré published a lavish folio edition of his collected works.[27]

Whether it was the appropriation of the scholarly folio format, or the mere fact of the collection of diverse vernacular texts into a scientific whole, this was too much for the physicians of the Paris medical faculty, who now launched a formal legal challenge to Paré's book. Although the book had already been published, the Faculty appealed to the Parlement of Paris, asking them to enforce the decree forbidding the sale of any medical book without the Faculty's approval. The Parlement prevaricated, asking all parties to put their opinion in writing; the book was in any case already all over Paris. This provoked Paré to a memorable riposte, a pamphlet in which he threw back the argument of his tormentors in their faces. For thirty years, he observed quite correctly, he had been publishing his works. The objections had nothing to do with the alleged indecency of his writings: rather, the physicians were trying to preserve a lucrative monopoly.

It was a shrewd thrust, and one that would have struck a chord with the surgeons and barbers excluded from recognition in the increasingly stratified world of Parisian medicine. By the time Paré was ready to publish a second edition tempers had cooled, and the text, with modest changes, was submitted to the Faculty for approval, as the decree of 1535 required. So it was something of a surprise when the Faculty raised new objections to the publication of a Latin translation in 1582. Having initially objected to their mysteries being shared with a vernacular audience, they now took exception to a Latin edition being translated by an unqualified surgeon. Publication had to be moved out of Paris, though Paré returned to his Paris printers for the definitive French edition of the complete works in 1585. When he died in 1590 he was the most published contemporary French medical author of the century.

Paré's travails tell us much about both the development of the medical profession and the increasing complexity of the medical marketplace. The Paris physicians were undoubtedly keen to defend their valuable prerogatives, but the publishers were also responding to the growth of a new market: for books that once would have been considered learned but now appealed to a more general audience. Most book owners who built a personal library of any size added to it a selection of medical texts.

This development of the market for technical and scientific books was not confined to the field of medicine. In all of the largest book markets, in France, Germany and Italy, booksellers were selling an increasing number of scholarly books in vernacular languages. Many were substantial tomes, published in folio and clearly intended for consultation and use, as well as to decorate a library.

The market for the scholarly vernacular was far less developed in peripheral print cultures, like England. These were large books, and it required considerable investment to bring them to the market.[28] It was far easier to accomplish this in the major continental centres of print, where publishers were accustomed to bearing the heavy investment costs of long Latin texts. The steady returns from such projects also generated profit that could be reinvested in large vernacular books – which, with a market restricted to a single language community, were inherently more risky. The failure of England's printers to establish a sizeable share in the international Latin trade meant that they did not accumulate the capital resources necessary to enter the market in significant categories of vernacular texts. In the larger continental publishing centres it was possible to set up a consortium of printers or booksellers to share costs and risk. In smaller, peripheral markets like England this was seldom attempted.

The medical marketplace

In 1523 a new surgeon appeared in Rome offering to provide a cure for the French pox (syphilis). His services were soon very much in demand. Despite the large fees he demanded, and the fact that he insisted on being paid in advance, many notables were prepared to undergo his prescribed treatment, which involved the use of 'certain fumigations'. 'He was a very learned man,' it was said, 'and he could talk marvellously about medical matters.' So great was his reputation that the Pope tried to retain him in his personal service. Wisely he declined and left Rome; and 'not many months later, all those he had cured fell so ill that they were a hundred times worse than before. If he had stayed, he would have been killed.'

Benvenuto Cellini, who records this incident in his autobiography, calls the surgeon a *ciumadore*, a charlatan.[29] But the surgeon seems to have been a highly educated and qualified physician, Jacopo Berengario da Carpi, *Practicus* of Surgery in the University of Bologna, a learned author whose commentary on the *Anatomy* of Mondino de' Liuzzi had been dedicated to Giulio de' Medici in 1521. Berengario was wise to abandon Rome before events exposed the chasm between his reputation as a learned theorist and his limitations as a practitioner.

Cases like this make it easy to understand why many held medical professionals in such low esteem. When Cellini himself contracted syphilis later in life he devised his own treatments and ignored the advice of physicians. Others drew on the wisdom of family and friends, or turned to the variety of healers and consultants that made up the varied and exotic hinterland of medical treatment.

This large and variegated medical marketplace encompassed learned medicine, certified surgeons and apothecaries, priests and healers. It flourished despite the best efforts of the medical profession to separate the different branches of the medical arts through formal training and certified qualifications. In the development of this medical marketplace print played a vital role, especially in eroding and eliding carefully constructed medical hierarchies. Through their printed books the unfashionable, heretical or simply untrained could reach out directly to their audience. Although Paracelsus was shunned by the medical establishment and forced to abandon his position in Basel, his works were extremely popular with the public, particularly in Germany.[30]

The trend towards increased stratification of the medical profession was a feature of all parts of Europe. In the main states of Italy physicians were organised into a college, which approved their qualification and asserted the right to examine the competence of barber-surgeons and apothecaries. In theory, the distinction between these callings was clear. Physicians, as specialists in internal medicine, avoided all manual activity. Surgeons and apothecaries were expected to refrain from diagnosis: their task was to carry out treatments prescribed by the physicians.

These careful distinctions were invariably elided in practice. In smaller towns a barber-surgeon might be the only available practitioner. Even in places where a physician practised, the humble surgeon was much cheaper. Often an intervention by a surgeon or apothecary followed a direct request from the patient. Men and women in pain were not concerned with the careful gradations of status that underpinned learned medicine; instead, they scoured the whole medical marketplace for relief and cures.

For the unlettered this often meant recourse to a local healer, or apothecary. Faith in local healers proved tenacious. As late as 1811, according to a

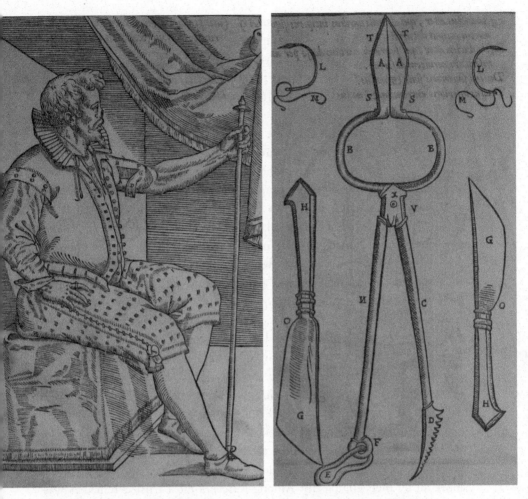

Fig. 62 a & b *De curtorum chirurgia*, 1597. Early plastic surgery. Gaspare Tagliacozzi demonstrates his groundbreaking techniques for the replacement of the nose, and the gruesome instruments needed to perform the operation. Loss of facial parts (from sword play or syphilis) was a sufficiently frequent occurrence to make this text a bestseller.

disapproving official report, the people of the Italian province of Molise and elsewhere 'are more prone to believe and obey the herbalist than the physician; they throw themselves into the arms of the charlatan, the cunning man and the astrologer-shepherd for diseases that they believe incurable, and which then become so in fact'.[31]

Even at this late date, the barriers between formal and informal medicine were not as clear cut as this may suggest. Practitioners of informal medicine also had their own specialism: one healer might be considered expert in curing fevers; another, headaches or pains in the joints. While the church authorities in Italy regarded with disapproval the prayers and incantations that accompanied these healing rituals they actively encouraged the practice of exorcism. Demands for exorcisms rose steadily in the sixteenth century and into the seventeenth.

For those who dwelt in cities the range of medical remedies was broader, but no less bewildering or treacherous. Those with funds consulted physicians or ordered potions from apothecaries. They sought advice from friends, and swapped tips on diet and purges. Increasingly they consulted books. The sixteenth century witnessed a vast upsurge in medical publication, a large part of it now in the vernacular. This was a literature that empowered the laity to take control of their own treatment. The distrust of medical professionals expressed by Cellini was widespread, and not in all cases fair, since the state of medical knowledge at that time meant that many conditions were simply incurable. But with doctors powerless to help them, readers turned to books that offered the prospect of a cure, often through the brewing of complex herbal and chemical concoctions. The publication of books of medical secrets enjoyed a tremendous vogue in the late sixteenth century, epitomised by the *Secrets* of Alessio Piemontese, a pseudonym for the Italian writer Girolamo Ruscelli.[32] According to Ruscelli, the 1,245 recipes he listed had been devised by a secret Academy established in Naples in the 1540s, though the existence of such a body is attested only in his book. Of the recipes, around a thousand were medical cures, the rest a miscellany of cosmetic and technical compounds. They are characterised above all by their complexity. Among Ruscelli's most trusted remedies was the oil of a red-haired dog. Alas for the dog, this could not be extracted while the donor was still alive. The dog should be seethed whole until it fell to pieces, and to the brew were then added scorpions, worms, various plants, hogs' and asses' marrow, in a definite order. The resulting ointment was effectual against many conditions, including gout. The complexity of the remedies did nothing to impede the book's popularity. Between its first translation into French in 1557 and the end of the century it went through a staggering thirty-eight editions.[33]

The success of Ruscelli's *Secrets* is testimony to the economic potential of bourgeois anxiety. But in fact the principles underlying his recipes – mystery and complexity – were common to all medicine. The Galenic universal cure, theriac, enjoyed a widespread vogue in the sixteenth century, challenged only by the new pretender: orvietan. Orvietan was the major stock in trade of the street vendor, or charlatan. It was touted by these ubiquitous travelling salesmen especially as an antidote to poison. This had a particular resonance in Italy where poison had played a prominent role in political culture since the infamous era of the Borgia Pope, Alexander VI. But the reputation of orvietan spread far and wide, especially in the seventeenth century when its ingredients (in fact a concoction of traditional herbs and a few spices) were revealed in print. In Italy the authorities responded by reinforcing the dignity of theriac, 'the regal antidote of antidotes'. All cities with a university or medical college prepared their own theriac, often in a civic public ceremony involving magistrates, physicians and ecclesiastical dignitaries. As ever, its potency lay in complexity. The sixty-four ingredients of the Salerno theriac trumped the forty-five of orvietan and restricted its availability to those with a certain level of disposable income. It continued to be recommended throughout the eighteenth century, its prestige and legendary healing powers enduring into the age of scientific medicine. Venice abandoned its public ceremony for the mixing of theriac only in 1842.[34]

The official patronage of theriac is a graphic demonstration of the complexity of a medical world that defies easy classification or stratification. The persistent pressure towards incorporation and professionalisation at the upper end of the discipline reflected only one aspect of this medical world: a determination that the dignity of academic medicine should be respected, and the attendant financial benefits defended. The market for academic medical texts in the sixteenth century was not overwhelmed by the surge in vernacular publications.[35] Instead the two flourished in tandem, supplying distinct but overlapping markets.

A fascinating insight into the impact of this medical publishing is provided by the health concerns of the Cecils, Elizabeth I's chief minister Lord Burghley and his son Robert Cecil, Earl of Salisbury who were members of a social group that read Latin, and certainly owned academic medical texts.[36] Yet their correspondence with friends, when it touches on medical matters, consists mostly of exchanging nostrums. Both Burghley and Salisbury practised pragmatic medicine. There is very little reference to humoral theory, and far more attention to diet. Salisbury was a precocious protagonist of the virtues of fruit, in contrast to the traditional meat and fish diet that Burghley favoured. Cecil was also a regular client of Stephen Higgens, a London apothecary with a very exclusive clientele. In the single year 1604–5 Higgens billed Salisbury for £62-worth of remedies.[37]

Those who could spent freely in the search for health, cure and pain relief. The printed word formed a buoyant part in this enormous medical marketplace. Ultimately, it must be admitted, it did little to improve the quality of life or chances of survival in a world where pain was an everyday, exhausting grief which, for the most part, could only be stoically endured.

CHAPTER 15

BUILDING A LIBRARY

IN 1598 the distinguished diplomat and scholar Sir Thomas Bodley wrote to the Vice-Chancellor of the University of Oxford offering to provide funds to re-establish a university library. It might seem strange that at this late date a university of Oxford's antiquity should lack a library, and this was not the first attempt to create a university collection. Fitful attempts to found a library in the fourteenth century had foundered as a result of the university's strongly collegiate structure, and it required a massive donation of over 280 volumes from Duke Humphrey of Gloucester in the 1430s and 1440s to provide a collection to match that of the better endowed colleges. This wonderful collection of manuscripts did not remain in the university's possession for long. The assault on monastic libraries at the time of the Reformation had sent a chill wind through the universities. The college libraries mostly survived, since most were non-monastic foundations, but the uncertainties and turbulence of the mid-Tudor period had a dampening effect on intellectual culture. The university libraries in Oxford and Cambridge fell into disuse. In Oxford the process of destruction was complete by January 1556, when the university made arrangements to sell off the library furniture. The books had already been dispersed, some to the college libraries.[1]

So Bodley's initiative was both timely and welcome. And for the next fifteen years he was able to orchestrate a remarkable programme of building and collecting.[2] Ably seconded by his long-suffering librarian, Thomas James, Bodley effected both a renovation of the original library building and a considerable extension to house new books. Bodley's original intention had been that he would provide for the fabric and thereby encourage others to fill the library by donations and bequests: this had been the main way the college libraries had accumulated books since their medieval beginnings. But with alumni donating mainly to the colleges, Bodley felt compelled to endow his library with new purchases. Soon James was having to cope with regular packages from London booksellers, all of which had to be catalogued and, in the case of the larger books, furnished with strong binding boards, clasps and chains. The impact was dramatic. By the time James published his second catalogue of the library in 1620 the Bodleian contained around 16,000 volumes.

This size of the collection was remarkable, and a new development of the seventeenth century. In the first age of print few institutional collections had advanced much beyond the size of the great Renaissance collections of manuscripts we encountered in the first chapter of this book. The library had struggled to find a role in the new age of print. The halting development and troubled sixteenth-century history of the Oxford University library is far more characteristic of the age than its later rapid development. Very seldom were institutions of learning able or willing to invest sufficiently to build collections. Institutional libraries continued to rely heavily on donations. They received many beautiful artefacts, manuscripts, and some working copies of texts, but not always those texts that students would be most eager to read to keep up with recent scholarship. These they would have to buy for themselves; and in the age of print they were increasingly able to do so.

Institutional libraries were valued especially for their extensive collections of manuscripts. Sir Thomas Bodley was eager that scholars visiting Oxford should be able to use his library, and many came from continental Europe.[3] Until well into the seventeenth century most of these foreign readers came to consult manuscripts, patiently enduring the library's irksome rule that an Oxford MA had to be present while they examined the text. In Bodley's old age Thomas James suffered a series of increasingly peremptory missives as the founder fretted about inappropriate use of the collection. Junior scholars were not to wander and browse, but must confine themselves to books necessary for their courses. Lurking suspicions of ill-intent are evident in the first version of the famous Bodleian oath, to be taken by all readers before admission to the library:

> You promise and solemnly engage before God . . . that whenever you shall enter the public library of the University, you will frame your mind to study in modesty and silence, and will use the books and other furniture in such manner that they may last as long as possible. Also that you will neither yourself in your own person steal, change, make erasures, deform, tear, cut, write notes in, interline, wilfully spoil, obliterate, defile, or in any other way retrench, ill-use, wear away or deteriorate any book or books, nor authorise any other person to do the like.[4]

A library of shadows

This and similar codes of practice represent a marked change in attitudes to the role of the library. The Renaissance library had been a convivial place; a place for meeting, conversation and display. It shared some of the characteristics of that other great repository of texts, the stationers' shop. The famous Florentine stationer Vespasiano presided over a space where scholars came to buy, to meet others interested in books, to exchange knowledge, borrow texts for copying, and engage scribes. The Renaissance library performed much the same social function for a slightly different clientele of scholars, diplomats and officials. These libraries offered opportunities for serious political conversation in a space where their host, the Renaissance prince, could display wealth and power through ownership of books.

By making ownership of books so much more common, print diminished the lustre of the Renaissance library. A scholar might still go to the Bodleian to read manuscripts, but collecting as a focus of princely magnificence diminished. In an age where few owned books, the collection of a Medici or Matthias Corvinus made a clear statement. Yet a century later, even a public official such as Antoine du Prat, *prévôt de Paris*, could own a thousand books.[5] In Oxford and Cambridge, scholars accumulated collections of two or three hundred books in the middle of the sixteenth century. This was equivalent in size to one of the more notable college libraries only fifty years before. Furthermore, the collections accumulated by private owners were in many respects more useful and often more up to date. Because institutional libraries acquired books mostly by donation, their collections had an inbuilt conservatism. There was also the likelihood that they would acquire duplicate copies of the same texts, and the terms of a bequest made disposal difficult.

With possession of texts spreading through society it required a connoisseur or scholar to appreciate the special magnificence of the greatest collections. The mere accumulation of texts was no longer enough to impress a casual visitor and the library receded as a focus for conspicuous princely wealth. Many of the great fifteenth- and sixteenth-century collections did not survive. Of those that did, many went through periods of conspicuous neglect. This is true of Fernando Colón's library in Seville, and even the Imperial collection in Vienna.[6] The Royal Library in Brussels had, in 1559, 666 printed books and 960 manuscripts. By 1683 there were 128 fewer items than a century before. In 1731, when fire consumed the building in which the library was housed, 500 of the most precious items were saved by being hurled out of a window.[7]

The changing role of the library can be seen most clearly in the decision of Philip II, against the wishes of his advisers, to site his library in the new monastery palace he was to build at El Escorial. The fabulous collection of manuscripts and printed books that the king accumulated was virtually unused for the three centuries after Philip's death. Philip envisaged his library as a private resource and repository of pious literature, not a place of meeting and conversation. In sixteenth-century court politics the library is seldom mentioned as a place of business: despite the now microscopic examination of the household government of Henry VIII the library never features as a location of significant power or discourse. Matthias Corvinus had had his library built next to his throne room, where his visitors could be impressed, but Henry's books were distributed between several of his palaces, and were shifted between them as occasion demanded.[8] This was not because Henry was not bookish. On the contrary, he was one of several sixteenth-century rulers who dabbled in writing and composition. It was a significant change, and not necessarily for the worse, that a Renaissance prince should pride himself on his education rather than his library.

The beginnings of the public library

In the sixteenth century the library also receded as a focus of public civic interest. Whereas in the fourteenth century the Republic of Venice had been prepared to invest heavily to secure Petrarch's library, a century later the gift of Cardinal Bessarion's famed collection of manuscripts had become a public embarrassment. After a hundred years had passed a home had still not been found that could provide the public access that had been a condition of the bequest.[9] This was not a unique example. In 1576 the city of Breslau received a significant bequest from their citizen Thomas Rehdiger of some 6,000 books, on condition that they be made available for public use. Rehdiger had lived a peripatetic life, and the collection was in Cologne at the time of his death. It took five years to transport the library back to Breslau, and many more before the promised public facility could be provided. It finally opened its doors in 1661, a full eighty-five years after the benefactor's death.[10]

The state of Bessarion's library was one of the main reasons why another prodigious Venetian collector, Domenico Grimani, refused entreaties to allow his books to be incorporated into the plan for a Venetian public collection.[11] Aldus Manutius and Erasmus both passed savage comment on such 'book buriers', who refused to lend manuscripts and sequestered them away in private collections. They were scarcely disinterested parties, because textual scholarship and scholarly printing depended on generous loans of prized manuscripts. But when Grimani made his dispositions for the future of his library in 1523 Bessarion's books were still mouldering in crates. His decision to give his books to the monastery of San Antonio, along with a generous cash sum for the creation of a building to hold them, seemed only prudent. Alas for his forethought, the library was burned down in the seventeenth century, taking with it all of Grimani's books, including the manuscripts of Pico della Mirandola, purchased by Grimani in 1498 as the basis of his collection.

The library as a cultural institution struggled to adapt to the new age of print. At the end of the sixteenth century the public library still lay some way in the future. This was true even of France, where the seventeenth and eighteenth centuries would witness a precocious development in access to books through public collections.[12] In the sixteenth century the establishment of a public collection depended on individual donors determined to endow a resource for their own local communities. Two examples from England are typical of this sort of initiative: the establishment of parochial libraries in Bury St Edmunds and Grantham.

Bury St Edmunds was a godly town with close connections to nearby Cambridge. In 1595, propelled by the preacher of St James's Church, Miles Mosse, citizens were induced to contribute books to a new parish library. This venture was strongly supported by pious citizens. In 1595 and 1596 some forty-one donors offered books, and within four years a collection of 200 volumes had been assembled.[13] It survives intact today in the care of Bury St Edmunds Cathedral Library (the parish church of St James having become the Cathedral in 1914).

The core of the collection was a range of Latin continental theology which was specially bought to stock the library. Donors presumably either provided money, or were instructed what to purchase. More characteristic donations were evident in the miscellaneous character of the library's other stock: some history, Bodin's *Six Books of the Commonwealth*, a valuable copy of Sebastian Münster's *Cosmography*. For unlearned users there were a small number of religious works in English: Jewel's *Apology*, some Calvin sermons and Bullinger's *Decades*. The core collection was intended for the use of the local clergy; it is impressive both for its range and coherence. The library owned several Latin bibles and a copy of the Antwerp Polyglot, a full range of the Church Fathers, and had comprehensive coverage of the Latin works of Calvin, Melanchthon, Bullinger and Peter Martyr Vermigli. This explains the dominance in this particular library of imported works, especially from two major centres of production, Basel and Geneva. The Church Fathers were represented by a magnificent series of editions published in Basel, though Athanasius was a Paris edition and Jerome the three-volume edition published in Antwerp. Interestingly the Latin edition of Calvin's *Institutes* was a Genevan import rather than the editions published in London. Those charged with making these purchases would have had recourse to the bookshops of Cambridge and London, where such books were readily available. In addition to his own publications Christophe Plantin supplied his London clients with mixed consignments of books from Basel, Geneva, Lyon and Zurich.[14] Presumably this was stock he had taken in exchange in transactions at the Frankfurt Fair.

A further window into the operations of this market is provided by the chained library at St Wulfram's Church, Grantham. In 1595 a local citizen, Francis Trigge, decided to create a library for his local town and undertook to supply books 'to the value of one hundred pounds or thereabouts'. For this he got about 300 books; apparently by the simple expedient of sending to Cambridge and seeing what was available.[15] The collection thus gives us an interesting snapshot of what could be provided by this buoyant market. Although the collection is less closely focused than that of Bury St Edmunds it reflects the same domination of the major continental centres of supply: Geneva, Basel and Antwerp all feature strongly.

Public men and private collections

The vast proportion of books published in the sixteenth century was purchased by individual buyers for their own use, and that of their families. During the course of the century a very large number of citizens from diverse walks of life accumulated increasingly significant collections. Of the contents of these collections we are becoming better informed, and not merely from the evidence of production, the basis of much of the evidence deployed in this book so far. We also have the opportunity to examine numerous surviving lists of individual collections, many of them compiled for purpose of valuation after the death of the owner. These inventories are by far the most numerous form of book list surviving from the period; archives and depositories across Europe contain several thousand, many of them still waiting to be discovered.

How can we make best use of this great mass of information? One approach is to examine, by decade, the average size of the collections recorded. This shows, much as one would expect, a steady rise in the average size of personal library collections as the century wears on.[16] The information for England shows that England's position on the periphery of the European book market was no obstacle to amassing a substantial collection of books. By the middle of the sixteenth century a scholarly collection of 100 titles was commonplace. By the 1570s and 1580s it was not unknown for relatively junior members of the universities to have this many; senior scholars had 300 or more.[17]

When John Bateman, a Fellow of Gonville and Caius College, Cambridge, died in 1559, the contents of his four-room chambers were valued at £48. His study housed a collection of 500 books.[18] Without repairing to the university or college library Bateman would have been able to consult a virtually complete range of standard editions of the Church Fathers. He had no fewer than twelve Latin bibles, two in Greek and six in Hebrew, and he owned numerous grammars. This represented a revolution in learning. Bateman had collected assiduously more recent controversial literature, and a fairly conventional sprinkling of the classics. There was also room in this busy life for recreation. The library boasted at least thirty books in English, including Chaucer, Gower and Lydgate, together with translations of Guevara and Quintus Curtius.

Fig. 63 The Library at the Plantin-Moretus print house. The busts and globe make a powerful statement affirming the humanist ideal of the civilising role of print. In fact much of the profit came from more mundane projects.

As this example makes plain, we are soon lured from the dry enumeration of statistics to an examination of contents. Here we can gather an enormous amount of information about what books sixteenth-century collectors owned. Sometimes, as with a theology student, a lawyer or a practising physician, we can infer (and sometimes prove from inspection of copies) that the books were consulted and well used. But this is not an inference that we can draw from all inventories. Neither can we assume that inventories offer a complete view of a book owner's reading matter.

The vast proportion of surviving inventories were compiled for valuation. They therefore did not detail what was of no value. The small books so important to several aspects of the trade – works of devotion, pamphlets and official edicts – scarcely feature in most inventories, or they are encompassed in a generic description of frustrating imprecision: 'other small books'; 'deux paquets de livres'. When plague came to Oxford in 1577 it carried off many scholars, and the assessors were overstretched. It is not difficult to see why they cut corners; but it is still frustrating that after listing 227 items of the library of James Reynolds the 228th item records 'a hundredth parchment old bookes'.[19] In fact, of the individual titles listed for members of Oxford University who died between 1507 and 1576, only 153 were books in English, and of these two-thirds were theological texts. What had become of the many thousands of vernacular titles that we know were published throughout Europe? Even allowing for the bias towards the scholarly in academic collections, Oxford and Cambridge testators must have had many of these texts. How many lurk behind laconic, frustrating formulas such as 'other old books', too cheap, or too common to merit separate valuation?

Fugitives

Cheap books for recreational use are frustratingly under-represented in inventories of personal collections, but they are not the only items missing: some books with intrinsic value might also be omitted from the written record. It was possible for precious items to be removed before the inventory was compiled. A family bible or Book of Hours was frequently bequeathed to a close relative or friend. Other items were omitted that could not be sold for quite different reasons. In 1577 an auction was held of the books of the schoolmaster of Bezièrs in southern France, Jean Dumas. Dumas had left the town in a hurry, probably because he was about to be exposed as a Calvinist. He left a collection of some size: around 250 books were put under the hammer.[20] The contents are of great interest, both for what Dumas owned and for what was missing. Dumas possessed an impressive collection of classical literature: the Greeks, Aristotle, the Roman histories (Sallust and Livy but not Tacitus), poetry and works of Cicero. He had modern humanist authors, but none of the Pléiade poets. He possessed some works of law; his five medical texts included a work by Galen. His scientific texts included a Copernicus. He owned Augustine and Aquinas, but there was no Protestant literature: no Protestant bible, no book of psalms, no works by Calvin or Luther. If Dumas was a Calvinist it is hard to credit that he did not own any of these works, in a collection of such size. Either he had rescued these precious items to take with him when he left town, or they had been disposed of; perhaps by Dumas to trusted friends. If not, the city authorities must have weeded the collection before they made up their list for auction.

Jean Dumas was an unabashed supporter of the new religion, but forbidden books could lurk in the most respected collections. This was all the more the case when the lists of forbidden books proclaimed a blanket ban on all the works written by disapproved authors. The Papal Index would have forbidden ownership of Melanchthon's grammatical and philological texts, simply because he was a known heretic. Even the most pious among Europe's scholarly community found this excessive. They were not set a particularly stringent example by Pope Sixtus V (Pope 1585–90), whose personal library of 1,600 items included twenty prohibited titles. These included more than ten works of the German jurist Joannes Oldendorpius and the *Bibliotheca universalis* of Conrad Gesner: an indispensable work of reference in any serious library.[21]

Beware pirates

Forbidden books were well represented in the library of Gian Vincenzo Pinelli, one of the greatest collectors of the late sixteenth century. Pinelli, a resident of Naples, began collecting soon after he moved to Padua, in northern Italy, in 1558. Over forty years he assembled a breathtaking collection of books and manuscripts, including an unrivalled assemblage of Greek manuscript texts.[22] Reaching into every field of learning and scholarship, the library also included several hundred vernacular works on contemporary French politics. As was customary in the larger libraries, these were collected into volumes by subject and bound.

Pinelli had many influential friends, which may have been why he had so little regard for the prohibitions of the Roman Index. An inventory taken in 1604 includes at least seventy-three books by prohibited non-Italian authors, including Erasmus, Bodin, Paracelsus, Rabelais and Sebastian Münster. The disapproved works of Italian literature he owned included texts by Aretino, Boccaccio and Machiavelli.[23]

Pinelli died in 1601, at which point his library entered a period of prolonged tribulation that illustrates vividly the threats to the survival of any sixteenth-century collection. The original intention had been for Pinelli's nephew to establish a library open to scholars at the family seat in Giuliano, outside Naples. Before this plan could be put into effect the Venetian government intervened to remove certain manuscripts they regarded as politically sensitive. The books were eventually loaded on to three ships for transportation through the Adriatic, but one was intercepted by pirates. When they discovered that the cases of freight contained nothing but books they threw several overboard. The abandoned ship was washed ashore and plundered by local fishermen. Of the thirty-three cases of books left on board the authorities could recover just twenty-two. The valuable volumes taken by the locals were dismembered and used to mend boats or provide primitive window coverings.

Barely had the remains of the collection made its way to Naples when Pinelli's nephew died. The idea of a permanent collection died with him. After prolonged litigation the collection was purchased at auction by Cardinal Borromeo for his new library in Milan (the Biblioteca Ambrosiana).[24] Borromeo's agents now made a careful selection for the long journey back to northern Italy, discarding items damaged by water or rodents, and books of less interest to their new owner. The following year the manuscripts and a selection of printed texts finally reached their new home.

Such was the fate of one of the great late Renaissance collections, at its peak well in excess of 6,000 printed books and 800 manuscripts. Nature, squabbles over inheritance and the dangers of transportation all posed formidable obstacles to survival. For other types of library the threat of destruction was more studied.

The spoils of war

Towards the end of the sixteenth century the Jesuit Order began to make imaginative use of the library as a tool of conversion, particularly in mission fields outside the main centres of European book production. One such example was the library created for the Jesuit College in Braunsberg (Braniewo) in northern Poland. The Jesuit College was founded in 1565 by the Prince Bishop of Warmia, Stanisław Hozjusz. Hozjusz was one of the great figures of the Polish Counter-Reformation, a diplomat and pugnacious polemicist whose published works achieved considerable popularity throughout Europe. Braunsberg was located perilously close to German East Prussia and had proved susceptible to Lutheran influence. The establishment of the Collegium Hosianum was a deliberate effort to counter the creeping spread of the Reformation. An important part of this missionary endeavour was the building of a library: over the next forty years a collection of almost 2,000 volumes was accumulated.

In 1626 the Swedish army of Gustavus Adolphus conquered Braunsberg as part of its triumphant campaign in the Baltic region. The army laid waste the town, but the library of the Jesuit College was treated with some care. The entire collection was crated up and sent to Uppsala where it was incorporated into the recently established university library: although the university had been founded in 1477 it had no library until 1620. The plunder of the Hosianum thus served a double purpose: to stock the new library and to deprive Polish Jesuits of their most powerful tool.

The collection has remained in Uppsala ever since, clearly distinguished by marks of ownership. Recently it has been the subject of a detailed catalogue.[25] We can see from this that the Hosianum accumulated most of its books on the German market. Over half the library's collection had been published in Germany, with Cologne predictably the provider of the largest consignment. This is a collection exclusively of Catholic works, so Wittenberg and Jena scarcely feature. Of the international centres Basel is well represented, but Geneva scarcely at all.

Interestingly, of the editions supplied from farther afield, northern Europe dominates even in this very Catholic collection. Antwerp supplied 150 books, more than Venice. Paris and Lyon each provide 100. Not all of these are contemporary publications. The 1,985 items in the Braunsberg collection include 336 incunabula and many publications from the first half of the sixteenth century. Many of the Parisian imprints date from the first decades of the sixteenth century, published at least half a century before they arrived in Braunsberg. These earlier texts must either have been accumulated from donation or by purchase on the second-hand market. In much the same way when Francis Trigge was buying his books for Grantham he obtained, presumably quite cheaply, a number of incunabula and a significant tranche of Paris imprints from the early part of the sixteenth century.[26]

The existence of this robust second-hand market represents a significant link with the practices of the medieval manuscript book trade. It also gave the sixteenth-century book world a more conservative character than would be obvious if we concentrated only on the most recently published books. Old books from the first century of print were simply too valuable to dispose of, even if the learning and knowledge they contained were seriously out of date. Old works of scholarship and pedagogy clogged up the shelves of libraries, the back rooms of bookshops and publishers' warehouses. There were some good aspects to this. A publisher like Plantin could help a rich young client build a library in a hurry, because he kept in stock most of his back catalogue. But publishers also held on to many thousand printed sheets of redundant learning simply because they could not sell them.[27] The second-hand market recycled other antiquated texts as ambitious donors like Francis Trigge sought to build a library quickly. There was always the risk that their agents would snap up job lots of texts of questionable contemporary relevance. It was another way in which the thrill of the new was diluted by the economic practicalities of sixteenth-century commerce.

The destruction of books

The destruction of the Jesuit library in Braunsberg was a deliberate act: a quite calculated attack on the cultural capital of an alien society. But at least the books survived. In this and subsequent centuries the conflicts between Europe's competing nation states would cause the destruction of much of the accumulated literary wealth of the first age of print. In the seventeenth century it was Germany, the historic heartland of print, which would be the major victim. The Thirty Years' War (1618–48) was a terrible blow to Europe's largest print world. The Swedish armies that ransacked Braunsberg also looted many German collections. The campaigns of Gustavus Adolphus initiated a massive exodus of books, continued by Swedish armies after his death. Erfurt, Eichsfeld, Mainz and Würzburg were all looted in 1631. Given this history of predatory collecting there is a certain poetic irony in the fact that the Swedish Royal Library lost three-quarters of its stock (18,000 books and 1,000 manuscripts) in a disastrous fire in 1658.[28] The most spectacular looting of the war was the seizure of the library of Heidelberg University, after the Catholic investiture of the Palatinate in 1622. Three thousand manuscripts and 12,000 printed books were appropriated for the Vatican library in Rome, where most still remain. At least they are well cared for.[29] What remained in Heidelberg was destroyed by the troops of Louis XIV in 1693.

Fire, flood and warfare: all took their toll on the accumulated cultural heritage of the first age of print. The University Library of Copenhagen was burned down in 1728. The Lisbon earthquake of 1755 destroyed the Royal Library of Portugal. The Public and University Library in Strasbourg was destroyed by German bombardment in 1870, despite promises that it would be spared. It was subsequently restocked through the donation of duplicates from German libraries, which accounts for the largely Germanic character of its early printed collections today.

This demonstration of the power of modern artillery was only a foretaste of the havoc wrought by the wars of the twentieth century. Collections in northern France suffered severe damage in the Great War of 1914–18, but nothing in comparison to the impact of aerial bombing in 1939–45. Victims of the conflict included the National Library of Belgrade, the Polish National Library and all the major libraries of Warsaw. The fighting in Italy destroyed more than twenty libraries, including the library of Naples University and the Public Library in Milan. In the intense fighting of the last years of the war many German universities lost their entire collections. Urban communities under bombardment could sometimes save their most precious manuscripts but seldom their printed books. The precious items moved to places of safety suffered further depredations and depletions in the chaotic period after Germany's defeat. The combined impact of Nazi looting and the appropriation of German collections in what became Communist Eastern Europe led to an enormous churning of library stock. Discovering what became of many early books is a continuing task even now, sixty years later.[30] The catalogue of the Berlin State Library, formerly one of the greatest of all collections, annotates many of its books with the cautious formula 'possibly lost in the war': they simply do not know. Certainly some Berlin books are in Cracow, and others in Saint Petersburg.

The destruction of the Second World War was so great that we can scarcely be surprised that many millions of old books were among its accidental victims. But sometimes destruction is more deliberate: as when libraries are targeted as repositories of a national cultural heritage. Between 1933 and 1945 it is estimated that the Nazi regime and its occupying troops destroyed as many as one hundred million books in Germany and occupied Europe. These may now seem like distant historical events, but the deliberate destruction of the National Library of Bucharest in the Romanian Revolution of 1989 and the destruction of the National and University Library of Bosnia in Sarajevo in 1992 occurred in very recent times. The occupation of Baghdad in 2003 was followed by wholesale looting of both the National Library and the National Museum of Iraq. The cultural consequences are still incalculable.

These terrible events have caused a cumulative attrition of the cultural legacy of the first age of print. Books that survived many hardships to reach the apparent safe haven of a major library perished in very recent times. We will never know quite what we have lost. But the chronicle of destruction is a bittersweet testimony to the power of books. Books preserve the accumulated, layered knowledge and wisdom of the human mind, with all its twists and turns, ignorance and false steps. For this reason books will always be loved, but also feared.

CHAPTER 16

WORD AND THE STREET

In 1989 workmen renovating a house in Delft made a most extraordinary discovery. Squirrelled away under the floorboards was a cache of old books. On further examination they turned out to be over four hundred years old. This was an old house, and the books had clearly been concealed, and then forgotten, at some point during the Dutch Revolt. All of them were forbidden Protestant works, and discovery could have landed their original owners in serious trouble. Their survival, undisturbed, through all the house's subsequent history is astonishing. But equally striking is the fact that, of the six books discovered, four were previously unknown.[1] No other copy has been traced in any library throughout the world.

It is almost impossible to know how many more of the publications of the sixteenth century may have disappeared altogether. Some books, like these heretical tracts, are scarce for a reason. If discovered at the time they were systematically destroyed. But many wholly uncontroversial books are also very rare; whole editions of school-books, catechisms and news books known to have been published have simply evaporated, used to death and discarded. The only systematic study of survival rates thus far accomplished is in this respect very revealing. Of all the books published in the French language in the sixteenth century, more than half are presently known in only one located copy.[2] If this is so, if so many books have survived in one example of several hundred printed, then how many have been lost altogether?

As a general rule, books published in the sixteenth century had the best chance of surviving if they made their way into libraries. Consequently certain categories of books had a far higher chance of survival: serious books, long books and big books, the sort of books a respectable citizen might wish his visitors to know that he owned. Large books in Latin had a particularly good chance of survival because they were less intensively used than vernacular handbooks that were read and consulted by the whole family. If these Latin tomes survived the death of their first owner then their prospects of longevity got better with every passing generation. Now they snooze away in libraries largely undisturbed.

With pamphlets of contemporary interest it was very different. Many survived only because a sixteenth-century purchaser gathered a handful together and bound them into a volume, making them more like their other, respectable books: in this way the literature of the streets was domesticated. But this occurred only with a fraction of those published. Overall less than 1 per cent of the total copies of books printed in the sixteenth century have survived to the present day. For pamphlets the figure is even lower.

Paper was too precious to waste. Books and pamphlets were torn up for wrapping, for stuffing bindings (and later furniture), and for use in the toilet. Blank spaces or the reverse sides of printed broadsheets were used for scribbling notes. Even valued texts grew out of date or dog-eared. Fire, damp, moths, mice, worms and time did the rest. Nineteenth-century revolutions and twentieth-century bombs picked off more of the survivors.

What remains is not then really representative of the whole published output of the sixteenth century. Most of the large, expensive books published then probably survive in at least one copy; sometimes many more. Books published in the fifteenth century, in the very first years of print, survive better than later publications, because contemporaries prized the new technology and started collecting them from the first years of their publication. Most of the first books published by Caxton in England have probably survived. But nobody, apart from a few men thought to be quite eccentric, collected the mundane everyday products of the press: broadsheet government orders, little sheets of songs, almanacs and calendars.

At this point print merged into the everyday world of communication and conversation that flowed easily from one medium to another: talk, letters and handwritten notices, public announcements, sermons, singing and plays.[3] The word on the street was seldom printed. But printers played their part. They listened and took note. Where there was a popular song, a good story, or a hideously shocking crime, they had a shrewd sense of what they could make of it.

To understand the world in which print existed we have to reconstruct this lost world of posters, pamphlets and pictures. No publisher could make their reputation with work of this sort. But they could make money. Many people, printers, sellers and writers, saw the potential of this market for news, sensation and excitement.

The power of prophecy

The sixteenth-century mind made little distinction between the everyday and the hereafter. In a world where God and the Devil were both seen as ceaselessly active, men and women scanned the most mundane events for signs of divine purpose. Great events were inevitably interpreted within a theological framework.

The iron grip of the ordinary in pre-modern societies is hard to comprehend today. The rhythm of the seasons and the vagaries of the weather were not just the determining patterns of existence: they were matters of life and death. A failed harvest could plunge millions over the narrow ledge that separated subsistence from starvation. The divine unpredictability of sunshine, hail, rain or thunder was the most tangible demonstration of humanity's utter helplessness in the face of God's mysterious will.

All of this was reflected in one of the most vibrant but ephemeral of all classes of printed literature, the market in calendars and prognostications. The impact of the seasons on the working round was deeply ingrained in what was still a fundamentally agricultural society. Even in towns, in an age when artificial heat and light was too expensive for the mundane tasks of the workshop, the working day was intensely seasonal. In the printer's workshop the press might be at work for twice as long in summer as in the dark winter months. Calendars were therefore fundamental to every working regime: they determined the rhythm of work and worship. Even before the age of print calendars were included in basic church handbooks and private devotional texts such as Books of Hours. They provided, one month on each page, a tabulation of the days, with festivals, saints' days and signs of the zodiac. Printed versions included a variety of other useful information such as annual markets and fairs.

It is easy to despise these calendars, amongst the most ephemeral of all sorts of print. But in their humble way they reflected a general awareness of the power of the celestial bodies to impact on everyday life; in this respect they provided a connection with far more sophisticated observers of the heavens: astronomers and cosmographers. In the sixteenth century the calendar also became a battleground. By 1578 Pope Gregory XIII had been convinced by his astrologers of what had long been suspected: that the calendar established by the Romans (the Julian calendar) had drifted away from the true seasons: the divergence was now of the order of ten days. The only remedy was for the calendar to leap forward ten days to make the correction. In 1582 the Pope made the necessary alteration. By a Papal Bull of 1 March it was decreed that

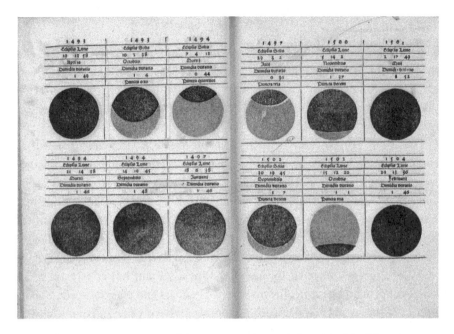

Fig. 64 Regiomontanus was one of the greatest and most influential of the fifteenth century astrologers. These pages of his calendar are from a section describing eclipses of the sun and the moon (Venice, August 1482).

4 October would be followed by the 15th. Catholic lands generally fell into line, though not necessarily on the prescribed days, but Protestant lands rejected the Gregorian calendar reform. The absurdity of different parts of Europe (in Germany, sometimes neighbouring territories) following different calendars persisted for many years. The last to make the change, England, only adopted the Gregorian calendar in 1752.

A similar tragicomic character can be detected in various efforts by Protestant jurisdictions to redesign the calendar, replacing saints' days with a new selection of Protestant heroes or notables of classical antiquity. The most dogged were the printers of Calvin's Geneva, who for several decades attached this alternative festal year to editions of the New Testament and Psalter. In the end the traditional calendar was too embedded in the annual round. The Protestant calendar now survives only as one of the ephemeral printed curiosities of the age.[4]

The calendar was also an important component of one other strand of astrological ephemera: the almanac. An almanac was technically a table of astrological events for the coming year. To this austere data was added useful information of the sort provided by calendars (festivals and fairs) and, in the age of print, an increasingly complex variety of prognostications, predictions derived from the planetary conjunctions for the coming year or years. Almanacs were extremely popular with publishers from the first age of print. Gutenberg included an almanac among his earliest publications: by 1470 printed prognostications can be documented for all the major zones of print production. The tradition developed most elegantly (and lucratively) in the Netherlands, where in 1469 the astronomer and physician Gaspar Laet initiated a series of annual publications that would be continued for the best part of a century.[5] The fact that the almanacs contained detailed predictions for the towns and provinces of the Low Countries did not limit their appeal. Editions of Laet's prognostications were also published in English for export.[6] A parallel French tradition was established in the *Shepherds' Calendar*, a perpetual almanac of considerable size and detail, which contained religious and moral advice as well as extensive tips on diet and nostrums for preserving good health.

The *Shepherds' Calendar* demonstrated the close connection between astronomy, the predictive science of astrology, and medicine. Just as medical science taught that human physiology comprised four humours corresponding with the elements, so the planets were ascribed attributes according to the same system. The science of astrology was based on the assumption of a close relationship between the planets and stars and all things on earth. By charting the relative movement of the planets the astrologer calculated influences on man and nature. The almanac's tables were a fundamental tool for doctor and astronomer alike. In 1437 the University of Paris decreed that every physician should possess a copy of the current almanac, so necessary was it deemed for medical diagnosis. The advent of printing made possible the generalisation of astronomical advice that had previously been the preserve of the rich.

Nostradamus

Throughout the sixteenth century the potency of astrology as a predictive tool was widely respected. Horoscopes were cast to determine the most propitious moment for a royal coronation or the laying of the foundation for a new building. Although the elite of scientific cosmographers regarded popular prognostications with something of the disdain humanists reserved for the indulgence trade, they certainly profited from the interest shown by Europe's rulers in more utilitarian astrology. Most of the major scientific cosmographers enjoyed royal support in return for astrological advice.

One man who successfully bridged the gap between the royal court and the world of popular print was the French physician Michel de Nostradamus. The son of a Provençal notary, Nostradamus was educated for a career in medicine. An early setback came when he was expelled by the Faculty of Medicine in Montpellier for practising as an apothecary, a manual trade, but this did not prevent Nostradamus establishing a considerable practice, and a growing reputation as an author. His eclectic works include both a paraphrase of Galen and the *Treatise on Sweets*, a volume that combines advice on recipes for facial make-up and the making of bonbons.[7]

By this point his interests had turned decisively away from medicine and towards the interpretation of celestial signs. In 1552 he issued what became the first of a series of annual almanacs and prognostications. The success of these modest volumes encouraged him to begin the project for which he is famous today: a series of elliptical French quatrains, containing 1,000 undated prophecies of future events. Published first at Avignon, then at Lyon, the fame of the prophecies quickly spread, particularly after Nostradamus was summoned to court to consult with the queen mother, Catherine de' Medici. Thereafter continuations and new editions followed in rapid profusion; so rapid, and indeed so similar in appearance are many of these volumes, that separating out different editions is a task of unusual complexity.[8] The French editions were published largely in Lyon, but Nostradamus also had an international following, with translations of his works into Italian, German and English. Nostradamus's discourse on the likely consequences of the eclipse of 1559 was, for instance, immediately republished by John Daye in London.[9] His death in 1566 brought to an end the annual sequence of almanacs, but did little to stem the popularity of the prophecies. In all, some 100 editions of his works are known to have appeared before the end of the sixteenth century.

The theatre of information

In 1601 the government of the ageing Queen Elizabeth of England faced a serious challenge to its authority. This came, unusually for a regime notable for the loyalty of its inner circle of trusted advisers, from the heart of the court. As the queen's long-standing trustees had left the scene one by one, a new generation jostled for power. With the old queen visibly failing, and the unacknowledged heir, James VI of Scotland, enigmatically distant, the stakes were high. By 1601 the emerging chief minister, Robert Cecil, had manoeuvred his rival, the Earl of Essex, Elizabeth's last favourite, into a position of frustrated isolation. Spurned by the queen, his military reputation in tatters, Essex contrived a hopeless, petulant and utterly foolhardy armed demonstration. A ramshackle band of retainers and aristocratic drifters marched on London before returning to Essex's house. Here they were disarmed and swiftly arrested.

To talk of an attempted coup is to dignify an affray that scarcely went beyond the tragicomic. But for the Privy Council it represented an opportunity to eliminate a political foe with a real capacity to engage the London crowd. Already on the day of the Earl's foray into London heralds had been dispatched to Cheapside and other places around London to proclaim him traitor. A proclamation to the same effect was issued the following day.[10] With the Earl safely in custody Cecil and his allies then staged an elaborate theatre to shape these confused events into a narrative where Essex's manic spasm was represented as a genuine threat to the political nation. First three Catholic priests were brought out of prison to be executed for treason. They were hanged, drawn and quartered as an exemplary spectacle. These three unfortunates had been condemned some time before, and then forgotten about. Most likely they were on the verge of being shipped to Wisbech, the remote fenland holding place for convicted Catholic priests. Now they became grisly props in an attempt to blacken Essex by association: to suggest that he was an agent of an international Catholic plot to divert the succession. If so, it was doomed to failure. Essex was too firmly associated in the public mind with the Protestant cause for this to take root. So at the last moment the Privy Council was forced to change tack, bringing to his trial a quite different and rather hastily compiled explanation of his treason. It was for this that Essex was condemned and executed on 25 February.

What is interesting about this episode is the very limited role played by print. The Privy Council were aware of the need to shape and educate popular opinion. Essex was known to be popular with the London crowd, and his execution provoked limited rumblings of discontent. In February a young lawyer was hanged at Smithfield for spreading libels. At the end of March the council was told of anonymous writings protesting against the execution of Essex. On 3 April the Lord Mayor sent to Cecil a libel that had been dropped at the Exchange. Almost certainly these notes of protest were handwritten. Compared to the barrage of print that accompanied the recent conflict between Henry IV of France and the Catholic League, or that which followed the assassination of the Prince of Orange, the small part played by print in these English events is striking.

The English publishing trade had developed considerably in the last decades of the sixteenth century, both in terms of output and the range of work it was

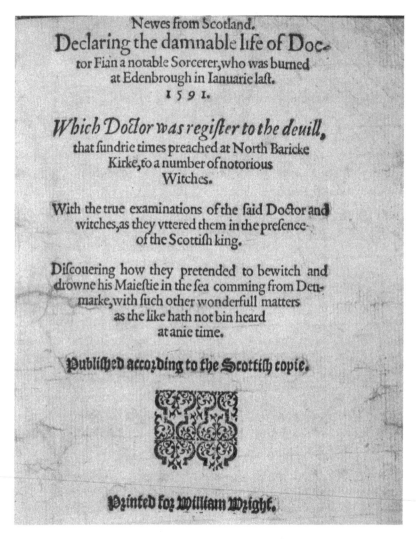

Newes from Scotland.

Declaring the damnable life of Doctor Fian a notable Sorcerer, who was burned
at Edenbrough in Ianuarie laſt.
1 5 9 1.

Which Doctor was regiſter to the deuill,
that ſundrie times preached at North Baricke
Kirke, to a number of notorious
Witches.

With the true examinations of the ſaid Doctor and
witches, as they vttered them in the preſence
of the Scottiſh king.

Diſcouering how they pretended to bewitch and
drowne his Maieſtie in the ſea comming from Deu-
marke, with ſuch other wonderfull matters
as the like hath not bin heard
at anie time.

𝕻ubliſh𝕖d acco𝕣ding to the 𝕾cottiſh copie.

𝕻𝕣inted fo𝕣 𝕸illiam 𝕸𝕣ight.

Fig. 65 a *News from Scotland.* This London pamphlet offers an account of a Scottish
witchcraft trial for the benefit of an English audience.

prepared to take on. But its overall shape and character was still discernibly
different from that of the major continental print industries. The slow
development of a market for domestic news pamphlets was one aspect
of this.[11] To a large extent this was an inevitable consequence of the
concentration of the entire industry in one location, London. The absence of a
provincial press made it difficult to develop a market for local regional news. To
publicise a monstrous birth or notorious crime in Chester, Hull or York, it was
necessary to send the manuscript to London and then have the printed sheets

Fig. 65 b *News from Scotland.* The illustration recapitulates the essentials of the narrative.

carted back again. For events where the interest lay in their immediacy and topicality this was a significant restraint on the publication of news pamphlets or broadsheets, the mainstay of the provincial press in many places around Europe.

This is not to say that there did not exist in England the same hunger for news evident in other parts of Europe. Successive English governments were only too aware that gossip and rumour were freely exchanged and could be very damaging: hence their determination that an official version of events should be publicly proclaimed. In the last decade of the sixteenth century enterprising London publishers printed a large number of English translations of French or Dutch news pamphlets, bringing to the English public news of the progress of the war on the continent, told from the perspective of Protestant allies in the war against Spain.[12] But this was foreign news. Despite the evident hunger for information, the English crown did not encourage the development of domestic news print, and London printers would certainly not stray into this area without encouragement. In England printed texts played a relatively marginal role in attempts to influence public opinion.[13]

This pattern continued into the seventeenth century. The first serial digests of news published in England, the corantos of the 1620s, consisted entirely of foreign news. These proved highly successful, so it is entirely characteristic of the Stuart monarchy's approach to the management of public opinion that, after these promising beginnings, an order of Star Chamber of 17 October 1632 prohibited the printing of all gazettes and news from foreign parts.[14] No further corantos were issued until 1638, when a monopoly on printing foreign news was granted to two stationers in return of a yearly payment of £10 towards the repair of St Paul's Cathedral. The re-founded corantos continued to deal exclusively with foreign news until 1641, by which time the Stuart monarchy had lost control of the London press.

Charles I was also at pains to uphold the Stationers' Company monopoly which inhibited provincial printing, restated by a Star Chamber decree of 1639. In the event the king would pay a heavy price for his assiduous attention to the prerogatives of the capital's printers, for as relations between the king and his subjects deteriorated towards open conflict, royal policy ensured that printing would be concentrated in the rebellious, parliamentarian capital. The difficulty of mobilising loyalist sentiment in the provinces was reinforced by the fact that the royal case could not be marshalled in print. It was hard to articulate the will of the county community where there was no printing to do so.[15] The establishment of Royalist presses in loyal towns once the war had begun, at Oxford and elsewhere, was very much a case of shutting the stable door after the horse had bolted.

Seeing and believing

The English print world was very particular, but the cautious development of print in the field of public information certainly reflected shared characteristics of European society. Much of public life in sixteenth-century Europe was built around the principle of bearing witness. Crowds gathered to hear a proclamation, to view a procession or to witness an execution. They heard sermons in church and gossiped in the marketplace. Much decision making and opinion forming was conducted in public, in groups, in the open air. Local populations were alerted to great events by the ringing of bells, the lighting of bonfires, or the gathering of crowds.[16] First news of great or memorable events was passed on by those who had witnessed them. Eyewitness accounts were then relayed by written dispatch.

It was by no means easy for printed accounts to make their way in this established world of letter writing and conversation. Where events had a largely exemplary character the accuracy of detail was not a critical issue. The report of an execution was arresting because of the hideous nature of the crime and the emblematic journey of the condemned from malefactor to penitent. Specific detail could be embroidered without reducing the force or value of the printed account. The same was to some extent true of accounts of natural disasters in faraway places. But the growth of interest in political news demanded new standards of credibility. News of great events or military victories was only of value if it were true.

The issues of credibility and public access raised by the wide dissemination of news dispatches were only solved in the seventeenth century.[17] In the polarised religious conflicts of the late sixteenth century Protestant and Catholic news networks were largely separate. This was partly because printers were reluctant to bring to the market anything except news of victories or the confusion of national enemies: natural prudence dictated that nothing be published that would offend the local authorities. News of Henry of Navarre's accession in 1589 was spread in at least forty pamphlets published in English. The ominous fact of his conversion to Catholicism in 1594 was greeted with deafening silence in London.[18]

In consequence English readers were far less likely to be presented with news from a malevolent Catholic source than from a friendly power: many English news pamphlets in this period were reprinted from Dutch originals.[19] This of course fundamentally undermined the credibility of pamphlets as news if bad news could never be shared.

For these reasons those in positions of political influence continued to prefer private networks of manuscript communication. These developed naturally from the news sources with which they were most familiar: ambassadorial dispatches and the exchange of letters between friends. Commercial manuscript newsletters enjoyed considerable success in this era, despite the growth of printed news sheets. In England they reached their heyday in the third decade of the seventeenth century.[20] In continental Europe they had been an established part of political and commercial society since the fifteenth century.[21]

The play's the thing

The complex relationship between print and oral culture is nowhere better displayed than in the development of drama: England's greatest and most distinctive contribution to sixteenth-century cultural life. The development of the open air theatre in London towards the end of the sixteenth century was extremely rapid. Between 1580 and 1620 London theatrical companies created a new form of public entertainment, where the work of some of the greatest

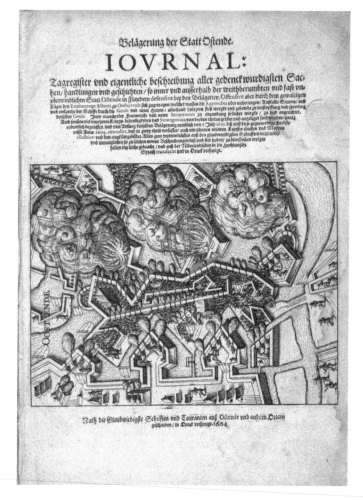

Fig. 66 The siege of Ostend. This early Journal was not a serial publication, but a pamphlet account of one of the critical events of the conflict between Spain and the northern Protestant powers. These events were followed by an interested public all across Europe – in this case in German translation.

dramatists was played to packed houses in new, purpose-built structures. This was a far cry from the boisterous (though hugely enjoyed) performances that had been offered by travelling players on extemporised temporary sets across most of Europe for the previous hundred years: performances that have left a limited impression in print.[22] The development of the London theatre was on an altogether different scale. By the last years of the sixteenth century some 15,000 customers could have attended a play every week: 10 per cent of the city's population.[23]

The development of the London theatre owed little to print. Between 1592 and 1609 the theatrical entrepreneur Philip Henslowe kept a detailed account book diary of the performances staged by his company. Of the 280 plays listed only thirty survive as a printed text.[24] Some very successful plays did merit a second life in print. Christopher Marlowe's *Massacre of Paris* was swiftly printed after its triumphant staging. Marlowe's *Dr Faustus* and Kyd's *Spanish Tragedy* both went through a number of printed editions, as did some of Shakespeare's history plays. But none achieved the success of steady Elizabethan bestsellers such as Dent's sermons or More and Dering's *Short Catechism for Householders*.[25]

There was no reason why a London publisher in search of profit (and what other sort was there?) should have thought of play texts as a promising way to make money. This was a project with high initiation costs. The publisher would have to pay something for the manuscript (if not as much as the author would have wished). By the time fees for registering the book with the Stationers had been paid, paper procured and wages paid to pressmen the profit margin on sales was extremely thin. Only if a play was sufficiently successful to merit a second or third edition was profit guaranteed. Takings on the first night of *The Massacre of Paris* were £3.14s. To print this or another play the publisher faced set-up costs of around £9 for an edition of 1,000 copies; even if it sold out completely (which might take several years) the potential profit was only around £6.[26] The economics were stark and daunting, and heavily weighted towards performance.

So the relative paucity of printed play texts may reflect publishers' scepticism about their profitability rather than fear on the part of the playwright or company that a printed version would make people less likely to come to the performance. Rather the contrary: the date of published texts of Shakespeare's plays in the 1590s may suggest that a print version was timed to coincide with a revival in the playhouse.[27] Shakespeare seems to have been keen that his plays should have a literary life, as well as an audience.

That said, the relationship between the printed play text and the performance seen on stage is by no means straightforward. Just as we have observed with sermons, it is difficult to assume that a printed text represents a literal transmission across media of what audiences would have seen enacted: in the pulpit or on the stage. The printed versions of the plays of Shakespeare (and Ben Jonson) are far too large to have fitted comfortably into the two hours thought customarily to have been the normal time allotted for theatrical performance. It may be that the plays printed contained passages that the author knew would not usually be performed.[28] The medium of print provided opportunities not available on the stage: to deepen character, to elaborate poetical, philosophical reflections that could be appreciated by the owner of a printed text who could follow the advice to 'read him therefore, and againe, and againe'.[29]

If the printed text was not the basis of the author's wealth – playwrights had this in common with other authors – it certainly helped build reputation. This change can be followed in the title-pages of the surviving play texts. The cluttered title-page of Marlowe's *Tamburlaine* in 1590 headlines the play's title and gives an elaborate and rather shambolic plot description, but does not mention the author. By 1594 the printed edition of *The Massacre of Paris* was proclaimed as 'written by Christopher Marlowe'. By 1598 an increasing number of Shakespeare's plays were published with his name on the title-page. The emergence of playwrights as respected literary figures is epitomised by the volumes of excerpts from play texts in the popular anthology *England's Parnassus* (1600) along with extracts from the leading Elizabethan poets. Shakespeare's plays were the most frequently represented. By embracing print he had secured his place in the canon of literary greatness even in his own lifetime.

Drama is a strangely hybrid medium. The oral performance has its origin in writing: the manuscript play text. It then takes wing in performance. It may then find a second audience (probably partially overlapping with the first) as literature. This hybrid character is deeply evocative of the fluid, transitional nature of communication in the sixteenth century. This was a world in which print had an important place, but did not yet rule the roost.

Mother Church

England was exceptional in the relatively modest part played by print in managing and mobilising opinion; we have seen that in France, the Low Countries and Italy the governing powers were active patrons of news print. But even here the printed word was only part of a culture of information that embraced many aspects of public communication. Print operated within a rich culture of ceremony, celebration and exchange of information. The exploitation of these diverse communication media was not the exclusive property of government. Indeed no one exploited it more effectively in its missionary efforts than the Jesuit Order.

The educational mission of the Jesuits has long been recognised as a key element in their success. Catechism schools provided the basic learning necessary to enter the newly founded Jesuit colleges, which provided an education universally acknowledged to be of the highest quality, even by confessional opponents. The foundation of a string of Jesuit colleges in France after 1559 was an important statement of intent in the fight against heresy. The Jesuits also made very active use of the press. When Emond Auger came to Lyon in 1563 he found himself pitched against a formidable adversary in Calvin's friend, Pierre Viret. Auger's preaching played a crucial role in restoring Catholic morale, leading in due course to the expulsion of the Calvinist preachers. Auger also recognised the value of print. To combat the flood of polemical Protestant pamphlets that had poured off the press since 1561 Auger published a series of his own sermons and tracts.[30] Providing the printers with alternative work played a critical role in breaking the link between print, profit and Protestantism that had converted so many Lyon publishers to an active role in the new movement. By 1567 the Calvinist Temple of Lyon was closed, and the city's presses denied to Protestant authors.

The Jesuits were everywhere respected as masters of theatre. The acting out of Latin plays was a key part of the curriculum in the Jesuit colleges. Public performances of these plays drew large crowds despite the use of the learned language; sometimes pamphlet synopses were distributed to the audience to allow them to follow the action.[31] The Jesuits never struggled to find printers: their copious popular writings made them important local patrons, and ensured that their play texts would also be taken on. They could sugar the pill by underwriting the cost, particularly for texts like play summaries that were intended to be given away rather than sold. This instance is a reminder that much of the printed ephemera of the sixteenth century was printed on demand for free distribution rather than sale. For publishers this made such work a more, rather than less attractive proposition.

The astute management of diverse forms of public engagement is evident in the public ceremonies that marked the completion of the building of the Jesuit house in Lisbon.[32] The Professed House of São Roque was founded in 1553 but not until the late 1580s was the building complete. Along with a church and residential quarters, the house boasted a public library housing a wide range of devotional, theological and historical works that were available to outside readers. The opportunity to proclaim the new eminence of the Jesuits in Lisbon came with the donation of a major collection of relics, including the skull of St Bridget of Ireland and the under-shirt of the Virgin Mary. These were introduced to the citizens of Lisbon in a spectacle on 25 January 1588, a parade that wound its way around the whole city, pausing on two occasions for the staging of edifying plays. The day of festivities had the desired effect. The Professed House was transformed into a major devotional centre and the moral supremacy of the Jesuits over competing ecclesiastical orders was assured.

There are few more apposite examples of the concerted orchestration of spiritual energy by astute manipulation of different media. Throughout Europe the interlocking dialogue of different modes of communication was a ubiquitous feature of the first age of print.

The Parisian Pepys

Let us end this book in the company of Pierre de L'Estoile, one of the sixteenth century's greatest diarists and a keen observer both of events and of the book trade.[33] L'Estoile was the son of a distinguished Parisian jurist and followed his father into the legal profession and royal service. In 1569 his family purchased for him the important office of Audiencier of the Chancellery of Paris. He would pass his whole life at the heart of the legal bureaucracy that dominated the capital's upper bourgeoisie.

From the time he returned to Paris on the completion of his education in 1565 to his death in 1612, L'Estoile left the city only once: to visit family properties in 1606. He thus lived through all the tumultuous events that unfolded in this dramatic period: the massacre of 1572, the League's expulsion of Henry III in 1588, the triumphant return of Henry IV. L'Estoile was an instinctive royalist, a scarcely disguised allegiance that brought him into considerable danger during the League ascendancy. At one point L'Estoile was shown a manuscript list with the names of prominent royalists marked out for retribution. Against their names was written a p (*pendu*), c (*chassé*, exiled) or d (*dagué*, to be stabbed). L'Estoile was in the third category: he was to be afforded the dignity of assassination rather than the humiliation of public execution. Fortunately he weathered this crisis to serve the new king into an increasingly cranky old age.

It is our great good fortune that L'Estoile had certain tastes that in his own day would have been regarded as distinctly eccentric. He liked to walk the streets, listening to gossip and noting the latest street songs. When he came home he would often transcribe them into his diary. An obsessive collector, L'Estoile also happily extended his collecting beyond the coins and curiosities of his fellow erudites to embrace the placards and brochures that littered the streets of Paris in these years. By 1607 he had filled some 1,200 scrapbooks with this material, including a priceless collection of illustrated political broadsheets. Scarcely thought worthy of more than passing attention in their day, they are now among the most prized unique items of the Bibliothèque Nationale in Paris.

L'Estoile paints a picture of a city abuzz with news, gossip and rumour, as events great and small are played out in the French capital's public space. News from abroad is received and analysed for its impact on France's turbulent politics. Strange and wondrous happenings are probed for their portents of God's purpose. L'Estoile reports news of the sack of Antwerp, Drake's return from his circumnavigation of the globe, the assassination of the Prince of Orange. His account of the subsequent interrogation of the assassin and his

Fig. 67 A news broadsheet from 1587. A remarkable bird discovered in England in 1586 is lauded in verse for the benefit of Dutch readers.

gruesome execution is so detailed it can only have come from a printed pamphlet. He offers a full account of the execution of Mary, Queen of Scots, and the torrent of epitaphs, verses and placards in which Parisians voiced their disapproval. The descent into the chaos of the League rebellion is fully and painfully chronicled. Although a committed royalist, L'Estoile thoroughly disapproved of the very public shows of favour showered by the king on his favourites. The subsequent feuds, duels and violent deaths of the young men raised up by the king are recorded without sympathy. The king's overt religiosity alternating with wild carousing left L'Estoile repelled and despairing. He had no doubt that the persistent criticisms of Catholic preachers were destroying the king's authority. The furious reaction to the assassination of Guise convulsed Paris and brought L'Estoile into personal danger. In the midst of these furies his judgement of the recently deceased Catherine de' Medici is unfairly offhand: 'she ate well, but did not understand matters of state'. Elsewhere he made clear that he admired Catherine's indefatigable spirit, exhibited in her insouciant reaction to publication of the violently abusive *Discours de la vie de Catherine de Medici*. Court gossip had it that the queen mother read it 'laughing with rage, and saying that if they had consulted her she would have given them lots more material'.[34]

L'Estoile endured the siege of Paris, and survived to witness the eventual submission of the city to Henry of Navarre. Through all of this L'Estoile recorded a torrent of public debate, pursued in placards, pasquils, verses, gossip, tracts, treatises and sermons. Many are assiduously recorded and transcribed into his diary. These contemporary responses to extraordinary events are often very funny, sometimes gross, but also often elaborate pastiches of considerable literary merit. Frequently it is by no means clear whether L'Estoile had his hands on a printed work, a handwritten sheet, or was simply recording something he had heard. Certainly many of the satires are too long and elaborate to fall into this last category, but the interweaving of print, manuscript and official declarations and declamatory sermons is otherwise intricate and difficult to disentangle. One anti-League tract circulated first in manuscript, and then, when it achieved currency in this form, was published as a pamphlet. Later, when the League achieved total domination of the Paris press, royalists had little choice but to resort to manuscript. L'Estoile was outraged that the Cardinal of Guise was able to change the printed account of the king's address at the Estates of Blois in 1588 to tone down criticism of the League. The following year at the height of the League agitation, L'Estoile managed to collect up 300 different tracts, all peddled in the streets. 'There was no little preacher who couldn't find a place in his sermon for a list of injuries against the King, no pedant so obscure that he didn't write a couple of sonnets on the subject, no minor printer who couldn't find a way to roll some new libellous and defamatory discourse off the press every day.'[35] They would have been cheap enough. The Duchess of Montpensier was observed riding through Paris, doling out pamphlets from baskets. Royalists like L'Estoile, meanwhile, were reduced to copying out verses for furtive distribution among like-minded friends. Some of L'Estoile's later appeared in the *Satyre Ménippée*, the master-work of royalist propaganda. 'I copied them myself in the evening, in my study, and let them fall into many good hands, more boldly than prudently.'[36]

Reading L'Estoile's assiduous copying, recording and collecting, we are the privileged witnesses of a vivid and extensive debate, conducted only in part in the medium of print. These were extraordinary times. Seldom was so large and sophisticated a place as Paris so consumed by political controversy over so long a period. Nevertheless what we see – and thanks to L'Estoile can document in unusual detail – is a heightened version of a far more general phenomenon. Print had not replaced more traditional means of communication, opinion forming and expressions of the communal will; but it certainly now played a prominent part in the theatre of information. Crucially this public discourse had passed out of the control of the powers that earlier in the century had willingly used print to promote their own authority. It was a development pregnant with consequences for the future, and for the emergence of a more confident and articulate public opinion.

This was the aspect of print culture that would most have surprised the humanist scholars of the fifteenth century who had celebrated the invention of movable type with such enthusiasm. For these scholars print offered the means to acquire larger numbers of texts for their own libraries. It is unlikely they would have approved the use to which it was put in the urgent public conflicts of the second half of the century.

The study of the Renaissance book world has brought on to the stage a large number of larger than life characters. The excitement of the new technology, the development of its capacities and the mania of collecting all encouraged men and women of an optimistic and entrepreneurial spirit to plunge into the business of books. Vespasiano da Bisticci and Pierre de L'Estoile were separated by a century in time and a sea change in European book culture, but they shared the same intellectual curiosity, zest for life, and sheer delight in a cornucopia of texts. Whether each man would have seen much of himself in the other is another matter. Vespasiano, factor of manuscripts for the great, would have had no inkling of the explosion of unrefined text; nor would he have been likely to approve an officer of the Paris court gathering up such material for his scrapbooks. From the distance of four centuries we have to be grateful for them both, assiduous in their promotion of book culture and in the recording of their recollections.

A Note on Sources: Mapping the Geography of Print

IT IS now fifty years since two French scholars, Lucien Febvre and Henri-Jean Martin, published their landmark study of the first era of printing: *L'Apparition du livre (The Coming of the Book)*.[1] Frequently reprinted and translated into every major language, *The Coming of the Book* helped crystallise an approach to book history which was eloquently pursued by another equally influential text, Elizabeth Eisenstein's *The Printing Press as an Agent of Change*. With this and a popular redaction, *The Printing Revolution in Early Modern Europe*, Eisenstein reformulated a view of the impact of print that has been the dominant motif of book history throughout the modern era; a view of print as an essential part of the modernising process, as a crucible of progress.[2]

This celebration of print reflects quite accurately the chorus of praise with which contemporaries greeted the new invention. Print, it was repeatedly proposed, had rescued the learning of the ancients from obscurity. The new technology 'had turned darkness into light'. As this book has demonstrated, this represented only one part of a far more complex reality. The humanist commentators of the sixteenth century have proved remarkably adept at persuading us to accept their ideological programme as a statement of historical reality.[3] In fact, as we have seen, the new book world involved a complex process of adaptation, restructuring and much heartache. The books that were often most successful were books of which humanists would scarcely have approved.

In fairness to scholars like Eisenstein and Henri-Jean Martin, much of this was far less clear when they wrote their books. Most scholars of the book have worked in the greatest collections, which naturally collected the finest books. The grubby, small books and pamphlets that made up the great bulk of production, and, as this book has argued, underpinned the economics of the industry, are scattered around thousands of different libraries.

Until very recently scholars attempting to study this massive outpouring of books have worked with very incomplete data. Put simply, it has been impossible to state with any confidence even basic facts about the early print world: such as how many books were printed, where, and by whom. For scholars working on British material this has been less apparent, because the small print output of London is reasonably fully documented. The pioneering work of Pollard and Redgrave, the *English Short Title Catalogue*, was first published as long ago as 1926.[4] But for many years this found no imitators. England comprised only around 4 per cent of the total print output of Europe, and Pollard and Redgrave found copies of most of the books in one of a small number of very large collections.[5] The larger, more dispersed print domains of continental Europe posed a far greater challenge. For some, such as Italy and Germany, a comprehensive census has been painstakingly compiled in the last thirty years. For others, like France and Spain, such a survey is only now being completed.

Ironically, it has been the next great information revolution – the internet – that has allowed this work on the first age of print to be pursued to a successful conclusion. The steady development of online library catalogues in the last twenty years has allowed scholars to draw together data from a mass of libraries around the world to create a master list of editions for each part of Europe – and hence for the whole of the first era of print. This also records, for the benefit of users, where all these often very rare books are to be found. The result is a total repertory of around 350,000 editions, and some 1.5 million surviving copies.[6]

For the entire sixteenth century, the largest market, by some distance, was the German-language zone of central Europe. The bibliographical survey of this area, the *VD 16*, documents some 100,000 books published in German-speaking lands during the course of the sixteenth century. This includes 7,000 books published in the Swiss Confederation, which encompassed one of the most important centres of the international book trade, Basel, and two smaller production centres of regional significance, Zurich and Berne. It excludes, however, German books published in places where German was not the predominant language (such as Copenhagen, or cities in parts of eastern Europe).

The Italian print world has been surveyed by the *Edit 16*, again now available as an online resource. This currently lists some 60,000 editions and copious data on surviving copies. Italian bibliography faced the formidable obstacle that there is no single Italian collection that could form the cornerstone of a bibliographical project. The *Edit 16* in fact incorporates data from 2,000 collections, some of them very small. As is the case for Germany with the *VD 16*, the survey is at present confined to libraries within Italy. To compare and group the dispersed surviving copies all items are provided with a unique edition identifier through the use of a fingerprinting system.[7] Italian books surviving uniquely in libraries outside Italy might add substantially to this total: the largest collection of sixteenth-century Italian books is in fact that of the British Library in London.

Bibliographers of France have been able to call upon two long-standing projects, both based on the work of Philippe Rénouard and the file notes left to the Bibliothèque Nationale in Paris. One offers a chronological survey of Paris imprints, and thus far extends to 1540; the other, an alphabetical survey of the output of individual printers, covers only the letters A and B.[8] These projects, and separate surveys of individual provincial printing centres, have now been partially overtaken by the global survey of the St Andrews French Book project.[9] This provides data on some 75,000 sixteenth-century editions published in the kingdom of France.

The St Andrews project team has also undertaken a fundamental renovation of the data available on publishing in the Low Countries. Here bibliography has been substantially shaped by the decision to treat the book heritage of Belgium and the Netherlands as separate entities. Though Nijhoff and Kronenberg had covered the whole of the Low Countries in their survey of post-incunabula (1501–40), the rest of Netherlandish publishing in the sixteenth century has been covered in separate projects. The *Typographia Batava* of Paul Valkema Blouw has made a reasonable job of capturing information on publishing in the northern Netherlands, but for the southern Netherlands the *Belgica typographica* notes only books located in Belgian libraries.[10] As a result it vastly understates the total output of presses in Antwerp and other important centres of typography. The St Andrews project has to some extent corrected this omission, and as a result can now present data on some 32,000 editions published in the Low Countries before 1601.

These recent researches confirm the importance of the Low Countries as a major centre of typographical production. The Swiss Confederation, the other major component of the central market, is important less for the absolute size of its print industry than for the quality of its scholarly editions. A total corpus of 11,000 editions is divided between the German-speaking cities, incorporated into *VD 16*, and the French-speaking area documented by Jean-François Gilmont's on-line resource (GLN 15–16).

An equivalent resource for Spain and Portugal is now close to completion. The work of a project led by Dr Alexander Wilkinson of University College,

Dublin, this will list around 18,000 editions for the Iberian kingdoms, including books printed in the satellite book world of Spanish colonial America.[11]

Print also expanded eastward to Poland, Bohemia and Hungary, and more haltingly, north to Scandinavia. The print domains of Denmark and Sweden have been surveyed by national bibliographical projects, as has the print output of Bohemia and Hungary.[12] Data for Poland is more fragmentary. In all cases, the more comprehensive searches of the Universal Short Title Catalogue have added many new items not represented in the published bibliographies. Collectively they make up a corpus of another 15,000 editions.

All of this data will, from 2011, be fully searchable through the online Universal Short Title Catalogue. This book has made much use of this developing data, particularly in its analysis of the evolving geography of print. But a full picture of the living, breathing world of authors, publishers and booksellers also relies on many hundreds of individual detailed studies, of printers, writers and texts. The debt this work owes to this enormous body of scholarship will be obvious, and is acknowledged in the accompanying bibliography. It is hoped that the Universal Short Title Catalogue will to some extent repay this debt by making available a vast new repository of data to all those interested in the diverse, complex and enthralling world of books.

APPENDIX:
A SUMMARY OF PRINTED OUTPUTS
THROUGHOUT EUROPE, 1450–1600

		Vernacular	Scholarly	Total
France		40,500	35,000	75,500
Italy		48,400	39,600	88,000
Germany		37,600	56,400	94,000
Switzerland		2,530	8,470	11,000
The Low Countries		17,896	14,021	31,917
	Subtotal	*146,926*	*153,491*	*300,417*
	Percentage of total	*81.99%*	*92.48%*	*87.03%*
England		13,463	1,664	15,127
Spain		12,960	5,040	18,000
Scandinavia		873	793	1,666
Eastern Europe		4,980	4,980	9,960
	Subtotal	*32,276*	*12,477*	*44,753*
	Percentage of total	*18.01%*	*7.52%*	*12.97%*
	Total	**179,202**	**165,968**	**345,170**

Acknowledgements

DURING THE course of work on this book I have accumulated many debts, and it is a pleasure to acknowledge help, advice and intellectual inspiration from many quarters. First and foremost, I owe a huge amount to all those who have worked over the years as part of the St Andrews Book project group, especially my long-term collaborators in this enterprise, Malcolm Walsby and Alexander Wilkinson. Philip John has now taken on the demanding role of co-ordinating technical work that underpins our data gathering and analysis. He has been joined on the project staff most recently by Graeme Kemp and Natasha Constantinidou.

I began the writing, and did much of the necessary preparatory work for this project, during a term as a visiting Fellow at All Souls College, Oxford. I am grateful to the Warden and Fellows, and to the staff of the Codrington Library, for providing such a stimulating and congenial environment in which to pursue these tasks. A survey of this nature inevitably draws on a wide range of detailed work from other scholars, and I have profited greatly from the opportunity to read the work of a whole host of scholars active in the very lively field of book history. Particular personal intellectual debts are owed to Alastair Duke, Falk Eisermann, Bruce Gordon, Lotte Hellinga, Ian Maclean, Jane Pettegree, and, at one further remove, Hugh Trevor-Roper and Simon Schama. I was privileged to hear both the two last named lecture when I was an undergraduate and I admired in both the recognition that the historian is also a storyteller. I hope this book makes a modest contribution to upholding this tradition.

Rona Johnston Gordon, Jane Pettegree, Peter Truesdale, Max von Habsburg, Sophie Mullins and Heather McCallum all read the complete first draft of this text, and I am grateful to them for the helpful suggestions that have contributed materially to the final product. I should also acknowledge the help of the library staff who over many years have made this work possible: fetching often unreasonable quantities of books, generating catalogue searches, answering my questions. During the course of fifteen years working on the history of books I have had the pleasure of working in many of the greatest collections of rare books. But this book would not have been possible had I only worked in these places. Many of the rarest books are tucked away in the most unlikely places. The fun of this work has been visiting some of these more eccentric resources, from the Library at Innerpeffray, tucked away up a farm track in rural Perthshire (a wonderful collection that deserves to be better known), to the small municipal library in France where I was invited to browse the rare book collection stored in the loft while my children amused themselves in the children's library below. My daughters Megan and Sophie have grown up with this project and I have been grateful for their tolerant and good-natured acceptance of 'holidays' built around visits to libraries. My wife Jane has not only shared some of the excitement of this work, but also sportingly coped with houseloads of graduate students and researchers as the work took shape.

This work would also not have been possible without the generous and sustained support provided to the St Andrews book project by the Arts and Humanities Research Council. For ten years they supported a project devoted exclusively to the culture and history of France; more recently they have supported the Universal Short Title Catalogue. In this altruistic commitment to recovering the common intellectual heritage of the shared European past they have captured something of the same pioneering spirit of the cultural world that is the subject of this book.

Andrew Pettegree
St Andrews, June 2009

ABBREVIATIONS

Benzing Josef Benzing, *Lutherbibliographie. Verzeichnis der gedruckten Schriften Martin Luthers bis zu dessen Tod* (2nd edn, Baden-Baden, Heitz, 1989)

BT Elly Cockx-Indestege, Geneviève Glorieux and Bart op de Beeck, *Belgica typographica 1541–1600: catalogus librorum impressorum ab anno MDXLI ad annum MDC in regionibus quae nunc Regni Belgarum partes sunt* (Nieuwkoop, de Graaf, 1968–94)

Edit 16 *Edit 16. Le edizioni italiane del XVI secolo: censimento nazionale* (5 vols, Roma: Istituto centrale per il catalogo unico delle biblioteche italiane e per le informazioni bibliografi che, 1989–)

FB Andrew Pettegree, Malcolm Walsby and Alexander Wilkinson, *FB. French Vernacular Books. Books Published in the French Language before 1601* (Leiden, Brill, 2007)

GLN 15–16 http://www.ville-ge.ch/musinfo/bd/bge/gln/. A bibliography of books published in the fifteenth and sixteenth centuries in the cities of Geneva, Lausanne and Neuchâtel, plus the city of Morges.

Göllner Carl Göllner, *Turcica: Die europäischen Türkendrucke des XVI. Jahrhunderts* (3 vols, Berlin, Akademie-Verlag, 1961–78)

IA *Index Aureliensis: catalogus librorum sedecimo saeculo impressorum* (14 vols, Baden-Baden, Koerner, 1962–2004)

IB Alexander Wilkinson, *IB. Books Printed in the Iberian Peninsula and in Spanish Abroad* (2 vols, Leiden, Brill, 2010)

ISTC Incunabula Short Title Catalogue. http://www.bl.uk/catalogues/istc

Knuttel	W.P.C. Knuttel, *Catalogus van de pamfletten-verzameling berustende in de Koninklijke Bibliotheek* (9 vols, The Hague, 1882–1920)
NB	Andrew Pettegree and Malcolm Walsby, *NB. Books Printed in the Low Countries before 1601* (2 vols, Leiden, Brill, 2011)
NK	Wouter Nijhoff and Maria Elizabeth Kronenberg, *Nederlandsche bibliographie van 1500 tot 1540* (3 vols, The Hague, Nijhoff, 1965–71; reprint of The Hague, 1919–42)
Shaaber	M.A. Shaaber, *Check-list of Works of British Authors Printed Abroad, in Languages other than English, to 1641* (New York, Bibliographical Society of America, 1975)
STC	A.W. Pollard and G.R. Redgrave, *A Short-title Catalogue of Books Printed in England, Scotland, & Ireland and of English Books Printed Abroad 1475–1640* (2nd edn, 3 vols, London, The Bibliographical Society, 1976–91)
TB	Paul Valkema Blouw, *Typographia Batava 1541–1600: repertorium van boeken gedrukt in Nederland tussen 1541 en 1600* (2 vols, Nieuwkoop, de Graaf, 1998)
VD 16	*VD 16. Verzeichnis der im deutschen Sprachbereich erschienenen Drucke des XVI. Jahrhunderts* (25 vols, Stuttgart, Hiersemann, 1983–2000)
VE 15	Falk Eisermann, *Verzeichnis der typographischen Einblattdrucke des 15. Jahrhunderts im Heiligen Römischen Reich Deutscher Nation: VE 15* (Wiesbaden, Reichert, 2004)
USTC	The Universal Short Title Catalogue, http://www.ustc.ac.uk/
Voet	Léon Voet, *The Plantin Press (1555–1589): A Bibliography of the Works Printed and Published by Christopher Plantin at Antwerp and Leiden* (6 vols, Amsterdam, Van Hoeve, 1980–83)

NOTES

Prelude

1. Marcantonio Sabellico, *De latinae linguae reparatione* (Venice, 1493).
2. The case is described in Ingeborg Jostock, *La Censure négociée. La contrôle du livre à Genève, 1560–1625* (Geneva, Droz, 2007), pp. 180–90.
3. For example the wonderful Pierre de L'Estoile (see Chapter 16).
4. The theme of the print revolution is most eloquently expounded by Elizabeth Eisenstein. See Elizabeth Eisenstein, *The Printing Press as an Agent of Change: Communications and Cultural Transformations in Early Modern Europe* (Cambridge, Cambridge University Press, 1979). Idem, *The Printing Revolution in Early Modern Europe* (Cambridge, Cambridge University Press, 1983). Eisenstein's optimistic agenda has not gone unchallenged. See particularly the debate between Eisenstein and Adrian Johns in the *American Historical Review*, 107 (2002), pp. 84–128.
5. The searches that lie behind the accumulation of this data are described at greater length in the note on sources at the end of this volume.

1: The Book Before Print

1. Marcus Tanner, *The Raven King. Matthias Corvinus and the Fate of his Lost Library* (New Haven, Yale University Press, 2008), pp. 204–6.
2. Bryan Ward-Perkins, *The Fall of Rome and the End of Civilization* (Oxford, Oxford University Press, 2005), pp. 151–63. Greg Woolf, 'Literacy or literacies in Rome?' in William A. Johnson and Holt N. Parker (eds), *Ancient Literacies. The Culture of Reading in Greece and Rome* (Oxford, Oxford University Press, 2009), pp. 46–68.
3. The evidence is summarised in Ward-Perkins, *The Fall of Rome*, pp. 154 ff.
4. L.D. Reynolds and N.G. Wilson, *Scribes and Scholars. A Guide to the Transmission of Greek and Latin Literature* (Oxford, Oxford University Press, 1968).
5. Christopher de Hamel, *A History of Illuminated Manuscripts* (2nd edn, London, Phaidon, 1994), p. 14.
6. Hilde de Ridder-Symoens, *A History of the University in Europe. Vol.1, Universities in the Middle Ages* (Cambridge, Cambridge University Press, 1992).
7. Graham Pollard, 'The pecia system in the medieval universities', in M.B. Parkes and Andrew G. Watson (eds), *Medieval Scribes, Manuscripts and Libraries. Essays Presented to N.R. Ker* (London, Scolar Press, 1978), pp. 145–61.

8. Richard H. Rouse and Mary A. Rouse, *Manuscripts and their Makers: Commercial Book Producers in Medieval Paris, 1200–1500* (London, Harvey Miller, 2000). Godfried Croenen and Peter Ainsworth, *Patrons, Authors and Workshops. Books and Book Production in Paris around 1400* (Louvain, Peeters 2006).

9. Berthold Louis Ullman, *The Humanism of Coluccio Salutati* (Padua, Antenore, 1963), pp. 129 ff.

10. London, British Library, Royal MS 19.D.11.

11. Rosemary Tzanaki, *Mandeville's Medieval Audiences. A Study of the Reception of the Book of Sir John Mandeville (1371–1550)* (Aldershot, Ashgate, 2003), pp. 4–5. Tzanaki notes the survival of around 300 manuscript copies.

12. De Hamel, *Illuminated Manuscripts*, p. 157.

13. Hanno Wijsman, 'Femmes, livres et éducation dans la dynastie Burgondo-Habsbourgeoise. Trois Marguerites à la loupe', in Jean-Marie Cauchies (ed.), *Marguerite d'York et son temps* (Neuchâtel, Centre Européen d'études Bourguignonnes, 2004), pp. 181–98.

14. Hanno Wijsman, *Handscriften voor het hertogdom. De mooiste verluchte manuscripten van Brabantse hertogen, edellieden, kloosterlingen en stedelingen* (Alphen, Uitgeverij Veerhuis, 2006).

15. Matins, lauds, prime, terce, sext, none, vespers and compline.

16. De Hamel, *Illuminated Manuscripts*, p. 168.

17. David McKitterick, *Print, Manuscript and the Search for Order, 1450–1830* (Cambridge, Cambridge University Press, 2003), pp. 48–52.

18. James Westphal Thompson (ed.), *The Frankfort Book Fair. The Francofordiense Emporium of Henri Estienne* (Chicago, Burt Franklin, 1911), p. 52.

19. William George and Emily Waters, *The Vespasiano memoirs: Lives of illustrious men of the XVth century by Vespasiano da Bisticci, Bookseller* (London, Routledge, 1926), p. 102.

20. Evidence for the size of these collections is helpfully summarised in Csaba Csapodi, *The Corvinian Library. History and Stock* (Budapest, Akadémiai Kiadó, 1973), pp. 25–9.

21. Tanner, *Raven King*, p. 141.

2: The Invention of Printing

1. For the eyewitness account see Martin Davies, 'Juan de Carvajal and early printing: the 42-line Bible and the Sweynheym and Pannartz Aquinas', *The Library*, 6th ser., 18 (1996), pp. 193–215, here 193–201.

2. The best introduction to Gutenberg by far is the monograph of Albert Kapr, *Johann Gutenberg. The Man and his Invention* (Aldershot, Scolar Press, 1996). See also Stephan Füssel, *Gutenberg and the Impact of Printing* (Aldershot, Ashgate 2005).

3. They are conveniently collected and translated in Douglas C. McMurtrie, *The Gutenberg Documents* (New York, Oxford University Press, 1941).

4. Albert C. Labriola and John W. Smeltz, *The Bible of the Poor. A Facsimile and Edition of the British Library Blockbook* (Pittsburgh, Duquesne University Press, 1990).

5. Carter Goodrich, *The Invention of Printing in China and its Spread Westward* (New York, Ronald Press, 1925).

6. Christopher de Hamel, 'Books of Hours: imaging the word', in John L. Sharpe and Kimberley van Kampen (eds), *The Bible as Book. The Manuscript Tradition* (London, British Library 1998), pp. 137–43.

7. Kapr, *Gutenberg*, pp. 180–3.

8. Aloys Ruppel, *Peter Schöffer aus Gernsheim* (Mainz, Gutenberg-Gesellschaft, 1937). Helmut Lehmann-Haupt, *Peter Schoeffer of Gernsheim and Mainz* (Rochester, NY, Leo Hart, 1950).

9. Paul Needham, 'The changing shape of the Vulgate Bible in fifteenth-century printing shops', in Kimberley van Kampen and Paul Saenger, *The Bible as Book. The First Printed Editions* (London, British Library, 1999), pp. 53–70.

10. Falk Eisermann, *Verzeichnis der typographischen Einblattdrucke des 15. Jahrhunderts im Heiligen Römischen Reich Deutscher Nation: VE 15* (Wiesbaden, Reichert, 2004) and see below, Chapter 6.

11. Arthur M. Hind, *An Introduction to a History of Woodcut* (London, Constable, 1935).

12. Richard Muther, *German Book Illustration of the Gothic Period and the Early Renaissance (1460–1530)* (Metuchen, NJ, Scarecrow Press, 1972).

13. Margaret M. Smith, *The Title-page: Its Early Development, 1460–1510* (London, British Library, 2000).

14. Hans-Jörg Künast, *Getruck zu Augspurg. Buchdruck und Buchhandel in Augsburg zwischen 1468 und 1555* (Tübingen, Niemeyer, 1997).

15. Oscar van Hase, *Die Koberger* (Wiesbaden, Breitkopf & Härtel, 1885).

16. Ibid., p. 54.

17. VE 15 A 44, W5, 10–19. Falk Eisermann, 'Auflagenhöhen von Einblattdrucken im 15. und frühen 16. Jahrhundert', in Volker Honemann et al., *Einblattdrucke des 15. und frühen 16. Jahrhunderts* (Tübingen, Niemeyer, 2000), pp. 143–77.

18. Henrick Mäkeler, *Das Rechnungsbuch des Speyerer Druckherrn Peter Drach d. M. (um 1450–1504)* (St Katharinen, Scripta Mercaturae, 2005).

19. Adrian Wilson, *The Making of the Nuremberg Chronicle* (Amsterdam, Nico Israel, 1976).

20. Ibid., p. 209.

3: Renaissance Encounters: The Crisis of Print

1. Filippo de Strata, *Polemic against Printing*, trans. Shelagh Grier with an introduction by Martin Lowry (Birmingham, Hayloft Press, 1986).

2. Jean-Marie Dureau, 'Les premiers ateliers français', in *Histoire de l'édition française* (4 vols, Paris, Promodis, 1982), I, pp. 163–75.

3. Richard Gascon, *Grand Commerce et vie urbaine au XVIe siècle. Lyon et ses marchands* (Paris, Ecole Pratique des Hautes Etudes, 1971).

4. P.M.H. Cuijpers, *Teksten als koopwaar. Vroege drukkers verkennen de markt* (Amsterdam, 1998). Anne Rouzet, *Dictionnaire des imprimeurs, libraires et éditeurs des XVe et XVIe siècles dans les limites géographiques de la Belgique actuelle* (Nieuwkoop, de Graaf, 1975).

5. George D. Painter, *William Caxton* (London, Chatto & Windus, 1976). N.F. Blake, *Caxton and his World* (London, House & Maxwell, 1969). H.S. Bennett, *English Books and Readers. I: 1475–1557* (Cambridge, Cambridge University Press, 1969), pp. 1–23.

6. Henry R. Plomer, *Wynkyn de Worde & his Contemporaries from the Death of Caxton to 1535* (London, Grafton, 1925).

7. For Italy see especially Victor Scholderer, *Fifty Essays in Fifteenth- and Sixteenth-century Bibliography* (Amsterdam, Hertzberger, 1966). There is a good introduction in Colin Clair, *A History of European Printing* (London, Academic Press, 1976), pp. 37–58.

8. For the early history of Venice printing see Martin Lowry, *Nicolas Jenson and the Rise of Venetian Publishing in Renaissance Europe* (Oxford, Blackwell, 1991). Leonardas Vytautas Gerulaitis, *Printing and Publishing in Fifteenth-century Venice* (Chicago, American Library Association, 1976) is insightful; though, as with all of these earlier works, the statistics are largely redundant.

9. Victor Scholderer, 'The petition of Sweynheym and Pannartz to Sixtus IV', *The Library*, 3rd ser., 6 (1915), pp. 186–90, reprinted in his *Fifty Essays*, pp. 72–3.

10. The figures come from ISTC. The Incunabula Short-Title Catalogue is a website hosted by the British Library. http://www.bl.uk/catalogues/istc. See also Lowry, *Nicolas Jenson*, pp. 106–9.

11. A point made eloquently by Mary A. Rouse and Richard H. Rouse, 'Backgrounds to print: aspects of the manuscript book in northern Europe of the fifteenth century', in their *Authentic Witnesses: Approaches to Medieval Texts and Manuscripts* (Notre Dame, IN, University of Notre Dame Press, 1991), pp. 449–66.

12. Melissa Conway, *The Diario of the Printing Press of San Jacopo di Ripoli, 1476–1484. Commentary and Transcription* (Florence, Olschki, 1999). Mary A. Rouse and Richard H. Rouse, *Cartolai, Illuminators, and Printers in Fifteenth-century Italy: The Evidence of the Ripoli Press* (Los Angeles, UCLA, 1988).

13. Victor Scholderer, 'Printers and readers in Italy in the fifteenth century', in his *Fifty Essays*, p. 207.

14. William A. Pettas, *The Giunti of Florence. Merchant Publishers of the Sixteenth Century* (San Francisco, B.M. Rosenthal, 1980).

15. Of the 264 editions published in Florence during these years, over 100 were editions of Savonarola's sermons.

16. Philippe Nieto, 'Géographie des impressions européennes du XVe siècle', *Revue française d'histoire du livre*, 118–21 (2004), pp. 125–73.

17. This pattern was repeated again and again. The press inaugurated in Udine in 1484 lasted only a couple of years. The next time a press worked in the town was 1592. Neil Harris, 'History of the Book in Italy', in Michael J. Suarez and Henry Woudhuysen (eds), *The Oxford Companion to the Book* (Oxford, Oxford University Press, 2010).

18. Paris and Lyon between them would be responsible for over 90 per cent of all books published in the kingdom. *FB*.

19. The six largest centres of production, Cologne, Basel, Augsburg, Nuremberg, Strasbourg and Leipzig between them accounted for 75 per cent of the books printed in Germany before 1501. ISTC.

20. Martha Tedeschi, 'Publish and perish. The career of Lienhart Holle in Ulm', in Sandra Hindman (ed.), *Printing the Written Word. The Social History of Books, circa 1450–1520* (Ithaca, NY, Cornell University Press, 1991), pp. 41–67.

21. ISTC lists nine works spread between these six places, printed between 1484 and 1485.

22. ISTC lists 75 works published between 1476 and 1493. De Colonia also printed a single work for Nicolaus Tegrimus at Nozzano (presumably a local bookseller there).

23. ISTC lists 33 editions divided between these four places of printing.

24. This section follows Lowry, *Nicolas Jenson*.

25. This data comes from an analysis of the online ISTC.

26. The collection was published 68 times in Germany, 41 in France and 13 times in the Low Countries, as against only 18 in Italy.

27. Of 450 fifteenth-century editions, all but 60 were published in the main northern centres of production, with France accounting for 281 editions.

28. The ISTC database lists 800 such fragments, probably indicative of at least as many separate printings.

29. The ISTC lists 93 editions of Petrarch, 31 editions of Dante, and 81 editions of the various works of Boccaccio.

30. Data from Howard Jones, *Printing the Classical Text* (Utrecht, de Graaf, 2004), adjusted to take into account the development of the ISTC database since publication of his work.

31. Martin Lowry, *The World of Aldus Manutius. Business and Scholarship in Renaissance Venice* (Oxford, Blackwell, 1979). David S. Zeidberg and Fiorella Gioffredi Superbi, *Aldus Manutius and Renaissance Culture* (Florence, Olschki, 1998).

32. Lowry, *World of Aldus Manutius*, p. 57.

33. Ibid., p. 217.

34. The details of the collapse can be found in ibid., pp. 128–9.

4: The Creation of a European Book Market

1. Paul Needham, 'Venetian printers and publishers in the fifteenth century', *La Bibliofilía* (1998), pp. 157–200.

2. Paul Needham has extracted from modern surveys of incunabula the highly suggestive finding that between 23 and 33 per cent of all fifteenth-century printed items in the libraries of these countries were printed in Venice. Ibid., p. 160.

3. Ibid., p. 161.

4. Alfred Hartmann and Beat R. Jenny, *Die Amerbachkorrespondenz* (10 vols, Basel, 1542–). Selections translated and edited by Barbara C. Halporn, *The Correspondence of Johann Amerbach. Early Printing in its Social Context* (Ann Arbor, University of Michigan Press, 2000).

5. Koberger to Amerbach, quoted in Curt F. Bühler, *The Fifteenth-Century Book. The Scribes, the Printers, the Decorators* (Philadelphia, University of Pennsylvania Press, 1960), p. 56.

6. Halporn, *Correspondence*, nos. 17–23, 40, 64.

7. Ibid., no. 39, and pp. 78–80.

8. Brigitte Moreau, *Inventaire chronologique des éditions parisiennes du XVIe siècle* (5 vols, Paris, F. Paillart/ Paris Musées, 1972–2004), though the data presented here is radically revised in *FB*.

9. *VD 16* A 4147.

10. Hilmar M. Pabel, *Herculean Labours. Erasmus and the Editing of St Jerome's Letters in the Renaissance* (Leiden, Brill, 2008).

11. Jean-François Gilmont, 'Printers by the rules', *The Library*, 6th ser., 2 (1980), pp. 129–55.

12. Halporn, *Correspondence*, no. 4.

13. Anne Rouzet, *Dictionnaire des imprimeurs, libraires et éditeurs des XVe et XVIe siècles dans les limites géographiques de la Belgique actuelle* (Nieuwkoop, de Graaf, 1975), pp. 239–40.

14. Examples in Moreau, *Inventaire chronologique*, though the practice here of grouping all variants under one entry can elide the relationship between printers, publishers and booksellers.

15. Halporn, *Correspondence*, no. 5.

16. Chapter 10, below.

17. Elizabeth Armstrong, *Before Copyright. The French Book-privilege System, 1498–1526* (Cambridge, Cambridge University Press, 1990).

18. Calvin to Francis Daniel, Paris, 22 April 1532: 'I will send you a hundred copies, or as many as you please'. *Letters of John Calvin selected from the Bonnet Edition* (Edinburgh, Banner of Truth, 1980), pp. 32–3.

19. *VD 16* R 1252.

20. Halporn, *Correspondence*, no. 241.

21. 'If it plese ony man spiritual or temporel to bye ony pyes of two and thre comemoracions of salisburi use empryntid after the forme of this present letter whiche ben wel and truly correct, late hym come to westmonester in to the almonesrye at the reed pale and he shal have them good chepe.' N.F. Blake, *Caxton and his World* (London, House & Maxwell, 1969), p. 193, plate 8.

22. Halporn, *Correspondence*, p. 119.

23. Ibid., nos. 43, 44.

24. Adrian Wilson, *The Making of the Nuremberg Chronicle* (Amsterdam, Nico Israel, 1976), pp. 229–37.

25. Halporn, *Correspondence*, no. 174.

26. Brian Richardson, *Printing, Writers and Readers in Renaissance Italy* (Cambridge, Cambridge University Press, 1999), p. 37.

27. On the Frankfurt Fair see especially Alexander Dietz, *Frankfurter Handelsgeschichte* (Frankfurt, Knauer 1921), III, pp. 1–178. Idem, *Zur Geschichte der Frankfurter Büchermesse, 1462–1792* (Frankfurt, Hanser, 1921). Bruno Recke, *Die Frankfurter Büchermesse* (Frankfurt, Stempel, 1951). A valuable account in English is the introduction to James Westphal Thompson (ed.), *The Frankfort Book Fair. The Francofordiense Emporium of Henri Estienne* (Chicago, Burt Franklin, 1911).

28. On the economic relationship between Frankfurt and Mainz see Stephan Füssel, *Gutenberg and the Impact of Printing* (Aldershot, Ashgate, 2003), p. 10. Albert Kapr, *Johann Gutenberg, The Man and his Invention* (Aldershot, Scolar Press, 1996).

29. The first printer settled in Frankfurt was Beatus Meurer, active for the short period 1511–12; there was no permanent press in the city before the arrival of Egenolph in 1530.

30. Friedrich Kapp, *Geschichte des deutschen Buchhandels bis in das 17. Jahrhundert* (Leipzig, Verlag des Börsenvereins, 1886), pp. 791–2.

31. Halporn, *Correspondence*, no. 43, p. 87.

32. Jean-François Gilmont, *John Calvin and the Printed Book* (Kirksville, MO, Truman State University Press, 2005), p. 221.

33. Halporn, *Correspondence*, letter 10, p. 28.

34. Graham A. Runnalls, 'La Vie, la mort et les livres de l'imprimeur-libraire parisien Jean Janot d'après son inventaire après décès (17 février 1522 [n.s.])', *Revue belge de philologie et d'histoire*, 78 (2000), pp. 797–850.

35. The data comes from the Erasmus Online database, a resource of the Erasmus Center for Early Modern Studies in Rotterdam.

36. Erasmus to Beatus Rhenanus, October 1518. Peter Bietenholz et al. (eds), *Collected Works of Erasmus* (Toronto, University of Toronto Press, 1974–), VI, *Correspondence*, no. 867, p. 155.

37. The early editions were divided between Paris, Antwerp, Venice, Strasbourg and Basel. The *Moriae Encomium* was printed a total of 42 times during Erasmus's lifetime; the first English edition was the English translation of 1549. *STC* 10500. Details of the continental editions in Erasmus Online.

38. Basel accounted for 373 of the 1,617 editions of Erasmus's works published during his lifetime, and 569 of the 2,576 editions published during the whole century. Erasmus Online.

39. Badius to Erasmus, 1512, in Bietenholz et al., *Correspondence*, no. 263.

40. The Erasmus Online database records 1,617 editions published between 1500 and 1536, so with an average print run of 1,000 copies this would imply a total output of 1.6 million copies.

41. These events are well described in Robert Coogan, *Erasmus, Lee and the Correction of the Vulgate: The Shaking of the Foundations* (Geneva, Droz, 1992).

42. Even as convinced an admirer as Peter Bietenholz notes 'the erratic vindictiveness' of Erasmus in old age. Peter G. Bietenholz, 'Printing and the Basel Reformation, 1517–65', in Jean-François Gilmont, *The Reformation and the Book* (Aldershot, Ashgate, 1996), p. 253.

43. Jean Lebeau, 'Erasme, Sebastian Franck et la tolérance', in *Erasmus, l'Alsace et son temps* (Strasbourg, Société Savante d'Alsace, 1971), pp. 117–38.

44. The ravages of time have claimed some of these treasures. Almost all the music books, for instance, are now gone, and the Protestant texts were removed in the seventeenth century. Catherine Weeks Chapman, 'Printed collections of polyphonic music owned by Ferdinand Columbus', *Journal of the American Musicological Society*, 21 (1968), pp. 34–84.

45. Henry Harrisse, *Excerpta Colombiniana; bibliographie de 400 pièces du 16e siècle; précédée d'une histoire de la Bibliothèque colombine et de son fondateur* (Paris, Welter, 1887). Klaus Wagner, 'Judicia Astrologica Colombiniana. Bibliographisches Verzeichnis einer Sammlung von Praktiken des 15. und 16. Jahrhunderts der Biblioteca Colombina Sevilla', *Archiv für Geschichte des Buchwesens*, 15 (1975), cols 1–98.

46. Klaus Wagner, 'Le Commerce du livre en France au début du XVIe siècle d'après les notes manuscrites de Fernando Colomb', *Bulletin du bibliophile*, 2 (1992), pp. 305–29.

47. Wagner, 'Commerce du livre', p. 324.

48. Ibid., p. 326.

49. *Catálogo Concordia de la Biblioteca de Hernando Colón* (2 vols, Madrid, 1993), nos. 402, 409, 412, 468 (bought London, 1522), nos. 427, 450, 458, 459, 454 (Nuremberg, 1521).

50. See in this context the inventory of stock of the Shrewsbury bookseller, Roger Ward. Alexander Rodger, 'Roger Ward's Shrewsbury stock: an inventory of 1585', *The Library*, 5th ser., 13 (1958), pp. 247–68.

51. Pierre Delsaerdt, 'A bookshop for a new age: the inventory of the bookshop of the Louvain bookseller Hieronymus Cloet, 1543', in Lotte Hellinga et al., *The Bookshop of the World. The Role of the Low Countries in the Book-Trade, 1473–1941* (Goy-Houten, de Graaf, 2001), pp. 75–86.

52. Happily they passed over texts that in more rigorous days would have caused him trouble: two French translations of the New Testament, and an evangelical text, *Le livre du vraye et parfait oraison*. The investigators might have mistaken this for an orthodox work of devotion.

5: Book Town Wittenberg

1. Venice, Rome, Florence and Milan (7,812 of 10,427 fifteenth-century editions published in Italy); Augsburg, Basel, Cologne, Leipzig, Nuremberg and Strasbourg (7,411 of 9,908 editions published in Germany); Paris, 3,174 and Lyon 1,422 of 5,270 editions published in France. ISTC.
2. 9,153 editions listed in *VD 16*, as against 7,755 for Leipzig, 7,645 for Cologne and 6,758 for Nuremberg.
3. Maria Grossmann, 'Wittenberg printing, early sixteenth century', *Sixteenth Century Essays and Studies*, 1 (1970), pp. 53–74.
4. Ibid. For detailed biographies see Christoph Reske, *Die Buchdrucker des 16. und 17. Jahrhunderts im deutschen Sprachgebiet: auf der Grundlage des gleichnamigen Werkes von Josef Benzing* (Wiesbaden, Harrassowitz, 2007).
5. Benzing no. 69.
6. *VE 15*.
7. John Flood, 'The printed book as a commercial commodity', *Gutenberg Jahrbuch*, 2001, p. 173. Paul Needham, *The Printer & the Pardoner* (Washington, Library of Congress, 1986), p. 31. Needham is describing a previously unknown indulgence certificate printed by William Caxton at Westminster, discovered in the binding of four other Caxton works now in the Library of Congress, Washington.
8. *VE 15*.
9. Benzing nos. 87 (Nuremberg), 89 (Basel). The first edition was presumably the broadsheet published by Jakob Thanner at Leipzig, Benzing no. 88.
10. Benzing, nos. 90–112.
11. *Eine Freiheit des Sermons päpstlichen Ablass und Gnade belangend*. Benzing, nos. 181–9.
12. Quoted in John Flood, 'The book in Reformation Germany', in Jean-François Gilmont (ed.), *The Reformation and the Book* (Aldershot, Ashgate, 1998), p. 36.
13. Lotter was nothing if not resilient: he resurfaced as the printer of Magdeburg during its resistance to Charles V (see Chapter 10). Reske, *Buchdrucker*, p. 580.
14. Heimo Reinitzer, *Biblia deutsch. Luthers Bibelübersetzung und ihre Tradition* (Ausstellung Herzog August Bibliothek Wolfenbüttel, 1983).
15. *Cranach im Detail. Buchschmuck Lucas Cranachs des Älteren und seiner Werkstatt* (Ausstellung Lutherhalle, Wittenberg, 1994).
16. *Gesetz und Gnade. Cranach, Luther und die Bilder* (Ausstellung, Eisenach, 1994).
17. Helmar Junghans, *Wittenberg als Lutherstadt* (Göttingen, Vandenhoeck & Ruprecht, 1979).
18. The figures come from an interrogation of *VD 16* and *Edit 16*.
19. Reinitzer, *Biblia deutsch*.
20. Hans-Joachim Köhler, *Hans-Joachim, Bibliographie der Flugschriften des 16. Jahrhunders. I: Das frühe 16. Jahrhundert (1501–1530)* (3 vols, Tübingen, 1991–96). Idem, *Flugschriften als Massenmedium der Reformationszeit* (Stuttgart, Klett-Cotta, 1981). See also the statistics presented in Mark U. Edwards, *Printing, Propaganda and Martin Luther* (Berkeley, University of California Press, 1994), p. 14.
21. The opposing points of view are laid out in Berndt Moeller, 'What was preached in German towns in the early Reformation?', in C. Scott Dixon, *The German Reformation. The Essential Readings* (Oxford, Blackwell, 1999), pp. 33–52. Susan C. Karant-Nunn, 'What was preached in German cities in the early years of the Reformation? *Wildwuchs* versus Lutheran unity', in Andrew Pettegree, *The Reformation. Critical Concepts in Historical Studies* (4 vols, London, Routledge, 2004), I, pp. 41–53.

22. Heinrich Richard Schmidt, *Reichsstädte, Reich und Reformation: korporative Religionspolitik 1521–1529/30* (Stuttgart, Steiner Verlag Wiesbaden, 1986).
23. Edwards, *Printing, Propaganda and Martin Luther*, p. 53.
24. Miriam Usher Chrisman, 'Reformation printing in Strasbourg', in Gilmont, *Reformation and the Book*, pp. 214–34. Paul A. Russell, *Lay Theology in the Reformation. Popular Pamphleteers in Southwest Germany, 1521–1525* (Cambridge, Cambridge University Press, 1986).
25. Miriam Usher Chrisman, *Lay Culture, Learned Culture. Books and Social Change in Strasbourg, 1480–1599* (New Haven, Yale University Press, 1982), p. 35. See also her *Conflicting Visions of Reform. German Lay Propaganda Pamphlets 1519–1530* (Boston, Humanities Press, 1996).
26. Benzing no. 3. *VD 16* L 3407.
27. After three further editions Froben's engagement with the printing of Luther's writings ended abruptly in 1519. Benzing nos. 239, 246, 393. *VD 16* L 3639, L 3842, L 5780.
28. *VD 16* B 5039, B 5095.
29. Reske, *Buchdrucker*, p. 183.
30. The figures come from online interrogation of *VD 16*.
31. Reske, *Buchdrucker*.
32. See for instance the oration preached by Melanchthon at Luther's funeral, *VD 16* M 3871–2 and other similar writings by Justus Jonas and Johannes Bugenhagen. *VD 16* B 9269–75, ZV 2696–7, J 899–905, ZV 8744, 8748, 8795, 20628. A number of these texts were subsequently translated into English: *An oracyon or precesce rehearced off Philipp Melanchton at the buryall of the Reverende man, Doctour Martyne Luther* (Wesel, Dereck van der Straten, 1546), *VD 16* ZV 25460.
33. Benzing lists 3,692 editions for the period of Luther's lifetime.
34. Nathan Rein, *The Chancery of God. Protestant Print, Polemic and Propaganda against the Empire, Magdeburg 1546–1551* (Aldershot, Ashgate, 2008).

6: Luther's Legacy

1. Francis Higman, *Piety and the People: Religious Printing in French, 1511–1551* (Aldershot, Ashgate, 1996), D 90–94.
2. M.A. Shaaber, *Check-list of Works of British Authors printed Abroad, in Languages other than English, to 1641* (New York, Bibliographical Society of America, 1975), F 41–103.
3. Manfred Vischer, *Bibliographie der Zürcher Druckschriften des 15. und 16. Jahrhunderts* (Baden-Baden, Koerner, 1991).
4. G.R. Potter, *Zwingli* (Cambridge, Cambridge University Press, 1976).
5. Chapter 10.
6. Adolf Fluri, *Beziehungen Berns zu den Buchdruckern in Basel, Zürich und Genf, 1476–1536* (Bern, 1913).
7. *ISTC*.
8. Wolfgang Undorf, 'The effects of a rational early modern book trade: the spread of early printed books in Scandinavia in the 15th century', *Gutenberg Jahrbuch*, 2001, pp. 168–71.
9. L. Nielsen, *Dansk bibliografi 1482–1550* (2nd edn, Copenhagen, Kongelige Bibliotek, 1996), no. 270. Other early Reformation tracts were published in Danish in Wittenberg (Nielsen 36, 172), Rostock (Nielsen 52, 81, 163, 230, 287) and Leipzig (Nielsen 207, 209, 213).
10. NK 412–14, 1436–41, 1687.
11. Anne Riising, 'The Book and the Reformation in Denmark and Norway, 1523–40', in Jean-François Gilmont, *The Reformation and the Book* (Aldershot, Ashgate, 1996), pp. 432–48.
12. L. Nielsen, *Dansk bibliografi 1551–1600* (Copenhagen, Gydendalske Boghandel, 1931–33).
13. Remi Kick, 'The book and the Reformation in the kingdom of Sweden, 1526–71', in Gilmont, *Reformation and the Book*, pp. 449–68.

14. I. Collijn, *Sveriges bibliografi intill ar 1600* (3 vols, Uppsala, 1927–38).
15. Eliska Ryznar and Murlin Croucher, *Books in Cezchoslovakia, Past and Present* (Wiesbaden, Otto Harrassowitz, 1989), pp. 1–20. Mirjam Bohatcová, 'The book and the Reformation in Bohemia and Moravia', in Gilmont, *Reformation and the Book*, pp. 385–409.
16. Mirham Bohatcová, 'Das Verhältnis der tschechischen und fremdsprachigen Drucke in Böhmen und Mähren von 15. Jahrhundert bis zum Jahre 1621', *Gutenberg Jahrbuch*, 1988, pp. 108–21. Idem, 'Der gegenwärtige Bearbeitunsstand der Druckproduction vom 15.–18. Jahrhundert in den böhmischen Ländern', *Gutenberg Jahrbuch*, 1987, pp. 265–78.
17. Alodia Kawecka-Gryczow and Janusz Tazbir, 'The book and the Reformation in Poland', in Gilmont, *Reformation and the Book*, pp. 410–31.
18. Gedeon Borsa, 'The book and the beginnings of the Reformation in Hungary', in Gilmont, *Reformation and the Book*, pp. 368–84.
19. Veturia Jugăreanu, *Bibliographie der siebenbürgischen Frühdrucke* (Baden-Baden, Koerner, 1959).
20. Erasmus's works were printed in fourteen different towns on the Iberian peninsula. Marcel Bataillon, *Erasmo y Espana* (Mexico City, Fondo de Cultura Económica, 1966). A. Gordon Kinder, 'Printing and Reformation ideas in Spain', in Gilmont, *Reformation and the Book*, pp. 292–318.
21. Clive Griffin, *The Crombergers of Seville. The History of a Printing and Merchant Dynasty* (Oxford, Oxford University Press, 1988).
22. Alastair Hamilton, *Heresy and Mysticism in Sixteenth-Century Spain: The Alumbrados* (Cambridge, James Clarke, 1992).
23. Especially from the Low Countries. Jean Peeters-Fontainas, *Bibliographie des impressions espagnoles des Pays-Bas méridionaux* (2 vols, Nieuwkoop, De Graaf, 1965).
24. Ugo Rozzo and Silvana Seidel Menchi, 'The book and the Reformation in Italy', in Gilmont, *Reformation and the Book*, pp. 319–67.
25. Ibid., p. 321.
26. Euan Cameron, 'Italy', in Andrew Pettegree (ed.), *The Early Reformation in Europe* (Cambridge, Cambridge University Press, 1992), p. 195.
27. Listed in Rozzo and Seidel Menchi, 'Book and the Reformation in Italy', pp. 346–54.
28. Ibid., pp. 337–43.
29. Emily Michelson, 'Luigi Lippomano, his vicars, and the reform of Verona from the pulpit', *Church History*, 78 (2009), pp.1–22.
30. Three editions, Venice, 1553–55. *Edit 16*.
31. Francis Higman, *Censorship and the Sorbonne* (Geneva, Droz, 1979), pp. 25–6.
32. B.T. Chambers, *Bibliography of French Bibles. Fifteenth- and Sixteenth-century French-language Editions of the Scriptures* (Geneva, Droz, 1983).
33. Robert Hari, 'Les Placards de 1534', in G. Berthoud (ed.), *Aspects de la propagande religieuse* (Geneva, Droz, 1957), pp. 79–142.
34. The definitive work on this circle is now Jonathan Reid, *King's Sister – Queen of Dissent: Marguerite of Navarre (1492–1549) and her Evangelical Network* (Leiden, Brill, 2009).
35. Higman, *Piety and the People*.
36. C.Ch.G. Visser, *Luther's geschriften in de nederlanden tot 1546* (Assen, Van Gorcum, 1969).
37. [Martin Luther], *Vanden eersten gebode* [Die thien geboden Gods] (Leiden, Seversz, 1521). NK 3463. [Martin Luther], *Nuttelijke bedenckenisse onser salicheyts* (Leiden, Seversz, n.d.). NK 263. [Martin Luther], *Van dat kersten gheloue eenlyefelike verclaringe van dat kersten gheloue* (Leiden, Seversz, n.d.). NK 2116.
38. There were some 400 printings of works of this character published between 1470 and 1540, mostly meditations on the life and passion of Jesus. Among many examples the following titles were especially popular: *Een devoet boexken van die heilige vijf wonden ons liefs Heren; Die passie ons liefs Heeren Jesu Christi; Dit zijn die XV bloetstortingen ons liefs heeren Jesu Christi.*

39. A.A. Den Hollander, *De Nederlandse Bijbelvertalingen, 1522-1545* (Nieukoop, de Graaf, 1997). See also his Biblia Sacra database, available online.

40. Jochen A. Führer, *Die kirchen- und die antireformatorische Religionspolitik Kaiser Karls V. in den siebzehn Provinzen der Niederlände 1515-1555* (Leiden, Brill, 2004). For reports of Münster in Germany see particularly Sigrun Häude, *In the Shadow of 'Savage Wolves'. Anabaptist Münster and the German Reformation during the 1530s* (Boston, Humanities Press, 2000).

41. P.M.H. Cuijpers, *Teksten als koopwaar. Vroege drukkers verkennen de markt* (Amsterdam, Amsterdam University, 1998).

42. Willem Heijting, 'Early Reformation literature from the printing shop of Mattheus Crom and Steven Mierdmans', *Nederlands Archief voor Kerkgeschiedenis*, 74 (1994), pp. 143-61.

43. Halporn, *Correspondence*, no. 43, pp. 87-9. *Catálogo Concordia de la Biblioteca de Hernando Colón* (2 vols, Madrid, 1993), nos. 402, 409, 412, 468 (bought London, 1522).

44. Lotte Hellinga, 'Importation of books printed on the continent into England and Scotland before *c.*1520', in Sandra Hindman (ed.), *Printing the Written Word. The Social History of Books, circa 1450-1520* (Ithaca, NY, Cornell University Press, 1991), pp. 205-24. Elizabeth Leedham-Green, 'University libraries and book-sellers', in Lotte Hellinga and J.B. Trapp (eds), *The Cambridge History of the Book in Britain. III: 1400-1557* (Cambridge, Cambridge University Press, 1999), pp. 316-53.

45. Henry R. Plomer, *Wynkyn de Worde & his Contemporaries from the Death of Caxton to 1535* (London, Grafton, 1925).

46. For instance at Cologne, Venice and Louvain. Shaaber, F 41-103.

47. David Daniell, *William Tyndale, a Biography* (New Haven, Yale University Press, 1994).

48. The Coverdale Bible in Cologne and the Matthew Bible in Antwerp.

49. S.L. Greenslade, *The Cambridge History of the Bible. Vol. 3, The West from the Reformation to the Present Day* (Cambridge, Cambridge University Press, 1963), p. 151.

50. William K. Sessions, *The First Printers at Ipswich in 1547-1548 and Worcester in 1549-1553* (York, privately printed, 1984).

51. Edward J. Baskerville, *A Chronological Bibliography of Propaganda and Polemic published in English between 1553 and 1558: From the Death of Edward VI to the Death of Mary I* (Philadelphia: American Philosophical Society, 1979). Andrew Pettegree, 'The Latin polemic of the Marian exiles', in his *Marian Protestantism. Six Studies* (Aldershot, Ashgate, 1996), pp. 118-28, 183-96.

7: First with the News

1. *VE 15*.

2. Stephan Füssel, *Emperor Maximilian and the Media of his Day. The Theuerdank of 1517* (Cologne, Taschen, 2003); published with a facsimile of the 1517 edition.

3. Idid., pp. 20-3. *VE 15* lists 128 broadsheets from the period before 1501. *VE 15* M 17-144.

4. Stephan Füssel, *Gutenberg and the Impact of Printing* (Aldershot, Ashgate, 2005), p. 156. See also Falk Eisermann, 'Buchdruck und politische Kommunikation. Ein neuer Fund zur frühen Publizistik Maximilians I.', *Gutenberg Jahrbuch*, 2002, pp. 77-83.

5. Wilberforce Eames, 'Columbus' letter on the discovery of America (1493-1497)', *Bulletin of the New York Public Library*, 28 (1924), pp. 595-9.

6. *VD 16* V 922-36, ZV 15198-99.

7. Francesco Trivellato, 'Merchants' letters across geographical and social boundaries', in Francisco Bethencourt and Florike Egmond (eds), *Correspondence and Cultural Exchange in Europe, 1400-1700* (Cambridge, Cambridge University Press, 2007), pp. 80-103.

8. Paul Roth, *Die neuen Zeitungen im 15. und 16. Jahrhundert* (Leipzig, Preisschr., Fürstl. jablonowskische Gesellschaft zu Leipzig, 1914).

9. Hans-Jörg Künast, *Getruck zu Augspurg. Buchdruck und Buchhandel in Augsburg zwischen 1468 und 1555* (Tübingen, Niemeyer, 1997).

10. Alastair Duke, 'Posters, pamphlets and prints. The ways and means of circulating dissident opinions on the eve of the Dutch Revolt', in his *Dissident Identities in the Early Modern Low Countries* (Aldershot, Ashgate, 2009), p. 169.

11. Jean-Pierre Seguin, 'L'Information à la fin du XVe siècle en France. Pièces d'actualité imprimées sous le règne de Charles VIII', *Arts et traditions populaires*, 4 (1956), pp. 309–30; 1–2 (1957) pp. 46–74, here nos. 4–5.

12. Ibid., nos. 7–32.

13. Ibid., p. 315.

14. Jean-Pierre Seguin, *L'Information en France de Louis XII à Henri II* (Geneva, Droz, 1961), Louis XII nos. 18–41. Michael Sherman, 'Political propaganda and Renaissance culture: French reactions to the League of Cambrai, 1509–1510', *Sixteenth Century Journal*, 8 (1977), pp. 97–128, an article based on material drawn from his unpublished dissertation: 'The selling of Louis XII: propaganda and popular culture in Renaissance France' (University of Chicago Ph.D. dissertation, 1974).

15. Jennifer Britnell, 'Antipapal writing in the reign of Louis XII: propaganda and self-promotion', in Jennifer Britnell and Richard Britnell (eds), *Vernacular Literature and Current Affairs in the Early Sixteenth Century: France, England and Scotland* (Aldershot, Ashgate, 2000), pp. 41–61.

16. Léon Voet, 'Abraham Verhoeren en de Antwerpse pers', *De Gulden Passer*, 31 (1953), pp. 1–37, here p. 17.

17. Aix-en-Provence, Bibliothèque Méjanes: Rés. S 25.

18. The colophon of the Aix copy shows that it was published on 15 March; the only other surviving copy, in the Bibliothèque Nationale in Paris, was published five days later, on 20 March. Paris BN: Rés. Lk7 10038.

19. Jean-Paul Barbier, *Bibliographie des discours politiques de Ronsard* (Geneva, Droz, 1984).

20. Füssel, *Gutenberg*, pp. 25–30.

21. *VE 15* C 14. Albert Kapr, *Johann Gutenberg. The Man and his Invention* (Aldershot, Scolar Press, 1996), pp. 189–97.

22. *VE 15* A 3–22, B 32–33, S 81–96; ISTC.

23. These works are conveniently listed in Carl Göllner, *Turcica: Die europäischen Türkendrucke des XVI. Jahrhunderts. I. Band MDI–MDL* (Berlin, Akademie-Verlag, 1961).

24. FB 7018–22.

25. Göllner, nos 246 ff.

26. Merten Sporer, *Ein new Lied von der Schlacht die von der ungerische Künig und der Türck miteinander ghetan haben. Im Speten thon* (1526). Göllner, 240. *Zway Schöne lieder das erst von dem Künig von Ungern wie er umkümen is* (1526). Göllner, nos 261–5.

27. Manuel Fernaández Alvarez, *Charles V* (London, Thames & Hudson, 1975), p. 123.

28. Göllner lists 148 items published in the two years 1565 and 1566. Göllner, nos 1060–207.

29. Albert Ganado and Maurice Agius-Vadalà, *A Study in Depth of 143 Maps representing the Great Siege of Malta of 1565* (Valletta, Bank of Valletta, 1994).

30. Göllner, nos 1527–32.

31. These events are vividly described in Iain Fenlon, *The Ceremonial City: History, Memory and Myth in Renaissance Venice* (New Haven, Yale University Press, 2007), pp. 175–91.

32. Göllner, nos. 1306–609. Dennis E. Rhodes, 'La battaglia di Lepanto e la stampa popolare a Venezia. Studio bibliografico', *Miscellanea Marciana*, 10–11 (1995–96), pp. 9–18.

33. Göllner, nos 1863–2463.

34. Tullio Bulgarelli, *Gli avvisi a stampa in Roma nel Cinquecento. Bibliografia, antologia* (Rome, Istituto di studi romani, 1967).

35. Four editions of this broadsheet were published in 1492: *VE 15* B 69–72.

36. E.L. Harrison, 'Virgil, Sebastian Brant, and Maximilian I', *Modern Language Review*, 76 (1981), pp. 99–115.

37. *VE 15* B 69–91.

38. H. Deresiewicz, 'Some sixteenth-century European earthquakes as depicted in contemporary sources', *Bulletin of the Seismological Society of America*, 72 (1982),pp. 507–23.

39. Irene Ewinkel, *De monstris: Deutung und Funktion von Wundergeburten auf Flugblättern im Deutschland des 16. Jahrhunderts* (Tübingen, Max Niemeyer, 1995); Jean Céard, *La Nature et les prodiges: L'Insolite au XVIe siècle, en France* (Geneva, Droz, 1977). For an introduction to the extensive literature on this subject see now Jennifer Spinks, 'Wondrous monsters: representing conjoined twins in early sixteenth-century German broadsheets', *Parergon*, 22 (2005), pp. 77–112. Idem, *Monstrous Births and Visual Culture in Sixteenth-century Germany* (London, Chatto & Pickering, 2009). Philip M. Soergel, 'The afterlives of monstrous infants in Reformation Germany', in Bruce Gordon and Peter Marshall (eds), *The Place of the Dead: Death and Remembrance in Late Medieval and Early Modern Europe* (Cambridge, Cambridge University Press, 2000), pp. 288–309.

40. A.W. Bates, *Emblematic Monsters: Unnatural Conceptions and Deformed Births in Early Modern Europe* (Amsterdam, Clio medica, 77, 2005).

41. H.-L. Baudrier and J. Baudrier, *Bibliographie lyonnaise. Recherches sur les imprimeurs, libraires, relieurs et fondeurs de lettres de Lyon au XVIe siècle* (12 vols, Lyon, Louis Brun, 1895–1921), III, 175–443, now much enhanced by the additional data in *FB*.

42. *FB* 5880–6012. *VD 16* B 5802–5804. Rudolf Schenda, *Die französische Prodigienliteratur in der zweiten Hälfte des 16. Jahrhunderts* (Munich, Hueber, 1961).

43. Rudolf Schenda, 'Die deutschen Prodigiensammlungen des 16. und 17. Jahrhunderts', *Archiv für Geschichte des Buchwesens*, 4 (1961–63), cols 637–710.

8: Polite Recreations

1. The volumes are part of the series printed by Jean Longis in Paris in the highly portable 16mo format. Tübingen University Library: Dk IV 32–5.

2. *FB* 651–1053, *VD 16* A 2111–46, *Edit 16* A 1380–445, *STC* 541–5, *IA* 104.214–104.520. A computation of the separate national bibliographies demonstrates that the *IA* is a very incomplete listing.

3. 1495. For the numerous sixteenth-century editions see *Edit 16* B 2731–69.

4. The various editions and their numerous reprints are listed at *Edit 16* A 2505–808.

5. For a flavour see the excellent modern edition and translation Torquato Tasso, *Jerusalem Delivered. Gerusalemme liberata*, ed. and transl. Anthony M. Esolen (Baltimore, MD, Johns Hopkins University Press, 2000).

6. Ludovico Ariosto, *Orlando Furioso*, trans. Guido Waldman (Oxford, Oxford University Press, 1974).

7. *FB* 6248–58. *IA* 121232–92.

8. *FB* 1702–34. *IA* 107316–596.

9. *FB* 6014–410. *VD 16* B 5812–47. *IA* 120152–4.

10. A point made by Neil Harris, 'History of the Book in Italy', in Michael J. Suarez and Henry Woudhuysen (eds), *The Oxford Companion to the Book* (Oxford, Oxford University Press, 2010).

11. Examples taken from Luther's works are conveniently presented in W.B. Lockwood, *An Informal History of the German Language* (Cambridge, Heffer, 1965), pp. 101–14. The Bible and Luther's other works were also still routinely published in the Low German used in north Germany and the Hanseatic ports. Heimo Reinitzer, *Biblia deutsch Luthers Bibelübersetzung und ihre Tradition* (Ausstellung Herzog August Bibliothek, Wolfenbüttel, 1983), pp. 126–7.

12. *Répertoire Bibliographique des livres imprimés en France au seizième siècle* (32 volumes, Baden-Baden, Koerner, 1968–80), IV, pp. 29–35; Malcolm Walsby, *The Printed Book in Brittany, 1480–1600* (Leiden, Brill, 2010), ch. 5.

13. I.D. McFarlane, *A Literary History of France. Renaissance France, 1470–1589* (London, Ernest Benn, 1974), pp. 135–42.

14. Francis M. Higman, *The Style of John Calvin in his French Polemical Treatises* (Oxford, Oxford University Press, 1967). Idem, *Jean Calvin. Three French Treatises* (London, Athlone, 1970).

15. *Jean Martin. Un Traducteur au temps de François Ier et de Henri II* (Paris, Presses de l'École Normale Supérieure, 1999). Dominique de Courcelles (ed.), *Traduire & adapter à la Renaissance* (Paris, l'École des Chartes, 1998).

16. Brian Richardson, *Printing, Writers and Readers in Renaissance Italy* (Cambridge, Cambridge University Press, 1999), p. 78.

17. Mary Beth Winn, *Anthoine Vérard, Parisian Publisher, 1485–1512* (Geneva, Droz, 1997).

18. Malcolm Walsby, 'La Voix de l'auteur? Autorité et identité dans les imprimés français au XVIe siècle', in A. Vanautgaerden and R. Gorris (eds), *L'Auteur à la Renaissance* (Turnhout, Brepols, 2009) pp. 65–81.

19. Richardson, *Printing, Writers and Readers*, p. 66.

20. *FB* 2578–675.

21. Richardson, *Printing, Writers and Readers*, p. 92. The Italian editions of Aretino's writings are listed at *Edit 16* A 2322–453.

22. Amedeo Quondam, 'Aretino e il libro: un repertorio, per una bibliografia', in *Pietro Aretino nel cinquecentario della nascita* (2 vols, Rome, Salerno, 1995), I, 197–230.

23. Richardson, *Printing, Writers and Readers*, pp. 93–4.

24. Ibid., pp. 73–4.

25. A useful table of the Spanish chivalric romances is provided in Henry Thomas, *Spanish and Portuguese Romances of Chivalry* (Cambridge, Cambridge University Press, 1920), pp. 147–8. Cf. Daniel Eisenberg and Maria Carmen Marín Pina, *Bibliografia de los libros de caballerías castellanos* (Zaragoza, Prensas Universitarias de Zargoza, 2000).

26. Irving A. Leonard, *Books of the Brave. Being an Account of Books and of Men in the Spanish Conquest and Settlement of the Sixteenth-Century New World* (2nd edn, Berkeley, University of California Press, 1992), p. 22.

27. Ibid., p. 26.

28. Ibid., pp. 68–9.

29. Ibid., p. 82.

30. Clive Griffin, *The Crombergers of Seville. The History of a Printing and Merchant Dynasty* (Oxford, Oxford University Press, 1988), pp. 70, 98, 152–3.

31. Irving A. Leonard, 'Romances of chivalry in the Spanish Indies. With some *registros* of shipments of books to the Spanish colonies', *University of California Publications in Modern Philology*, 16 (1933), pp. 217–372.

32. Particularly noteworthy in this connection is the sequence of popular texts published in a cheap quarto edition by the Paris bookseller Nicolas Bonfons between 1570 and 1586. These include *L'Hystoire des nobles et vaillans Cheualiers Milles & Amys* (n.d.); *La terrible et merveilleuse vie de Robert le diable* (n.d.); *Ogier le dannoys* (n.d.); *L'Histoire du noble preux & vaillant Cheualier Guillaume de Palerne. Et de la belle Melior* (n.d.); *Histoire des merveilleux faicts du preux & vaillant chevalier Artus de Bretaigne* (1584); *Histoire des hauts et chevaleureux faicts d'armes de Meliadus* (1584); *Histoire de Morgant le géant* (1584); *Histoire du noble Tristan, Prince de Leonnois, Chevalier de la Table Ronde* (1586); *L'Histoire de Melusine fille du roy d'Albanie et de madame Pressine* (n.d); *Histoire du preux et vaillant chevalier Meurvin* (n.d). There is a superb sequence of these extremely rare works in the Musée Condé, Chantilly. For the seventeenth century, *L'Histoire de Melusine, nouvellement imprimée* (Troyes, 1699). Alfred Morin, *Catalogue descriptif de la bibliothèque bleue de Troyes* (Geneva, Droz, 1974).

33. Stephen Rawles, 'The earliest editions of Nicolas de Herberay's translations of Amadis de Gaule', *The Library*, 6th ser., 3 (1981), pp. 91–108. Jean-Marc Chatelain, 'L'Illustration d'*Amadis de Gaule* dans les éditions françaises du XVIe siècle', in Nicole Cazauran and Michel Bideaux (eds), *Les Amadis en France au XVIe siècle* (Paris, Cahiers Victor Saulnier, 2000), pp. 41–52.

34. In editions by Jean Poupy and Jean Parent in Paris, Benoist Rigaud and François Didier in Lyon, and Henry Heyndricx in Antwerp.
35. Books I (1590), II (1593) and V (1598). A full sequence of the first four books was finally published only in 1618 and 1619. *STC* 541–4. For Amadis in English see the introduction by Helen Moore to *Amadis de Gaule. Translated by Anthony Munday* (Aldershot, Ashgate, 2004).
36. This theme is carefully elucidated in John J. O'Connor, *Amadis de Gaule and its Influence on Elizabethan Literature* (New Brunswick, Rutgers University Press, 1970).
37. Diana Robin, *Publishing Women. Salons, the Presses and the Counter-Reformation in Sixteenth-century Italy* (Chicago, University of Chicago Press, 2007).
38. Paul Grendler, *The Roman Inquisition and the Venetian Press, 1540–1605* (Princeton, NJ, Princeton University Press, 1977), p. 82.
39. F. Lesure, *Répertoire international des sources musicales. Recueils imprimés XVIe–XVIIe siècles. Tom. 1, Liste chronologique* (München, G. Henle, 1960).
40. Richard J. Agee, *The Gardano Music Printing Firms, 1569–1611* (Rochester, NY, University of Rochester Press, 1998).
41. Daniel Heartz, *Pierre Attaingant: Royal Printer of Music* (Berkeley, University of California Press, 1969).
42. F. Lesure and G. Thibault, *Bibliographie des éditions d'Adrian Le Roy et Robert Ballard (1551–1598)* (Paris, Société française de musicologie, 1955).
43. Laurent Guillo, *Les Éditions musicales de la renaissance lyonnaise* (Paris, Klincksieck, 1991). Henri Vanhulst, *Catalogue des éditions de musique publiées à Louvain par Pierre Phalèse et ses fils 1545–1578* (Brussels, Palais des académies, 1990).
44. Lesure, *Répertoire*, lists around 1,650 collections, each of which would have had four separate parts (each a separate book).
45. For an example of a fine collection that seems no longer to be extant see Michael G. Brennan, 'Sir Charles Somerset's music books (1622)', *Music & Letters*, 74 (1993), pp. 501–18.

9: At School

1. *Collected Works of Erasmus*, XXIV, pp. 661–91. G. H. Bantock, *Studies in the History of Educational Theory. I: Artifice and Nature, 1350–1765* (London, Allen & Unwin, 1980), pp. 53–73.
2. *Collected Works of Erasmus*, XXV, pp. 269–89.
3. Harry Carter and H.D.L. Vervliet, *Civilité Types* (Oxford, Oxford Bibliographical Society, 1966).
4. Steven Ozment, *Three Behaim Boys. Growing up in Early Modern Germany* (New Haven, Yale University Press, 1990), pp. 97, 109, 125, 131, 135–6, 137, 143.
5. H. Anders, 'The Elizabethan ABC and the catechism', *The Library*, 4th ser., 16 (1935), pp. 32–48.
6. H. de Ridder Symoens (ed.), *A History of the University in Europe. II: Universities in Early Modern Europe (1500–1800)* (Cambridge, Cambridge University Press, 1996).
7. Karin Maag, *Seminary or University? The Genevan Academy and Reformed Higher Education, 1560–1620* (Aldershot, Ashgate, 1995).
8. Paul F. Grendler, *Schooling in Renaissance Italy. Literacy and Learning, 1300–1660* (Baltimore, MD, Johns Hopkins University Press, 1989).
9. Anthony Grafton, and Lisa Jardine, *From Humanism to the Humanities. Education and the Liberal Arts in Fifteenth- and Sixteenth-century Europe* (London, Duckworth, 1986), pp. 140–1. For further evidence of English ownership of Erasmus see Elizabeth Leedham-Green, 'University libraries and book-sellers' in Lotte Hellinga and J.B. Trapp (eds), *The Cambridge History of the book in Britain, III: 1400–1557* (Cambridge, Cambridge University Press, 1999), pp. 343–4.

10. The annual salary was usually around 60 ducats per annum. Grendler, *Schooling in Renaissance Italy*, p. 17.
11. Ibid., pp. 43–5.
12. Ibid., pp. 212 ff.
13. USTC, incorporating data from other online resources: *Edit 16, VD 16, FB*. For the fifteenth century, ISTC and Howard Jones, *Printing the Classical Text* (Utrecht, de Graaf, 2004).
14. George Huppert, *Public Schools in Renaissance France* (Urbana, University of Illinois Press, 1984), p. 5.
15. *FB* 18322–435.
16. Huppert, *Public Schools*, pp. 53–4.
17. Ibid., p. 52.
18. Malcolm Seaborne, *The English School: Its Architecture and Organization, 1370–1870* (Toronto, University of Toronto Press, 1971).
19. Jonathan Arnold, *Humanism and Reform in Early Tudor England* (London, I.B. Tauris, 2007).
20. Seaborne, *The English School*, p. 19.
21. Gwendolen Woodward and R. A. Christophers, *The Chained Library of the Royal Grammar School, Guildford, Catalogue* (Guildford, Royal Grammar School, 1972).
22. Claire Cross, *The Free Grammar School of Leicester* (Leicester Department of English Local History Occasional Papers, 4, 1953), pp. 26–7.
23. J. Basil Oldham, *A History of Shrewsbury School, 1552–1952* (Oxford, Blackwell, 1952).
24. Grendler, *Schooling in Renaissance Italy*, p. 309.
25. Andrew W. Tuer, *History of the Horn Book* (New York, Benjamin Blom, 1897).
26. Grendler, *Schooling in Renaissance Italy*, pp. 142 ff.
27. New York, Morgan Library: E.2/45/A/XVIe.
28. Ian Green, *The Christian's ABC. Catechisms and Catechizing in England, c.1530–1740* (Oxford, Oxford University Press, 1996).
29. Gerard van Thienen and John Goldfinch, *Incunabula Printed in the Low Countries: A Census* (Nieuwkoop, de Graaf, 1999).
30. Grendler, *Schooling in Renaissance Italy*, pp. 188–91, 413–16.
31. *FB* 23968–4173 for Guevara in French. *STC* 12425–451. *VD 16* G 4008–25.
32. In Venice marginally more boys (53 per cent) followed the vernacular in 1587 than the Latin curriculum.
33. Huppert, *Public Schools*, p. 53.
34. Cross, *Free Grammar School of Leicester*, pp. 26–7.
35. Huppert, *Public Schools*, pp. 132–3.
36. Grendler, *Schooling in Renaissance Italy*, p. 337.
37. Ibid., p. 44.
38. Susan Broomhall, *Women and the Book Trade in Sixteenth-century France* (Aldershot, Ashgate, 2002).
39. Lowell Green, 'The education of women in the Reformation', *History of Education Quarterly*, 19 (1979), pp. 93–116.
40. *VD 16* A 989–98.
41. *VD 16* M 7171.
42. Christopher Boyd Brown, *Singing the Gospel: Lutheran Hymns and the Success of the Reformation* (Cambridge, MA, Harvard University Press, 2005).
43. Green, 'Education of women'.
44. David Cressy, *Literacy and the Social Order: Reading and Writing in Tudor and Stuart England* (Cambridge, Cambridge University Press, 1980). R.A. Houston, *Literacy in Early Modern Europe: Culture and Education, 1500–1800* (London, Longman, 1988).
45. Grendler, *Schooling in Renaissance Italy*, p. 86.

46. Evidence summarised in Geoffrey Parker, *The Dutch Revolt* (London, Allen Lane, 1977), p. 21.
47. Hanno Wijsman, 'Historiography and history in transition. Production, reception and contextualisation of the Chroniques of Enguerrand de Monstrelet in manuscript and print', in Graeme Kemp and Malcolm Walsby (eds), *The Book in Transition. The Printed Book in the Post-Incunabula Age, 1500–1640* (Leiden, Brill, 2011).
48. Bruce Gordon, 'The changing face of Protestant history and identity in the sixteenth century', in his *Protestant History and Identity in Sixteenth-Century Europe* (2 vols, Aldershot, Ashgate, 1996), pp. 1–22. Alexandra Kess, *Johann Sleidan and the Protestant Vision of History* (Aldershot, Ashgate, 2008).
49. *FB* 8064–121.
50. Véronique Benhaïm, 'Les Thresors d'Amadis', in Nicole Cazauran and Michel Bideaux (eds), *Les Amadis en France au XVIe siècle* (Paris, Cahiers Victor Saulnier, 2000), pp. 157–81. The *Treasures* was published in English a full twenty years before the text of the romance. *STC* 545.
51. For a sampling of the numerous editions *IA* 100926–101321.

10: The Literature of Conflict

1. James Atkinson, *The Trial of Luther* (London, Batsford, 1971), p. 95.
2. At Louvain and Liège in the Low Countries, Ingolstadt and Mainz in Germany, and of course in Rome itself. Ibid., pp. 83, 92.
3. Richard Friedenthal, *Luther* (London, Weidenfeld & Nicolson, 1967), p. 251.
4. J.M. de Bujanda, Francis M. Higman and James K. Farge, *Index de l'Université de Paris: 1544, 1545, 1547, 1549, 1551, 1556* (Sherbrooke, Centre d'études de la Renaissance, 1985). J.M. de Bujanda, *Index de l'Université de Louvain: 1546, 1550, 1558* (Sherbrooke, Centre d'études de la Renaissance, 1986).
5. J.M. de Bujanda, *Index de Venise, 1549, de Venise et Milan, 1554* (Sherbrooke, Centre d'études de la Renaissance, 1987); *Index de l'Inquisition espagnole: 1551, 1554, 1559* (Sherbrooke, Centre d'études de la Renaissance, 1984). J.M. de Bujanda, *Index de Rome: 1557, 1559, 1564: les premiers index romains et l'index du Concile de Trente* (Sherbrooke, Centre d'études de la Renaissance, 1990).
6. E. Baskerville, *A Chronological Bibliography of Propaganda and Polemic Published in English between 1553 and 1558* (Philadelphia, American Philosophical Society, 1979). Andrew Pettegree, *Emden and the Dutch Revolt. Exile and the Development of Reformed Protestantism* (Oxford, Clarendon Press, 1992).
7. The standard bibliography is now Jean-François Gilmont and Rodolphe Peter, *Bibliotheca Calviniana. Les oeuvres de Jean Calvin publiées au XVIe siècle* (3 vols, Geneva, Droz, 1991–2000).
8. The scribes were supplied by the Bourse Française, the body that provided poor relief for the immigrant French. Jeannine E. Olson, *Calvin and Social Welfare. Deacons and the Bourse française* (Selinsgrove, PA, Susquehanna University Press, 1989), p. 34.
9. See the table presented as an appendix to Jean-François Gilmont, *John Calvin and the Printed Book* (Kirksville, MO, Truman State University Press, 2005), pp. 293–5.
10. Cited in Alastair Duke, Gillian Lewis and Andrew Pettegree (eds), *Calvinism in Europe. A Collection of Documents* (Manchester, Manchester University Press, 1992), pp. 60–6, along with extracts from the Edict of Châteaubriant.
11. Olson, *Calvin and Social Welfare*. H-L. Schlaepfer, 'Laurent de Normandie', in G. Berthoud (ed.), *Aspects de la propagande religieuse* (Geneva, Droz, 1957), pp. 176–230.
12. Eugénie Droz, 'Antoine Vincent. La propagande protestante par le psautier', in Berthoud (ed.), *Aspects de la propagande religieuse*, pp. 276–93.
13. See on these presses Andrew Pettegree, *The French Book and the European Book World* (Leiden, Brill, 2007), chs 3 & 4.

14. *Cantique de victoire pour l'eglise de Lyon. A Lyon, Le jour de la victoire, dernier du mois d'Avril. 1562* [Lyon, Jean Saugrain, 1562]. *FB* 35606. Aix-en-Provence, Bibliothèque Méjanes: Rec D 9 (1358).

15. Mark U. Edwards, *Printing, Propaganda and Martin Luther* (Berkeley, University of California Press, 1994), pp. 14–36.

16. Francis Higman, *Piety and the People. Religious Printing in French, 1511–1551* (Aldershot, Ashgate, 1996).

17. Luc Racaut, *Hatred in Print, Catholic Propaganda and Protestant Identity during the French Wars of Religion* (Aldershot, Ashgate, 2002).

18. Antoine du Val, *Mirouer des Calvinistes*, fol. 28v. Quoted Racaut, *Hatred in Print*, p. 87.

19. Norman Davies, *A History of Europe* (Oxford, Oxford University Press, 1996), pp. 500–1.

20. Marcus van Vaernewijck, *Van die beroerlicke tijden*, quoted in Duke et al., *Calvinism in Europe*, pp. 145–7.

21. *Catechismus, ofte onderwijsinghe in de christelicke leere, gelijck in die kercken ende scholen der Cheur vorstelicken Paltz ghedreven oft gheleert wordt* (Delft, Harman Schinckel, 1566). W. Heijting, *De catechismi en confessies in de nederlandse reformatie tot 1585* (Nieuwkoop, de Graaf, 1989), B.12.4, illustrated II, p. 184. The reference is to Matthew 13.44: 'The Kingdom of God is like a treasure hidden in the field.'

22. J.M. De Bujanda, *Index d'Anvers 1569, 1570, 1571* (Sherbrooke, Centre d'études de la Renaissance, 1988).

23. Leon Voet, *The Golden Compasses: A History and Evaluation of the Printing and Publishing Activities of the Officina Plantiniana at Antwerp* (Amsterdam, Van Gendt, 1969–72). Colin Clair, *Christopher Plantin* (London, Cassell, 1960).

24. Clair, *Plantin*, pp. 23–8.

25. Colin Clair, 'Christopher Plantin's trade connections with England and Scotland', *The Library*, 5th ser., 14 (1959), pp. 28–45

26. Clair, *Plantin*, pp. 130–3.

27. *TB* II 499–501, 514–24.

28. See the statistic tables provided by John Barnard and Maureen Bell for John Barnard and D.F. McKenzie (eds), *The Cambridge History of the Book in Britain. Volume IV: 1557–1695* (Cambridge, Cambridge University Press, 2002), here pp. 781–2.

29. Peter Milward, *Religious Controversies of the Elizabethan Age. A Survey of Printed Sources* (London, Scolar Press, 1978), no. 5.

30. Bartholomew Clerke, *Fidelis servi, subdito infideli responsio* (London, John Daye, 1573). *STC* 5407. George Ackworth, *De visibili Romanarchia contra Nich. Sanderi libri duo* (London, John Daye, 1573). *STC* 99.

31. Patrick Collinson, *The Elizabethan Puritan Movement* (London, Jonathan Cape, 1967), pp. 71–83.

32. In this case the dissidents turned to an old friend of English Protestantism since the time of the Marian exile, Gellius Ctematius in Emden. Pettegree, *Emden and the Dutch Revolt*, nos. 175–81.

33. *STC* 4711–13, 10392, 10847, 10848, 10850.

34. *STC* 3802, 13377, 17278.4, 17278.5, 19394.

35. Summarised in Milward, *Religious Controversies*, pp. 86–93.

36. *TB* II 544–8.

37. *STC* 18548.5–564.5.

38. Ian Green, *Print and Protestantism in early Modern England* (Oxford, Oxford University Press, 2000).

39. Ian Green, *The Christian's ABC. Catechisms and Catechizing in England, c.1530–1740* (Oxford, Oxford University Press, 1996).

40. James Raven, *The Business of Books. Booksellers and the English Book Trade* (New Haven, Yale University Press, 2007), p. 47.

41. Beautifully described in Heiko Oberman, *Luther. Man between God and the Devil* (New Haven, Yale University Press, 1989), pp. 3–12.

42. Over the five years 1546–51 Magdeburg's presses turned out over 400 works, almost exclusively short pamphlets in support of the Protestant cause. Nathan Rein, *The Chancery of God. Protestant Print, Polemic and Propaganda against the Empire, Magdeburg 1546–1551* (Aldershot, Ashgate, 2008). For the contribution of Flaccius see *VD 16* F 1244–1574.

43. Mary Jane Haemig and Robert Kolb, 'Preaching in Lutheran pulpits in the age of confessionalization', in Robert Kolb (ed.), *Lutheran Ecclesiastical Culture 1550–1675* (Leiden, Brill, 2008), p. 125.

44. Christopher Boyd Brown, *Singing the Gospel: Lutheran Hymns and the Success of the Reformation* (Cambridge, MA, Harvard University Press, 2005). Rebecca Wagner Oettinger, *Music as Propaganda in the German Reformation* (Aldershot, Ashgate, 2001).

45. Christopher Boyd Brown, 'Devotional life in hymns, liturgy, music and prayer', in Kolb, *Lutheran Ecclesiastical Culture*, p. 225.

46. Brown, 'Devotional life', p. 234.

47. Ibid., p. 236.

48. Robert Scribner, 'Incombustible Luther: the image of the Reformer in early modern Germany', in his *Popular Culture and Popular Movements in Reformation Germany* (London, Hambledon Press, 1987), pp. 323–53.

49. Illustrated ibid., pp. 342, 344.

50. Paul F. Grendler, *The Roman Inquisition and the Venetian Press* (Princeton, NJ, Princeton University Press, 1977), p. 133.

11: The Search for Order

1. Among them Pierre de Ronsard, Jean-Antoine de Baïf, Claude Doron, Pontus de Tyard, Guy du Faur (Pibrac), Philippe Desportes and Jacques Davy du Perron. Mark Greengrass, *Governing Passions. Peace and Reform in the French Kingdom, 1576–1585* (Oxford, Oxford University Press, 2007).

2. *Discours des Triomphes et Resiouissances faicts par la Serenissime Seigneurie de Venise, à l'entrée heureuse de Henry de Valois, troisiesme de ce nom, Treschrestien Roy de France & de Pologne* [Lyon, Michel Jove, 1574]; *La Somptueuse et Magnifique entrée du Tres-Chrestien Roy Henry III en la cité de Mantoüe* [Paris, Nicolas Chesneau, 1576]. *FB* 3417, 11276, 50519, 50520, 20823.

3. *FB* 44042–282. Amyot's translation was also the basis for the famous English version of North.

4. *FB* 30497–501.

5. Greengrass, *Governing Passions*, pp. 199–200.

6. 'Belles paroles enrichies d'exemples et sentences tirees de Platon, Aristote et de Plutarque.' Ibid., p. 150.

7. *FB* 51623–5, 51629.

8. *FB* 13150 and many subsequent editions.

9. Arnaud Sorbin, *Le Vray Reveille-matin pour la deffense de la majesté de Charles IX* (n.p., 1574). Sydney Anglo, *Machiavelli, the First Century. Studies in Enthusiasm, Hostility and Irrelevance* (Oxford, Clarendon Press, 2005), p. 268.

10. Robert von Friedeburg, *Self-Defence and Religious Strife in Early Modern Europe. England and Germany, 1530–1680* (Aldershot, Ashgate, 2002).

11. Nathan Rein, *The Chancery of God. Protestant Print, Polemic and Propaganda against the Empire, Magdeburg 1564–1551* (Aldershot, Ashgate, 2008), p. 23.

12. *VD 16* K 432–49.

13. W.S. Hudson, *John Ponet (1516–1556) Advocate of Limited Monarchy* (Chicago, University of Chicago Press, 1942).

14. Robert M. Kingdon, *Myths About the St Bartholomew's Day Massacres, 1572–1576* (Cambridge, MA, Harvard University Press, 1988); Ralph Giesey, 'The Monarchomach

triumvirs: Hotman, Beza and Mornay', *Bibliothèque d'Humanisme et Renaissance*, 32 (1970), pp. 41–56. Quentin Skinner, *The Foundations of Modern Political Thought* (Cambridge, Cambridge University Press, 1978).

15. D.R. Kelley, *François Hotman: A Revolutionary's Ordeal* (Princeton, NJ, Princeton University Press, 1973).

16. George Garnett (ed.), *Vindiciae contra Tyrannos* (Cambridge, Cambridge University Press, 1994).

17. *The Rights of Magistrates* went through at least seven editions in the first decade: *FB* 4154–7, 4160, 4162, 4166.

18. Anglo, *Machiavelli*, pp. 183–225.

19. Sergio Bertelli and Piero Innocenti, *Bibliografia Machiavelliana* (Verona, 1979).

20. *FB* 35750–784.

21. Nicole Cazauran (ed.), *Discours merveilleux: de la vie, actions et deportements de Catherine de Médici, Royne-mère* (Geneva, Droz, 1995).

22. Anglo, *Machiavelli*, p. 306.

23. Raymond A. Mentzer, *Family Survival and Confessional Identity among the Provincial Huguenot Nobility* (West Lafayette, IN, Purdue University Press, 1994).

24. Martin van Gelderen, *The Political Thought of the Dutch Revolt, 1555–1590* (Cambridge, Cambridge University Press, 1992).

25. For a flavour see Julian H. Franklin, 'Sovereignty and the mixed constitution: Bodin and his critics', in J.H. Burns (ed.), *The Cambridge History of Political Thought, 1450–1700* (Cambridge, Cambridge University Press, 1991), pp. 299–328.

26. *FB* 6146–51, 6153–8, 6161–2, 6171–3, 6177–8.

27. Rodolph Crahay, *Bibliographie critique des éditions anciennes de Jean Bodin* (Brussels, Académie Royale de Belgique, 1992). Julian H. Franklin (ed.), *Jean Bodin* (Aldershot, Ashgate, 2006).

28. Lauren Kim, 'French royal acts printed before 1601: a bibliographical study' (University of St Andrews Ph.D. dissertation, 2007).

29. The financial ordinance of Saint-Germain was printed seven times immediately after promulgation in 1561 and a further eleven times over the next six years. Fiscal measures in 1574, 1594 and 1595 were published between ten and thirteen times.

30. The details of the Loire tolls were mostly the work of Eloi Gibier of Orleans who published around 250 editions of these small handbooks. *FB* 41753–999.

31. The position was held successively by Robert Estienne, Féderic Morel and his son, also Féderic.

32. A rare example of a (broadsheet) provincial reprint of this sort is illustrated in Andrew Pettegree, *The French Book and the European Book World* (Leiden, Brill, 2007), p. 273.

33. *FB* 27871–86, 28271–82. Kim, 'French royal acts'.

34. Voet 121–563. Plantin's file copy can still be seen, carefully archived in the Museum Plantin-Moretus in Antwerp.

35. Voet 186.

36. Voet 186, 190, 204.

37. Voet 426, 429.

38. Voet 456, 496, 517, 520.

39. Voet 269.

40. Voet 268, 287, 316, 478.

41. Described in *Répertoire bibliographique des livres imprimés en France du seizième siècle* (32 volumes, Baden-Baden, Koerner, 1968–1980), XII, pp. 51 ff.

42. We are not helped by the decision of the German national bibliography, the *VD 16*, specifically to exclude single-sheet items.

43. Manfred Vischer, *Zürcher Einblattdrucke des 16. Jahrhunderts* (Baden-Baden, Koerner, 2001).

44. *Répertoire bibliographique*, XIII, p. 28.

45. As an introduction to the copious literature on this subject, Alison Adams and Anthony J. Harper (eds), *The Emblem in Renaissance and Baroque Europe* (Leiden, Brill, 1992).
46. Visser, Arnoud, 'Escaping the Reformation in the republic of letters: confessional silence in Latin emblem books', *Church History and Religious Culture*, 88 (2008), pp. 139–67, here p. 150.
47. *IA* 102865–3051, now greatly augmented.
48. Alison Adams, Stephen Rawles and Alison Saunders, *A Bibliography of French Emblem Books* (2 vols, Geneva, Droz, 1999–2002). Alison Saunders, *The Sixteenth-century French Emblem Book. A Decorative and Useful Genre* (Geneva, Droz, 1988).
49. Voet 1476–87 (Junius), 2168–74 (Sambucus).
50. Wolfgang Klose (ed.), *Stammbücher des 16. Jahrhunderts* (Wiesbaden, Otto Harrassowitz, 1989).
51. Wolfgang Klose, *Corpus alborum amicorum. Beschreibendes Verzeichnis der Stammbücher des 16. Jahrhunderts* (Stuttgart, Hiersemann, 1988), p. 364.

12: Market Forces

1. GLN 15–16 records 4,491 editions published in Geneva, Lausanne and Neuchâtel in the fifteenth and sixteenth centuries. ISTC and *VD 16* respectively give 847 and 6,577 editions for Basel.
2. An analysis of the data newly gathered for *NB*.
3. *FB*, replacing the incomplete data of the *Répertoire bibliographique des livres imprimés en France au seizième siècle* (32 volumes, Baden-Baden, Koerner, 1968–1980). Some summary totals for vernacular production are presented in Andrew Pettegree, *The French Book and the European Book World* (Leiden, Brill, 2007), p. 264.
4. The splendid quality of this work is now beautifully evoked by Hendrik D.L. Vervliet, *The Palaeotypography of the French Renaissance. Selected Papers on Sixteenth-Century Typefaces* (Leiden, Brill, 2008).
5. Denis Pallier, *Recherches sur l'imprimerie à Paris pendant la Ligue (1585–1594)* (Geneva, Droz, 1976), enhanced by *FB*.
6. Graham A. Runnalls, 'La Vie, la mort et les livres de l'imprimeur-libraire parisien Jean Janot d'après son inventaire après décès (17 février 1522 [n.s.])', *Revue belge de philologie et d'histoire*, 78 (2000), pp. 797–850.
7. This was true also of the secular *Farces*, published as short epitome, around which the players would presumably extemporise a longer performance. Three collections of these farces are known: one now in the British Library, one in the Bibliothèque Nationale in Paris, one (the *Recueil* Cohen) in private hands. Together they comprise around 150 editions; the fact that there is no overlap between the three suggests the probable size of the original trade. Gustave Cohen, *Recueil de farces françaises inédites du XVIe siècle* (Cambridge, MA, Medieval Academy of America, 1949).
8. Georges Wildenstein, 'L'Imprimeur-libraire Richard Breton et son inventaire après décès', *Bibliothèque d'Humanisme et Renaissance*, 21 (1959), pp. 364–79. See also Barbara Diefendorf, *Beneath the Cross: Catholics and Huguenots in Sixteenth-Century Paris* (New York, Oxford University Press, 1991), pp. 132–7.
9. Francis Higman, Yann Morvant and Marc Vial, 'A bookseller's world: the inventaire of Vincent Réal', in Andrew Pettegree, Paul Nelles and Philip Conner (eds), *The Sixteenth-Century French Religious Book* (Aldershot, Ashgate, 2001), pp. 303–18.
10. William A. Pettas, *The Giunti of Florence. Merchant Publishers of the Sixteenth Century* (San Francisco, B.M. Rosenthal, 1980).
11. Paul F. Grendler, *The Roman Inquisition and the Venetian Press* (Princeton, NJ, Princeton University Press, 1977), p. 16.
12. An analysis based on the data presented in Gustav Schwetschte (ed.), *Codex Nundinarius: Germaniae literatae bisecularis. Mess-Jahrbücher des deutschen Buchhandels von dem*

Erscheinen des ersten Mess-Kataloges in Jahre 1564 bis zu der Gründung des Buchhändlervereins im Jahre 1765 (Nieuwkoop, de Graaf, 1963).

13. Grendler, *Roman Inquisition*, p. 186.

14. Data from an analysis of *VD 16*.

15. Christoph Reske, *Die Buchdrucker des 16. und 17. Jahrhunderts im deutschen Sprachgebiet* is organised topographically; data on output is available through the *VD 16* place of publication index.

16. James Westphal Thompson, *The Frankfort Book Fair: The Francofordiense Emporium of Henri Estienne* (Chicago, Burt Franklin, 1911), pp. 34–8.

17. For a survey of the output of vernacular recreational literature in Germany see also Walter Röll, 'Zur Verbreitung deutscher Erzähltexte in den hundert Jahren nach der Erfindung des Buchdrucks', *Gutenberg Jahrbuch*, 1987, pp. 158–65.

18. Grendler, *Roman Inquisition*, p. 16.

19. John Barnard and Maureen Bell, Statistic tables', in John Barnard and D.F. McKenzie (eds), *The Cambridge History of the Book in Britain, Volume IV: 1557–1695* (Cambridge, Cambridge University Press, 2002), pp. 779–82.

20. Cyprian Blagden, *The Stationers' Company: A History, 1403–1959* (London, Allen & Unwin, 1960).

21. A sense of how impressive can be obtained by browsing E.S. Leedham-Green, *Books in Cambridge Inventories: Book Lists from Vice-Chancellor's Court Probate Inventories in the Tudor and Stuart Periods* (2 vols, Cambridge, Cambridge University Press, 1986) and R.J. Fehrenbach and E.S. Leedham-Green, *Private Libraries in Renaissance England: A Collection and Catalogue of Tudor and Early Stuart Book-Lists* (6 vols, Binghamton, NY, Medieval & Renaissance Texts & Studies, 1992–), the equivalent resource for Oxford.

22. Alexander Rodger, 'Roger Ward's Shrewsbury stock: an inventory of 1585', *The Library*, 5th ser., 13 (1958), pp. 247–68.

23. Ward stocked works by Viret, de Bèze, Gualter and Ochino, as well as at least a dozen separate works by Calvin.

24. *IB*.

25. Grendler, *Roman Inquisition*, p. 16.

26. Henri Lapeyre, *Une Famille de marchands: les Ruiz. Contribution à l'étude du commerce entre la France et l'Espagne au temps de Philippe II* (Paris, A. Colin, 1955). Christian Péligry, 'Les Éditeurs Lyonnais et le marché espagnol aux XVIe et XVIIe siècles', in *Livre et lecture en Espagne et en France sous l'ancien régime* (Paris, editions A.D.P.F, 1981), pp. 85–95.

27. Clive Griffin, *Journeymen-Printers, Heresy and the Inquisition in Sixteenth-Century Spain* (Oxford, Oxford University Press, 2005).

28. Ian Maclean, 'Murder, debt and retribution in the Italico-Franco-Spanish book trade: the Beraud–Michel–Ruiz affair, 1586–91', in his *Learning and the European Marketplace: Essays in Early Modern Book History* (Leiden, Brill, 2009).

29. Lapeyre, *Les Ruiz*, p. 570.

30. Malcolm Walsby, *The Printed Book in Brittany, 1480–1600* (Leiden, Brill, 2010).

31. Jean Peeters-Fontainas, *Bibliographie des impressions espagnoles des Pays-Bas méridionaux* (2 vols, Nieuwkoop, de Graaf, 1965).

32. Colin Clair, *Christopher Plantin* (London, Cassell, 1960), pp. 87–104.

33. L. Nielsen, *Dansk bibliografi 1551–1600* (Copenhagen, Gydendalske Boghandel, 1931–33), enhanced by the searches of the St Andrews USTC project.

34. *STC* gives a total of 13 items for the press, 11 in the single year 1508.

35. Alastair J. Mann, *The Scottish Book Trade, 1500–1720. Print Commerce and Print Control in Early Modern Scotland* (East Linton, Tuckwell, 2000).

36. H.G. Aldis, *A List of Books printed in Scotland before 1700* (Edinburgh, National Library of Scotland, 1970). The vast majority were printed in Edinburgh, with a handful in Stirling and St Andrews. These were mostly the responsibility of small branch offices set up by the Edinburgh printer Robert Lekpreuik.

37. Jonquil Bevan, 'Scotland', in *Cambridge History of the Book in Britain*, IV pp. 687–700. See esp. p. 698: 'Bookselling, rather than book production, was the motive force in the expansion of the trade in Scotland'.

38. Alexsandor Stipcevic, 'Aspectes de la production du livre croate au XVe siècle', in Henrik Heger and Janine Matillon (eds), *Les Croates et la civilisation du livre* (Paris, Presses de l'Université de Paris-Sorbonne, 1986), pp. 27–33.

39. Veturia Jugăreanu, *Bibliographie der siebenbürgischen Frühdrucke* (Baden-Baden, Koerner, 1959).

40. Marvin J. Heller, *The Sixteenth-century Hebrew Book. An Abridged Thesaurus* (2 vols, Leiden, Brill, 2004), I, pp. xliii–xlix.

41. Ibid., pp. 252–3.

42. Clive Griffin, *The Crombergers of Seville. The History of a Printing and Merchant Dynasty* (Oxford, Oxford University Press, 1988), pp. 82–97.

43. Jaime Lara, *Christian Texts for Aztecs. Art and Liturgy in Colonial Mexico* (Notre Dame, IN, University of Notre Dame Press, 2008).

44. Joaquín Garcia Icazbalceta, *Bibliografia Mexicana del signo XVI* (2nd edn, Mexico City, Fondo de Cultura Economica, 1954) lists 179 items fully described, a further 85 not known from surviving copies and 48 from fragments. Carlos E. Castañeda, 'The beginning of printing in America', *Hispanic American Historical Review*, 20 (1940), pp. 671–85.

45. Hugh Amory and David D. Hall, *A History of the Book in America. I; The Colonial Book in the Atlantic World* (Cambridge, Cambridge University Press, 2000). Isaiah Thomas, *The History of Printing in America* (New York, Weathervane Books, 1970).

13: Science and Exploration

1. Owen Gingerich, *The Book Nobody Read. In Pursuit of the Revolutions of Nicolaus Copernicus* (London, Heinemann, 2004).

2. For a useful introduction to scientific publishing, and to the classification of subject material, see Margaret Bingham Stillwell, *The Awakening Interest in Science during the First Century of Printing, 1450–1550* (New York, Bibliographical Society of America, 1970).

3. Between 1511 and 1536 Basel printers published 373 editions of the works of Erasmus, almost a quarter of all the editions published during his lifetime. Erasmus Online.

4. Martin Steinmann, *Johannes Oporinus. Ein Basler Buchdrucker um die Mitte des 16. Jahrhunderts* (Basel, Helbing & Lichtenhahn, 1967).

5. Anna Pavord, *The Naming of Names. The Search for Order in the World of Plants* (London, Bloomsbury, 2005) pp. 150–5.

6. Sara J. Schechner, *Comets, Popular Culture and the Birth of Modern Cosmology* (Princeton, NJ, Princeton University Press, 1997), p. 46.

7. Paolo Zambelli (ed.), *Astrologi hallucinati. Stars and the End of the World in Luther's Time* (Berlin, de Gruyter, 1986).

8. Owen Gingerich, *An Annotated Census of Copernicus' De revolutionibus (Nuremberg, 1543 and Basel, 1566)* (Leiden, Brill, 2002). Gingerich offers an entertaining and insightful account of this research in *The Book Nobody Read*.

9. Gingerich compiled a list of thirty-two astronomers who might plausibly have been expected to own a copy of Copernicus; surviving autograph copies prove that at least half did so. Gingerich, *Book Nobody Read*, p. 128.

10. Ibid., pp. 82, 94–6.

11. Rosemary Tzanaki, *Mandeville's Medieval Audiences. A Study of the Reception of the Book of Sir John Mandeville (1371–1550)* (Aldershot, Ashgate, 2003). For sixteenth-century editions see Shaaber, M 90–158. *VD 16* J 625–7. *FB* 36062–82. *STC* 17246–54.

12. *VD 16* V 923–30.

13. *FB* 50670–765.

14. The following paragraphs follow Frank Lestringant, *Mapping the Renaissance World: The Geographical Imagination in the Age of Discovery* (Berkeley, University of California Press, 1994).

15. André Thevet, *Cosmographie de Levant* (Lyon, Jean de Tournes and Guillaume Gazeau, 1554). There was also an Antwerp edition of 1555. *FB* 49225-7.

16. Thevet would probably have had access to the definitive edition published on the Froben press at Basel in 1542. *VD 16* R 2615.

17. André Thevet, *Les Singularitez de la France antarctique* (Paris, heirs of Maurice de La Porte, 1557). Again there was a very rapid Antwerp reprint. *FB* 49228-30.

18. Lestringant, *Mapping the Renaissance World*, pp. 62–3. Héret is known principally for his translations of Alexander of Aphrodisias and Dares Phrygius.

19. Polydore Vergil, *De inventoribus rerum*.

20. Leonard, *Books of the Brave*, pp. 36–64.

21. André Thevet, *La Cosmographie universelle* (Paris, Guillaume Chaudière, 1575). *FB* 49234-5.

22. Jean de Léry, *Histoire d'un voyage faict en la terre de Bresil* (La Rochelle [= Geneva], Antoine Chuppin, 1578). *FB* 34334.

23. *FB* 34334-44.

24. *Les Vrais Pourtraits et vies des hommes illustres grecz, latins et payens* (Paris, Widow Kerver and Guillaume Chaudière, 1584). *FB* 49237.

25. Cited in Matthew McLean, *The Cosmographia of Sebastian Münster. Describing the World in the Reformation* (Aldershot, Ashgate, 2007), p. 133.

26. Anthony Grafton, 'José de Acosta: Renaissance historiography and New World humanity', in John Jeffries Martin (ed.), *The Renaissance World* (London, Routledge, 2007), pp. 166–88.

27. Nicholas Crane, *Mercator. The Man who Mapped the Planet* (London, Weidenfeld & Nicolson, 2002).

28. This early world view is illustrated in ibid., p. 52.

29. P.D.A. Harvey, *Maps in Tudor England* (London, Public Record Office, 1993). David Buisseret, *The Mapmakers' Quest: Depicting New Worlds in Renaissance Europe* (Oxford, Oxford University Press, 2003), pp. 64–7. Idem, *Monarchs, Ministers, and Maps: The Emergence of Cartography as a Tool of Government in Early Modern Europe* (Chicago, University of Chicago Press, 1992).

30. *Abraham Ortelius, Theatrum orbis terrarum: Antwerp 1570*, with an introduction by R.A. Skelton (Amsterdam, Meridian, 1964).

31. Illustrated Buisseret, *Mapmakers' Quest*, p. 40.

32. There is an evocative facsimile: *Georg Braun, Cities of the World*, introduction by Lelio Pagani (Leicester, Magna Books, 1990). Buisseret, *Mapmakers' Quest*, pp. 171–4.

33. McLean, *Cosmographia*.

34. Pavord, *Naming of Names*.

35. *VD 16* 6689–92. The further sixteenth-century editions published in Germany are *VD 16* M 6693–719.

36. McLean, *Cosmographia*, p. 174.

37. *FB* 38867.

38. Pavord, *Naming of Names*, pp. 93–160.

39. Strasbourg, Johann Schott. *VD 16* B 8499.

40. Basel, Michael Isengrin. *VD 16* F 3242.

41. London, Mierdman, 1551. *STC* 24365. Subsequent elaborations were published (in English) by Arnold Birckman at Cologne, *STC* 24366, 24567.

42. Pavord, *Naming of Names*, pp. 243 ff.

43. *Joyfull newes out of the Newe Found worlde*, *STC* 18005-7. *FB* 38131-2.

44. *FB* 46328-9.

45. La Croix du Maine, *Premier volume de la bibliotheque de la Croix du Maine* (Paris, Abel L'Angelier, 1584).

46. Paul Nelles, 'The library as an instrument of discovery: Gabriel Naudé and the uses of history', in D. R. Kelley (ed.), *History and the Disciplines* (Rochester, NY, University of Rochester Press, 1997), pp. 41–57.

47. Ann Blair, 'Annotating and indexing natural philosophy', in Marina Frasca-Spada and Nick Jardine (eds), *Books and the Sciences in History* (Cambridge, Cambridge University Press, 2000), pp. 69–89.

48. Blair, 'Annotating and indexing', p. 79 and figure 4.4.

49. Wolfram Zaunmüller, *Bibliographisches Handbuch der Sprachwörterbücher: ein internationales Verzeichnis von 5600 Wörterbüchern der Jahre 1460-1958 für mehr als 500 Sprachen und Dialekte* (New York, Hafner, 1958). Margarete Lindemann, *Die französischen Wörterbücher von den Anfängen bis 1600: Entstehung und typologische Beschreibung* (Tübingen, Niemeyer, 1994). F. Claes, *Lijst van Nederlandse woordenlijsten en woordenboeken gedrukt tot 1600* (Nieuwkoop, de Graaf, 1974).

50. Albert Labarre, *Bibliographie du dictionarium d'Ambrogio Calepino: (1502-1779)* (Baden-Baden, Koerner, 1975).

14: Healing

1. Harry S. Shelley, 'Cutting for the stone', *Journal of the History of Medicine and Allied Sciences*, 13 (1958), pp. 50–67.

2. Charles L. Cooke, 'Calvin's illnesses and their relation to Christian vocation', in Timothy George (ed.), *John Calvin and the Church. A Prism of Reform* (Louisville, KY, Westminster John Knox, 1990), pp. 59–70.

3. Margaret Bingham Stillwell, *The Awakening Interest in Science During the First Century of Printing, 1450-1550* (New York, Bibliographical Society of America, 1970), no. 331. Stillwell describes it as 'the first organised treatise on medicine to be printed'. Four editions were published before 1500. ISTC.

4. Barbara C. Halporn, *The Correspondence of Johann Amerbach. Early Printing in its Social Context* (Ann Arbor, University of Michigan Press, 2000), no. 219.

5. Lotte Hellinga, 'Medical incunabula', in Robin Myers and Michael Harris (eds), *Medicine, Mortality and the Book Trade* (London, St Paul's Bibliographies, 1998), pp. 73–86. Stillwell, *Awakening Interest in Science*, nos. 255–558.

6. Stillwell, *Awakening Interest in Science*, nos. 374, 375.

7. Richard J. Durling, 'A chronological census of Renaissance editions and translations of Galen', *Journal of the Warburg and Courtauld Institute*, 24 (1961), pp. 230–305.

8. Ibid., pp. 238–9.

9. FB 22159–95.

10. Amsterdam experienced plague on ten occasions during the sixteenth century; Leiden was afflicted in sixteen separate years. Leo Noordegraaf and Gerrit Valk, *De Gave Gods. De pest in Holland vanaf de late middeleeuwen* (Bergen, Octavo, 1988). The data is summarised in Andrew Cunningham and Ole Peter Grell, *The Four Horsemen of the Apocalypse. Religion, War, Famine and Death in Reformation Europe* (Cambridge, Cambridge University Press, 2000), pp. 275–6.

11. Paul Slack, *The Impact of Plague in Tudor and Stuart England* (London, Routledge, 1985), pp. 53–78.

12. A fine introduction to this subject is William Naphy and Andrew Spicer, *The Black Death and a History of Plagues, 1345-1730* (Stroud, Tempus, 2000). See also Cunningham and Grell, *Four Horsemen of the Apocalypse*, pp. 272–304.

13. Quoted Cunningham and Grell, *Four Horsemen of the Apocalypse*, p. 281.

14. Ibid., p. 280.

15. Noordegraaf and Valk, *De Gave Gods*. In England the spots on the back or chest were known as 'God's tokens'. Slack, *Impact of Plague*, pp. 25–6.

16. William Naphy, 'Plague-spreading and a magisterially controlled fear', in Naphy and Penny Roberts (eds), *Fear in Early Modern Society* (Manchester, Manchester University Press, 1997), pp. 28–43.

17. Jane Stevens Crawshaw, *Islands of Isolation. Fighting the Plague in Early Modern Venice* (Aldershot, Ashgate, 2012). I am grateful to Dr Crawshaw for permission to cite her work in advance of publication.

18. Martin Steinmann, *Johannes Oporinus. Ein Basler Buchdrucker um die Mitte des 16. Jahrhunderts* (Basel, Helbing & Lichtenhahn, 1967).

19. C.D. O'Malley, *Andreas Vesalius of Brussels, 1514-1564* (Berkeley, University of California Press, 1964).

20. Ibid., p. 47.

21. Harry Clark, 'Foiling the pirates: the preparation and publication of Andreas Vesalius's *De humani corporis fabrica*', *Library Quarterly*, 51 (1981), pp. 301-11. Harvey Cushing, *A Bio-bibliography of Andreas Vesalius* (New York, Schuman, 1943). Cf. Elly Cockx-Indestege, *Andreas Vesalius, a Belgian Census: Contribution towards a New Edition of H.W. Cushing's Bibliography* (Brussels, Royal Library Albert I, 1994).

22. Steinmann, *Oporinus*.

23. On the role of Basel as a centre of scholarly printing see now especially Frank Hieronymus, *Theophrast und Galen – Celsus und Paracelsus. Medizin, Naturphilosphie und Kirchenreform im Basler Buchdruck bis zum Dreissigjährigen Krieg* (4 vols, Basel, Universitätsbibliothek, 2005).

24. *Christiania restituta* ([Vienne], 1553). Of the 800 or 1,000 printed, just three survive, now in Paris, Bibliothèque Nationale; Vienna, Oesterreichische Nationalbibliothek; and Edinburgh University Library. John F. Fulton and Madeline E. Stanton, *Michael Servetus, Humanist and Martyr* (New York, Herbert Reichner, 1953), pp. 84–6.

25. Janet Doe, *A Bibliography of the Works of Ambroise Paré: premier chirugien & conseiller du roy* (Chicago, University of Chicago Press, 1937).

26. FB 40671–95.

27. FB 40684.

28. It is interesting in this connection that whereas the first edition of William Turner's herbal was published in London (by the Dutch printer Steven Mierdman, in 1551), subsequent enlarged editions were printed in Cologne. STC 24365, 24366, 24367.

29. The story is retold in the foreword to David Gentilcore, *Healers and Healing in Early Modern Italy* (Manchester, Manchester University Press, 1998), p. vii.

30. VD 16 P 365–726. Interestingly, his works made their way into French first through editions published in the Low Countries. FB 40560–8.

31. Gentilcore, *Healers and Healing*, p. 73.

32. John Ferguson, 'The Secrets of Alexis. A sixteenth-century collection of medical and technical receipts', *Proceedings of the Royal Society of Medicine*, 24 (1930), pp. 225–46. William Eamon, *Science and the Secrets of Nature: Books of Secrets in Medieval and Early Modern Culture* (Princeton, NJ, Princeton University Press, 1994).

33. *Les secrets de reverend signeur Alexis Piemontois, contenans excellens remedes contre plusieurs maladies, playes et autres accidens* (Antwerp, Christophe Plantin, 1557). FB 46900–39.

34. Gentilcore, *Healers and Healing*, p. 115.

35. Ian Maclean, *Learning and the European Marketplace: Essays in Early Modern Book History* (Leiden, Brill, 2009).

36. Caroline Bowden, 'The library of Mildred Cooke Cecil, Lady Burghley', *The Library*, 6th ser., 1 (2005), pp. 3–29.

37. This paragraph draws on a presentation by Pauline Cross of her research project, 'The Health of the Cecils (c.1550–c.1660)', funded by the Wellcome Trust.

15: Building a Library

1. Kristian Jensen, 'Universities and colleges', in Elisabeth Leedham-Green and Teresa Webber (eds), *The Cambridge History of Libraries in Britain and Ireland: Vol. I: to 1640* (Cambridge, Cambridge University Press, 2006), pp. 345–62.

2. Ian Philip, *The Bodleian Library in the Seventeenth and Eighteenth Centuries* (Oxford, Clarendon Press, 1983).

3. Mary Clapinson, 'The Bodleian Library and its readers, 1602–1652', *Bodleian Library Record*, 19 (1), (2006), pp. 30–46.

4. Ibid., pp. 36–7.

5. M. Connat and J. Mégret, 'Inventaire de la bibliothèque des du Prat', *Bibliothèque d'Humanisme et Renaissance*, 3 (1943), pp. 72–128.

6. Anthony Hobson, *Great Libraries* (London, Weidenfeld & Nicolson, 1970), pp. 109, 143.

7. Ibid., p. 98

8. The books accumulated by Henry VIII are now catalogued in James P. Carley (ed.), *The Libraries of King Henry VIII* (London, British Library, 2000).

9. Lotte Labowsky, *Bessarion's Library and the Biblioteca Marciana. Six Early Inventories* (Rome, Edizioni di storia e letteratura, 1979), p. 92.

10. Norman Davies and Roger Moorhouse, *Microcosm. Portrait of a Central European City* (London, Jonathan Cape, 2002), p. 172.

11. Martin Lowry, 'Two great Venetian libraries in the age of Aldus Manutius', *Bulletin of the John Rylands Library*, 57 (1974–75), pp. 128–66.

12. *Histoire des Bibliothèques françaises: 2. Les bibliothèques sous l'ancien régime, 1530–1789* (Paris, Promodis, 1988). See also Andrew Pettegree, 'Rare books and revolutionaries. The French bibliothèques municipales', in his *The French Book and the European Book World* (Leiden, Brill, 2007), pp. 1–16.

13. The collection is analysed (with a transcription) in John Craig, *Reformation, Politics and Polemics. The Growth of Protestantism in East Anglian Market Towns, 1500–1610* (Aldershot, Ashgate, 2001), pp. 205–12.

14. Colin Clair, 'Christopher Plantin's trade connections with England and Scotland', *The Library*, 5th ser., 14 (1959), pp. 28–45.

15. John Glenn and David Walsh, *Catalogue of the Francis Trigge Chained Library, St Wulfram's Church, Grantham* (Cambridge, Brewer, 1988).

16. Albert Labarre, *Le Livre dans la vie amiénoise du seizième siècle* (Paris, Béatrice-Nauwelaerts, 1971), pp. 139–45. Brian Richardson, *Printing, Writers and Readers in Renaissance Italy* (Cambridge, Cambridge University Press, 1999) pp. 118–21.

17. E.S. Leedham-Green, *Books in Cambridge Inventories: Book Lists from Vice-Chancellor's Court Probate Inventories in the Tudor and Stuart Periods* (2 vols, Cambridge, Cambridge University Press, 1986). The equivalent records for Oxford are studied in the series R.J. Fehrenbach and E.S. Leedham-Green, *Private Libraries in Renaissance England: A Collection and Catalogue of Tudor and Early Stuart Book-lists* (6 vols, Binghamton, NY, Medieval & Renaissance Texts & Studies, 1992–).

18. Leedham-Green, *Books in Cambridge Inventories*, I, pp. 234–44.

19. Fehrenbach and Leedham-Green, *Private Libraries in Renaissance England*, no. 127.

20. Pierre Jourda, 'La Bibliothèque d'un régent calviniste (1577)', in *Mélanges d'histoire littéraire de la Renaissance offerts à Henri Chamard* (Paris, Librarie Nizet, 1951), pp. 269–73.

21. Paul Grendler, *The Roman Inquisition and the Venetian Press, 1540–1605* (Princeton, NJ, Princeton University Press, 1977), p. 290

22. Marcella Grendler, 'A Greek collection in Padua: the library of Gian Vincenzo Pinelli (1535–1601)', *Renaissance Quarterly*, 33 (1980), pp. 386–416; idem, 'Book collecting in Counter-Reformation Italy: the library of Gian Vincezo Pinelli (1535–1601)', *Journal of Library History*, 16 (1981), pp. 144–51.

23. The prohibited titles are discussed in Grendler, *Roman Inquisition*, p. 289 and listed pp. 321–4.

24. Anthony Hobson, 'A sale by candle in 1608', *The Library*, 5th ser., 26 (1971), pp. 215–33.

25. Josef Trypucko, *The Catalogue of the Book Collection of the Jesuit College in Braniewo held in the University Library in Uppsala* (3 vols, Warsaw/Uppsala, Uppsala Universitetsbibliotek, 2007), p. 547.

26. Glenn and Walsh, *Trigge Chained Library*, nos. 76, 77, 151, 157, 160, 190, 271, 278. The earliest Paris item was an incunabulum of 1477 (no. 215).

27. See the example of the stock of the Lyon publisher Symphorien Beraud documented in Chapter 12.

28. These and other examples are taken from the introduction to James Raven (ed.), *Lost Libraries. The Destruction of Great Book Collections Since Antiquity* (Basingstoke, Palgrave, 2004), pp. 1–40.

29. Elmar Mittler, *Bibliotheca Palatina: Katalog zur Ausstellung vom 8. Juli bis 2. November 1986* (Heidelberg, Braus, 1986).

30. Owen Gingerich offers an amusing and illuminating account of the emergence of several lost copies of Copernicus from hiding places in Eastern Europe. Owen Gingerich, *The Book Nobody Read. In Pursuit of the Revolutions of Nicolaus Copernicus* (London, Heinemann, 2004), pp. 220–38.

16: Word and the Street

1. Alastair Duke, 'Posters, pamphlets and prints', in his *Dissident Identities in the Early Modern Low Countries* (Aldershot, Ashgate, 2009), p. 160. Henk van Nierop, 'Ketterij uit Utopia: verboden zestiende-eeuwse boeken', *NRC Handelsblad*, Supplement, 24 February 1989.

2. According to the data collected for *FB*.

3. Adam Fox, *Oral and Literate Culture in England, 1500–1700* (Oxford, Oxford University Press, 2000).

4. Eugénie Droz, 'Le Calendrier genevois, agent de la propagande', in her *Chemins de l'herésie. Textes et documents* (4 vols, Geneva, Slatkine, 1970–76), II, pp. 433–56.

5. ISTC; *NK* 1297–1307, 3330–56, *BT* 1749–54, *FB* 32459–70.

6. *NK* 1303–1305, 3357, *STC* 470.2, 470.3, 471, 471.5. On English almanacs see E.F. Bosanquet, *English Printed Almanacks and Prognostications to 1600* (London, Bibliographical Society, 1917).

7. *FB* 39564.

8. *FB* 39561–677. Michel Chomarat and Jean-Paul Laroche, *Bibliographie Nostradamus; XVIe, XVIIe, XVIIIe siècles* (Baden-Baden, Koerner, 1989).

9. *STC* 18694. Chomarat and Laroche, *Bibliographie*, 38. Other English editions of the year were *STC* 492, 492.2. Chomarat and Laroche, *Bibliographie*, 34, 35.

10. Paul L. Hughes and James F. Larkin (eds), *Tudor Royal Proclamations* (3 vols, New Haven, Yale University Press, 1964–69), III, no. 808. Paul Hammer, 'The smiling crocodile: the earl of Essex and late-Elizabethan "popularity" ', in Steve Pincus and Peter Lake (eds), *The Public Sphere in Early Modern England* (Manchester, Manchester University Press, 2007), pp. 95–115.

11. Richard Streckfuss, 'News before newspapers', *Journalism and Mass Communication*, 75 (1998), pp. 84–97.

12. Lisa Ferraro Parmelee, *Good Newes from Fraunce. French Anti-League Propaganda in Late Elizabethan England* (Rochester, NY, University of Rochester Press, 1996).

13. This is certainly the judgement of the leading specialist on the period. See Joad Raymond, *Pamphlets and Pamphleteering in Early Modern Britain* (Cambridge, Cambridge University Press, 2003).

14. Ibid., p. 149. F. Dahl, *A Bibliography of English Corantos and Periodical Newsbooks 1620-1642* (London, Bibliographical Society, 1952).

15. F. Levy, 'How information spread among the gentry, 1550-1640', *Journal of British Studies*, 21 (1982), pp. 11-34. It is also interesting to note that the title of John Morrill's book changes from The Revolt *of* the Provinces to the Revolt *in* the Provinces in the second edition. *The Revolt of the Provinces: Conservatives and Radicals in the English Civil War, 1630-1650* (London, Longman, 1980).

16. David Cressy, *Bonfires and Bells. National Memory and the Protestant Calendar in Elizabethan and Stuart England* (London, Weidenfeld & Nicolson, 1989).

17. David Randall, *Credibility in Elizabethan and Early Stuart Military News* (London, Pickering & Chatto, 2008).

18. Streckfuss, 'News before newspapers', p. 93.

19. Though sometimes pamphlets made their way into English through the intermediary language of French. *STC 17659: Articles of the peace* (1607). 'All being faithfully translated out of high Dutch into French, and out the same into English'.

20. Randall, *Credibility*, p. 86.

21. For the European marketplace of political *avvisi* see Zuszsa Barbarics and Renate Pieper, 'Handwritten newsletters as a means of communication in early modern Europe', in Francisco Bethencourt and Florike Egmond (eds), *Correspondence and Cultural Exchange in Europe, 1400-1700* (Cambridge, Cambridge University Press, 2007), pp. 53-79.

22. For the publication of play texts across Europe see Julie Stone Peters, *Theatre of the Book, 1480-1880. Print, Text and Performance in Europe* (Oxford, Oxford University Press, 2000), pp. 15-40.

23. Andrew Gurr, *The Shakespearean Stage, 1574-1642* (Cambridge, Cambridge University Press, 1970), p. 140.

24. Neil Carson, *A Companion to Henslowe's Diary* (Cambridge, Cambridge University Press, 1988), pp. 82-4.

25. The comparison is developed in Peter W.M. Blayney, 'The publication of playbooks', in John D. Cox and David Scott Kastan (eds), *A New History of Early English Drama* (New York, Columbia University Press, 1997), pp. 383-422.

26. Blaney, 'Publication of playbooks', pp. 407-12.

27. Lukas Erne, *Shakespeare as Literary Dramatist* (Cambridge, Cambridge University Press, 2003), pp. 78-100.

28. This is the controversial argument of Erne, ibid.

29. Ibid., p. 233.

30. *FB* 2129-96. A. Lynn Martin, *The Jesuit Mind. The Mentality of an Elite in Early Modern France* (Ithaca, NY, Cornell University Press, 1988).

31. Jean-Marie Valentin, *Les Jésuites et le théâtre (1554-1680): Contribution à l'histoire culturelle du monde catholique dans le Saint-Empire Romain Germanique* (Bern, Lang, 2001).

32. Liam M. Brockley, 'Jesuit pastoral theater on an urban stage: Lisbon, 1588-1593', *Journal of Early Modern History*, 9 (2005), pp. 3-50.

33. His diary is edited by Louis Raymond Lefevre, *Journal de L'Estoile* (Paris, Gallimard, 1943). A brisk selection of excerpts in English translation is available as Nancy Lyman Roelker, *The Paris of Henry of Navarre as seen by Pierre de L'Estoile* (Cambridge, MA, Harvard University Press, 1958).

34. Roelker, *Paris of Henry of Navarre*, p. 36

35. Ibid., p. 177.

36. Ibid., p. 176.

A Note on Sources: Mapping the Geography of Print

1. Lucian Febvre and Henri-Jean Martin, *L' Apparition du livre* (Paris, Albin Michel, 1958). *The Coming of the Book. The Impact of Printing, 1458-1800* (London, N.L.B., 1976).

2. Elizabeth Eisenstein, *The Printing Press as an Agent of Change: Communications and Cultural Transformations in Early Modern Europe* (Cambridge, Cambridge University Press, 1979). Idem, *The Printing Revolution in Early Modern Europe* (Cambridge, Cambridge University Press, 1983).

3. Anthony Grafton and Lisa Jardine, *From Humanism to the Humanities. Education and the Liberal Arts in Fifteenth- and Sixteenth-Century Europe* (London, Duckworth, 1986).

4. A.W. Pollard and G.R. Redgrave, *A Short-Title Catalogue of Books Printed in England, Scotland, & Ireland and of English Books Printed Abroad 1475–1640* (2nd edn, 3 vols, London, Bibliographical Society, 1976–91).

5. Around 80 per cent of the items in the first edition of the *STC* were located in either the British Library or the Bodleian Library, Oxford.

6. The Universal Short Title Catalogue, planned to go online in 2011. See table in appendix, p. 357.

7. A system described in Neil Harris, 'Tribal lays and the history of the fingerprint', in David J. Shaw, *Many into One: Problems and Opportunities in Creating Shared Catalogues of Older Books* (London, Consortium of European Research Libraries, 2006), pp. 21–71.

8. Bridgette Moreau, *Inventaire chronologique des éditions parisiennes du XVIe siècle* (5 vols, Paris, F. Paillart/Paris Musées, 1972–2004). Philippe Renouard, *Imprimeurs & libraires parisiens du XVIe siècle* (Paris, Service des travaux historiques de la ville de Paris/ Paris Musées, 1964–).

9. Andrew Pettegree, Malcolm Walsby and Alexander Wilkinson, *FB. French Vernacular Books. Books Published in the French language before 1601* (Leiden, Brill, 2007).

10. Wouter Nijhoff and Maria Elizabeth Kronenberg, *Nederlandsche bibliographie van 1500 tot 1540* (3 vols, 's-Gravenhage, Nijhoff, 1965–71; reprint of The Hague, 1919–1942). Paul Valkema Blouw, *Typographia Batava 1541–1600: repertorium van boeken gedrukt in Nederland tussen 1541 en 1600* (2 vols, Nieuwkoop, de Graaf, 1998). Elly Cockx-Indestege, Geneviève Glorieux and Bart op de Beeck, *Belgica typographica 1541–1600: catalogus librorum impressorum ab anno MDXLI ad annum MDC in regionibus quae nunc Regni Belgarum partes sunt* (Nieuwkoop, de Graaf, 1968–94).

11. Alexander Wilkinson, *IB. Books printed in the Iberian Peninsula and in Spanish Abroad* (2 vols, Leiden, Brill, 2010).

12. L. Nielsen, *Dansk bibliografi 1482–1550* (2nd edn, Copenhagen, Kongelige Bibliotek, 1996). Idem, *Dansk bibliografi 1551–1600* (Copenhagen, Gydendalske Boghandel, 1931–33). I. Collijn, *Sveriges bibliografi intill ar 1600* (3 vols, Uppsala, Svenska litteratursällskapet, 1927–38). G. Borsa et al., *Régi Magyaroszaki Nyomtatvanyook 1473–1600. Res litteraria Hungariae vetus operum impressorum 1473–1600* (Budapest, 1971). Zd. V. Tobolka and Fr. Horak, *Knihopis ceskych a slovenskych tisku od doby nejstarsi az do konce XVIII. Stoleti* (Prague, 1925–67).

BIBLIOGRAPHY

Bibliographical handbooks

Aldis, H.G., *A List of Books printed in Scotland before 1700* (Edinburgh, National Library of Scotland, 1970)

Allison, A.F. and D.M. Rogers, *The Contemporary Printed Literature of the English Counter-Reformation between 1558–1640: An Annotated Catalogue* (Brookfield, VT, Scolar Press, 1989–94)

Baudrier, H.-L. and J. Baudrier, *Bibliographie lyonnaise. Recherches sur les imprimeurs, libraires, relieurs et fondeurs de lettres de Lyon au XVIe siècle* (12 vols, Lyon, Louis Brun, 1895–1921)

Benzing, Josef, *Lutherbibliographie. Verzeichnis der gedruckten Schriften Martin Luthers bis zu dessen Tod* (2nd edn, Baden-Baden, Heitz, 1989)

Borsa, G. et al., *Régi Magyaroszaki Nyomtatvanyook 1473–1600. Res litteraria Hungariae vetus operum impressorum 1473–1600* (Budapest, 1971)

Cockx-Indestege, Elly, Geneviève Glorieux and Bart op de Beeck, *Belgica typographica 1541–1600: catalogus librorum impressorum ab anno MDXLI ad annum MDC in regionibus quae nunc Regni Belgarum partes sunt* (Nieuwkoop, de Graaf, 1968–94)

Collijn, I., *Sveriges bibliografi intill ar 1600* (3 vols, Uppsala, Svenska litteratursällskapet, 1927–38)

Edit 16. Le edizioni italiane del XVI secolo: censimento nazionale (5 vols, Roma, Istituto centrale per il catalogo unico delle biblioteche italiane e per le informazioni bibliografiche, 1989–)

Eisermann, Falk, *Verzeichnis der typographischen Einblattdrucke des 15. Jahrhunderts im Heiligen Römischen Reich Deutscher Nation: VE 15* (Wiesbaden, Reichert, 2004)

Heller, Marvin J., *The Sixteenth-Century Hebrew Book. An Abridged Thesaurus* (2 vols, Leiden, Brill, 2004)

Icazbalceta, Joaquín Garcia, *Bibliografia Mexicana del signo XVI* (2nd edn, Mexico City, 1954)

Index Aureliensis: catalogus librorum sedecimo saeculo impressorum (14 vols, Baden-Baden, Koerner, 1962–2004)

Knuttel, W.P.C., *Catalogus van de pamfletten-verzameling berustende in de Koninklijke Bibliotheek* (9 vols, The Hague, 1882–1920)

Moreau, Bridgette, *Inventaire chronologique des éditions parisiennes du XVIe siècle* (5 vols, Paris, F. Paillart/ Paris Musées, 1972–2004)

Nielsen, L., *Dansk bibliografi 1482–1550* (2nd edn, Copenhagen, Kongelige Bibliotek, 1996)

Nielsen, L., *Dansk bibliografi 1551–1600* (Copenhagen, Gydendalske Boghandel, 1931–33)

Nijhoff, Wouter and Maria Elizabeth Kronenberg, *Nederlandsche bibliographie van 1500 tot 1540* (3 vols, The Hagne, Nijhoff, 1965–71; reprint of The Hague, 1919–42)

Peeters-Fontainas, Jean, *Bibliographie des impressions espagnoles des Pays-Bas méridionaux* (2 vols, Nieuwkoop, de Graaf, 1965)

Pettegree, Andrew and Malcolm Walsby, *NB. Books printed in the Low Countries before 1601* (2 vols, Leiden, Brill, 2011)

Pettegree, Andrew, Malcolm Walsby and Alexander Wilkinson, *FB. French Vernacular Books. Books published in the French language before 1601* (Leiden, Brill, 2007)

Pollard, A.W. and G.R. Redgrave, *A Short-title Catalogue of Books printed in England, Scotland, & Ireland and of English Books printed Abroad 1475–1640* (2nd edn, 3 vols, London, Bibliographical Society, 1976–91)

Renouard, Philippe, *Imprimeurs & libraires parisiens du XVIe siècle* (Paris, Service des travaux historiques de la ville de Paris/ Paris Musées, 1964–)

Répertoire bibliographique des livres imprimés en France au seizième siècle (30 vols, Baden-Baden, Heitz, 1968–80)

Rouzet, Anne, *Dictionnaire des imprimeurs, libraires et éditeurs des XVe et XVIe siècles dans les limites géographiques de la Belgique actuelle* (Nieuwkoop, de Graaf, 1975)

Shaaber, M.A., *Check-list of works of British Authors printed Abroad, in Languages other than English, to 1641* (New York, Bibliographical Society of America, 1975)

Tobolka, Zd. V. and Fr. Horak, *Knihopis ceskych a slovenskych tisku od doby nejstarsi az do konce XVIII. Stoleti* (Prague, 1925–67)

Valkema Blouw, Paul, *Typographia Batava 1541–1600: repertorium van boeken gedrukt in Nederland tussen 1541 en 1600* (2 vols, Nieuwkoop, de Graaf, 1998)

Van Thienen, Gerard and John Goldfinch, *Incunabula printed in the Low Countries: A Census* (Nieuwkoop, de Graaf, 1999)

VD 16. Verzeichnis der im deutschen Sprachbereich erschienenen Drucke des XVI. Jahrhunderts (25 vols, Stuttgart, Hiersemann, 1983–2000)

Voet, Léon, *The Plantin Press (1555–1589): A Bibliography of the Works printed and published by Christopher Plantin at Antwerp and Leiden* (6 vols, Amsterdam, Van Hoeve, 1980–83)

Wilkinson, Alexander, *IB. Books printed in the Iberian Peninsula and in Spanish Abroad* (2 vols, Leiden, Brill, 2010)

General works

Bennett, H.S., *English Books and Readers, 1475–1640* (3 vols, Cambridge, Cambridge University Press, 1969)

Cavallo, Guglielmo and Roger Chartier, *A History of Reading in the West* (Cambridge, Polity Press, 1999)

Clair, Colin, *A History of European Printing* (London, Academic Press, 1976).

Eisenstein, Elizabeth, *The Printing Press as an Agent of Change: Communications and Cultural Transformations in Early Modern Europe* (Cambridge, Cambridge University Press, 1979)

Eisenstein, Elizabeth, *The Printing Revolution in Early Modern Europe* (Cambridge, Cambridge University Press, 1983)

Febvre, Lucian and Henri-Jean Martin, *The Coming of the Book. The Impact of Printing, 1458–1800* (London, Verso, 1976)

Gaskell, Philip, *A New Introduction to Bibliography* (Oxford, Oxford University Press, 1972)

Steinberg, S.H. *Five Hundred Years of Printing* (London, Penguin, 1955)

1: The Book before Print

Anglo, Sydney, *The Martial Arts in Renaissance Europe* (New Haven, Yale University Press, 2000)

Berkovits, Ilona, *Illuminated Manuscripts from the Library of Matthias Corvinus* (Budapest, Corvina Press, 1964)

Bloomfield, M.W., *Incipits of Latin Works on the Virtues and Vices, 1100–1500 AD: Including a Section of Incipits of Works on the Pater Noster* (Cambridge, MA, Mediaeval Academy of America, 1979)

Bühler, Curt F., *The Fifteenth-century Book. The Scribes, the Printers, the Decorators* (Philadelphia, PA, University of Pennsylvania Press, 1960)

Croenen, Godfried and Peter Ainsworth, *Patrons, Authors and Workshops. Books and Book Production in Paris around 1400* (Louvain, Peeters, 2006)

Csapodi, Csaba, *The Corvinian Library. History and Stock* (Budapest, Akadémiai Kiadó, 1973)

Duffy, Eamon, *Marking the Hours. English People and their Prayers, 1240–1570* (New Haven, Yale University Press, 2006)

George, William and Emily Waters, *The Vespasiano Memoirs: Lives of Illustrious Men of the XVth Century by Vespasiano da Bisticci, Bookseller* (London, Routledge, 1926), p. 102.

Goodrich, Carter, *The Invention of Printing in China and its Spread Westward* (New York, Ronald Press, 1925)

Hamel, Christopher de, 'Books of Hours: imaging the word', in John L. Sharpe and Kimberley van Kampen (eds), *The Bible as Book. The Manuscript Tradition* (London, British Library, 1998), pp. 137–43

Hamel, Christopher de, *A History of Illuminated Manuscripts* (2nd edn, London, Phaidon, 1994)

Hindman, Sandra and James Douglas Farquhar, *Pen to Press: Illustrated Manuscripts and Printed Books in the First Century of Printing* (College Park, University of Maryland Press, 1977)

Hughes, A., *Mediaeval Manuscripts for Mass and Office, a Guide to their Organisation and Terminology* (Toronto, University of Toronto Press, 1982)

Ker, N.H., *Mediaeval Libraries of Great Britain* (2nd edn, London, Royal Historical Society, 1964)

Martin, Henri-Jean and Roger Chartier, *Histoire de l'édition française. Le livre conquérant. Du Moyen Age au milieu du XVIIe siècle* (Paris, Promodis, 1982)

Neddermeyer, Uwe, *Von der Handschrift zum gedruckten Buch: Schriftlichkeit und Leseinteresse im Mittelalter und in der frühen Neuzeit: quantitative und qualitative Aspekte* (Wiesbaden, Otto Harrassowitz, 1998)

Pollard, Graham, 'The pecia stystem in the medieval universities', in M.B. Parkes and Andrew G. Watson (eds), *Mediaeval Scribes, Manuscripts and Libraries. Essays Presented to N.R. Ker* (London, Scolar Press, 1978), pp. 145–61

Reynolds, L.D. and N.G. Wilson, *Scribes and Scholars. A Guide to the Transmission of Greek and Latin Literature* (Oxford, Oxford University Press, 1968)

Ridder-Symoens, Hilde de, *A History of the University in Europe. Vol.1, Universities in the Middle Ages* (Cambridge, Cambridge University Press, 1992)

Rouse, Mary A. and Rouse, Richard H., *Cartolai, Illuminators, and Printers in Fifteenth-century Italy: The Evidence of the Ripoli Press* (Los Angeles, UCLA, 1988)

Rouse, Richard H., and Rouse, Mary A., *Manuscripts and their Makers: Commercial Book Producers in Medieval Paris, 1200–1500* (London, Harvey Miller, 2000)

Sutton, Anne F. and Livia Visser-Fuchs, *Richard III's Books. Ideals and Reality in the Life and Library of a Mediaeval Prince* (Stroud, Sutton, 1997)

Tanner, Marcus, *The Raven King. Matthias Corvinus and the Fate of his Lost Library* (New Haven, Yale University Press, 2008)

Thorp, Nigel, *The Glory of the Page: Medieval & Renaissance Illuminated Manuscripts from Glasgow University Library* (London, Glasgow University Library, 1987)

Tzanaki, Rosemary, *Mandeville's Mediaeval Audiences. A Study of the Reception of the Book of Sir John Mandeville (1371–1550)* (Aldershot, Ashgate, 2003)

Ullman, Berthold Louis, *The Humanism of Coluccio Salutati* (Padua, Antenore, 1963)

Ward-Perkins, Bryan, *The Fall of Rome and the End of Civilization* (Oxford, Oxford University Press, 2005)

Wijsman, Hanno, *Handschriften voor het hertogdom. De mooiste verluchte manuscripten van Brabantse hertogen, edellieden, kloosterlingen en stedelingen* (Alphen, Uitgeverij Veerhuis, 2006)

Woolf, Greg, 'Literacy or literacies in Rome?', in William A. Johnson and Holt N. Parker (eds), *Ancient Literacies. The Culture of Reading in Greece and Rome* (Oxford, Oxford University Press, 2009), pp. 46–68

2: The Invention of Printing

Davies, Martin, 'Juan de Carvajal and early printing: the 42-line Bible and the Sweynheym and Pannartz Aquinas', *The Library*, 6th ser., 18 (1996), pp. 193–215

Eisermann, Falk, 'Auflagenhöhen von Einblattdrucken im 15. und frühen 16. Jahrhundert', in Volker Honemann et al. (eds), *Einblattdrucke des 15. und frühen 16. Jahrhunderts* (Tübingen, Niemeyer, 2000), pp. 143–77.

Füssel, Stephan, *Gutenberg and the Impact of Printing* (Aldershot, Ashgate, 2005)

Gilmont, Jean-François, 'Printers by the rules', *The Library*, 6th ser., 2 (1980), pp. 129–55

Hase, Oscar van, *Die Koberger* (Wiesbaden, Breitkopf & Härtel, 1885)

Hellinga, Lotte, 'Printing types and the printed word: considerations around new insights into the beginning of printing', *Archiv für Geschichte des Buchwesens*, 53 (2003), pp. 249–65

Hellinga-Querido, Lotte and Clemens de Wolf, *Laurens Janszoon Coster was zijn naam* (Haarlem, Enschedé, 1988)

Hind, Arthur M., *An Introduction to a History of Woodcut* (London, Constable, 1935)

Jensen, Kristian (ed.), *Incunabula and their Readers: Printing, Selling and Using Books in the Fifteenth Century* (London, British Library, 2003)

Kapr, Albert, *Johann Gutenberg. The Man and his Invention* (Aldershot, Scolar Press, 1996)

Künast, Hans-Jörg, *Getruck zu Augspurg. Buchdruck und Buchhandel in Augsburg zwischen 1468 und 1555* (Tübingen, Niemeyer, 1997)

Lehmann-Haupt, Helmut, *Peter Schoeffer of Gernsheim and Mainz* (Rochester, Loe Hart, 1950)

McMurtrie, Douglas C., *The Gutenberg Documents* (New York, Oxford University Press, 1941)

Mäkeler, Henrick, *Das Rechnungsbuch des Speyerer Druckherrn Peter Drach d. M. (um 1450–1504)* (St Katharinen, Scripta Mercaturae, 2005)

Muther, Richard, *German Book Illustration of the Gothic Period and the Early Renaissance (1460–1530)* (Metuchen, NJ, Scarecrow Press, 1972)

Needham, Paul, 'The changing shape of the Vulgate Bible in fifteenth-century printing shops', in Kimberley van Kampen and Paul Saenger (eds), *The Bible as Book, the First Printed Editions* (London, British Library, 1998), pp. 53–70

Ruppel, Aloys, *Peter Schöffer aus Gernsheim* (Mainz, Gutenberg Gesellschaft, 1937).

Scholderer, Victor, 'The petition of Sweynheym and Pannartz to Sixtus IV', *The Library*, 3rd ser., 6 (1915), pp. 186–90

Smith, Margaret M., *The Title-page: Its Early Development, 1460–1510* (London, British Library, 2000)

Wilson, Adrian, *The Making of the Nuremberg Chronicle* (Amsterdam, Nico Israel, 1976)

3: Renaissance Encounters: The Crisis of Print

Amram, David Weerner, *The Makers of Hebrew Books in Italy* (London, Holland Press, 1963)

Blake, N.F., *Caxton and his World* (London, House & Maxwell, 1969)

Conway, Melissa, *The Diario of the Printing Press of San Jacopo di Ripoli, 1476–1484. Commentary and Transcription* (Florence, Olschki, 1999)

Gerulaitis, Leonardas Vytautas, *Printing and Publishing in Fifteenth-Century Venice* (Chicago, American Library Association, 1976)

Goldschmidt, E. Ph., *Mediaeval Texts and their First Appearance in Print* (London, Bibliographical Society, 1943)

Harris, Neil, 'History of the Book in Italy', in Michael J. Suarez and Henry Woudhuysen (eds), *The Oxford Companion to the Book* (Oxford, Oxford University Press, 2010)

Jones, Howard, *Printing the Classical Text* (Utrecht, de Graaf, 2004)

Lowry, Martin, 'The New Academy of Aldus Manutius: a Renaissance dream', *Bulletin of the John Rylands University Library of Manchester*, 58 (1976), pp. 378–420

Lowry, Martin, *Nicolas Jenson and the Rise of Venetian Publishing in Renaissance Europe* (Oxford, Blackwell, 1991)

Lowry, Martin, *The World of Aldus Manutius. Business and Scholarship in Renaissance Venice* (Oxford, Blackwell, 1979)

Needham, Paul, *The Printer & the Pardoner* (Washington, Library of Congress, 1986)

Needham, Paul, 'Venetian printers and publishers in the fifteenth century', *La Bibliofilia* (1998), pp. 157–200

Nieto, Philippe, 'Géographie des impressions européennes du XVe siècle', *Revue française d'histoire du livre*, 118–21 (2004), pp. 125–73

Noakes, Susan, 'The development of the book market in late quattrocento Italy: printers' failures and the role of the middleman', *Journal of Mediaeval and Renaissance Studies*, 11 (1981), pp. 23–55, here 44–5

Painter, George D., *William Caxton* (London, Chatto & Windus, 1976)

Plomer, Henry R. *Wynkyn de Worde & his Contemporaries from the Death of Caxton to 1535* (London, Grafton, 1925)

Rouse, Mary A. and Richard H. Rouse, 'Backgrounds to print: aspects of the manuscript book in northern Europe of the fifteenth century', in their *Authentic Witnesses: Approaches to Medieval Texts and Manuscripts* (Notre Dame, IN, University of Notre Dame Press, 1991)

Scholderer, Victor, *Fifty Essays in Fifteenth- and Sixteenth-century Bibliography* (Amsterdam, Hertzberger, 1966)

Strata, Filippo de, *Polemic Against Printing* (Birmingham, Hayloft Press, 1986)

Tedeschi, Martha, 'Publish and perish. The career of Lienhart Holle in Ulm', in Sandra Hindman (ed.), *Printing the Written Word. The Social History of Books, circa 1450–1520* (Ithaca, NY, Cornell University Press, 1991), pp. 41–67.

Zeidberg, David S. and Fiorella Gioffredi Superbi, *Aldus Manutius and Renaissance Culture* (Florence, Olschki, 1998)

4: The Creation of a European Book Market

Armstrong, Elizabeth, *Before Copyright. The French Book-privilege System, 1498–1526* (Cambridge, Cambridge University Press, 1990)

Broomhall, Susan, *Women and the Book Trade in the Sixteenth-century France* (Aldershot, Ashgate, 2002)

Coogan, Robert, *Erasmus, Lee and the Correction of the Vulgate: The Shaking of the Foundations* (Geneva, Droz, 1992)

Cuijpers, P.M.H., *Teksten als koopwaar. Vroege drukkers verkennen de markt* (Amsterdam, University of Amsterdam, 1998)

Delsaerdt, Pierre, 'A bookshop for a new age: the inventory of the bookshop of the Louvain bookseller Hieronymus Cloet, 1543', in Lotte Hellinga et al., *The Bookshop of the World. The Role of the Low Countries in the Book Trade, 1473–1941* (Goy-Houten, de Graaf, 2001), pp. 75–86.

Dietz, Alexander, *Frankfurter Handelsgeschichte* (Frankfurt, Knauer, 1921)

Dietz, Alexander, *Zur Geschichte der Frankfurter Büchermesse, 1462–1792* (Frankfurt, Hauser, 1921)

Halporn, Barbara C., *The Correspondence of Johann Amerbach. Early Printing in its Social Context* (Ann Arbor, University of Michigan Press, 2000)

Harrisse, Henry, *Excerpta Colombiniana; bibliographie de 400 pièces du 16e siècle; précédée d'une histoire de la Bibliothèque colombine et de son fondateur* (Paris, Welter, 1887)

Hartmann, Alfred and Beat R. Jenny, *Die Amerbachkorrespondenz* (10 vols, Basel, 1942–)

McKitterick, David, *Print, Manuscript and the Search for Order, 1450–1830* (Cambridge, Cambridge University Press, 2003)

Pabel, Hilmar M., *Herculean Labours. Erasmus and the Editing of St Jerome's Letters in the Renaissance* (Leiden, Brill, 2008).

Pollard, Graham and Albert Ehrman, *The Distribution of Books by Catalogue from the Invention of Printing to AD 1800* (Cambridge, Roxburghe Club, 1965)

Recke, Bruno, *Die Frankfurter Büchermesse* (Frankfurt, Stempel, 1951)

Thompson, James Westphal (ed.), *The Frankfort Book Fair. The Francofordiense Emporium of Henri Estienne* (Chicago, Burt Franklin, 1911)

Vervliet, Hendrik D.L., *Post-incunabula and their Publishers in the Low Countries* (The Hague, Martinus Nijhoff, 1978)

Wagner, Klaus, 'Le Commerce du livre en France au début du XVIe siècle d'après les notes manuscrites de Fernando Colomb', *Bulletin du bibliophile*, 2 (1992), pp. 305–29

Winn, Mary Beth, *Anthoine Vérard, Parisian Publisher, 1485–1512* (Geneva, Droz, 1997)

5: Book Town Wittenberg

Chrisman, Miriam Usher, *Conflicting Visions of Reform. German Lay Propaganda Pamphlets 1519–1530* (Boston, Humanities Press, 1996)

Chrisman, Miriam Usher, *Lay Culture, Learned Culture. Books and Social Change in Strasbourg, 1480–1599* (New Haven, Yale University Press, 1982)

Cranach im Detail. Buchschmuck Lucas Cranachs des Älteren und seiner Werkstatt (Ausstellung Lutherhalle Wittenberg, 1994)

Edwards, Mark U., *Printing, Propaganda and Martin Luther* (Berkeley, University of California Press, 1994)

Gesetz und Gnade. Cranach, Luther und die Bilder (Ausstellung Eisenach, 1994)

Junghans, Helmar, *Wittenberg als Lutherstadt* (Göttingen, Vandenhoeck & Ruprecht, 1979)

Köhler, Hans-Joachim, *Bibliographie der Flugschriften des 16. Jahrhunders. I: Das frühe 16. Jahrhundert (1501–1530)* (3 vols, Tübingen, Bibliotheca Academica, 1991–96)

Köhler, Hans-Joachim, *Flugschriften als Massenmedium der Reformationszeit* (Stuttgart, Klett-Cotta, 1981)

Matheson, Peter, *The Rhetoric of the Reformation* (Edinburgh, T. & T. Clark, 1998)

Reinitzer, Heimo, *Biblia deutsch. Luthers Bibelübersetzung und ihre Tradition* (Ausstellung Herzog August Bibliothek Wolfenbüttel, 1983)

O'Sullivan, Orlaith (ed.), *The Bible as Book. The Reformation* (London, British Library, 2000)

Reske, Christoph, *Die Buchdrucker des 16. und 17. Jahrhunderts im deutschen Sprachgebiet: auf der Grundlage des gleichnamigen Werkes von Josef Benzing* (Wiesbaden, Harrassowitz, 2007)

Robinson-Hammerstein, Helga (ed.), *The Transmission of Ideas in the Lutheran Reformation* (Dublin, Irish Academic Press, 1989)

Scribner, R., *For the Sake of Simple Folk. Popular Propaganda for the German Reformation* (Cambridge, Cambridge University Press, 1981)

Weiss, Ulman (ed.), *Flugschriften der Reformationszeit* (Tübingen, Bibliotheca academica, 2001)

6: Luther's Legacy

Baskerville, Edward J., *A Chronological Bibliography of Propaganda and Polemic published in English between 1553 and 1558: From the Death of Edward VI to the Death of Mary I* (Philadelphia, American Philosophical Society, 1979)

Bohatcová, Mirham, 'Der gegenwärtige Bearbeitungsstand der Druckproduktion vom 15.–18. Jahrhundert in den böhmischen Ländern', *Gutenberg Jahrbuch*, 1987, pp. 265–78

Bohatcová, Mirham, 'Das Verhältnis der tschechischen und fremdsprachigen Drucke in Böhmen und Mähren vom 15. Jahrhundert bis zum Jahre 1621', *Gutenberg Jahrbuch*, 1988, pp. 108–21

Bouwman, André et al., *Stad van Boeken. Handschriften en Druk in Leiden, 1260–2000* (Leiden, Primavera, 2007)

Chambers, B.T., *Bibliography of French Bibles. Fifteenth- and Sixteenth-century French-Language Editions of the Scriptures* (Geneva, Droz, 1983)

Den Hollander, A.A., *De Nederlandse Bijbelvertalingen, 1522–1545* (Nieuwkoop, de Graaf, 1997)

Fühner, Jochen A. *Die kirchen- und die antireformatorische Religionspolitik Kaiser Karls V. in den siebzehn Provinzen der Niederlande 1515–1555* (Leiden, Brill, 2004)

Gilmont, Jean-François, *Le Livre réformé au XVIe siècle* (Paris, Bibliothèque nationale de France, 2005)

Gilmont, Jean-François, *The Reformation and the Book* (Aldershot, Ashgate, 1996)

Grendler, Paul F., *Culture and Censorship in Late Renaissance Italy and France* (London, Variorum, 1981)

Grendler, Paul F., *The Roman Inquisition and the Venetian Press* (Princeton, NJ, Princeton University Press, 1977).

Griffin, Clive, *The Crombergers of Seville. The History of a Printing and Merchant Dynasty* (Oxford, Oxford University Press, 1988)

Hamilton, Alastair, *Heresy and Mysticism in Sixteenth-century Spain: The Alumbrados* (Cambridge, James Clarke, 1992)

Hari, Robert, 'Les Placards de 1534', in G. Berthoud (ed.), *Aspects de la propagande religieuse* (Geneva, Droz, 1957), pp. 79–142

Higman, Francis M. *Censorship and the Sorbonne: A Bibliographical Study of Books in French Censured by the Faculty of Theology of the University of Paris, 1520–1551* (Geneva, Droz, 1979)

Higman, Francis, *Lire et découvrir: la circulation des idées au temps de la Réforme* (Geneva, Droz, 1998)

Higman, Francis, *Piety and the People: Religious Printing in French, 1511–1551* (Aldershot, Ashgate, 1996)

Leedham-Green, Elizabeth, 'University libraries and book-sellers', in Lotte Hellinga and J.B. Trapp (eds), *The Cambridge History of the Book in Britain. III: 1400–1557* (Cambridge, Cambridge University Press, 1999), pp. 316–53

Michelson, Emily, 'Luigi Lippomano, his Vicars, and the Reform of Verona from the Pulpit', *Church History*, 78 (2009), pp. 1–22

Pettegree, Andrew, 'The Latin polemic of the Marian exiles', in his *Marian Protestantism. Six Studies* (Aldershot, Ashgate, 1996), pp. 118–28, 183–96

Sessions, William K., *The First Printers at Ipswich in 1547–1548 and Worcester in 1549–1553* (York, privately printed, 1984)

Shaaber, M.A., *Check-list of Works of British Authors Printed Abroad, in Languages other than English, to 1641* (New York, Bibliographical Society of America, 1975)

Staedtke, Joachim, *Heinrich Bullinger Bibliographie. Beschreibendes Verzeichnis der gedruckten Werke von Heinrich Bullinger* (Zürich, Theologischer Verlag, 1972)

Visser, C.Ch.G., *Luther's geschriften in de nederlanden tot 1546* (Assen, Van Gorcum, 1969)

Vischer, Manfred, *Bibliographie der Zürcher Druckschriften des 15. und 16. Jahrhunderts* (Baden-Baden, Koerner, 1991)

7: First with the News

Barbier, Jean-Paul, *Bibliographie des discours politiques de Ronsard* (Geneva, Droz, 1984)

Bates, A.W., *Emblematic Monsters: Unnatural Conceptions and Deformed Births in Early Modern Europe* (Amsterdam, Clio medica, 77, 2005)

Bulgarelli, Tullio, *Gli avvisi a stampa in Roma nel Cinquecento. Bibliografia, antologia* (Rome, Istituto di studi romani, 1967)

Deresiewicz, H., 'Some sixteenth-century European earthquakes as depicted in contemporary sources', *Bulletin of the Seismological Society of America*, 72 (1982), pp. 507–23

Duke, Alastair, 'Posters, pamphlets and prints. The ways and means of circulating dissident opinions on the eve of the Dutch Revolt', in his *Dissident Identities in the Early Modern Low Countries* (Aldershot, Ashgate, 2009), pp. 157–77

Eames, Wilberforce, 'Columbus' letter on the discovery of America (1493–97)', *Bulletin of the New York Public Library* (1924), pp. 595–9

Eisermann, Falk, 'Buchdruck und politische Kommunikation. Ein neuer Fund zur frühen Publizistik Maximilians I', *Gutenberg Jahrbuch*, 2002, pp. 77–83

Fenlon, Iain, *The Ceremonial City: History, Memory and Myth in Renaissance Venice* (New Haven, Yale University Press, 2007)

Fenlon, Iain, 'Lepanto: music, ceremony and celebration in Counter-Reformation Rome', in his *Music and Culture in Late Renaissance Italy* (Oxford, Oxford University Press, 2002), pp. 139–61

Ganado, Albert and Maurice Agius-Vadalà, *A Study in Depth of 143 Maps representing the great Siege of Malta of 1565* (Valletta, Bank of Valletta, 1994)

Göllner, Carl, *Turcica: Die europäischen Türkendrucke des XVI. Jahrhunderts. I. Band MDI-MDL* (Berlin, Akademie-Verlag, 1961)

Gunn, Steven, David Grummitt and Hans Cools, *War, State, and Society in England and the Netherlands 1477–1559* (Oxford, Oxford University Press, 2007)

Harrison, E.L., 'Virgil, Sebastian Brant, and Maximilian I', *The Modern Language Review*, 76 (1981), pp. 99–115

Harrisse, Henry, *Bibliotheca Americana Vetustissima: A Description of Works Relating to America, Published Between the Years 1492 and 1551* (New York, Philes, 1866)

Roth, Paul, *Die neuen Zeitungen im 15. und 16. Jahrhundert* (Leipzig, Preisschr., Fürstl. jablonowskische Gesellschaft zu Leipzig, 1914)

Schenda, Rudolf, 'Die deutschen Prodigiensammlungen des 16. und 17. Jahrhunderts', *Archiv für Geschichte des Buchwesens*, 4 (1961–63), cols 637–710

Schenda, Rudolf, *Die französische Prodigienliteratur in der zweiten Hälfte des 16. Jahrhunderts* (Munich, Hueber, 1961)

Soergel, Philip M., 'The afterlives of monstrous infants in Reformation Germany', in Bruce Gordon and Peter Marshall (eds), *The Place of the Dead: Death and Remembrance in Late Medieval and Early Modern Europe* (Cambridge, Cambridge University Press, 2000), pp. 288–309

Spinks, Jennifer, 'Wondrous monsters: representing conjoined twins in early sixteenth-century German broadsheets', *Parergon*, 22 (2005), pp. 77–112

Spinks, Jennifer, *Monstrous Births and Visual Culture in Sixteenth-century Germany* (London, Chatto & Pickering, 2009)

Trivellato, Francesca, 'Merchants' letters across geographical and social boundaries', in Francisco Bethencourt and Florike Egmond (eds), *Correspondence and Cultural Exchange in Europe, 1400–1700* (Cambridge, Cambridge University Press, 2007), pp. 80–103

Voet, Léon, 'Abraham Verhoeren en de Antwerpse pers', *De Gulden Passer*, 31 (1953), pp. 1–37

8: Polite Recreations

Agee, Richard J., *The Gardano Music Printing Firms, 1569–1611* (Rochester, NY, University of Rochester Press, 1998)

Benhaïm, Véronique, 'Les Thresors d'Amadis', in Nicole Cazauran and Michel Bideaux (eds), *Les Amadis en France au XVIe siècle* (Paris, Cahiers Victor Saulnier, 2000), pp. 157–81.

Brennan, Michael G., 'Sir Charles Somerset's music books (1622)', *Music & Letters*, 74 (1993), pp. 501–18

Brown, Howard Mayer, *Instrumental Music printed before 1600. A Bibliography* (Cambridge, MA, Harvard University Press, 1965)

Chatelain, Jean-Marc, 'L'Illustration d'*Amadis de Gaule* dans les éditions françaises du XVIe siècle', in Nicole Cazauran and Michel Bideaux (eds), *Les Amadis en France au XVIe siècle* (Paris, Cahiers Victor Saulnier, 2000), pp. 41–52

Courcelles, Dominique de (ed.), *Traduire & adapter à la Renaissance* (Paris, l'École des Chartes, 1998)

Eisenberg, Daniel and Maria Carmen Marín Pina, *Bibliografía de los libros de caballerías castellanos* (Zaragoza, Prensas universitarias de Zaragoza, 2000)

Goodman, Jennifer R., *Chivalry and Exploration, 1298–1630* (Woodbridge, Boydell, 1998)

Guillo, Laurent, *Les Éditions musicales de la renaissance lyonnaise* (Paris, Klincksieck, 1991)

Heartz, Daniel, *Pierre Attaignant: Royal Printer of Music* (Berkeley, University of California Press, 1969)

Jean Martin. Un traducteur au temps de François Ier et de Henri II (Paris, Presses de l'Ecole Normale Supérieure, 1999)

Leonard, Irving A., *Books of the Brave. Being an Account of Books and of Men in the Spanish Conquest and Settlement of the Sixteenth-century New World* (2nd edn, Berkeley, University of California Press, 1992)

Leonard, Irving A., 'Romances of chivalry in the Spanish Indies. With some *registros* of shipments of books to the Spanish colonies', *University of California Publications in Modern Philology*, 16 (1933), pp. 217–372

Lesure, F. *Répertoire international des sources musicales. Recueils imprimés XVIe–XVIIe siècles. Tom. 1, Liste chronologique* (Munich, G. Henle, 1960)

Lesure, F. and G. Thibault, *Bibliographie des éditions d'Adrian Le Roy et Robert Ballard (1551–1598)* (Paris, Société Française de Musicologie, 1955)

O'Connor, John J., *Amadis de Gaule and its Influence on Elizabethan Literature* (New Brunswick, Rutgers University Press, 1970)

Pettas, William A., *The Giunti of Florence. Merchant Publishers of the Sixteenth Century* (San Francisco, B.M. Rosenthal, 1980)

Quondam, Amedeo, 'Aretino e il libro: un repertorio, per una bibliografia', in *Pietro Aretino nel cinquecentario della nascita* (2 vols, Rome, Salerno, 1995), I, pp. 197–230

Rawles, Stephen, 'The earliest editions of Nicolas de Herberay's translations of Amadis de Gaule', *The Library*, 6th ser., 3 (1981), pp. 91–108

Richardson, Brian, *Printing, Writers and Readers in Renaissance Italy* (Cambridge, Cambridge University Press, 1999)

Robin, Diana, *Publishing Women. Salons, the Presses and the Counter-Reformation in Sixteenth-century Italy* (Chicago, University of Chicago Press, 2007)

Thomas, Henry, *Spanish and Portuguese Romances of Chivalry* (Cambridge, Cambridge University Press, 1920), pp. 147–8

Vanhulst, Henri, *Catalogue des éditions de musique publiées à Louvain par Pierre Phalèse et ses fils 1545–1578* (Brussels, Palais des Académies, 1990)

Walsby, Malcolm, 'La Voix de l'auteur? Autorité et identité dans les imprimés français au XVIe siècle', in A. Vanautgaerden and R. Gorris (eds), *L'Auteur à la Renaissance* (Turnhout, Brepols, 2009) pp. 65–81

9: At School

Anders, H. 'The Elizabethan ABC and the catechism', *The Library*, 4th ser., 16 (1935), pp. 32–48

Arnold, Jonathan, *Humanism and Reform in Early Tudor England* (London, I.B. Tauris, 2007)

Bantock, G. H., *Studies in the History of Educational Theory. I: Artifice and Nature, 1350–1765* (London, Allen & Unwin, 1980)

Benhaïm, Véronique, 'Les Thresors d'Amadis', in Nicole Cazauran and Michel Bideaux (eds), *Les Amadis en France au XVIe siècle* (Paris, Cahiers Victor Saulnier, 2000), pp. 157–181

Carter, Harry and H.D.L. Vervliet, *Civilité Types* (Oxford, Oxford Bibliographical Society, 1966)

Cressy, David, *Literacy and the Social Order: Reading and Writing in Tudor and Stuart England* (Cambridge, Cambridge University Press, 1980)

Cross, M. Claire, *The Free Grammar School of Leicester* (Leicester Department of English Local History Occasional Papers, 4, 1953)

Fletcher, John M., 'Change and resistance to change: a consideration of the development of English and German universities during the sixteenth century', *History of Universities*, 1 (1981), pp. 1–36

Gordon, Bruce, 'The changing face of Protestant history and identity in the sixteenth century', in his *Protestant History and Identity in Sixteenth-century Europe* (2 vols, Aldershot, Ashgate, 1996), pp. 1–22

Grafton, Anthony and Lisa Jardine, *From Humanism to the Humanities. Education and the Liberal Arts in Fifteenth- and Sixteenth-century Europe* (London, Duckworth, 1986)

Green, Ian, *The Christian's ABC. Catechisms and Catechizing in England, c.1530–1740* (Oxford, Oxford University Press, 1996)

Grendler, Paul F., *Schooling in Renaissance Italy. Literacy and Learning, 1300–1660* (Baltimore, Johns Hopkins University Press, 1989)

Houston, R.A., *Literacy in Early Modern Europe: Culture and Education, 1500–1800* (London, Longman, 1988)

Huppert, George, *Public Schools in Renaissance France* (Urbana, University of Illinois Press, 1984)

Kess, Alexandra, *Johann Sleidan and the Protestant Vision of History* (Aldershot, Ashgate, 2008)

Maag, Karin, *Seminary or University? The Genevan Academy and Reformed Higher Education, 1560–1620* (Aldershot, Ashgate, 1995)

Oastler, C.L., *John Day, the Elizabethan Printer* (Oxford, Oxford Bibliographical Society, 1975)

Ridder Symoens, H. de (ed.), *A History of the University in Europe. II: Universities in Early Modern Europe (1500–1800)* (Cambridge, Cambridge University Press, 1996)

Seaborne, Malcolm, *The English School: Its Architecture and Organization, 1370–1870* (Toronto, University of Toronto Press, 1971)

Tuer, Andrew W., *History of the Horn Book* (New York, Benjamin Blom, 1897)

Wijsman, Hanno, 'Historiography and history in transition. Production, reception and contextualisation of the Chroniques of Enguerrand de Monstrelet in manuscript and print', in Graeme Kemp and Malcolm Walsby (eds), *The Book in Transition. The Printed Book in the Post-Incunabula Age, 1500–1640* (Leiden, Brill, 2011)

Wijsman, Hanno, *Handschriften voor het hertogdom. De mooiste verluchte manuscripten van Brabantse hertogen, edellieden, kloosterlingen en stedelingen* (Alphen, Veerhuis, 2006)

Woodward, Gwendolen and R. A. Christophers, *The Chained Library of the Royal Grammar School, Guildford, Catalogue* (Guildford, Royal Grammar School, 1972)

10: The Literature of Conflict

Atkinson, James, *The Trial of Luther* (London, Batsford, 1971)

Baskerville, E., *A Chronological Bibliography of Propaganda and Polemic published in English between 1553 and 1558* (Philadelphia, American Philosophical Society, 1979)

Brown, Christopher Boyd, *Singing the Gospel: Lutheran Hymns and the Success of the Reformation* (Cambridge, MA, Harvard University Press, 2005)

Bujanda, J.M. De, Francis M. Higman and James K. Farge, *Index de l'Université de Paris: 1544, 1545,1547, 1549, 1551, 1556* (Sherbrooke: Centre d'études de la Renaissance, 1985)

Clair, Colin, *Christopher Plantin* (London, Cassell, 1960)

Droz, Eugénie, 'Antoine Vincent. La propagande protestante par le psautier', in G. Berthoud (ed.), *Aspects de la propagande religieuse* (Geneva, Droz, 1957), pp. 276–93

Fragnito, Gigliola (ed.), *Church, Censorship and Culture in Early Modern Italy* (Cambridge, Cambridge University Press, 2001)

Friedenthal, Richard, *Luther* (London, Weidenfeld & Nicolson, 1967)

Gilmont, Jean-François and Peter Rodolphe, *Bibliotheca Calviniana. Les oeuvres de Jean Calvin publiées au XVIe siècle* (3 vols, Geneva, Droz, 1991–2000)

Gilmont, Jean-François, *John Calvin and the Printed Book* (Kirksville, MO, Truman State University Press, 2005)

Green, Ian, *Print and Protestantism in Early Modern England* (Oxford, Oxford University Press, 2000)

Grendler, Paul, *The Roman Inquisition and the Venetian Press, 1540–1605* (Princeton, NJ, Princeton University Press, 1977)

Higman, Francis, *Piety and the People. Religious Printing in French, 1511–1551* (Aldershot, Ashgate, 1996)

Jostock, Ingeborg, *La Censure négociée. La contrôle du livre à Genève, 1560–1625* (Geneva, Droz, 2007)

Kolb, Robert (ed.), *Lutheran Ecclesiastical Culture, 1550–1675* (Leiden, Brill, 2008)

Milward, Peter, *Religious Controversies of the Elizabethan Age. A Survey of Printed Sources* (London, Scolar Press, 1978)

Oettinger, Rebecca Wagner, *Music as Propaganda in the German Reformation* (Aldershot, Ashgate, 2001)

Pallier, Denis, *Recherches sur l'imprimerie à Paris pendant la Ligue (1585–1594)* (Geneva, Droz, 1976)

Pettegree, Andrew, *Emden and the Dutch Revolt. Exile and the Development of Reformed Protestantism* (Oxford, Clarendon Press, 1992)

Pettegree, Andrew, *The French Book and the European Book World* (Leiden, Brill, 2007)

Racaut, Luc, *Hatred in Print: Catholic Propaganda and Protestant Identity during the French Wars of Religion* (Aldershot, Ashgate, 2002)

Raven, James, *The Business of Books. Booksellers and the English Book Trade* (New Haven, Yale University Press, 2007)

Rein, Nathan, *The Chancery of God. Protestant Print, Polemic and Propaganda Against the Empire, Magdeburg 1546–1551* (Aldershot, Ashgate, 2008)

Schlaepfer, H.-L., 'Laurent de Normandie', in G. Berthoud (ed.), *Aspects de la propagande religieuse* (Geneva, Droz, 1957), pp. 176–230

Voet, Leon, *The Golden Compasses: A History and Evaluation of the Printing and Publishing Activities of the Officina Plantiniana at Antwerp* (Amsterdam, van Gendt, 1969–72)

11: The Search for Order

Adams, Alison and Anthony J. Harper (eds), *The Emblem in Renaissance and Baroque Europe* (Leiden, Brill, 1992)

Adams, Alison, Stephen Rawles and Alison Saunders, *A Bibliography of French Emblem Books* (2 vols, Geneva, Droz, 1999–2002)

Anglo, Sydney, *Machiavelli, the First Century. Studies in Enthusiasm, Hostility and Irrelevance* (Oxford, Clarendon Press, 2005)

Bertelli, Sergio and Piero Innocenti, *Bibliografia Machiavelliana* (Verona, Valdonega, 1979)

Cazauran, Nicole (ed.), *Discours merveilleux: de la vie, actions et deportements de Catherine de Médici, Royne-mère* (Geneva, Droz, 1995)

Crahay, Rodolph, *Bibliographie critique des éditions anciennes de Jean Bodin* (Brussels, Académie Royale de Belgique, 1992)

Franklin, Julian H., *Jean Bodin* (Aldershot, Ashgate, 2006)

Friedeburg, Robert von, *Self-Defence and Religious Strife in Early Modern Europe. England and Germany, 1530–1680* (Aldershot, Ashgate, 2002)

Garnett, George (ed.), *Vindiciae contra Tyrannos* (Cambridge, Cambridge University Press, 1994)

Giesey, Ralph, 'The Monarchomach triumvirs: Hotman, Beza and Mornay', *Bibliothèque d'Humanisme et Renaissance*, 32 (1970), pp. 41–56

Greengrass, Mark, *Governing Passions. Peace and Reform in the French Kingdom, 1576–1585* (Oxford, Oxford University Press, 2007)

Kingdon, Robert M., *Myths about the St Bartholomew's Day Massacres, 1572–1576* (Cambridge, MA, Harvard University Press, 1988)

Klose, Wolfgang, *Corpus alborum amicorum. Beschreibendes Verzeichnis der Stammbücher des 16. Jahrhunderts* (Stuttgart, Hiersemann, 1988)

Klose, Wolfgang (ed.), *Stammbücher des 16. Jahrhunderts* (Wiesbaden, Otto Harrassowitz, 1989)

Saunders, Alison, *The Sixteenth-century French Emblem Book. A Decorative and Useful Genre* (Geneva, Droz, 1988)

Skinner, Quentin, *The Foundations of Modern Political Thought* (Cambridge, Cambridge University Press, 1978)

Van Gelderen, Martin, *The Political Thought of the Dutch Revolt, 1555–1590* (Cambridge, Cambridge University Press, 1992).

Vischer, Manfred, *Zürcher Einblattdrucke des 16. Jahrhunderts* (Baden-Baden, Koerner, 2001)

Visser, Arnoud, 'Escaping the reformation in the republic of letters: confessional silence in Latin emblem books', *Church History and Religious Culture*, 88 (2008), pp. 139–67

12: Market Forces

Amory, Hugh and David D. Hall, *A History of the Book in America. I; The Colonial Book in the Atlantic World* (Cambridge, Cambridge University Press, 2000)

Blagden, Cyprian, *The Stationers' Company: A History, 1403–1959* (London, Allen & Unwin, 1960)

Castañeda, Carlos E., 'The beginning of printing in America', *Hispanic American Historical Review*, 20 (1940), pp. 671–85

Clair, Colin, 'Christopher Plantin's trade connections with England and Scotland', *The Library*, 5th ser., 14 (1959), pp. 28–45

Griffin, Clive, *Journeymen-Printers, Heresy and the Inquisition in Sixteenth-century Spain* (Oxford, Oxford University Press, 2005)

Higman, Francis, Yann Morvant and Marc Vial, 'A bookseller's world: the inventaire of Vincent Réal', in Andrew Pettegree, Paul Nelles and Philip Conner (eds), *The Sixteenth-century French Religious Book* (Aldershot, Ashgate, 2001), pp. 303–18

Jugareanu, Veturia, *Bibliographie des siebenbürgischen Frühdrucke* (Baden-Baden, Koerner, 1959)

Lapeyre, Henri, *Une Famille de marchands: les Ruiz. Contribution à l'étude du commerce entre la France et l'Espagne au temps de Philippe II* (Paris, A. Colin, 1955)

Lara, Jaime, *Christian Texts for Aztecs. Art and Liturgy in Colonial Mexico* (Notre Dame, IN, University of Notre Dame Press, 2008)

Maclean, Ian, 'Murder, debt and retribution in the Italico-Franco-Spanish book trade: the Beraud–Michel–Ruiz affair, 1586–91', in his *Learning and the European Marketplace: Essays in Early Modern Book History* (Leiden, Brill, 2009)

Mann, Alastair J., *The Scottish Book Trade, 1500–1720. Print Commerce and Print Control in Early Modern Scotland* (East Linton, Tuckwell, 2000)

Péligry, Christian, 'Les Éditeurs Lyonnais et le marché espagnol aux XVIe et XVIIe siècles', in *Livre et lecture en Espagne et en France sous l'ancien régime* (Paris, editions ADPF, 1981), pp. 85–95

Rodger, Alexander, 'Roger Ward's Shrewsbury Stock: an inventory of 1585', *The Library*, 5th ser., 13 (1958), pp. 247–68

Röll, Walter, 'Zur Verbreitung deutscher Erzähltexte in den hundert Jahren nach der Erfindung des Buchdrucks', *Gutenberg Jahrbuch*, 1987, pp. 158–65

Runnalls, Graham A., 'La Vie, la mort et les livres de l'imprimeur-libraire parisien Jean Janot d'après son inventaire après décès (17 février 1522 [n.s.])', *Revue belge de philologie et d'histoire*, 78 (2000), pp. 797–850

Schwetschte, Gustav (ed.), *Codex Nundinarius: Germaniae Literatae Bisecularis. Mess-Jahrbücher des Deutschen Buchhandels von dem Erscheinen des ersten Mess-Kataloges in Jahre 1564 bis zu der Gründung des Buchhändlervereins im Jahre 1765* (Nieuwkoop, de Graaf, 1963)

Vervliet, Hendrik D.L., *The Palaeotypography of the French Renaissance. Selected Papers on Sixteenth-century Typefaces* (Leiden, Brill, 2008)

Walsby, Malcolm, *The Printed Book in Brittany, 1486–1600* (Leiden, Brill, 2010)

Wildenstein Georges, 'L'Imprimeur-libraire Richard Breton et son inventaire après décès', *Bibliothèque d'Humanisme et Renaissance*, 21 (1959), pp. 364–79

13: Science and Exploration

Blair, Ann, 'Annotating and indexing natural philosophy', in Marina Frasca-Spada and Nick Jardine (eds), *Books and the Sciences in History* (Cambridge, Cambridge University Press, 2000), pp. 69–89

Buisseret, David, *The Mapmakers' Quest: Depicting New Worlds in Renaissance Europe* (Oxford, Oxford University Press, 2003)

Buisseret, David, *Monarchs, Ministers, and Maps: The Emergence of Cartography as a Tool of Government in Early Modern Europe* (Chicago, University of Chicago Press, 1992)

Campbell, Mary B. *The Witness and the Other World: Exotic European Travel Writing, 400–1600* (Ithaca, NY, Cornell University Press, 1988)

Chomarat, Michel and Jean-Paul Laroche, *Bibliographie Nostradamus; XVIe, XVIIe, XVIIIe siècles* (Baden-Baden: Koerner, 1989)

Claes, F., *Lijst van Nederlandse woordenlijsten en woordenboeken gedrukt tot 1600* (Nieuwkoop, de Graaf, 1974)

Crane, Nicholas, *Mercator. The Man who Mapped the Planet* (London, Weidenfeld & Nicolson, 2002)

Frasca-Spada, Marina and Nick Jardine, *Books and the Sciences in History* (Cambridge, Cambridge University Press, 2000)

Gingerich, Owen, *An Annotated Census of Copernicus' De revolutionibus (Nuremberg, 1543 and Basel, 1566)* (Leiden, Brill, 2002)

Gingerich, Owen, *The Book Nobody Read. In Pursuit of the Revolutions of Nicolaus Copernicus* (London, Heinemann, 2004)

Grafton, Anthony, 'José de Acosta: Renaissance historiography and New World humanity', in John Jeffries Martin (ed.), *The Renaissance World* (London, Routledge, 2007), pp. 166–88

Harvey, P.D.A., *Maps in Tudor England* (London, Public Record Office, 1993)

Kearney, Hugh, *Science and Change, 1500–1700* (London, Weidenfeld and Nicolson, 1971)

Labarre, Albert, *Bibliographie du dictionarium d'Ambrogio Calepino: (1502–1779)* (Baden-Baden, Koerner, 1975)

Lestringant, Frank, *Mapping the Renaissance World. The Geographical Imagination in the Age of Discovery* (Berkeley, University of California, 1994)

Lindemann, Margarete, *Die französischen Wörterbücher von den Anfängen bis 1600: Entstehung und typologische Beschreibung* (Tübingen, Niemeyer, 1994)

McLean, Matthew, *The Cosmographia of Sebastian Münster. Describing the World in the Reformation* (Aldershot, Ashgate, 2007)

Marr, Alexander, 'A Renaissance library rediscovered: the "Repertorium librorum Mathematica" of Jean I du Temps', *The Library*, 7th ser., 9 (2008), pp. 428–70

Nelles, Paul 'The library as an instrument of discovery: Gabriel Naudé and the uses of History', in D. R. Kelley (ed.), *History and the Disciplines* (Rochester, NY, University of Rochester Press, 1997), pp. 41–57

Pavord, Anna, *The Naming of Names. The Search for Order in the World of Plants* (London, Bloomsbury, 2005)

Schechner, Sara J., *Comets, Popular Culture and the Birth of Modern Cosmology* (Princeton, NJ, Princeton University Press, 1997)

Steinmann, Martin, *Johannes Oporinus. Ein Basler Buchdrucker um die Mitte des 16. Jahrhunderts* (Basel, Helbing & Lichtenhahn, 1967)

Stillwell, Margaret Bingham, *The Awakening Interest in Science During the First Century of Printing, 1450-1550* (New York, Bibliographical Society of America, 1970)

Stipcevic, Alexsandor, 'Aspectes de la production du livre croate au XVe siècle', in Henrik Heger and Janine Matillon (eds), *Les Croates et la civilisation du livre* (Paris, Presses de l'Université de Paris-Sorbonne, 1986), pp. 27–33

Wightman, W.P.D., *Science in a Renaissance Society* (London, Hutchinson, 1972)

Zambelli, Paolo (ed.), *Astrologi hallucinati. Stars and the End of the World in Luther's Time* (Berlin, de Gruyter, 1986)

Zaunmüller, Wolfram, *Bibliographisches Handbuch der Sprachwörterbücher: ein internationales Verzeichnis von 5600 Wörterbüchern der Jahre 1460-1958 für mehr als 500 Sprachen und Dialekte* (New York, Hafner, 1958)

14: Healing

Bowden, Caroline, 'The library of Mildred Cooke Cecil, Lady Burghley', *The Library*, 6 (1) (2005), pp. 3–29.

Brockliss, Laurence and Colin Jones, *The Medical World of Early Modern France* (Oxford, Oxford University Press, 1997)

Broomhall, Susan, *Women's Medical Work in Early Modern France* (Manchester, Manchester University Press, 2004)

Clark, Harry, 'Foiling the pirates: the preparation and publication of Andreas Vesalius's *De humani corporis fabrica*', *Library Quarterly*, 51 (1981), pp. 301–11

Cockx-Indestege, Elly, *Andreas Vesalius, a Belgian Census: Contribution towards a New Edition of H.W. Cushing's Bibliography* (Brussels, Royal Library Albert I, 1994)

Crawshaw, Jane Stevens, *Islands of Isolation. Fighting the Plague in Early Modern Venice* (Aldershot, Ashgate, forthcoming in 2012)

Cunningham, Andrew and Ole Peter Grell, *The Four Horsemen of the Apocalypse. Religion, War, Famine and Death in Reformation Europe* (Cambridge, Cambridge University Press, 2000)

Cushing, Harvey, *A Bio-bibliography of Andreas Vesalius* (New York, Schuman, 1943)

Doe, Janet, *A Bibliography of the Works of Ambroise Paré: premier chirugien & conseiller du roy* (Chicago, University of Chicago Press, 1937)

Eamon, William, *Science and the Secrets of Nature: Books of Secrets in Medieval and Early Modern Culture* (Princeton, NJ, Princeton University Press, 1994)

Ferguson, John, 'The secrets of Alexis. A sixteenth-century collection of medical and technical receipts', *Proceedings of the Royal Society of Medicine*, 24 (1930), pp. 225–46

Fulton, John F. and Madeline E. Stanton, *Michael Servetus, Humanist and Martyr* (New York, Herbert Reichner, 1953)

Gentilcore, David, *Healers and Healing in Early Modern Italy* (Manchester, Manchester University Press, 1998)

Hellinga, Lotte, 'Medical incunabula', in Robin Myers and Michael Harris (eds), *Medicine, Mortality and the Book Trade* (London, St Paul's Bibliographies, 1998), pp. 73–86

Hieronymus, Frank, *Theophrast und Galen – Celsus und Paracelsus. Medizin, Naturphilosphie und Kirchenreform im Basler Buchdruck bis zum Dreissigjährigen Krieg* (4 vols, Universitätsbibliothek, Basel, 2005)

Maclean, Ian, *Learning and the European Marketplace: Essays in Early Modern Book History* (Leiden, Brill, 2009)

Naphy, William and Andrew Spicer, *The Black Death and a History of Plagues, 1345–1730*, (Stroud, Tempus, 2000)

O'Malley, C.D., *Andreas Vesalius of Brussels, 1514–1564* (Berkeley, University of California Press, 1964)

Rey, Roselyne, *The History of Pain* (Cambridge, MA, Harvard University Press, 1995)

Siraisi, Nancy G., *History, Medicine and the Traditions of Renaissance Learning* (Ann Arbor, University of Michigan Press, 2007)

Siraisi, Nancy G., *Medieval & Early Renaissance Medicine. An Introduction to Knowledge and Practice* (Chicago, University of Chicago Press, 1990)

Slack, Paul, *The Impact of Plague in Tudor and Stuart England* (London, Routledge, 1985)

Wear, A., R.K. French and I.M. Lonie, *The Medical Renaissance of the Sixteenth Century* (Cambridge, Cambridge University Press, 1985)

Webster, Charles, *Health, Medicine and Mortality in the Sixteenth Century* (Cambridge, Cambridge University Press, 1979)

15: Building a Library

Carley, James P. (ed.), *The Libraries of King Henry VIII* (London, British Library, 2000)

Clapinson, Mary, 'The Bodleian Library and its readers, 1602–1652', *Bodleian Library Record*, 19 (1) (2006), pp. 30–46

Connat, M. and J. Mégret, 'Inventaire de la bibliothèque des du Prat', *Bibliothèque d'humanisme et renaissance*, 3 (1943), pp. 72–128

Craig, John, *Reformation, Politics and Polemics. The Growth of Protestantism in East Anglian Market Towns, 1500–1610* (Aldershot, Ashgate, 2001)

Dahl, F., *A Bibliography of English Corantos and Periodical Newsbooks 1620–1642* (London, Bibliographical Society, 1952)

Fehrenbach, R.J. and E.S. Leedham-Green, *Private Libraries in Renaissance England: A Collection and Catalogue of Tudor and Early Stuart Book-lists* (6 vols, Binghamton, NY, Medieval & Renaissance Texts & Studies, 1992–)

Glenn, John and David Walsh, *Catalogue of the Francis Trigge Chained Library, St Wulfram's Church, Grantham* (Cambridge, Brewer, 1988)

Grendler, Marcella, 'Book collecting in Counter-Reformation Italy: The Library of Gian Vincezo Pinelli (1535–1601)', *Journal of Library History*, 16 (1981), pp. 144–51

Grendler, Marcella, 'A Greek collection in Padua: the library of Gian Vincenzo Pinelli (1535–1601)', *Renaissance Quarterly*, 33 (1980), pp. 386–416

Harris, Neil, 'Tribal lays and the history of the fingerprint', in David J. Shaw (ed.), *Many into One: Problems and Opportunities in Creating Shared Catalogues of Older Books* (London, Consortium of European Research Libraries, 2006), pp. 21–71

Histoire des bibliothèques françaises: 2. Les bibliothèques sous l'ancien régime, 1530–1789 (Paris, Promodis, 1988)

Hobson, Anthony, *Great Libraries* (London, Weidenfeld & Nicolson, 1970)

Hobson, Anthony, 'A sale by candle in 1608', *The Library*, 5th ser., 26 (1971), pp. 215–33

Jensen, Kristian, 'Universities and colleges', in Elizabeth Leedham-Green and Teresa Webber (eds), *The Cambridge History of Libraries in Britain and Ireland, Vol. I: to 1640* (Cambridge, Cambridge University Press, 2006), pp. 345–62

Jourda, Pierre, 'La Bibliothèque d'un régent calviniste (1577)', in *Mélanges d'histoire littéraire de la Renaissance offerts à Henri Chamard* (Paris, Librairie Nizet, 1951), pp. 269–73

Labarre, Albert, *Le Livre dans la vie amiénoise du seizième siècle* (Paris, Béatrice-Nauwelaerts, 1971)

Labowsky, Lotte, *Bessarion's Library and the Biblioteca Marciana. Six Early Inventories* (Rome, Edizioni di storia e letteratura, 1979)

Leedham-Green, E.S., *Books in Cambridge Inventories: Book Lists from Vice-Chancellor's Court Probate Inventories in the Tudor and Stuart Periods* (2 vols, Cambridge, Cambridge University Press, 1986)

Lowry, Martin, 'Two great Venetian libraries in the age of Aldus Manutius', *Bulletin of the John Rylands Library*, 57 (1974–75), pp. 128–66

Mittler, Elmar, *Bibliotheca Palatina: Katalog zur Ausstellung vom 8. Juli bis 2. November 1986* (Heidelberg, Braus, 1986)

Philip, Ian, *The Bodleian Library in the Seventeenth and Eighteenth Centuries* (Oxford, Clarendon Press, 1983)

Raven, James (ed.), *Lost Libraries. The Destruction of Great Book Collections since Antiquity* (Basingstoke, Palgrave, 2004)

Streckfuss, Richard, 'News before newspapers', *Journalism and Mass Communication*, 75 (1998), pp. 84–97

Trypucko, Josef, *The Catalogue of the Book Collection of the Jesuit College in Braniewo Held in the University Library in Uppsala* (3 vols, Warsaw/ Uppsala, Uppsala Universitetsbibliotek, 2007)

16: Word and the Street

Barbarics, Zuszsa and Renate Pieper, 'Handwritten newsletters as a means of communication in early modern Europe', in Francisco Bethencourt and Florike Egmond (eds), *Correspondence and Cultural Exchange in Europe, 1400–1700* (Cambridge, Cambridge University Press, 2007), pp. 53–79

Blayney, Peter W.M., 'The publication of playbooks', in John D. Cox and David Scott Kastan (eds), *A New History of Early English Drama* (New York, Columbia University Press, 1997), pp. 383–422

Bosanquet, E.F., *English Printed Almanacks and Prognostications to 1600* (London, Bibliographical Society, 1917)

Brockley, Liam M., 'Jesuit pastoral theater on an urban stage: Lisbon, 1588–1593', *Journal of Early Modern History*, 9 (2005), pp. 3–50

Carson, Neil, *A Companion to Henslowe's Diary* (Cambridge, Cambridge University Press, 1988)

Chomarat, Michel and Jean-Paul Laroche, *Bibliographie Nostradamus: XVIe, XVIIe, XVIIIe siècles* (Baden-Baden, Koerner, 1989)

Cressy, David, *Bonfires and Bells. National Memory and the Protestant Calendar in Elizabethan and Stuart England* (London, Weidenfeld & Nicolson, 1989)

Droz, Eugénie, 'Le Calendrier genevois, agent de la propagande', in her *Chemins de l'hérésie. Textes et documents* (4 vols, Geneva, Slatkine, 1970–76), II, pp. 433–56

Duke, Alastair, 'Posters, pamphlets and prints', in his *Dissident Identities in the Early Modern Low Countries* (Aldershot, Ashgate, 2009), pp. 157–77

Erne, Lukas, *Shakespeare as Literary Dramatist* (Cambridge, Cambridge University Press, 2003)

Fox, Adam, *Oral and Literate Culture in England, 1500–1700* (Oxford, Clarendon Press, 2000)

Gurr, Andrew, *The Shakespearean Stage, 1574–1642* (Cambridge, Cambridge University Press, 1970)

Hammer, Paul, 'The smiling crocodile: the earl of Essex and late-Elizabethan "popularity"', in Steve Pincus and Peter Lake (eds), *The public sphere in early modern England* (Manchester, Manchester University Press, 2007), pp. 95–115.

Love, Harold, *Scribal Publication in Seventeenth-century England* (Oxford, Clarendon Press, 1993)

Martin, A. Lynn, *The Jesuit Mind. The Mentality of an Elite in Early Modern France* (Ithaca, NY, Cornell University Press, 1988)

Nierop, Henk van, 'Ketterij uit Utopia: verboden zestiende-eeuwse boeken', NRC Handelsblad, Supplement, 24 February 1989

Parmelee, Lisa Ferraro, Good Newes from Fraunce. French Anti-League Propaganda in Late Elizabethan England (Rochester, NY, University of Rochester Press, 1996)

Randall, David, Credibility in Elizabethan and Early Stuart Military News (London, Pickering & Chatto, 2008)

Raymond, Joad, Pamphlets and Pamphleteering in Early Modern Britain (Cambridge, Cambridge University Press, 2003)

Roelker, Nancy Lyman, The Paris of Henry of Navarre as seen by Pierre de L'Estoile (Cambridge, MA, Harvard University Press, 1958)

Stone Peters, Julie, Theatre of the Book, 1480–1880. Print, Text and Performance in Europe (Oxford, Oxford University Press, 2000)

Valentin, Jean-Marie, Les Jésuites et le théâtre (1554–1680): contribution à l'histoire culturelle du monde catholique dans le Saint-Empire Romain Germanique (Bern, Lang, 2001)

INDEX